Instructional Strategies for Students With Mild, Moderate, and Severe Intellectual Disability

This book is dedicated in loving memory of my parents, Lillian and Michael. They instilled in me a deep understanding and appreciation of compassion for others, dedication to a task, and the importance of family. My parents always believed in me and held me to a high personal standard. I only hope that I have lived up to their expectations.

RMG
December 2016

This book is dedicated to my children, who inspire me to be a better teacher educator and researcher—to improve teaching and learning for all students; my parents who were committed and passionate educators; and my husband for this continual support.

ECB
December 2016

Instructional Strategies for Students With Mild, Moderate, and Severe Intellectual Disability

Edited by

Richard M. Gargiulo
Professor Emeritus, University of Alabama at Birmingham

Emily C. Bouck
Michigan State University

Los Angeles | London | New Delhi
Singapore | Washington DC | Melbourne

FOR INFORMATION:

SAGE Publications, Inc.
2455 Teller Road
Thousand Oaks, California 91320
E-mail: order@sagepub.com

SAGE Publications Ltd.
1 Oliver's Yard
55 City Road
London EC1Y 1SP
United Kingdom

SAGE Publications India Pvt. Ltd.
B 1/I 1 Mohan Cooperative Industrial Area
Mathura Road, New Delhi 110 044
India

SAGE Publications Asia-Pacific Pte. Ltd.
3 Church Street
#10-04 Samsung Hub
Singapore 049483

Copyright © 2018 by SAGE Publications, Inc.

Printed in the United States of America

ISBN 978-1-5063-0666-7

This book is printed on acid-free paper.

Acquisitions Editor: Terri Accomazzo
Editorial Assistant: Erik Helton
Production Editor: Olivia Weber-Stenis
Copy Editor: Melinda Masson
Typesetter: Hurix Systems Pvt. Ltd.
Proofreader: Laura Webb
Indexer: Naomi Linzer
Cover Designer: Anupama Krishnan
Marketing Manager: Kara Kindstrom

17 18 19 20 21 10 9 8 7 6 5 4 3 2 1

Brief Contents

Detailed Contents

Foreword

My first teaching job was in a self-contained classroom for adolescents with mild to moderate intellectual disability in West Texas. Prior to accepting this job, I had received teacher preparation in a graduate degree program in intellectual disability and emotional disturbance. All of my students that first year were Hispanic boys who were classified as educable mentally retarded, and they were with me all day, every day, in a self-contained classroom. Thank goodness the field has changed somewhat dramatically since those days in the late 1970s. We have done away with the term *mental retardation*; we definitely do not refer to individuals as "educable" (EMR) or "trainable" (TMR), two descriptors used regularly to describe students with various degrees of intellectual disability; and we are aware that many of the assessment instruments used to identify individuals were biased. Yes, indeed, the field of educating students with intellectual disability has changed dramatically from terminology to the way many services are provided. Today there are fewer self-contained classrooms and special schools for students in this category and many more opportunities for students to receive their education in inclusive settings with their typical peers.

Not all changes in the field of intellectual disability have been positive, the one change that I consider the most negative being the growing disinterest in this population of individuals. Over the past twenty-five years, the field of intellectual disability has been diminished in special education. This has been the result of many different factors, including the growth of several other disability categories such as autism spectrum disorders and dyslexia, the negative connotations associated with intellectual disability, an increased awareness that many measurement instruments used to identify intellectual disability were biased, and an increased awareness of the disproportionality of certain groups of individuals from minority populations. Regardless of the reasons why there has been a decrease in the reported prevalence of this disability, the fact remains that many children and adults continue to experience intellectual disability in likely the same frequency as before, and these individuals need the attention of professionals who are knowledgeable about appropriate assessments and interventions.

Instructional Strategies for Students With Mild, Moderate, and Severe Intellectual Disability is a book that is long overdue. The fact that less attention has been paid to individuals with intellectual disability has resulted in less research, fewer professionals trained to work with this population, and fewer available textbooks to provide the necessary information for people to be effective teachers of children and young adults with intellectual disability. The addition of this book to the field should help reverse some of those negative consequences and once again call attention to a very important segment of special education.

The book is organized in a very systematic way to shepherd the reader from the historical roots of the field of intellectual disability, through different developmental periods, from preschool years through young adulthood. The initial section lays the foundation for the book by discussing terminology, classifications, and etiology. Including this information in the beginning chapters ensures the reader will have a firm understanding of intellectual disability before studying specific needs of different developmental periods. Following the foundational material provided in the early chapters are sections on different chronological age groups, highlighting much needed information about characteristics and needs of individuals with intellectual disability at different periods of their lives. Sequencing the book in this manner gives the reader an opportunity to grow along with individuals with intellectual disability to better understand the needs of this group, at various times in the life span. This approach allows teachers and prospective teachers to gain an understanding of the needs of each group and how meeting those needs enables individuals to develop higher levels of skills through appropriate, evidence-based instruction.

The editors, Dr. Gargiulo and Dr. Bouck, have assembled some of the leading professionals in teacher preparation and research for individuals with intellectual disability in the country. Indeed, authors of chapters represent the top researchers and teachers who prepare professionals for working with this population. By bringing together such a strong author team, the co-editors have ensured the inclusion of the most up-to-date and evidence-based information available. The book will have a positive impact on a field that is in need of something that will bring a renewed interest in intellectual disability. Mission accomplished.

Tom E. C. Smith
University Professor
University of Arkansas
September 2016

Preface

Our Purpose

In this book, we, as editors, strove for two unique but critical features—a life span approach coupled with a focus on the continuum of intellectual disability. We elected to adopt a life span approach so teacher educators could better prepare their students to support learners with intellectual disability across their development. We also felt it was important for teachers to understand the developmental sequence necessary to ensure success throughout the school years. We believe that providing pre-service and in-service teachers with the knowledge of developmentally appropriate instruction for students with intellectual disability makes them better able to plan and deliver high-quality academic, functional, and behavioral education. As editors, we also purposefully chose to focus across the continuum of students with intellectual disability. Today's teachers are increasingly educating students with mild, moderate, and severe intellectual disability within their classrooms. Thus, our goal in crafting this book was to equip educators with fundamentally sound, research-based tactics and strategies designed to increase the efficiency and effectiveness of learning among individuals with intellectual disability across both the age- and ability-level spectrum.

Audience

Instructional Strategies for Students With Mild, Moderate, and Severe Intellectual Disability was written for multiple audiences, although the primary audience is intended to be in-service and pre-service teachers who plan or desire to educate students with intellectual disability. However, *Instructional Strategies for Students With Mild, Moderate, and Severe Intellectual Disability* can easily serve as a reference work for school administrators, curriculum specialists, and related service providers.

Of course, this textbook can support anyone who needs to better understand students with intellectual disability from preschool through adolescence.

Hopefully, this book can also be a resource for parents who are seeking additional information to support the education of their own children with an intellectual disability.

ORGANIZATION OF THE TEXT

This textbook is organized into five parts spanning thirteen chapters. Ten chapters are, for the most part, organized around specific age ranges. As you will note, the chapters in the textbook, outside of Chapters 1, 2, and 3, are not structured in such a manner that an instructor must teach or experience the content in the order of the chapters. Instead, the textbook is organized so that individual instructors can teach the chapters, and others can interact with the book, in their particular order of choosing.

Chapter 1. Understanding Intellectual Disability

Chapter 2. Foundational Concepts: Etiology of Intellectual Disability and Characteristics of Students With Intellectual Disability

Chapter 3. Educational Issues Affecting Students With Intellectual Disability

Chapter 4. Assessing and Evaluating Students With Intellectual Disability

Chapter 5. Behavioral Interventions for Students With Intellectual Disability

Chapter 6. Assistive Technology for Students With Intellectual Disability

Chapter 7. Teaching Academic Skills to Preschool Students With Intellectual Disability

Chapter 8. Life Skills for Preschool Students With Intellectual Disability

Chapter 9. Teaching Academic Skills to Elementary-Age Students With Intellectual Disability

Chapter 10. Life Skills for Elementary-Age Students With Intellectual Disability

Chapter 11. Teaching Academic Skills to Secondary Students With Intellectual Disability

FEATURES

The chapters are similarly structured at the beginning and the end. Each one begins with **Learning Objectives** and ends with a **Chapter Summary, Review Questions,** and a list of **Organizations and Professional Associations** (and accompanying websites) related to the chapter content. Each chapter also contains many figures and tables to help illuminate and support the content being presented for a range of audiences, but with special attention to pre-service teachers. Additionally, the content in the chapters is grounded, to the greatest extent possible, in research. Given the current, and appropriate, era of attention to research-based or research-supported practice, it is important for future and current educators to understand the research base, and at times the lack thereof, behind the education of students with intellectual disability.

PEDAGOGICAL AIDS AND HIGH-INTEREST FEATURES

Our goal in writing this book was to create the kind of textbook we would want to use as instructors responsible for a course on teaching students with intellectual disability (a methods course) while also being sensitive to the needs of our students. Instructors will appreciate a chapter correlation grid whereby chapter content is aligned with the CEC (Council for Exceptional Children) Initial Special Education Developmental Disabilities Specialty Set standards.

ACKNOWLEDGMENTS

When we started this book, we knew it was to be a truly collaborative experience—not just between the two of us but also among the chapter authors, the team at SAGE, and our reviewers. We would first like to express our deep appreciation to the chapter authors; without these experts and wonderful colleagues, this book would not be as good as we believe it to be. We gratefully acknowledge the contributions of Amanda Boutout, David F. Cihak, Ginevra R. Courtade, Samuel A. DiGangi, Teresa Taber Doughty, Joan Grim, Robert C. Pennington, Megan Purcell, Karrie A. Shogren, Jordan Shurr, Cate C. Smith, Kylan Turner, and Michael L. Wehmeyer. These dedicated authors worked hard and did so across multiple contexts, including sending us several revisions and answering last-minute inquiries while always remaining consummate professionals. Thank you!

We also must express our deepest appreciation to our editor, Terri Accomazzo, and her editorial assistant, Erik Helton, for continuing to guide and support us throughout the writing process while overlooking our occasional errors with a pleasant and "no problem" attitude. We are grateful for your belief in this project.

We would also like to acknowledge the multiple reviewers who reviewed different chapters as well as the initial prospectus. Their input strengthened the textbook, and we know it is better because they encouraged us to make it better. Thank you to Lynne Bejoian, Montclair State University; Nancy Burton, Concord University; Kaybeth Calabria, Franciscan University of Steubenville; Ellen Duchaine, Texas State University; Maryann Dudzinski, Valparaiso University; Kate Esposito, California State University, Dominguez Hills; Marita Flagler, Shippensburg University; Sara Flanagan, University of Kentucky; Pamela Gent, Clarion University; and Adam Halpern, Hofstra University.

About the Editors

Richard M. Gargiulo

Dr. Gargiulo always wanted to be a teacher. He began working toward this goal at Hiram Scott College in Scottsbluff, Nebraska, where he received an undergraduate degree in elementary education and English. Three years later, Richard was teaching fourth graders in the Milwaukee public schools while working toward a master's degree in intellectual disability at the University of Wisconsin–Milwaukee. At the conclusion of his first year of teaching, he was asked to teach a class of young children with intellectual disability and for the next three years essentially became an early childhood special educator. It was at this point in Richard's career that he decided to earn a doctorate. He resigned his teaching position and moved to Madison, Wisconsin, where he pursued a PhD in the areas of human learning, child development, and behavioral disabilities. Upon receiving his degree, Dr. Gargiulo accepted a faculty position in the Department of Special Education at Bowling Green State University (Ohio), where for the next eight years he was a teacher educator. In 1982, he moved to Birmingham, Alabama, and joined the faculty of the University of Alabama at Birmingham (UAB), where, until his retirement, he served as a professor in the Department of Curriculum and Instruction. In November 2014, Dr. Gargiulo was awarded Professor Emeritus status by the board of trustees of the University of Alabama system.

Richard has had a rich and rewarding professional career spanning more than four decades. During the course of this journey, he twice served as president of the Alabama Federation, Council for Exceptional Children (CEC), and is a past president of the CEC Division of International Special Education and Services (DISES) and the CEC Division on Autism and Developmental Disabilities (DADD). Currently, Richard serves as the Southeast representative to the board of directors of DADD. He has lectured abroad extensively and was a Fulbright Scholar to the Czech Republic in 1991. In 2007, he was invited to serve as a Distinguished Visiting Professor at Charles University in Prague, Czech Republic.

Teaching has always been his passion. In 1999, he was honored with UAB's President's Award for Excellence in Teaching. In 2007, he received the Jasper Harvey Award from the Alabama Federation of the CEC in recognition of being named the outstanding special education teacher educator in Alabama.

With a background in both educational psychology and special education, Dr. Gargiulo's research has appeared in a wide variety of professional journals including *Child Development, Journal of Educational Research, Journal of Learning Disabilities, American Journal of Mental Deficiency, Childhood Education, Journal of Visual Impairment and Blindness, British Journal of Developmental Psychology, Journal of Special Education, Early Childhood Education Journal, International Journal of Clinical Neuropsychology,* and *International Journal of Special Education,* among many others.

In addition to the present text, Richard has authored or co-authored eleven books, several with multiple editions, ranging in topics from counseling parents of children with disabilities to child abuse, early childhood education, early childhood special education, and, most recently, teaching in inclusive classrooms.

Emily C. Bouck

Dr. Bouck is an associate professor of special education in the Department of Counseling, Educational Psychology, and Special Education at Michigan State University, from which she received her doctorate in special education. Dr. Bouck is the author of numerous peer-reviewed journal articles and chapters relating to her two main areas of research—mathematics education for students with disabilities and functional life skills education for students with disabilities—with a central theme of assistive technology throughout both areas. She is also the author of *Assistive Technology* and *Special Education in Contemporary Society* (joining Richard Gargiulo on the sixth edition of his text), both published by SAGE. Emily is a past president of the Council for Exceptional Children Division on Autism and Developmental Disabilities and has also been active in the Technology and Media Division. Dr. Bouck has taught courses on assistive technology; social, legal, and ethical issues in special education; special education methods; and doctoral seminars. She has experience working with a range of students with disabilities in school settings from preschool through age 26.

About the Contributors

E. Amanda Boutot, PhD, BCBA-D, is an associate professor of special education at Texas State University (San Marcos) where she is the coordinator of the autism and applied behavior analysis master's program. Amanda received her PhD in special education at the University of Texas at Austin. Dr. Boutot has numerous publications including articles in the *Journal of Applied Behavior Analysis, Focus on Autism and Other Developmental Disabilities, Education and Training in Autism and Developmental Disabilities*, and *Research in Autism Spectrum Disorders*. She has also authored several book chapters and two books including *Autism Encyclopedia: The Complete Guide to Autism Spectrum Disorders* and *Autism Spectrum Disorders: Foundations, Characteristics, and Effective Strategies*. Amanda recently completed the Play and Language (PAL) Program for Early Autism Intervention, a comprehensive curriculum and assessment for children with or suspected of having autism or other developmental disabilities. Dr. Boutot has presented nationally and internationally and has been an invited or keynote speaker in Bulgaria and Turkey. She currently serves as a past president of the Division on Autism and Developmental Disabilities of the Council for Exceptional Children.

David F. Cihak, PhD, is a professor of special education at the University of Tennessee where he serves as program coordinator of the special education and education technology program and teaches courses regarding characteristics and methods for students with severe disabilities, characteristics and methods for students' autism spectrum disorders, applied behavior analysis for teachers, and single-subject research designs. David brings over twenty years of experience in teacher education in the area of special education as both a teacher and teacher educator. He has taught students with high- and low-incidence disabilities at the elementary, middle, and high school levels. He has published over fifty data-based research studies focused on remedying classroom-based problems associated with academic and social/behavioral problems of individuals with severe disabilities and autism resulting in greater competency, community access, and acceptance. His research interests include the use of effective instructional and behavioral strategies, specifically video, augmented, mobile, and context-aware technologies for improving educational, functional, and social/communicative outcomes for students in classroom and community settings. David is also currently examining instructional technologies (for example, apps, augmented and context-aware reality) to facilitate the acquisition, generalization, and maintenance of functional digital media skills to improve digital inclusion and independence.

Ginevra R. Courtade, PhD, is an associate professor in special education at the University of Louisville. Dr. Courtade has worked in the field of moderate to severe disabilities for fifteen years. Her work focuses specifically on teaching academics to students with moderate to severe disabilities and preparing teachers to instruct students in the general education curriculum using evidence-based practices. Ginevra has numerous publications to her credit, including *Early Literacy Skills Builder, Teaching to Standards: Science, Aligning IEPs to the Common Core State Standards*, and *Six Successful Strategies for Teaching Common Core State Standards to Students With Moderate to Severe Disabilities*.

Dr. Courtade received her bachelor's degree in psychology from the State University of New York at Buffalo, her master's degree in special education from D'Youville College, and her doctoral degree in special education from the University of North Carolina at Charlotte. Prior to her current position, Ginevra spent two years at West Virginia University, where she served as an assistant professor in special education.

Currently, Dr. Courtade works closely with the Kentucky Department of Education to provide training and support to new teachers of students with moderate to severe disabilities. She also trains teachers nationally to implement academic curricula for their students.

Samuel A. DiGangi, PhD, BCBA-D, is an associate professor of special education in the Division of Educational Leadership and Innovation at Mary Lou Fulton Teachers College at Arizona State University (ASU). Dr. DiGangi directs the master of education in curriculum and instruction, applied behavior analysis program. Sam's research and teaching interests include the learning technologies of social and academic behavior, specifically the development, evaluation, and refinement of evidence-based techniques for use by teachers, parents, and practitioners. Dr. DiGangi's approach integrates applied behavior analysis, functional behavior assessment, visual analysis of data, and curriculum-based evaluation.

Dr. DiGangi has served as associate vice president of University Technology and executive director of the ASU Applied Learning Technologies Institute. He has led numerous sponsored projects and joint ventures centering on positive behavior intervention and supports, classroom behavior management, and adaptive/assistive technologies to enable and advance learning. Sam strives to foster innovation in design and implementation of instructional environments and approaches to enhance classroom-based and distance education at the local, national, and global levels.

Teresa Taber Doughty, PhD, is dean of the College of Education and a professor of special education at the University of Texas at Arlington. She previously served as an associate dean and professor of special education at Purdue University where she prepared pre-service teachers and graduate students for the field of special education. Her research focuses on assistive technologies, instructional and inclusive practices, applied behavior analysis, stimulus control, and community-based instruction. Teresa brings over thirty years of experience in special education and has published approximately sixty data-based research studies, chapters, monographs, articles, and manuals in her field. Dr. Taber Doughty currently serves on the Board of Visitors of the Council for the Accreditation of Educator Preparation (CAEP) and as the executive director for the Division of Autism and Developmental Disabilities of the Council for Exceptional Children.

Joan Grim, BS, MS, was a special education teacher and administrator in the Knox County, Tennessee, schools from 1979 until 2001. She taught children with a variety of disabilities across all ages as well as a noncategorical preschool class for five years before becoming a special education school administrator. After completing coursework for her PhD, Joan began teaching in the special education program at the University of Tennessee. Her professional focus is preparing pre-service special educators to teach preschool and school-age children with comprehensive disabilities in inclusive public schools. Dr. Grim is the 2016–2017 president-elect of the Tennessee Council for Exceptional Children.

Robert C. Pennington, PhD, BCBA-D, is an associate professor at the University of Louisville in the Department of Special Education. He has over twenty-five years of experience working with individuals with disabilities, their families, and teachers. He graduated from the University of Kentucky in 2010 and has had accepted for publication thirty peer-reviewed articles and book chapters related to working with persons with autism spectrum disorders and intellectual disability. Robert is passionate about the dissemination of research-based practice and has provided nearly 200 refereed and invited presentations to practitioners. He currently sits on five journal editorial boards and on multiple advisory panels including the Kentucky Advisory Council on Autism Spectrum Disorders. His current research interests involve behavior analytic communication instruction and expanding writing repertoires for students with significant intellectual disability.

Megan Purcell, PhD, is a clinical assistant professor in human development and family studies in the College of Health and Human Sciences at Purdue University. She completed her graduate training in early childhood special education and family studies at the University of Kansas. Her research and teaching are intertwined and drive her preparation of providers who will serve young children with and without disabilities and their families. Through best practice and the implementation of the DEC Recommended Practices, Megan seeks to increase positive outcomes for children and families. Her ultimate goal is to work with and prepare current and future early childhood educators and early interventionists to provide highly effective, inclusive services for all children to achieve the best possible outcomes.

Karrie A. Shogren, PhD, is a professor in the Department of Special Education, director of the Kansas University Center on Developmental Disabilities, and associate director of the Beach Center on Disability, all at the University of Kansas. Dr. Shogren's research focuses on self-determination and systems of support for students with disabilities. Karrie has published over 100 articles in peer-reviewed journals, is the author or co-author of ten books, and is one of the co-authors of *Intellectual Disability: Definition, Classification, and Systems of Supports*, the eleventh edition of the American Association on Intellectual and Developmental Disabilities' seminal definition of *intellectual disability* (formerly *mental retardation*), as well as the Supports Intensity Scale—Children's and Adult Version. Dr. Shogren has received grant funding from several sources, including the Institute of Education Sciences (IES) and National Institute on Disability, Independent Living, and Rehabilitation Research (NIDILRR). Dr. Shogren is co-editor of *Inclusion* and *Remedial and Special Education*.

Jordan Shurr, PhD, is an associate professor in the Department of Counseling and Special Education at Central Michigan University in Mount Pleasant. He teaches coursework in special education, specifically in intellectual disability, transition, and inclusion. Dr. Shurr is engaged in local, national, and international service through school training and research partnerships, professional journal and conference reviews, national board leadership, and international education and training collaborations. Jordan's areas of research specialization include literacy access for students with significant disabilities, technology supports, and critical issues within the profession of teaching students with significant disabilities. Dr. Shurr has fifteen-plus years of combined experience in classroom teaching, teacher education, educational research, assistive technology consultation, and camp inclusion.

Cate C. Smith, PhD, is an assistant professor in special education at Appalachian State University. She received MS and PhD degrees in special education from the University of Tennessee as well as a graduate certificate in evaluation, statistics, and measurement. Her work with students and practitioners focuses on using assistive technology and mobile platforms such as the iPad to improve academic and functional skills for students with moderate to significant intellectual and developmental disabilities including autism spectrum disorders. Cate's research includes investigating the use of mobile technology to improve independent functioning that results in greater academic enrichment, socialization, independent living, community access, and post-school outcomes for students with moderate to significant disabilities. She has authored research papers in peer-reviewed journals such as *Focus on Autism and Other Developmental Disabilities* and the *Journal of Special Education Technology*. Dr. Smith teaches undergraduate and graduate courses on assessment, intervention, inclusion, and assistive technology for students with mild to moderate and significant disabilities.

Kylan Turner, PhD, BCBA-D, has worked with children with autism spectrum disorders (ASD) for over fifteen years. Kylan was selected as a Leadership Education in Neurodevelopmental and Related Disabilities Fellow specializing in ASD from 2009 to 2011 and developed and disseminated a training curriculum focused on applied behavior analytic (ABA) intervention to community organizations throughout Pennsylvania. She graduated with her PhD in special education in 2012 from the University of Pittsburgh. Dr. Turner is a Board Certified Behavior Analyst, teaches graduate-level courses on ASD and ABA, and supervises students seeking fieldwork hours at Arizona State University. Her research interests include evaluations of behavioral interventions with the goal of identifying the most effective treatments for children with

ASD. Kylan specializes in the development of behavioral interventions provided through parent training to address sleep and feeding behavior problems in children with ASD.

Michael L. Wehmeyer, PhD, is Ross and Mariana Beach Distinguished Professor of Special Education and director and senior scientist at the Beach Center on Disability, both at the University of Kansas. He is the author or co-author of more than 370 peer-reviewed journal articles or book chapters and has authored, co-authored, edited, or co-edited thirty-six books on disability- and education-related issues, including issues pertaining to self-determination, positive psychology and disability, transition to adulthood, the education and inclusion of students with severe disabilities, and technology use by people with cognitive disabilities. Dr. Wehmeyer is past president and a Fellow of the American Association on Intellectual and Developmental Disabilities (AAIDD); past president of the Council for Exceptional Children's (CEC) Division on Career Development and Transition; Fellow of the American Psychological Association's (APA) Intellectual and Developmental Disabilities Division; and vice president for the Americas and a Fellow of the International Association for the Scientific Study of Intellectual and Developmental Disabilities. Michael has been recognized for his research and service with awards from numerous associations and organizations, including, recently, the APA Distinguished Contributions to the Advancement of Disability Issues in Psychology Award, the AAIDD Research Award, the Distinguished Researcher Award for lifetime contributions to research in intellectual disability by The Arc of the United States, the Burton Blatt Humanitarian Award from the CEC Division on Autism and Developmental Disabilities, and the CEC Special Education Research Award for 2016. He earned his PhD in human development and communication sciences from the University of Texas at Dallas, where he received a 2014 Distinguished Alumni Award.

PART I

Perspectives on Intellectual Disability

CHAPTER 1

Understanding Intellectual Disability

Richard M. Gargiulo and Emily C. Bouck

Learning Objectives

After reading Chapter 1, you should be able to:

- Discuss society's changing views of individuals with intellectual disability.
- Describe how intellectual ability and adaptive behavior are assessed.
- Summarize the key elements of the AAIDD definitions of intellectual disability from 1961 to 2010.
- List four ways of classifying individuals with intellectual disability.
- Explain why the number of individuals with intellectual disability has decreased over the years.

Intellectual disability is a very powerful term. It is also an emotionally laden label, one that conjures up various images of people with intellectual disability. What do you think of when someone says "intellectual disability"? Do you immediately think of the character from the movie *Radio*, *The Other Sister*, or *I Am Sam*? Maybe you recall meeting a young girl with Down syndrome when you volunteered to help during last year's Special Olympics, or perhaps you recollect how you felt when a group of adults with intellectual disability sat by you in a restaurant. Often our images of individuals with an intellectual disability are based on stereotypes resulting from limited contact and exposure. Consequently, many of us are susceptible to inaccuracies, misconceptions, and erroneous beliefs about this population. As a result, people with intellectual disability frequently encounter prejudice, ignorance, and, in some instances, outright discrimination simply because society has identified them as "different." Yet despite the diversity represented by this group, we firmly believe that children and adults with intellectual disability are first and foremost people who are more like their typically developing peers than they are different. In fact, very few ever fit the images and stereotypes commonly portrayed by the media.

Until very recently, individuals with an intellectual disability were often identified as *mentally retarded*—a pejorative, stigmatizing, and highly offensive label (commonly referred to in some circles as the "R" word). Today, the terminology of choice is *intellectual disability*. The acceptance of this new terminology has been championed by the premier professional organization in the field—the American Association on Intellectual and Developmental Disabilities.

THE "R" WORD—WHAT'S THE BIG DEAL?

Point

As young children, we were taught that "sticks and stones may break my bones but words will never hurt me." We repeated this saying to ourselves whenever we were teased by other kids. As we grew older, though, some of us started to realize the truth. Words are powerful; they can and often do hurt. Many times, they leave emotional scars that, unlike broken bones, don't always heal with the passage of time. Sometimes, words that aren't necessarily meant to offend can cause great pain. In fact, many words used by some children, as well as adults, perpetuate stereotypes and hurt the feelings of the recipient. One of these words is the "R" word. As the mother of a child with Down syndrome, I cannot bring myself to use this word. It is way too painful. The term in question begins with *R* and rhymes with *yard*. On any given school day, students carelessly toss this word around without giving it a second thought. For many individuals, it is just an expression; yet there are significant negative connotations associated with it. Have you ever said, "That's so '*R*' worded," or "You're such an '*R* word*?*" Many people don't realize that this word sends a message that it's all right to make fun of individuals with disabilities or, worse yet, to disregard them completely. Next time, remember another phrase: "Think before you speak."

Counterpoint

How does a word such as *retarded* take on such a negative connotation? If we stopped using the word, wouldn't it just be replaced by another inappropriate term such as *stupid, dumb, idiot,* or *imbecile*? Using words to label people for good or bad is part of who we are as a society and is done extensively by the government, in our schools, and throughout our communities. So if using a word like *retarded* to label a person has such negative connotations, why do we keep doing it? The reason is simple. The problem isn't with the word per se, or any other controversial term for that matter; it is the intent behind the use of the word. Sure, you can eliminate *retarded* from your vocabulary, but it will most likely just be replaced by another word with equally negative values unless we eliminate the intent. In fact, this has been the case throughout history. The chronology of the word *retarded* began with *feebleminded* and then evolved to *idiot, imbecile,* and *moron.* These are all words that are now considered pejorative and inappropriate in today's society. So, what will be the next term to replace *retarded*? Or will we finally realize that it isn't the word that hurts? It's the power we give the word.

Reflection

What do you think? Is it just the word, or is it the meaning and value associated with the term *retarded*? If we didn't use this term, would it simply be replaced by another (possibly less offensive) word?

SOURCE: Adapted from M. Hardman, C. Drew, and M. Egan, *Human Exceptionality*, 11th ed. (Belmont, CA: Wadsworth/Cengage Learning, 2014), p. 213.

The term *intellectual disability* is currently preferred by many policy makers, advocates, parents, service providers, teachers, and scholars. It is generally seen as less offensive to persons with this disability and is also consistent with contemporary Canadian and European terminology. The United States recently adopted this position. In October 2010, legislation was enacted (PL 111–256, commonly known as Rosa's law) that removed the terms *mental retardation* and *mentally retarded* from federal health, education, and labor statutes. In their place, we now find the designation *intellectual disability* to be the preferred language.

The goal of this chapter is to examine basic issues and concepts necessary for understanding intellectual disability and individuals with this disability. In this chapter, we will examine historical foundations, evolving definitions, identification, and assessment procedures along with classification models and the prevalence of intellectual disability.

Historical Perspectives on Intellectual Disability

It is generally believed that individuals with intellectual disability have been present in all societies throughout the ages. Historically speaking, the field of intellectual disability resembles an ever-changing mosaic influenced by the socio-political and economic climate of the times. Attitudes toward and understanding of intellectual disability have also affected the treatment of people with intellectual disability. Intellectual disability is a field that is continually evolving—from the ignorance of antiquity to the highly scientific and legal foundations of the early twenty-first century. Along this pathway, people with intellectual disability have had to endure and battle myths, fear, superstition, attempts at extermination, and educational and social segregation before arriving at today's policy of normalization and inclusion (Richards, Brady, & Taylor, 2015).

EARLY CIVILIZATIONS

Early written records from the era of the Greek and Roman empires make reference to citizens with intellectual disability. In some instances, these accounts date back to almost 1550 B.C. (Lindman & McIntyre, 1961). In many ways, the Greek and Roman societies were highly advanced and civilized, but the treatment of infants with disabilities would be judged cruel and barbaric by today's standards. Scheerenberger's (1983) detailed account of the history of intellectual disability reveals, for example, that in the city-state of Sparta, which placed a premium on physical strength and intellectual ability, **eugenics** and **infanticide** were common, everyday occurrences. Only the brightest and strongest of citizens were encouraged to have children. Newborns were examined by a council of inspectors, and babies thought to be defective or inferior were thrown from a cliff to die on the rocks below.

The early days of the Roman Republic mirrored the practices of the Greeks. Deformed infants were routinely allowed to perish—but only during the first eight days of life. Fathers held complete control over their children and could do whatever they wished, including selling or killing them. This doctrine of *patria potestas* is unparalleled in any other society.

THE MIDDLE AGES

From the fall of the Roman Empire in A.D. 476 to the beginning of the Renaissance in the 1300s, religion became a dominant social force, heralding a period of more humane treatment of individuals with disabilities. Churches established monasteries and asylums as sanctuaries for persons with intellectual disability. Children with intellectual disability were often called *les enfants du bon Dieu* ("the children of God"). Infanticide was rarely practiced because the largely agrarian societies required many workers in the fields. In some instances, individuals thought to have an intellectual disability found their way into castles where, though protected and shown favor, they served as buffoons and court jesters entertaining the nobility (Gargiulo, 1985). King Henry II of England enacted a policy in the twelfth century, *de praerogativa regis* ("of the king's prerogative"), whereby "natural fools" became the king's wards (Drew & Hardman, 2007).

At the same time, it was an era in which fear and superstition ran rampant. People with intellectual disability were frequently thought to be "filled with Satan" and to possess demonic powers, which often led to torture and death for practicing witchcraft. It was not uncommon for individuals with intellectual disability to be sent to prison and kept in chains because they were perceived to be a danger to society and their behavior was seen as unalterable.

It is important to note that when scholars and researchers talk about individuals with intellectual disability at this point in history, they are generally referring to those with more severe intellectual disability. Many persons with milder forms of intellectual disability could function adequately in the simple agrarian economies of that day and thus were not recognized or labeled as intellectually disabled. Their behavior was not viewed as different from that of their peers, many of whom were also illiterate yet capable of manual labor.

According to Hickson, Blackman, and Reis (1995), conditions and services for persons with intellectual disability did not greatly improve during the Renaissance (1350–1550). However, the social climate of the Renaissance set the stage for later events that would directly affect individuals with intellectual disability. A spirit of inquiry and openness took hold, along with a philosophy of humanism; Europe was on the verge of change.

EARLY OPTIMISM

The "modern" period in the history of intellectual disability traces its roots to the early nineteenth century. Scientific advances of this era helped to more clearly define the field of intellectual disability. Jean-Étienne Dominique

Esquirol (1782–1840), for example, differentiated between mental illness, which he termed *dementia*, and intellectual disability, which he called *amentia*. He also proposed a two-level classification system of intellectual disability: imbeciles and idiots. Imbeciles, in contemporary terminology, were persons with mild intellectual disability and higher-functioning individuals with moderate intellectual disability. Those identified by Esquirol as idiots would likely be characterized today as individuals with severe or profound intellectual disability (Scheerenberger, 1983).

It was during this period that the groundbreaking work of Jean-Marc Gaspard Itard (1774–1838) occurred. His pioneering efforts with Victor, the so-called *homme sauvage* or "wild man," earned him the title *Father of Special Education*. Itard's systematic attempts at educating Victor, whom he believed to be a victim of social/educational deprivation, signals the start of the notion that individuals with intellectual disability are capable of learning—however limited it may be.

Edouard Seguin (1812–1880) was inspired by the work of his mentor, Itard. Based on his religious convictions, Seguin was a fervent advocate for the education of children with intellectual disability. He was firmly convinced that highly structured and systematic sensorimotor instruction involving positive reinforcement and modeling would lead to improvement. His educational model, which he believed applicable to all children with intellectual disability regardless of severity, stressed physiological and moral education. In 1837, Seguin established the first school in Paris for the education of children with intellectual disability.

Because of the political turmoil in France in the mid-1800s, Seguin immigrated in 1848 to the United States, where he played a principal role in helping to establish residential facilities for persons with intellectual disability in several states. In 1876, the Association of Medical Officers of American Institutions for Idiotic and Feeble-Minded Persons was established, with Seguin serving as its first president. This association was the forerunner of today's American Association on Intellectual and Developmental Disabilities.

Beginning in the mid-nineteenth century, residential institutions began to dot the American landscape. In 1848, Samuel Gridley Howe (1801–1876) successfully lobbied the Massachusetts legislature and secured funding to establish the first residential facility for individuals with intellectual disability. Howe, a physician who was serving as the director of the Perkins Institution for the

Blind, located this residential school in a wing of the institution and initially offered services to ten "idiot" children (Scheerenberger, 1983). Howe believed that institutions should be kept small. Along with other advocates and social activists of his time, he was optimistic the persons with intellectual disability could be rehabilitated and eventually reintegrated into the mainstream of community life. For various reasons, however, this did not occur, and enthusiasm was eventually replaced with pessimism.

PROTECTION AND PESSIMISM

The late nineteenth and early twentieth centuries witnessed the development of large, geographically isolated institutions for individuals with intellectual disability. The focus of these facilities changed as the invigorating optimism of the early 1800s generally gave way to disillusionment, fear, and pessimism (Morrison & Polloway, 1995). Institutions were overcrowded and understaffed. Their mission shifted from one of education and rehabilitation, as espoused by Seguin and others, to a new custodial role. Caring concern was slowly replaced by an unjustified concern with protecting society from individuals with intellectual disability.

The public's regressive attitude toward persons with intellectual disability was fueled by two publications: *"The Jukes": A Study in Crime, Pauperism, Disease and Heredity* (Dugdale, 1877) and *The Kallikak Family: A Study in the Heredity of Feeblemindedness* (Goddard, 1912). The underlying thesis of these two books is that intellectual disability—or *feeblemindedness*, as it was then called—is inherited. It was generally believed that crime, poverty, and a host of other social ailments were directly due to the overpopulation of individuals with intellectual disability. Decades later, Goddard's questionable research into the descendants of a Revolutionary War soldier known by the pseudonym Martin Kallikak also supported the erroneous belief that intellectual disability results solely from heredity. Collectively, such publications reinforced the hypothesis that intellectual disability and social problems are correlated, thereby justifying the removal of these individuals from society and their sterilization. In the early 1900s, many states enacted legislation enforcing sterilization of citizens with intellectual disability. In 1927, the U.S. Supreme Court in *Buck v. Bell* upheld the constitutionality of these enactments.

One of the unfortunate consequences of this shift in societal attitude was that institutions became permanent residences for people with intellectual disability; thus, they were no longer prepared for their eventual return to society (Drew & Hardman, 2007). Education and training functions virtually disappeared, and only the most rudimentary care was provided. Over time, these institutions deteriorated, becoming warehouses for society's unwanted citizens. Living conditions were harsh and often deplorable. This situation was poignantly captured by Blatt and Kaplan (1966) in their classic photographic essay on institutional life, *Christmas in Purgatory*.

Beginning in the 1960s, a highly visible call for more humane and normalized living arrangements for people with intellectual disability was issued. Initiated in Sweden by Bengt Nirje (1969), the principle of **normalization** emphasizes "making available to the mentally retarded [intellectually disabled] patterns and conditions of everyday life which are as close as possible to the norms and patterns of the mainstream of society" (p. 181). In the United States, the idea that persons with intellectual disability have a right to culturally normative experiences was championed by Wolfensberger (1972). This concept, coupled with a renaissance of societal concern for individuals with intellectual disability, helped to facilitate a movement, beginning in the 1970s, toward **deinstitutionalization** and more community-based services for individuals with intellectual disability. Today, legislative as well as legal action has resulted in more normalized lifestyles and greater access to all aspects of society for our fellow citizens with intellectual disability.

THE EMERGENCE OF PUBLIC EDUCATION FOR STUDENTS WITH INTELLECTUAL DISABILITY

Although institutions were firmly established as part of the American social fabric in the late 1800s, public education for children with intellectual disability was virtually nonexistent. The first public school class for "slow learning" youngsters was formed in Providence, Rhode Island, at the very end of the nineteenth century. These programs were largely segregated or self-contained classes and would remain so for the better part of the twentieth century. Classes for higher-functioning pupils with intellectual disability began to grow, in part as a result of the popularizing of intelligence testing. Scheerenberger (1983) reports that by 1930, sixteen states had enacted either mandatory or permissive legislation regarding special classes for children with intellectual disability. By 1952, forty-six of the forty-eight states provided an education to children with intellectual disability. Students with severe or profound intellectual disability, however, were largely excluded from public education. This pattern was to change beginning in the late 1950s and 1960s, thanks in part to the advocacy and initiatives of well-organized parent groups. The National Association of Parents and Friends of Mentally Retarded Children, formed in 1950, was especially influential in securing rights for children with intellectual disability (Hickson et al., 1995). This group was the forerunner of today's very active and politically powerful association known simply as The Arc.

The 1960s and 1970s marked the beginning of an era of national concern for the rights of individuals, a focus that continues today. People with intellectual disability would benefit from this attention. Aided by the actions of President John F. Kennedy, who had a sister with intellectual disability, enlightened social policies, new educational programs, and a national research agenda were all forthcoming. At the same time, advances in the field of psychology and education demonstrated that, to some degree, all individuals with intellectual disability are capable of learning. Professionals also began a movement toward less restrictive and more integrated educational placements for students with intellectual disability—an emphasis with a very contemporary flavor. But perhaps the principal legacy of this era, which is foundational to today's educational programming, is a greater acceptance of persons with intellectual disability and their right, as fellow citizens, to live their lives in the most normalized fashion.

IDENTIFICATION AND ASSESSMENT OF INTELLECTUAL DISABILITY

The constructs of intelligence and adaptive behavior play key roles in our understanding of the concept of intellectual disability. Yet both of these terms are somewhat difficult to define and assess. For the sake of clarity, we will discuss each concept separately; but remember they are intricately interrelated and provide the foundation for contemporary thinking about intellectual disability.

INTELLECTUAL ABILITY

The question of what constitutes intelligence and how to describe it has challenged educators, psychologists, and thinkers throughout the years. Even today, there is disagreement among professionals as to the meaning of this term and the best way of measuring intelligence. Intelligence is perhaps best thought of as a construct or theoretical abstraction; it is not a visible entity but rather a human trait whose existence is inferred based on a person's performance on certain types of cognitive tasks. Because no one has ever seen intelligence and we have only deduced its presence, professionals have come to the realization that they are "attempting to explain one of the most complex and elusive components of human functioning" (Beirne-Smith, Patton, & Kim, 2006, p. 95).

These difficulties notwithstanding, a great amount of effort has been expended on trying to accurately assess intellectual functioning. The most common way of determining an individual's cognitive ability is through an IQ or intelligence test. Two of the more widely used individually administered IQ measures are the Wechsler Intelligence Scale for Children (5th ed.), or WISC-V (Wechsler, 2014), and the fifth edition of the original work of Binet and Simon from the early twentieth century, the Stanford-Binet Intelligence Scales (Roid, 2003). Some psychologists and psychometrists rely on the Kaufman Assessment Battery for Children (Kaufman & Kaufman, 2004), especially when evaluating youngsters from culturally and linguistically diverse backgrounds.

Data gleaned from the WISC-V, the Stanford-Binet V, and similar measures are thought to represent a sample of an individual's intellectual skills and abilities. These data are usually summarized as an IQ score. Originally, an IQ was defined as a ratio between the person's mental age (MA or developmental level) and chronological age (CA) multiplied by 100. For instance, a student whose chronological age is 10 but who performs on an IQ test like a typical 5-year-old would have an IQ of 50; if accompanied by deficits in adaptive behavior, this individual would very likely be identified as having an intellectual disability. Today, deviation IQs or standard scores have replaced intelligence quotients in most professional circles. A standard score is nothing more than an expression of how far a particular raw score deviates from a specific reference point such as the test mean. Standard scores are often expressed as standard deviations. One standard deviation on both the Stanford-Binet V and the WISC-V is equivalent to 15 IQ points. Both tests have a mean IQ of 100.

Although IQ testing is very common in schools, the issue of assessing someone's intelligence, especially if a special education placement may result, is somewhat controversial. Cautionary flags and reasons for concern tend to focus on these issues:

- Potential for cultural bias. Intellectual assessments are often criticized because of their highly verbal nature and reflection of middle-class Anglo standards.

- Stability of IQ. An IQ test only reports a person's performance at a particular point in time; intelligence is not static but capable of changing, and in some cases, the change can be significant.

- Overemphasis on IQ scores. An IQ score is not the sole indicator of an individual's ability, nor is it a measure of the person's worth; yet IQ is often stressed at the expense of other factors such as motivation or adaptive skills.

ADAPTIVE BEHAVIOR

The notion of adaptive behavior was first introduced in the 1973 AAIDD definition of intellectual disability. It was retained in the 1983 description and is the underpinning of the most recent AAIDD definitions. **Adaptive behavior** is seen as "the degree to which, and the efficiency with which, the individual meets the standards of maturation, learning, personal independence, and/or social responsibility that are expected for his or her age level and cultural group" (Grossman, 1983, p. 11). In continuing this thinking, Luckasson et al. (2002) describe adaptive behavior as "the collection of conceptual, social, and practical skills that have been learned by people in order to function in their everyday society" (p. 73). Stated another way, it is how well a person copes with the everyday demands and requirements of his or her environment. According to Luckasson and her colleagues, adaptive behavior is seen as significant limitations in the expression or performance of conceptual (for example, reading and writing, money concepts), social (for example, obeying laws, following rules), and practical (for example, eating, dressing oneself, meal preparation, occupational abilities) adaptive skills. (See Table 1.1.)

The idea of context is also important for understanding the concept of adaptive behavior. Because behavior is strongly influenced by cultural factors, age and situation appropriateness must always be considered within the setting in which it occurs. For example, a teenage girl who uses her fingers while eating might be viewed as exhibiting inappropriate behavior; however, this behavior is only maladaptive when considered within the context of Western cultures.

It is not always easy to assess adaptive behavior. It is usually measured via direct observation, structured interviews, or standardized scales. Information may be obtained from family members, teachers, caregivers, or other professionals. AAIDD is currently developing the Diagnostic Adaptive Behavior

TABLE 1.1 2002 AAIDD Adaptive Skill Areas

SKILL AREA	EXAMPLES OF BEHAVIOR
Conceptual	• Language (receptive and expressive) • Reading and writing • Money concepts • Self-direction
Social	• Interpersonal • Responsibility • Self-esteem • Gullibility (likelihood of being tricked or manipulated) • Naiveté • Follows rules • Obeys laws • Avoids victimization

Practical	• Activities of daily living:
	  ○ Eating
	  ○ Transfer/mobility
	  ○ Toileting
	  ○ Dressing
	• Instrumental activities of daily living:
	  ○ Meal preparation
	  ○ Housekeeping
	  ○ Transportation
	  ○ Taking medication
	  ○ Money management
	  ○ Telephone use
	  ○ Occupational skills
	  ○ Maintains safe environments

SOURCE: Adapted from *Mental Retardation: Definition, Classification, and Systems of Supports*, 10th ed. (Washington, DC: American Association on Mental Retardation, 2002), p. 42.

Scale (DABS) as a standardized measure of adaptive behavior. Based on the three adaptive skill areas (conceptual, social, and practical), this new instrument is being normed on individuals in the chronological age range of 4–21 years old with and without intellectual disability. Designed as a diagnostic test, the DABS seeks to provide a precise cutoff point for persons deemed to have "significant limitations" in adaptive behavior (American Association on Intellectual and Developmental Disabilities, 2015). As you will now learn, these limitations represent key components of the most recent AAIDD definitions of intellectual disability.

EVOLVING DEFINITIONS OF INTELLECTUAL DISABILITY

Intellectual disability is a complex and multifaceted concept. It has been studied by psychologists, sociologists, educators, physicians, and many other professionals. This multidisciplinary interest in and investigation of intellectual disability, while beneficial, has significantly contributed to problems of conceptual and definitional clarity (Drew & Hardman, 2007). Yet, by its very nature, intellectual disability cannot be studied independently of other disciplines. We fully agree with Drew and his colleague that there is considerable merit in a multidisciplinary approach; however, we must not lose sight of what should be our central focus, the individual with an intellectual disability.

HISTORICAL INTERPRETATIONS

Over the years, the American Association on Intellectual and Developmental Disabilities (AAIDD) has put forth several different interpretations of intellectual disability. We will briefly examine some of these early definitions to gain a better appreciation of how our understanding of this disability has evolved.

1961 AAIDD Definition. AAIDD's sixth definition appeared in 1961 and was widely accepted by professionals. At this point in time, intellectual disability was described as "subaverage general intellectual functioning which originates during the developmental period and is associated with impairments in adaptive behavior" (Heber, 1961, p. 3). Let us analyze the meaning of these phrases. *Subaverage general intellectual functioning* is defined as an intelligence quotient (IQ) greater than one **standard deviation** (SD) (a statistic describing variance from the mean or average score of a particular group) below the mean for a given age group. In 1961, this was interpreted to be an IQ below 85 or 84 depending on which standardized IQ test was used. The *developmental period* extended from birth to approximately age 16. The criterion of *impairments in adaptive behavior* is a critical and unique aspect of this definition. The inclusion of this factor establishes dual criteria for identifying someone as having an intellectual disability (Scheerenberger, 1987). Adaptive behavior, which Heber introduced, refers to an individual's ability to meet the social requirements of

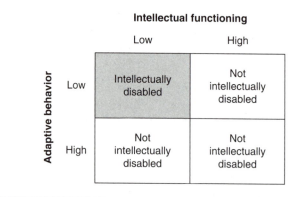

NOTE: Classification of an individual as intellectually disabled requires both low intellectual functioning and deficits in adaptive behavior.

his or her community that are appropriate for his or her chronological age; it is an indication of independence and social competency. Thus, according to Heber's definition, a person with an IQ of 79 who did not exhibit a significant impairment in adaptive behavior could not be identified as having an intellectual disability. (See Figure 1.1.)

1973 AAIDD Definition. Herbert Grossman chaired a committee charged with revising the 1961 AAIDD definition. Grossman's (1973) definition viewed intellectual disability as "significantly subaverage general intellectual functioning existing concurrently with deficits in adaptive behavior, and manifested during the developmental period" (p. 11). Though paralleling its predecessor, the Grossman definition is conceptually distinct. First, the 1973 definition refers to significantly subaverage intellectual ability. Operationally, intellectual disability was psychometrically redefined as performance at least two standard deviations below the mean. This more conservative approach considered the upper IQ limit to be 70 or 68 (again, depending on whether the Stanford-Binet Intelligence Scales [SD = 16 points] or the Wechsler Intelligence Scale for Children [SD = 15 points] was used). Statistically speaking, this represents the lower 2.27 percent of the population instead of the approximately 16 percent included in the Heber definition. (See Figure 1.2.) Adopting this standard eliminated the classification of "borderline" intellectual disability incorporated in Heber's conceptual scheme.

FIGURE 1.2 The Normal Curve: A Theoretical Distribution of Intelligence

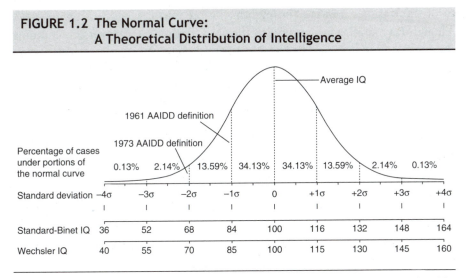

NOTE: The 1961 AAIDD definition defines mental intellectual disability as an IQ lower than 85 (84) on a standardized measure of intelligence. The 1973 AAIDD definition defines intellectual disability as an IQ lower than 70 (68). Later versions allow for professional judgment when considering intellectual performance.

The Grossman definition also sought to clarify the relationship between adaptive behavior and intellectual functioning. This definition attempted to focus greater attention on adaptive behavior and described it as the ability of an individual to meet "the standards of personal independence and social responsibility expected of his [or her] age and cultural group" (Grossman, 1973, p. 11). Adaptive behavior was to be considered within the context of the person's age and sociocultural group. Grossman's work attempted to strengthen the link between IQ and adaptive behavior in an effort to reduce the number of pupils identified with intellectual disability solely on the basis of their IQ. The 1973 definition also extended the concept of the developmental period to age 18 to more accurately reflect when most people complete their education. Although this definition forms the foundation for the current federal definition of intellectual disability, some educators were concerned that lowering the IQ threshold to 68 (70) could possibly deny a special education to students who otherwise would have been eligible. It was feared that these children would be misclassified and inappropriately placed and thus "drown in the mainstream" (Scheerenberger, 1987).

1983 AAIDD Definition. In 1983, AAIDD published yet another revision to its manual on terminology and classification. Once again, Grossman led the organization's efforts. The eighth edition mirrors its 1973 predecessor. Though very similar in wording to the 1973 definition, this version contains some important changes. The 1983 Grossman edition suggests using a range of 70–75 when describing the upper limits of intellectual performance on a standardized measure of intelligence rather than a strict cutoff of 70. An IQ score of 70 is intended only as a guideline.

Flexibility is the key to understanding the operation of this definition. The clinical judgment of the professional now plays an important role when making a diagnosis of intellectual disability.

1992 AAIDD Definition. In May 1992, Ruth Luckasson and her colleagues crafted a new definition of intellectual disability, which was published in *Mental Retardation: Definition, Classification, and Systems of Supports.* According to this manual,

> Mental retardation [intellectual disability] refers to substantial limitations in present functioning. It is characterized by significantly subaverage intellectual functioning existing concurrently with related limitations in two or more of the following applicable adaptive skill areas: communication, self-care, home living, social skills, community use, self-direction, health and safety, functional academics, leisure, and work. Mental retardation [intellectual disability] manifests before age 18. (p. 5)

Application of this definition requires careful consideration of the following four essential assumptions:

1. Valid assessment considers cultural and linguistic diversity as well as differences in communication and behavioral factors.

2. The existence of limitations in adaptive skills occurs within the context of community environments typical of the individual's age peers and is indexed to the person's individualized needs for supports.

3. Specific adaptive limitations often coexist with strengths in other adaptive skills or other personal capabilities.

4. With appropriate supports over a sustained period, the life functioning of the person with mental retardation [intellectual disability] will generally improve. (Luckasson et al., 1992, p. 5)

The 1992 AAIDD definition is a highly functional definition. It portrays intellectual disability as a relationship among three key elements: the individual, the environment, and the type of support required for maximum functioning in various settings. It essentially reflects the "fit" between the person's capabilities and the structure and expectations of the environment. This ninth version also represents a conceptual shift away from viewing intellectual disability as an inherent trait to a perspective that considers the person's present level of functioning and the supports needed to improve it. The interaction among the individual, the environment, and support is perhaps best conceptualized as an equilateral triangle because it shows the equality among the three elements or sides.

The 1992 AAIDD description of intellectual disability stresses functioning in one's community rather than just focusing on the clinical aspect of the individual such as IQ or adaptive behavior (Smith, Polloway, Patton, & Dowdy, 2008). This definition is an optimistic one; it assumes that a person's performance will improve over time when appropriate supports are provided. Though certainly a unique portrayal of intellectual disability, this definition, like its predecessors, retains an emphasis on intellectual performance coupled with impairments in adaptive skills.

CONTEMPORARY VIEWPOINTS

2002 AAIDD Definition. As times have changed, so has our understanding of the construct of intellectual disability. The 2002 AAIDD definition represents another effort in our evolving understanding of intellectual disability. The purpose of the tenth edition was to "create a contemporary system of diagnosis, classification, and systems of support for the disability currently known as mental retardation [intellectual disability]" (Luckasson et al., 2002, p. xii).

This definition states that "mental retardation [intellectual disability] is a disability characterized by significant limitations both in intellectual functioning and in adaptive behavior as expressed in conceptual, social, and practical adaptive skills. This disability originates before age 18" (Luckasson et al., 2002, p. 1).

Accompanying this description are five assumptions considered essential when applying this definition:

- Limitations in present functioning must be considered within the context of community environments typical of the individual's age, peers, and culture.

- Valid assessment considers cultural and linguistic diversity as well as differences in communication and sensory, motor, and behavioral factors.

- Within an individual, limitations often coexist with strengths.

- An important purpose of describing limitations is to develop a profile of needed supports.

- With appropriate personalized supports over a sustained period, the life functioning of the person with mental retardation [intellectual disability] will generally improve. (Luckasson et al., 2002, p. 1)

Like its predecessor, the 2002 AAIDD definition retains a positive perspective toward individuals with intellectual disability while continuing to acknowledge the significance of adaptive behavior and systems of support. It also preserves the idea that intellectual disability is a "function of the relationship among individual functioning, supports, and contexts" (Wehmeyer, 2003, p. 276). This conceptualization of intellectual disability, while not flawless, represents a logical step in the continuing challenge of advancing our understanding of the concept of intellectual disability.

2010 AAIDD Definition. The eleventh AAIDD definition (Schalock et al., 2010) both reiterates and strengthens key concepts found in the 2002 definition of intellectual disability. Developed by a committee of eighteen medical and legal scholars as well as policy makers, educators, and other professionals, the 2010 definition emphasizes the abilities and assets of individuals with intellectual disability rather than their deficits or limitations.

Intellectual disability is viewed as a state of functioning rather than an inherent trait. As in earlier definitions, one of the goals of the 2010 definition is to maximize support services so as to allow persons with intellectual disability to participate fully in all aspects of daily life.

The description of intellectual disability in the 2010 manual mirrors the wording found in the tenth edition, as do the five accompanying assumptions. The eleventh edition also retains the emphasis on adaptive behavior while stressing systems of support. The term *mental retardation*, however, is replaced by the more contemporary label *intellectual disability*. This term is less pejorative while also reflecting a social–ecological understanding of disability (Schalock, 2015). The committee notes, however, that despite the change in terminology, the term *intellectual disability* refers to the same population of individuals who were recognized previously as being mentally retarded (Schalock et al., 2010).

The latest AAIDD definition reflects best practices and new thinking about classifying individuals with intellectual disability. Rather than using intellectual functioning as a basis for classifying persons with cognitive limitations, the 2010 definition encourages professionals and service providers to classify on the basis of various dimensions of human functioning—intellectual abilities, adaptive behavior, health, participation, and context. *Human functioning* is essentially viewed as "an umbrella term for all life activities and encompasses body structures and functions, personal activities, and participation, which in turn are influenced by one's health and environmental or contextual factors" (Schalock et al., 2010, p. 15). This multidimensional perspective allows one to classify depending on the questions being asked (for example, "Is this person competent to be a self-advocate, maintain a bank account, or have sexual relations?") and the specific purpose of the classification system. Classification is then linked to personalized systems of support for that individual (Schalock, 2015).

CLASSIFICATION OF INDIVIDUALS WITH INTELLECTUAL DISABILITY

A classification system is a convenient way for differentiating among individuals who share a common characteristic—in this instance, intellectual disability. Of course, we must remember that there is a great degree of variability among members of this population despite the fact that they share a common label. Because intellectual disability exists along a continuum, there have been numerous proposals on how to classify people with this disability. Like definitions of intellectual disability, classification models tend to vary according to a particular focus. We will examine several systems—some vintage ones along with the most contemporary thinking in this area.

AN ETIOLOGICAL PERSPECTIVE

Traditionally, individuals with intellectual disability have been classified based on known or presumed medical/biological causes. This etiological orientation assumes that intellectual disability is a consequence of a disease process or biological defect. Examples include intellectual disability that is due to infections such as rubella (German measles) or maternal syphilis, chromosomal abnormalities such as Down syndrome, or metabolic disorders such as phenylketonuria (PKU). (These examples and others will be more fully explored in Chapter 2.) Although useful for physicians and other health care workers, this classification scheme has limited applicability for nonmedical practitioners.

INTELLECTUAL DEFICITS

A long-standing and popular classification scheme among psychologists and educators is one based on the severity of intellectual impairment as determined by an IQ test. This model is one of the most widely cited in the professional literature and, until recently, reflected the position of AAIDD dating back to the 1973 Grossman definition of intellectual disability. According to this system, deficits in intellectual functioning and related impairments in adaptive behavior result in individuals being classified into one of four levels of intellectual disability—mild, moderate, severe, or profound—with *mild* representing the highest level of performance for persons thought to have an intellectual disability and *profound* the lowest. Intellectual competency is often the primary variable used in constructing these discriminations; Table 1.2 presents the IQ ranges typically used.

AN EDUCATIONAL PERSPECTIVE

Another classification system popular with educators since the 1960s is to classify students with intellectual disability on the basis of expected or anticipated educational accomplishments. Generally speaking, special education teachers

TABLE 1.2 Classification of Intellectual Disability According to Measured Intelligence		
CLASSIFICATION LEVEL	**MEASURED IQ**	**SD BELOW MEAN**
Mild intellectual disability	55-70	2 to 3
Moderate intellectual disability	40-55	3 to 4
Severe intellectual disability	25-40	4 to 5
Profound intellectual disability	Under 25	More than 5

NOTE: IQ scores are approximate.
SD = standard deviation.

classified learners into two groups: **educable mentally retarded (EMR)** or **trainable mentally retarded (TMR)**. These designations are roughly equivalent to the AAIDD labels of *mild* and *moderate intellectual disability*, with IQs ranging from about 50–55 to 70–75 and 35–40 to 50–55, respectively. (Before the enactment of PL 94–142, public schools rarely served individuals with IQs lower than 35; therefore, these students were not labeled according to this system.) As you might expect, the term *educable* implies that a pupil has some, albeit limited, academic potential; *trainable* implies that a child is incapable of learning but possibly could be trained in nonacademic areas. Over the years, professionals have learned that these prognostic labels, which represent an "educability quotient," are inaccurate and present a false dichotomy; we affirm that all children are capable of learning when presented with the appropriate circumstances. The notion of presumed academic achievement has slowly fallen out of favor in professional circles. These terms are currently considered pejorative and tend to perpetuate stereotypical and prejudicial attitudes.

LEVELS OF SUPPORT

In the early nineties, AAIDD (Luckasson et al., 1992), in a dramatic and controversial maneuver, shifted from a classification model based on severity of intellectual impairment to one based on the type and extent of needed supports. This scheme, retained in the 2002 definition by Luckasson et al., classifies individuals with intellectual disability according to the **level of support**—intermittent, limited, extensive, or pervasive—needed to effectively function across adaptive skill areas in various natural settings, rather than according to their deficits. In fact, AAIDD recommends abandoning references to severity. Table 1.3 describes the four classification levels endorsed by AAIDD.

The aim of this approach is to explain an individual's functional (rather than intellectual) limitations in terms of the amount of support he or she requires to achieve optimal growth and development at home, at school, at the workplace, and in other community settings (Beirne-Smith et al., 2006). This model, which represents more than a mere substitution for the previous AAIDD IQ-based classification scheme, extends the concept of support beyond the intensity of needed support to include the type of support system required. **Natural supports** typically include family members, friends, teachers, and co-workers. **Formal supports** are usually thought of as government-funded social programs like Social Security payments or health care programs, habilitation

TABLE 1.3 Classification of Intellectual Disability According to Intensities of Support

SUPPORT LEVEL	DESCRIPTION	EXAMPLES
Intermittent	Supports on an as-needed or episodic basis. Person does not always need the support(s), or person needs short-term supports during life span transitions. When provided, intermittent supports may be of high or low intensity.	• Loss of employment • Acute medical crisis
Limited	Supports characterized by consistency over time, time-limited but not intermittent; may require fewer staff and less cost than more intense levels of support.	• Job training • Transitioning from school to adult status
Extensive	Supports characterized by regular involvement (e.g., daily) in at least some environments (such as work or home) and not time-limited.	• Ongoing home living assistance
Pervasive	Supports characterized by their constancy and high intensity; provided across all environments, potential life-sustaining nature. Pervasive supports typically involve more staff and intrusiveness than extensive or time-limited supports.	• Chronic medical situation

SOURCE: Adapted from *Mental Retardation: Definition, Classification, and Systems of Supports,* 10th ed. (Washington, DC: American Association on Mental Retardation, 2002), p. 152.

services, and even the efforts of groups like the Council for Exceptional Children or The Arc, a national advocacy organization on intellectual disability. It is difficult to say how professionals, school systems, and other groups will respond to this new way of thinking about classifying people with intellectual disability.

PREVALENCE OF INTELLECTUAL DISABILITY

How many students in the United States have an intellectual disability? Answering this question first requires that we define the term *prevalence*. **Prevalence** refers to the total number of individuals with a particular disability existing in the population at a given time. Prevalence is typically expressed as a percentage of the population exhibiting this specific disability—in this instance, the percentage of pupils with intellectual disability enrolled in special education classes. According to data from the U.S. Department of Education (2015), 415,200 children between the ages of 6 and 21 were identified as intellectually disabled and receiving a special education during the 2013–2014 school year. These students represent approximately 7.1 percent of all pupils with disabilities but less than 1 percent of the total school-age population. Although a figure of approximately 415,000 may seem large, over the years the number of students classified as having an intellectual disability has decreased significantly for a variety of reasons ranging from the benefits of prevention and early intervention, to changing definitions, to improved referral tactics (see Figure 1.3). The reasons for this decrease are likely due to the benefits of prevention and early intervention, to changing definitions, and to improved referral tactics, as well as the impact of litigation (discussed in Chapter 3) and the placement of higher-functioning individuals with intellectual disability into programs for pupils with learning disabilities. Perhaps the most compelling reason for fewer students being identified as intellectually disabled is a reluctance among professionals to identify (or misidentify) someone as having an intellectual disability if he or she is from a culturally or linguistically diverse group (Gargiulo, 2012).

The federal government also reports data on the number of preschoolers receiving a special education. According to the U.S. Department of Education (2015), approximately 14,200 preschoolers (youngsters ages 3–5) are

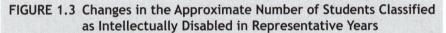

FIGURE 1.3 Changes in the Approximate Number of Students Classified as Intellectually Disabled in Representative Years

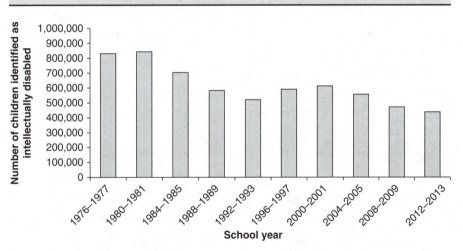

NOTE: Enrollment figures represent pupils ages 6-21 served under Part B and Chapter 1.

SOURCE: Various U.S. Department of Education Annual Reports to Congress on the Implementation of the Individuals with Disabilities Education Act.

recognized as intellectually disabled. This figure represents 1.9 percent of all young children with a disability.

Within the population of individuals identified as having an intellectual disability, persons with a mild intellectual disability, to use a familiar or common term, constitute the largest proportion. It is estimated that approximately 90 percent of students with intellectual disability function at the mild level (IQ between 50 and 70–75). The remaining 10 percent are classified as exhibiting moderate, severe, or profound intellectual disability (Hardman, Drew, & Egan, 2014).

Chapter Summary

- Our understanding of intellectual disability reflects changing attitudes toward persons with intellectual disability as well as the prevailing economic and sociopolitical climate of the times.

- Intelligence is a theoretical construct whose existence can only be inferred on the basis of a person's performance on certain types of cognitive tests that only represent a sample of the person's intellectual skills and abilities.

- Contemporary practice considers intellectual disability to be the result of interactions among the person, the environment, and those supports required to maximize the individual's performance in particular settings or environments.

- Some models group persons with intellectual disability according to the etiology or cause of the disability; others label persons according to the severity of their cognitive impairment, such as mildly or severely intellectually disabled.

- Educators sometimes identify students with intellectual disability as educable mentally retarded (EMR) or trainable mentally retarded (TMR), terms now considered pejorative.

- The 2002 AAIDD definition classifies individuals with intellectual disability on the basis of the extent or levels of support they require to function effectively across adaptive skill areas in various natural settings, such as home, school, or job.

- Currently, approximately 7 percent of all students with disabilities, or about 1 percent of the total school-age population, are recognized as being intellectually disabled.

- The vast majority of persons with intellectual disability have an IQ between 50 and 70–75.

Review Questions

1. How has society's view and understanding of persons with intellectual disability changed over the centuries?

2. Why is the assessment of intelligence such a controversial issue?

3. What is adaptive behavior, and how is it assessed?

4. How has the definition of intellectual disability changed over the past several decades?

5. Identify the three key elements of the 1992 AAIDD definition of intellectual disability. How are they conceptually interrelated?

6. List four different strategies for classifying individuals with intellectual disability.

7. What factors have contributed to the gradual reduction in the number of students classified as intellectually disabled?

Key Terms

eugenics (page 6)
infanticide (page 6)
normalization (page 10)
deinstitutionalization (page 10)
adaptive behavior (page 13)
standard deviation (SD) (page 15)
educable mentally retarded (EMR) (page 23)

trainable mentally retarded (TMR) (page 23)
level of support (page 23)
natural supports (page 23)
formal supports (page 23)
prevalence (page 24)

Organizations Concerned With Intellectual Disability

American Association on Intellectual and Developmental Disabilities

https://aaidd.org/

The Arc (formerly the Association for Retarded Citizens of the United States)

www.thearc.org

Division on Autism and Developmental Disabilities, Council for Exceptional Children

www.daddcec.org

National Down Syndrome Congress

www.ndsccenter.org

National Down Syndrome Society

http://ndss.org

CHAPTER 2

Foundational Concepts

Etiology of Intellectual Disability and Characteristics of Students With Intellectual Disability

Richard M. Gargiulo and Emily C. Bouck

Learning Objectives

After reading Chapter 2, you should be able to:

- Describe pre-, peri-, and postnatal causes of intellectual disability.
- Summarize representative learning and social/behavioral characteristics of students with intellectual disability.

Determining the cause, or **etiology**, of an intellectual disability is a difficult process. Multiple reasons are typically involved, and frequently the cause is unknown. In fact, in only about half of all cases of intellectual disability can a specific cause be cited. Generally speaking, the less severe the disability, the greater the likelihood that a particular cause cannot be determined (Smith, Polloway, Taber-Doughty, Patton, & Dowdy, 2016; Turnbull, Turnbull, Wehmeyer, & Shogren, 2016).

Although scientists and other researchers are unable to determine the etiology of intellectual disability in every instance, we do know a great deal about what causes, or is at least implicated as, possible etiological factors. Investigators have designed several different schemes or models for classifying known and/or suspected causes of intellectual disability. For the purpose of this discussion, we have adopted the American Association on Intellectual and Developmental Disabilities (AAIDD) format (Luckasson et al., 2002) for categorizing etiological factors typically associated with intellectual disability. The 2002 AAIDD model, as well as the 2010 conceptualization, designates three main sources of possible causes of intellectual disability that are based on the time of onset: **prenatal** (occurring before birth), **perinatal** (occurring around the time of birth), and **postnatal** (occurring after birth). Table 2.1 (page 32) identifies some of the variables that could possibly lead to an intellectual disability.

Prenatal Causes of Intellectual Disability

Even a quick glance at Table 2.1 suggests that many different factors, of various origins, contribute to the possibility that a developing fetus may be at risk for intellectual disability. In some instances, intellectual disability will be an inescapable fact; in other cases, it is highly probable. Fortunately, researchers are making great strides in the areas of detection and prevention of certain types of intellectual disability.

CHROMOSOMAL ABNORMALITIES

Down syndrome, the most common and perhaps best-known genetic disorder, was first described by Dr. John Langdon Down in 1866; however, it was not until 1959 that Down syndrome was linked to a chromosomal abnormality (Lejune, Gautier, & Turpin, 1959). Most people have forty-six chromosomes arranged in twenty-three pairs; people with Down syndrome have forty-seven. Chromosomes are rod- or threadlike bodies that carry the genes that provide the blueprint or building blocks for development. The most common type of Down syndrome, accounting for approximately 90 percent of cases, is known as trisomy 21. In this instance, an extra chromosome becomes attached to the twenty-first pair, with the result that there are three (tri) chromosomes at this particular site.

Scientists are uncertain as to exactly what causes Down syndrome. Thyroid problems, drugs, and exposure to radiation are all suspected, but there appears to be a strong link between maternal age and Down syndrome (Roizen, 2013). It is estimated that at age 25, the incidence of Down syndrome is 1 out of 1,250 births; at age 30, it is approximately 1 in 1,000 births; at age 35, it is nearly 1 in 400 births; at age 40, it is about 1 in 100 births; and at age 45, the risk is 1 out of 30 births (Fergus, 2016; March of Dimes, 2015a). It is important to note that maternal age itself does *not* cause Down syndrome, only that there is a strong correlation. Down syndrome affects all racial and socioeconomic groups equally.

Physicians will frequently offer diagnostic testing procedures capable of detecting chromosomal abnormalities like Down syndrome to women who will be age 35 or older on their due date or those whose blood screening is abnormal. **Chorionic villus sampling (CVS)** is one example. It is typically performed at about ten to twelve weeks of gestation while **amniocentesis** is more common during the second trimester of pregnancy.

With CVS, a small sample of chorionic villi (tiny fingerlike projections that make up the placenta) is removed from the placenta and analyzed for chromosomal or genetic birth defects with results typically available within a few days. Although CVS carries a higher risk for a miscarriage than amniocentesis, detection of problems occurs earlier in fetal development. It is considered the safest invasive diagnostic procedure prior to the fourteenth week of pregnancy (Schonberg, 2013). Amniocentesis, on the other hand, is usually done at about fifteen to eighteen weeks in the pregnancy. A small amount (1–2 ounces) of amniotic fluid is withdrawn via a needle from the sac surrounding the fetus. This fluid is then analyzed and a determination made, usually within ten to fourteen days, if the baby portrays atypical chromosomal development (Schonberg, 2013).

In the vast majority of instances, these prenatal biochemical analyses do not reveal the presence of a disorder or defect. When the results are positive, however, and indicate that the fetus has, for example, Down syndrome, parents are confronted with a decision as to whether to terminate the pregnancy (called an elective or **therapeutic abortion**) or to begin planning and preparation for an infant who will most likely have a disability. These are very difficult and often painful decisions involving a variety of moral and ethical dilemmas.

TABLE 2.1 Possible Causes of Intellectual Disability

PRENATAL FACTORS	EXAMPLES	PERINATAL FACTORS	EXAMPLES	POSTNATAL FACTORS	EXAMPLES
Chromosomal abnormalities	• Down syndrome • Fragile X syndrome • Prader-Willi syndrome	Gestational disorders	• Low birth weight • Prematurity	Infections and intoxicants	• Child abuse/neglect • Head trauma • Malnutrition • Environmental deprivation
Metabolic and nutritional disorders	• Phenylketonuria • Tay-Sachs disease • Galactosemia	Neonatal complications	• Hypoxia • Birth trauma • Seizures • Respiratory distress • Breech delivery • Prolonged delivery	Environmental factors	• Lead poisoning • Encephalitis • Meningitis • Reye's syndrome
Maternal infections	• Rubella • Syphilis • HIV (AIDS) • Cytomegalovirus • Rh incompatibility • Toxoplasmosis			Brain damage	• Neurofibromatosis • Tuberous sclerosis
Environmental conditions	• Fetal alcohol syndrome • Illicit drug use				
Unknown influences	• Anencephaly • Hydrocephalus • Microcephaly				

SOURCE: R. Gargiulo, *Special Education in Contemporary Society*, 5th ed. (Thousand Oaks, CA: Sage, 2015), p. 171.

Down syndrome most often results in mild to moderate intellectual disability. In some instances, however, individuals may have a severe intellectual disability, and in other situations, near normal intelligence is possible. Besides intellectual disability, this chromosomal aberration frequently results in other health concerns such as heart defects, hearing loss, intestinal malformations, vision problems, and an increased risk for thyroid difficulties and childhood leukemia (March of Dimes, 2015a; National Down Syndrome Society, 2015b).

People with Down syndrome have distinctive physical characteristics. Among the most commonly observed features are an upper slant of the eyes, short stature, a flat nose, somewhat smaller ears and nose, an enlarged and sometimes protruding tongue, short fingers, reduced muscle tone, and a single crease (simian crease) across the palm of the hand (people without Down syndrome have parallel lines). Most individuals with Down syndrome will exhibit some, but not all, of these identifying characteristics.

Life expectancies for people with Down syndrome have increased dramatically. In the 1920s and 1930s, the life span for a child with Down syndrome was generally less than ten years; today, thanks to advances in medicine and health care, large numbers of individuals with Down syndrome are living to age 60 (Roizen, 2013). With advancing chronological age, however, individuals with Down syndrome face a greater risk for developing Alzheimer's disease (National Down Syndrome Society, 2015a).

Fragile X syndrome is one of the more recently identified conditions linked to intellectual disability. This syndrome affects approximately 1 in 4,000 males and about 1 in 6,000 to 8,000 females, making it one of the leading inherited causes of intellectual disability (Batshaw, Gropman, & Lanpher, 2013; March of Dimes, 2015b). Because of the involvement of the X chromosome, this condition, which is caused by an abnormal or defective gene, predominantly affects males, although females can be carriers of the gene that causes it. Fragile X occurs in all racial and ethnic groups.

Individuals who have this disorder have a deficiency in the structure of the X chromosome of the twenty-third pair. Under a microscope, one of the "arms" of the X chromosome appears pinched or weakened and thus fragile. Females, who have two X chromosomes, are less susceptible to the defective gene; males, who have one X and one Y chromosome, are substantially at risk.

Typical characteristics associated with this syndrome include cognitive deficits of varying degrees, a long narrow face, large ears, poor muscle tone, a prominent forehead, and a large head circumference. At puberty, enlarged testicles are present (March of Dimes, 2015b). Behaviorally, individuals with fragile X syndrome typically exhibit attention disorders, self-stimulatory behaviors, and speech and language problems. About one-third of females with this disorder evidence significant intellectual disability while other girls have learning disabilities. The fragile X syndrome also appears to be associated with other disabilities such as autism spectrum disorders and disorders of attention (National Fragile X Foundation, 2015).

Prader-Willi syndrome is a chromosomal abnormality associated with genetic mutations of the fifteenth chromosome—typically contributed by the father. In a minority of instances, the entire paternal chromosome is missing, and the mother contributes both fifteenth chromosomes. Considered a "rare" disorder, Prader-Willi syndrome occurs in about 1 out of every 12,000–15,000 individuals. Prader-Willi syndrome can equally be found in males and females and across all races (Prader-Willi Syndrome Association, 2016b).

The paternal genes lacking in persons with Prader-Willi syndrome play a significant role in the regulation of appetite. In fact, this syndrome is the leading genetic cause of obesity. Prader-Willi syndrome is considered a multistage syndrome. In the first stage, the infant exhibits low muscle tone (hypotonia) and feeding difficulties. Beginning at approximately 18–36 months of age, the youngster experiences significant weight gain without an increase in caloric intake. As the child approaches school age, there is an abnormal interest in food and increased appetite.

Later, the individual exhibits an insatiable appetite and aggressive food-seeking behavior. This obsession with food requires strict regulation, control, and dietary management. The onset of this classical phase of Prader-Willi syndrome is variable, and can appear as early as age 3 or in adolescence (Prader-Willi Syndrome Association, 2016a).

Children with Prader-Willi syndrome typically evidence mild to moderate intellectual disability; however, some individuals exhibit IQs within the normal range. In addition to concerns about weight, children with Prader-Willi syndrome are at risk for other health issues such as short stature, sleep disturbances, incomplete sexual development, and vision defects, as well as developmental delays and behavior problems (Prader-Willi Syndrome Association, 2016a, 2016b; Simpson, 2013).

METABOLIC AND NUTRITIONAL DISORDERS

Phenylketonuria, more commonly known by its acronym, **PKU**, is an example of an inborn error of metabolism. It is a recessive trait, meaning that both parents have to be carriers of the defective gene. When this occurs, there is a 25 percent chance that the infant will be born with PKU. There is an equal probability, however, that the baby will be healthy (and a 50 percent chance it will be an asymptomatic carrier) (March of Dimes, 2015c). In the United Sates, PKU appears in about 1 out of every 10,000 births and is more common among whites of European descent (Pellegrino, 2013).

PKU affects the way an infant's body processes or metabolizes protein. Affected babies lack the liver enzyme needed to process phenylalanine, which is common in many high-protein foods such as meat and dairy products. As a result of this deficiency, phenylalanine accumulates in the bloodstream and becomes toxic. This metabolic malfunction, if not promptly treated, leads to brain damage and intellectual disability, which is often severe.

Elevated levels of phenylalanine can be detected in the blood and urine of newborns within the first few days of life. All states now mandate screening for this disorder. If unusually high levels of phenylalanine are found, the infant is placed on a special diet, reducing the intake of protein. Researchers have found that if dietary restrictions are introduced shortly after birth, the devastating consequences of PKU are significantly minimized (Batshaw & Lanpher, 2013). Current thinking suggests that dietary restrictions should be maintained throughout the person's life (National Institutes of Health, 2015). As individuals with PKU age, dietary control can become more difficult. Of particular concern are women of childbearing age who have PKU. The metabolic imbalances within these women can cause serious consequences to the developing fetus. In more than 90 percent of these pregnancies, babies are born with intellectual disability and heart defects, and they are usually of low birth weight. However, returning to an individualized, restricted diet prior to pregnancy and maintaining it throughout pregnancy usually results in a healthy baby (Batshaw & Lanpher, 2013).

Awareness of this concern has resulted in warning labels on many popular food items such as diet soft drinks and some low-fat foods ("Caution: product contains phenylalanine").

Galactosemia is another example of an inborn error of metabolism. In this disorder, infants are unable to process galactose, a form of sugar typically found in milk and other food products. Manifestation of this condition in newborns typically includes jaundice, liver damage, heightened susceptibility to infections, failure to thrive, vomiting, and cataracts, along with impaired intellectual functioning (Drew & Hardman, 2007). If galactosemia is detected early, a diet that avoids milk and other dairy products as well as certain legumes (for example, dried peas and garbanzo beans) is initiated. These dietary restrictions may substantially reduce the serious consequences associated with this disorder (Richards, Brady, & Taylor, 2015).

MATERNAL INFECTIONS

Viruses and infections often cause intellectual disability and a host of other problems. While pregnant, a woman and her developing child are very susceptible to a wide variety of potentially damaging infections. Exposure during the first trimester of pregnancy usually results in severe consequences. **Rubella** (German measles) is a good example of this type of infection. This mild but highly contagious illness has been linked to intellectual disability, vision and hearing defects, heart problems, and low birth weight. Rubella is one of the leading causes of multiple impairments in children. With the introduction of a rubella vaccine in 1969, instances of rubella-related disabilities have substantially decreased.

Sexually transmitted diseases such as gonorrhea and **syphilis** are capable of crossing the placenta and attacking the central nervous system of the developing fetus. In contrast to rubella, the risk to the unborn child is greater at the later stages of fetal development.

Acquired immune deficiency syndrome (AIDS), which is attributed to the human immunodeficiency virus (HIV), is another probable cause of intellectual disability and other developmental delays. Generally transmitted via unprotected sexual intercourse with an infected person, exposure to contaminated blood or bodily fluids, or the sharing of hypodermic needles, HIV crosses the placenta and affects the central nervous system while also damaging the immune system, leaving the fetus substantially at risk for opportunistic infections. Pediatric AIDS is suspected of being a leading infectious cause of intellectual disability. At the same time, HIV is the single most preventable cause of infectious intellectual disability.

Maternal–fetal **Rh incompatibility**, although technically not an infection, is another potential cause of intellectual disability. At one time, this disease was a leading cause of intellectual disability; however, thanks to preventive efforts, this is no longer the case. Simply stated, Rh disease is a blood group incompatibility between a mother and her unborn child. This discrepancy is the result of the Rh factor, a protein found on the surface of red blood cells. Rh-positive blood contains this protein; Rh-negative blood cells do not.

Rh incompatibility often leads to serious consequences such as intellectual disability, cerebral palsy, epilepsy, and other neonatal complications. The problem arises when an Rh-negative mother carries an Rh-positive baby, which causes her to produce antibodies against any future Rh-positive fetus. For this reason, Rh-negative women today generally receive an injection of Rh immunoglobulin (Rhlg) within seventy-two hours of delivering an Rh-positive baby. In the vast majority of cases, this procedure prevents the production of antibodies, thus preventing problems in any future pregnancies (National Heart, Lung, and Blood Institute, 2015).

Toxoplasmosis is a further example of maternal infection that typically poses grave risks to an unborn child. Toxoplasmosis is contracted through exposure to cat fecal matter; it is also present in undercooked or raw meat and raw eggs. If the mother is exposed to this parasitic infection during pregnancy, especially in the third trimester, it is very likely that fetal infection will occur. Infected infants may be born with an intellectual disability, cerebral palsy, damaged retinas leading to blindness, microcephaly (unusually small head), enlarged liver and spleen, jaundice, and other very serious complications. Antibiotics seem to provide some defense for both mother and child.

Our final illustration of maternal infections is **cytomegalovirus (CMV)**, an especially common virus that is part of the herpes group. Most women have been exposed to this virus at some time in their lives and thus develop immunity. If initial exposure occurs during pregnancy, however, the fetus may be severely affected. CMV often leads to brain damage and thus intellectual disability, blindness, and hearing impairments.

ENVIRONMENTAL CONTRIBUTIONS

Many unsafe maternal behaviors—among them, smoking, illicit drug use (for example, cocaine, heroin), and the consumption of alcohol before and during pregnancy—have been linked to impaired fetal development. The use of alcohol, in particular, has captured the attention of scientists and researchers for many years. In 1973, the term **fetal alcohol syndrome**, or **FAS**, was first coined (Jones, Smith, Ulleland, & Streissguth, 1973). Today, **fetal alcohol spectrum disorder (FASD)** is one of the leading causes of intellectual disability in the United States. Each year an estimated 40,000 babies are born with some degree of alcohol-associated damage or defect (Kids Health, 2015; National Organization on Fetal Alcohol Syndrome, 2015). It is important to note that there is no known safe level of alcohol consumption during pregnancy (Paulson, 2013).

Depending on the amount, duration, and timing of alcohol consumption, damage to the central nervous system and developing brain of the unborn child is not uncommon. FAS, a more severe manifestation of FASD, is characterized by a variety of physical deformities, including facial abnormalities, heart defects, low birth weight, and motor dysfunctions. In addition to mild to moderate intellectual disability, attention disorders, memory difficulties, and behavioral problems are usually present. Less severe and subtler forms of alcohol-related damage are recognized as **partial fetal alcohol syndrome (pFAS)**. The effects of alcohol consumption last a lifetime; yet this condition is completely preventable (National Organization on Fetal Alcohol Syndrome, 2015; Paulson, 2013).

UNKNOWN INFLUENCES

Several types of cranial malformations are the result of unknown prenatal factors. **Anencephaly** is but one illustration. In this condition, the entire brain or a large portion of it fails to develop properly, with devastating consequences for the infant. A more common condition is **microcephaly**, characterized by an unusually small head and severe to profound intellectual disability. **Hydrocephalus** is a disorder associated with the interference or blockage of the flow of cerebrospinal fluid, resulting in an accumulation of excess fluid that typically leads to an enlarged cranial cavity and potentially damaging compression on the brain. Doctors can surgically implant shunts that remove the excess fluid, thereby minimizing the pressure on the infant's brain and consequently the severe effects of this condition.

PERINATAL CAUSES OF INTELLECTUAL DISABILITY

GESTATIONAL DISORDERS

The two most common problems associated with gestational disorders are **low birth weight** and **premature birth**. Prematurity is generally defined as a birth that occurs prior to thirty-six weeks of gestation. Low birth weight is defined as less than 5 pounds, 8 ounces (2,500 grams), and very low birth weight as less than 3 pounds, 5 ounces (1,500 grams). In the majority of instances, but not all, low-birth-weight infants are premature. Not all babies with gestational disorders will have a disability or encounter future difficulties in school. However, some of these children may develop subtle learning problems, some may have an intellectual disability, and still others may have sensory and motor impairments.

NEONATAL COMPLICATIONS

Complications surrounding the birth process may cause intellectual disability and other developmental delays. One common example is **anoxia** (oxygen deprivation) or **hypoxia** (insufficient oxygen). Anoxia may occur because of damage to the umbilical cord or as a result of a prolonged and difficult delivery. Obstetrical or **birth trauma**, such as the improper use of forceps, may cause excessive pressure on the skull, which in turn may damage a portion of the infant's brain. A **breech presentation** is another illustration of a neonatal problem. In a breech delivery, the infant exits the birth canal buttocks first instead of the more typical headfirst presentation. This fetal delivery position raises concerns about the possibility of damage to the umbilical cord and a heightened threat of injury to the baby's head because of the greater intensity and frequency of uterine contractions later in the birth process. Worries about the infant's skull also arise when a **precipitous birth** (one lasting less than two hours) occurs. The gentle molding of the skull may not take place during a precipitous birth, thus increasing the risk of tissue damage and intellectual disability (Drew & Hardman, 2007).

POSTNATAL CAUSES OF INTELLECTUAL DISABILITY

INFECTIONS AND INTOXICANTS

Lead and mercury are two examples of environmental toxins that can cause intellectual disability. **Lead poisoning** is a serious public health problem.

Because of its highly toxic nature, lead is no longer used in the manufacturing of gasoline or paint. But even though it is no longer commercially available, some youngsters are still at risk for lead poisoning. Children who live in older homes or apartments may ingest lead by eating peeling paint chips containing lead. Lead poisoning can cause seizures, brain damage, and disorders of the central nervous system.

Infections represent another source of concern for young children. **Meningitis**, most commonly caused by a viral infection, leads to damage to the covering of the brain known as the meninges. Meningitis may result from complications associated with typical childhood diseases such as mumps, measles, or chicken pox. Because it is capable of causing brain damage, intellectual disability is a distinct possibility. Equally devastating is **encephalitis**, which is an inflammation of the brain tissue. Encephalitis may cause damage to the central nervous system and can result from complications of infections typically associated with childhood such as mumps or measles.

ENVIRONMENTAL FACTORS

A wide variety of environmental or psychosocial influences are often associated with intellectual disability, especially instances of mild intellectual disability. Debilitating factors may include nutritional problems, adverse living conditions, inadequate health care, and a lack of early cognitive stimulation. Many of these factors are associated with lower socioeconomic status. Child abuse and neglect along with head trauma resulting from automobile accidents or play-related injuries are also potential contributing factors. Of course, not all children exposed to these traumatic postnatal situations become intellectually disabled. These illustrations represent only evidence correlated with, but *not* necessarily causes of, intellectual disability. It is perhaps best to think of these variables as interacting risk factors, with some children being more vulnerable than others. Fortunately, most children exposed to these unfavorable circumstances develop normally.

Although a large portion of intellectual disability is attributed to environmental factors, contemporary thinking suggests that intellectual disabilities associated with psychosocial influences are the result of interaction between environmental and genetic or biological contributions (Shapiro & Batshaw, 2013). Stated another way, a youngster's genetic endowment provides a range of intellectual opportunity that is then mediated by the environment to which that individual is exposed.

Learning Characteristics of Students With Intellectual Disability

When discussing characteristics common to students with intellectual disability, it is important to remember that although, as a group, they may exhibit a particular feature, not all individuals identified as intellectually disabled will share this characteristic. Persons with intellectual disability are an especially heterogeneous population; interindividual differences are considerable. Many factors influence individual behavior and functioning—among them, chronological age, the severity and etiology of the disability, and educational opportunities. We caution you to remember that the following descriptions represent generalizations and are only useful for framing this discussion. Finally, in several ways, learners with intellectual disability are more like their typically developing counterparts than they are different, sharing many of the same social, emotional, and physical needs.

The most common defining characteristic of someone identified as intellectually disabled is impaired cognitive functioning, which, you may recall, can vary greatly. Investigators are typically not concerned with the person's intellectual ability per se but rather are concerned with the impact that lower IQ has on the individual's ability to learn, acquire concepts, process information, and apply knowledge in various settings such as school and community. Scientists do not yet fully understand the complexity of the learning process in human beings. Learning is a difficult concept to define—in many ways, it is unique to the individual—and is composed of many interrelated cognitive processes. Learning, then, is not a unitary variable. We have chosen, therefore, to briefly examine several of the characteristics that researchers believe influence learning. In subsequent chapters of this textbook, we identify instructional strategies and interventions designed to enhance the performance of students, across the life span, who evidence deficits in these particular learning characteristics.

ATTENTION

Attention, a multidimensional concept, plays a key role in learning. Many of the learning difficulties of students with intellectual disability are thought to be due to attentional deficits. Before learning a task, a person must be able to attend to its relevant attributes. Individuals with an intellectual disability often experience difficulty focusing their attention, maintaining it, and selectively attending to relevant stimuli. They often ignore the salient attributes of a task but instead focus on its irrelevant features. It may well be that pupils with intellectual disability perform poorly on certain learning tasks because they do not know how to attend to the critical aspects or dimensions of the problem (Alevriadou & Grouios, 2007; Richards et al., 2015).

MEMORY

Memory, an important component of learning, is often impaired in children with intellectual disability. As you might expect, the more severe the cognitive impairment, the greater the deficits in memory (Owens, 2009). **Short-term memory** (information stored for a few seconds or hours) is especially problematic for individuals with intellectual disability such as following teacher directions given in sequence or sequential job tasks from an employer. **Working memory**, on the other hand, refers to the ability to retain information while simultaneously performing another cognitive task (Jarrold & Brock, 2012). Recalling an address while listening to directions illustrates this process. Research suggests that working memory in students with intellectual disability is significantly poorer in comparison to their typically developing classmates (Richards et al., 2015).

ACADEMIC PERFORMANCE

Most students with intellectual disability encounter difficulties in their academic work. Generally, this deficiency is seen across all subject areas, but reading appears to be the weakest area, especially reading comprehension (Taylor, Smiley, & Richards, 2015). Pupils identified as intellectually disabled are also deficient in mathematics, but their performance is more in line with their mental age (Hardman, Drew, & Egan, 2014). Remember, just because a student is academically unsuccessful does not mean that he or she cannot excel in other school endeavors such as athletics or the arts.

MOTIVATION

Motivational factors are crucial for understanding the discrepancy that often exists between an individual's performance and his or her actual ability. It is not unusual for students with intellectual disability to approach a learning situation with heightened anxiety. A history of failure in earlier encounters contributes to this generalized feeling of apprehension; consequently, pupils seem to be less goal oriented and lacking in motivation.

Past experiences with failure typically lead individuals with intellectual disability to exhibit an **external locus of control**; that is, they are likely to believe that the consequences or outcomes of their behavior are the result of circumstances and events beyond their personal control, rather than their own efforts (Shogren, Bovaird, Palmer, & Wehmeyer, 2010). Repeated episodes of failure also give rise to a related concept, **learned helplessness**—the perception that no matter how much effort they put forth, failure is inevitable. ("No matter how hard I try, I won't be successful!") This expectancy of failure frequently causes students with intellectual disability to stop trying, even when the task is one they are capable of completing. Educators sometimes refer to this behavior as the "pencil-down syndrome."

Accumulated experiences with failure also result in a style of learning and problem solving characterized as **outer-directedness**, or a loss of confidence and trust in one's own abilities and solutions and a reliance on others for cues and guidance (Bybee & Zigler, 1998). While not solely limited to individuals with intellectual disability, this overreliance on others contributes to a lack of motivation and increased dependence. Once again, the origin of this behavior can be traced to the debilitating effects of repeated failure.

GENERALIZATION

It is not unusual for individuals with intellectual disability to experience difficulty in transferring or **generalizing** knowledge acquired in one context to new or different settings. In a large number of instances, learning in someone with an intellectual disability is situation specific; that is, once a particular skill or behavior is mastered, the individual has difficulty duplicating the skill when confronted with novel circumstances—different cues, different people, or different environments (Richards et al., 2015). For example, an adolescent with intellectual disability who can successfully determine correct change from a purchase in the school cafeteria might experience difficulty when counting his or her change at a grocery store or a restaurant. Therefore, teachers must systematically plan for generalization; typically, it does not occur automatically. Generalization of responses can be facilitated, for example, by using concrete materials rather than abstract representations, by providing instruction in various settings where the strategies or skill will typically be used, by incorporating a variety of examples and materials, or by simply informing the pupils of the multiple applications that are possible.

LANGUAGE DEVELOPMENT

Speech and language development are closely related to cognitive functioning. In fact, speech and language difficulties are more common among individuals with intellectual disability than in their typically developing counterparts (Gleason & Ratner, 2013). Given the association between intellectual ability and speech and language, it is not surprising that students with intellectual disability experience a great deal of difficulty with academic tasks, such as reading, that require verbal and language competency.

Speech disorders are typical among individuals with intellectual disability (Taylor et al., 2015). These may include errors of articulation such as additions or distortions, fluency disorders such as stuttering, and voice disorders such as hypernasal speech or concerns about loudness. In fact, speech and language difficulties are a fairly common secondary disability among students with intellectual disability (Gargiulo, 2015).

Despite the prevalence of speech disorders, language problems are receiving increased attention from professionals because deficits in this arena are highly debilitating. There is a strong correlation between intellectual ability and language development—the higher the IQ, the less pervasive the language disorder. Although children with intellectual disability, especially those with higher IQs, acquire language in the same fashion as their typically developing peers, development occurs more slowly, their vocabulary is more limited, and grammatical structure and sentence complexity are often impaired (Owens, 2014). Yet language is crucial for the independent functioning of individuals with an intellectual disability. Deficits in this area can significantly impede social development and hinder peer relationships (Friend & Bursuck, 2015).

SOCIAL AND BEHAVIORAL CHARACTERISTICS OF STUDENTS WITH INTELLECTUAL DISABILITY

The ability to get along with other people is an important skill; and it is just as significant for individuals who are intellectually disabled as it is for those without an intellectual disability. In fact, in some situations, social adeptness or proficiency may be as important as, if not more important than, intellectual ability. In the area of employment, for example, when workers with intellectual or other developmental disabilities experience difficulty on the job, it is

TABLE 2.2 Representative Learning and Behavioral Characteristics of Learners With Intellectual Disability

DIMENSION	ASSOCIATED ATTRIBUTES AND FEATURES
Attention	• Inability to attend to critical or relevant features of a task • Diminished attention span • Difficulty ignoring distracting stimuli
Memory	• Deficits in memory correlated with severity of intellectual disability • Limitations in ability to selectively process and store information • Inefficient rehearsal strategies • Difficulty with short-term (working) memory is common—recalling directions in sequence presented seconds earlier
Motivation	• History of and a generalized expectancy for failure—learned helplessness—effort is unrewarded; failure is inevitable • Exhibit external locus of control—belief that outcomes of behavior are the result of circumstances (fate, chance) beyond personal control rather than own efforts • Evidence outer-directedness, a loss of confidence and a distrust of own abilities, reliance on others for cues and guidance
Generalization	• Difficulty applying knowledge or skill to new tasks, situations, or settings • Problem in using previous experience in novel situations • Teachers must explicitly plan for generalization; typically it does not automatically occur
Language Development	• Follow same sequence of language acquisition as typical individuals, albeit at a slower pace • Strong correlation between intellectual ability and language development—the higher the IQ, the less pervasive the language difficulty • Speech disorders (articulation errors, stuttering) more common than in peers without intellectual disability • Vocabulary is often limited • Grammatical structure and sentence complexity are often impaired
Academic Development	• Generally exhibit difficulties in all academic areas with reading being the weakest • Problem-solving difficulties in arithmetic
Social Development	• Typically lacking in social competence • Rejection by peers and classmates is common—poor interpersonal skills • Frequently exhibit socially inappropriate or immature behavior—difficulty establishing and maintaining friendships • Diminished self-esteem coupled with low self-concept

SOURCE: Adapted from R. Gargiulo and D. Metcalf, *Teaching in Today's Inclusive Classrooms*, 3rd ed. (Boston, MA: Cengage Learning, 2017), p. 84.

frequently due to problems of social interactions with coworkers and supervisors rather than job performance per se (Hendricks & Wehman, 2009).

Individuals with intellectual disability often exhibit poor interpersonal skills and socially inappropriate or immature behavior; as a result, they frequently encounter rejection by peers and classmates. It is not unusual for individuals with intellectual disability to lack the social competency necessary to establish and maintain appropriate interpersonal relations (Friend & Bursuck, 2015; Vaughn, Bos, & Schumm, 2014). The success or failure of students with intellectual disability who are placed in general education classrooms is often determined by their social skills. This lack of social ability can pose significant difficulties as increasing numbers of individuals with intellectual disability are seizing the opportunity to participate in more normalized environments. Direct social skill instruction is one way of enhancing the social development of persons with an intellectual disability. Behavior modification techniques can reduce inappropriate social behaviors while establishing more desirable and acceptable behaviors. The modeling of the appropriate behavior of classmates is another way that students with intellectual disability can acquire more socially attractive behaviors, which in turn can lead to greater peer acceptance.

Table 2.2 presents a summary of select learning and behavioral characteristics of individuals with intellectual disability.

Chapter Summary

Etiology of Intellectual Disability

- One way of categorizing etiological factors is on the basis of time of onset: before birth (prenatal), around the time of birth (perinatal), or after birth (postnatal).

Characteristics of Individuals with Intellectual Disability

- Common behaviors of persons with intellectual disability include attention deficits, or difficulty focusing and attending to relevant stimuli, and memory problems.

- Past experiences with failure frequently lead individuals with intellectual disability to doubt their own abilities and thus exhibit an external locus of control.

- Recurring episodes of failure also give rise to learned helplessness. These accumulated instances of failure frequently result in a loss of confidence and trust in one's own problem-solving abilities and a reliance on others for direction and guidance. This behavior is identified as outer-directedness.

- Individuals with intellectual impairments also often exhibit poor interpersonal skills and socially inappropriate or immature behaviors.

Review Questions

1. Intellectual disability is often the result of various etiological factors. List two possible prenatal, perinatal, and postnatal contributions of intellectual disability.

2. How do learned helplessness, outer-directedness, and generalizing affect learning in students with intellectual disability?

3. What are some of the common learning and behavioral characteristics of individuals with intellectual disability?

Key Terms

etiology (page 29)
prenatal (page 30)
perinatal (page 30)
postnatal (page 30)
Down syndrome (page 30)
chorionic villus sampling (CVS) (page 31)
amniocentesis (page 31)
therapeutic abortion (page 31)
fragile X syndrome (page 33)
Prader-Willi syndrome (page 34)

phenylketonuria (PKU) (page 35)
galactosemia (page 36)
rubella (page 36)
syphilis (page 36)
acquired immune deficiency syndrome (AIDS) (page 36)
Rh incompatibility (page 37)
toxoplasmosis (page 37)
cytomegalovirus (CMV) (page 37)
fetal alcohol syndrome (FAS) (page 38)

fetal alcohol spectrum disorders
(FASD) (page 38)

partial fetal alcohol syndrome
(pFAS) (page 38)

anencephaly (page 38)

microcephaly (page 38)

hydrocephalus (page 38)

low birth weight (page 39)

premature birth (page 39)

anoxia (page 39)

hypoxia (page 39)

birth trauma (page 39)

breech presentation (page 39)

precipitous birth (page 39)

lead poisoning (page 39)

meningitis (page 40)

encephalitis (page 40)

short-term memory (page 42)

working memory (page 42)

external locus of control (page 43)

learned helplessness (page 43)

outer-directedness (page 43)

generalizing (page 43)

Organizations Concerned With Intellectual Disability

American Association on Intellectual and Developmental Disabilities

https://aaidd.org/

The Arc (formerly the Association for Retarded Citizens of the United States)

www.thearc.org

Division on Autism and Developmental Disabilities, Council for Exceptional Children

www.daddcec.org

National Down Syndrome Congress

www.ndsccenter.org

National Down Syndrome Society

http://ndss.org

CHAPTER 3

Educational Issues Affecting Students With Intellectual Disability

Emily C. Bouck and Richard M. Gargiulo

Learning Objectives

After reading Chapter 3, you should be able to:

- Explain key legislation and policies influencing the education of students with intellectual disability and the impact of the different pieces of legislation or policy on the education of learners with intellectual disability.

- List the key components to be included in an individualized education program.

- Describe contemporary issues impacting the education of students with disabilities and how these issues influence the education of students with intellectual disability.

- Explain what is a functional curriculum and what is an academic or standards-based curriculum.

The education of students with intellectual disability, like the education of all students, is impacted by a variety of factors. In this chapter, we will consider both historical and contemporary factors impacting the education of students with intellectual disability, including legislation and policy, multi-tiered systems of support, and the accountability system. This chapter will also discuss some of the fundamental questions regarding the education of students with intellectual disability: what to teach and where to teach it.

LEGISLATION AND POLICY AFFECTING STUDENTS WITH INTELLECTUAL DISABILITY

Federal education-related legislation and policy affects students with disabilities, including students with intellectual disability. The two most common education-related laws and policies affecting students with intellectual disability, like all students with disabilities, are the Every Student Succeeds Act (2015)—the reauthorization of the Elementary and Secondary Education Act (formerly known as the No Child Left Behind Act of 2001)—and the Individuals with Disabilities Education Improvement Act of 2004. Section 504 of the Rehabilitation Act of 1973 also impacts the education of pupils with disabilities.

NO CHILD LEFT BEHIND ACT

No Child Left Behind (NCLB) (PL 107–110) was the 2001 reauthorization of the Elementary and Secondary Education Act (ESEA). ESEA (PL 89–10) was the federal education law originally signed into effect in 1965 that provided federal funds to schools in return for following federal education guidelines (Yell, 2016). NCLB (2002) was built upon four pillars: stronger accountability, greater local control, use of proven (scientifically based) educational methods, and greater choice for parents (Turnbull, 2005). The goals of NCLB were (a) *all* students will achieve high academic standards and be proficient in mathematics and reading by the 2013–2014 school year; (b) highly qualified teachers will teach all students; (c) all schools and classrooms will be safe, including drug free, and advantageous to learning; (d) students who are English learners will be proficient in English; and (e) 100 percent of students will graduate from high school (Turnbull, 2005; Yell, 2016).

NCLB is probably best known for its focus on accountability, including the 100 percent proficiency rate by the target date, as well as the schools making

adequate yearly progress (AYP). In other words, NCLB (2002) required that schools continue to make progress in raising the percentage of students proficient in reading and mathematics, as measured by yearly state standardized assessments, and the AYP had to occur for not just all students but also specific subgroups of students, including students with disabilities (Yell, 2016). Under NCLB, all students in Grades 3 through 8, and once again in high school, were to take a standardized statewide assessment in reading and mathematics. Within NCLB were sanctions for schools that fail to make AYP, for all students as well as the specific, targeted subpopulations within a school (that is, students with disabilities, students from economically disadvantaged backgrounds, students who are English learners, and students from diverse racial and ethnic groups) (Simpson, LaCava, & Graner, 2004; Yell, 2016). With the accountability, schools must also have 95 percent of their students, and students in each subpopulation, take the standardized statewide assessment. Participation in the accountability systems and options for standardized statewide assessments will be discussed in greater detail later in this chapter.

Beyond accountability and participation in statewide assessments, other facets of NCLB affect students with intellectual disability. Under NCLB, all teachers must be highly qualified to teach core academic subjects, including mathematics, literacy (for example, English, reading), science, foreign language, the arts, and the different areas of social studies (for example, history, civics, government) (Yell, 2016). Although states define *highly qualified teachers* under NCLB, the basic guidelines include holding a bachelor's degree, being certified or licensed in the area(s) they teach, and demonstrating competency, such as by passing a test (Yell, 2016). There were special considerations for students with intellectual disability and their teachers. For students with intellectual disability who receive instruction at an elementary level and take an alternate assessment, a highly qualified teacher, even at the secondary level, would need to have passed the elementary subject matter test (Yell, 2016).

However, for students with an intellectual disability who receive instruction in core content areas from special education teachers above an elementary level, each teacher would need to be highly qualified in each subject matter; the same is true for general education teachers. NCLB also required paraprofessionals who provide instructional support to be highly qualified (National Education Association, 2015; Yell, 2016).

A final issue to discuss relative to NCLB is the use of **scientifically based** practices or instruction (Wakeman, Browder, Meier, & McColl, 2007). Under

NCLB, schools were to provide students with scientifically based instruction and educational practices; scientifically based practices are those that are supported by empirical, rigorous research (Yell, 2016). The use of scientifically based practices extends to instruction as well as assessment, progress monitoring, classroom and behavior management, and teachers' professional development (Yell, 2016). The What Works Clearinghouse (http://ies.ed.gov/ncee/wwc/) was established by the U.S. Department of Education to evaluate and provide information on scientifically based practices for educators (Simpson et al., 2004).

EVERY STUDENT SUCCEEDS ACT

As noted, the Every Student Succeeds Act (ESSA) (PL 114–95) was signed into law on December 10, 2015, and is the reauthorization of the Elementary and Secondary Education Act. Hence ESSA replaces NCLB. ESSA retains many aspects of NCLB, although some changes are noted in the new legislation. For example, ESSA continues to have students tested once a year in Grades 3–8 and then once in high school for literacy and mathematics and requires that achievement data be disaggregated by different subgroups (e.g., disability status, race). ESSA, however, eliminates the definition of a highly qualified teacher (Gargiulo & Bouck, 2018). Subtle changes to ESSA also occurred with regards to alternate assessments. Previously, 1 percent of students could take an alternate assessment and have the scores counted in a school's AYP. With ESSA, 1 percent of students—at the state level—can be assessed with an alternate assessment; the 1 percent cap is for those students who would fall under new state-developed definitions of "students with the most significant cognitive disabilities." ESSA also explicitly references universal design for learning, which will be discussed in greater depth later in the chapter (Gargiulo & Bouck, 2018).

INDIVIDUALS WITH DISABILITIES EDUCATION IMPROVEMENT ACT

The Individuals with Disabilities Education Improvement Act of 2004 (IDEA 2004), first signed into law in 1975 as the Education for All Handicapped Children Act (PL 94–142), is the federal law governing the education of students with disabilities. States receive federal funding for the education of *all* students with disabilities in exchange for passing state laws that, at a minimum, offer the same rights and protections as IDEA. IDEA consists of four major parts: Part A provides definitions and goals, Part B focuses on the education of students with disabilities aged 3–21, Part C addresses the education of children with disabilities from birth until age 3, and Part D provides grants relative to the education of students with disabilities (Yell, 2016).

Throughout this chapter, we will focus on Part B of IDEA, the part focused on students between 3 and 21 years of age. States can provide an education for students beyond age 21 (Michigan, for example, provides an education until 26 years of age for students with disabilities), but the federal government only requires educational services until age 21. Generally, people speak of IDEA as focused on six major principles or provisions: (a) zero reject, (b) nondiscriminatory identification and evaluation, (c) **free appropriate public education (FAPE)**, (d) **least restrictive environment (LRE)**, (e) procedural safeguards or due process, and (f) parental participation (Smith, 2005; Yell, 2016). (See Table 3.1.) Together, these provisions provide for a free appropriate public education for *all* students with disabilities who qualify to be provided in the least restrictive environment; the services and educational programs provided to each student with disabilities are written into a legal document referred to as an **individualized education program (IEP)**. Schools are to actively seek out, identify, and evaluate—in a nondiscriminatory manner—all students who have or are suspected of having one of the following disabilities: autism spectrum disorder, deafness, deaf-blindness, developmental delay, hearing impairment, intellectual disability, multiple disabilities, orthopedic impairments, other health impairment, emotional disturbance, specific learning disability, speech or language impairment, traumatic brain injury, and visual impairment including blindness (Yell, 2016). IDEA also provides students with disabilities who qualify protections in terms of due process and a system of procedural safeguards. Under IDEA, parents are to be active participants in all aspects of the education of students with a disability, as well as take responsibility for their child's education (Turnbull, 2005; Yell, 2016).

When IDEA was reauthorized in 2004, it was aligned with NCLB (Turnbull, 2005). For example, IDEA 2004 emphasized the participation of students with disabilities in each state's accountability system; alternate assessments (discussed later in this chapter) were an option for students with severe disabilities, like students with intellectual disability, to participate in the accountability system. IDEA also stipulated the services and education provided to

TABLE 3.1 Expanded Information on Aspects of IDEA 2004

PRINCIPLE FROM IDEA 2004	INTERPRETATION
Zero reject	• Schools must actively seek out all students to evaluate (e.g., child find system). • All students who qualify under IDEA are to be given a free appropriate public education.
Nondiscriminatory evaluation	• Evaluations used to determine eligibility must be fair and accurate (that is, not culturally biased). • Parents or schools can request an initial evaluation.
Free appropriate public education (FAPE)	• Eligible students receive a free (that is, no cost to the parents) education that is appropriate for each individual. • The education provided must consist of what is listed in the individualized education program (IEP).
Least restrictive environment (LRE)	• Students are educated to the maximum extent possible with their peers without disabilities. • A continuum of placement options exists, from inclusion in general education classes to separate classes, separate schools, and homebound or hospital instruction.
Procedural safeguards	• Safeguards are in place to protect students with disabilities and their parents (for example, parents must consent to services for them to be provided). • Procedures allow for due process hearings when disagreements occur between parents and schools.
Parental participation	• Parents are to be actively involved in the education of their child with a disability, including consenting to evaluations and services. • Parents are to receive reports about their child's progress toward meeting his or her IEP goals.

SOURCE: Adapted from M. Yell, *The Law and Special Education,* 4th ed. (Boston, MA: Pearson Education, 2016).

students with disabilities in their IEP be, to the extent practical, based on scientifically based research or evidence, as well as support teacher professional development focusing on scientifically based practices (Turnbull, 2005). The 2004 reauthorization also required highly qualified special education teachers and supported the safe schools principle of NCLB through the provision of moving students to an interim alternative educational setting for up to 45 school days given specific violations (for example, drugs, weapons), as well as creating a more stringent manifestation determination process (Smith, 2005; Turnbull, 2005). See Table 3.2 for additional changes to IDEA in the 2004 reauthorization.

TABLE 3.2 Examples of Additional Changes to IDEA in the 2004 Reauthorization

- Allowed IEP team members to be excused if parents and the school personnel agree provided the team member's part is not being modified
- Removed the requirement for short-term objectives under annual goals in an IEP for students who were not taking an alternate assessment
- Allowed changes to be made to an IEP without convening if the school personnel and parents agree
- Allowed schools to seek reimbursement for attorney fees from parents for frivolous lawsuits
- Prohibited states from requiring that students with learning disabilities be determined through an ability-achievement discrepancy model; allowed learning disabilities eligibility through response to intervention
- Removed surgically implanted assistive technology as devices covered under assistive technology in IDEA

SOURCES: T. E. C. Smith, "IDEA 2004: Another Round in the Reauthorization Process," *Remedial and Special Education*, 26(6), 2005, pp. 314-319; M. Yell, *The Law and Special Education*, 3rd ed. (Boston, MA: Pearson Education, 2012).

SECTION 504 OF THE REHABILITATION ACT OF 1973

Section 504 of the Rehabilitation Act of 1973 (PL 93–112) prohibits the discrimination of individuals with disabilities by entities that receive federal funding. This includes almost all public schools, including PK–12 and institutions of higher education. Unlike IDEA, Section 504 more broadly defines a disability. Like IDEA, Section 504 does guarantee a student with a disability a free appropriate public education. Often, FAPE under Section 504 focuses on a comparable educational experience for students with and without disabilities and the provision of reasonable **accommodations** to students with disabilities (Aron & Loprest, 2012; Yell, 2016). It is important to note that while all students with disabilities found eligible under IDEA are covered under Section 504, not all students covered under Section 504 are eligible for the rights and protections provided by IDEA (Gargiulo, 2015; Rosenfeld, 1996).

LITIGATION

In addition to the federal policy impacting the education of students with intellectual disability, litigation is influential. To recall from a civics lesson, legislation occurs when the legislative branch of the government (that is, Congress) passes a law (for example, PL 94–142) and then the president, the executive branch of the government, signs it. This is referred to as statutory law (Yell, 2016). An administrative agency then takes the law or act and creates regulations; for example, the

Code of Federal Regulations (CFR) for IDEA is Title 34, Subtitle B, Chapter III, Parts 300 and 301 (see http://idea.ed.gov/download/finalregulations.pdf). In contrast, litigation (that is, lawsuits) creates case law, which occurs when the judicial branch of the government interprets laws or regulations (Yell, 2016).

Historical pieces of litigation involving children with disabilities helped frame the education of not just students with intellectual disability but all students with disabilities. Prior to the passing of PL 94–142, the court ruling in *Pennsylvania Association for Retarded Children (PARC) v. Commonwealth of Pennsylvania* stated that a free public education was to be provided to all students with intellectual disability between the ages of 6 and 21. The 1972 ruling in *PARC* also involved that students with intellectual disability should be educated in programs likes those for children without a disability (Yell, 2016). In the 1979 ruling of *Larry P. v. Riles*, the court stated that IQ tests cannot be used to determine placement in classes for students with educable mental retardation (mild intellectual disability) for African Americans. Also in 1979, *Armstrong v. Kline* upheld that schools cannot limit the number of days education is provided to students with severe disabilities, if long summer breaks would result in denial of a free appropriate public education. In other words, it supported extended-school-year education for students with severe disabilities. Finally, *Daniel R. R. v. State Board of Education* in 1989 resulted in a new two-prong test for evaluating least restrictive environment compliance: "can education in the general education classroom with supplementary aids and services be achieved satisfactorily?, and if a student is placed in a more restrictive environment setting, is the student integrated to the maximum extent appropriate?" (Yell, 2016, p. 248). Of course, litigation continues into today.

INDIVIDUALIZED EDUCATION PROGRAMS

An individualized education program (IEP) is an important element in the education of students with disabilities. It is within this document that all the services, programming, accommodations, and goals for a student exist. Procedural and substantive requirements exist for IEPs, including involving parents (that is, procedural) and ensuring that IEPs are written in such a manner as to confer "meaningful educational benefit" (that is, substantive) (Yell, 2016, p. 213). IEPs are developed during IEP team meetings, which are to consist of, at a minimum, a special educator, a general education teacher, a local educational agency representative who can commit to services, an individual to interpret any evaluations, parents or guardians, and the student, as appropriate. Additional individuals can be invited as needed (for example, related service providers, such as speech–language pathologists or school social workers) or as requested by the parents (Gartin & Murdick, 2005; Yell, 2016). Each IEP must contain, at a minimum, eight parts. (See Table 3.3 for IEP components.)

One of the most challenging parts of IEP development is writing measurable annual goals (both functional and academic). Annual goals consist of three components: (a) an observable, measurable target behavior; (b) the circumstances in which a target behavior is measured (setting, materials); and (c) the goal or mastery criterion (Yell, 2016). After writing annual goals, IEP teams are to measure those goals. IEP teams are expected to continually monitor student process on meeting IEP goals and revising those goals as necessary (Yell, 2016). See Table 3.4 for some sample IEP goals for students with intellectual disability.

CONTEMPORARY EDUCATIONAL ISSUES

Federal laws and legislation impact the education of students with disabilities. Current or contemporary educational issues, to some degree, also impact their education. Some of the contemporary educational issues examined in this chapter include multi-tiered systems of support, evidence-based practices, the Common Core State Standards, accountability, and universal design for learning. Even if a contemporary issue does not appear to immediately impact pupils with intellectual disability, such as response to intervention, such practices in school are indirectly affecting the education of *all* students with disabilities.

TABLE 3.3 IEP Components From IDEA 2004

1. Present level of academic achievement and functional performance (PLAAFP). The PLAAFP provides baseline information about a student's performance, his or her needs, and access to the general education curriculum.
2. Measurable annual goals; one goal for each area of need identified in the PLAAFP. Short-term objectives are only required for students who take an alternate assessment.
3. Information on how and when the student's progress toward each annual goal will be measured and reported to parents.
4. Educational services, including special education (e.g., instruction, consultation), related services (e.g., speech and language), and supplementary aids and services (e.g., assistive technology) provided, including where, how often, and for how long.
5. Amount of time, if any, a student does not participate in general education.
6. Student's participation in the accountability system (e.g., general large scale with accommodations, alternate assessment) and accommodations on assessments.
7. Start date for IEP and its duration (e.g., one year).
8. For students over the age of 16, or younger based on state laws, transition services.

SOURCE: Adapted from M. Yell, *The Law and Special Education*, 4th ed. (Boston, MA: Pearson Education, 2016).

TABLE 3.4 Sample IEP Annual Goals

AREA OF SUPPORT	GOAL
Employment/ Independent Living	• Using picture prompts, John will complete two- to three-step prevocational jobs with no more than two verbal prompts in three out of three trials. • When approaching a peer in the classroom at the start of the school day, Mia will use her augmentative and alternative communication device to initiate a greeting in 75 percent of the observed interactions.
Behavior	• In the classroom, when presented with a nonpreferred typical activity (circle time, reading worksheet, math pages), Jeni will use pretaught self-calming strategies (e.g., breathe deep, ask to take a break) or perform the requested task without displaying behaviors of leaving the room without permission, throwing away materials, or yelling 80 percent of the time.
Mathematics	• When presented with a math assignment, Curt will correctly solve two-digit addition problems with or without use of concrete manipulatives in four out of five trials. • When grocery shopping during community-based instruction, Devon will correctly use the "round to the next dollar" strategy for items selected in four out of five trials.
Language Arts/Literacy	• When evaluated at the end of the school year, Lexi will select and read books written in English at the fourth-grade level with at least 50 words read correctly per minute. • When out in the community with his class for community-based instruction, Humberto will recognize safety symbols and words, such as STOP, in three out of five trials.

SOURCE: Adapted from G. Gibb and T. Dyches, *IEPs: Writing Quality Individualized Education Programs* (Boston, MA: Pearson Education, 2016).

MULTI-TIERED SYSTEMS OF SUPPORT

A **multi-tiered system of support (MTSS)** is a service delivery model or framework whose purpose is to provide students with the services they need through continual monitoring. In other words, MTSS is a problem-solving approach that tries to support students academically and behaviorally based on data-based decisions (Cusumano Algozzine, & Algozzine, 2014; Harlacher, Sakelaris, & Kattelman, 2014). The MTSS involves providing support at multiple levels, often referred to as tiers (Sailor, 2015).

Response to intervention (RTI) and **positive behavior interventions and supports (PBIS)** are multi-tiered systems of support (Sailor, 2015). RTI was introduced in IDEA 2004 as an alternate means of identifying students with learning disabilities, in opposition to the ability–achievement discrepancy model. With RTI, students would be considered to have a learning disability if they failed to respond to scientifically based or research-based interventions. RTI in practice is often used more broadly as a pre-referral strategy for identifying students with disabilities or finding students who struggle and providing additional supports (Gargiulo, 2015; Gargiulo & Metcalf, 2017; Sailor, 2015).

RTI typically involves three or four tiers of supporting students academically (see Figure 3.1). Within RTI, all students receive universal or primary intervention, referred to as Tier 1. Tier 1 involves the provision of high-quality (that is, evidence-based) instruction to all students with screening. Students who fail to respond to the universal instruction would receive additional instruction or support, referred to as Tier 2. The support in Tier 2 is more intensive, typically conducted in smaller groups, and involves more frequent progress monitoring. Students who then fail to respond to the Tier 2 intervention would move into Tier 3, which provides the most intensive and individualized interventions. Depending on the RTI model, Tier 3 could result in special education or referral for special education evaluation (Burns & Gibbons, 2012; Gargiulo, 2015).

FIGURE 3.1 A Three-Tier Response-to-Intervention Model

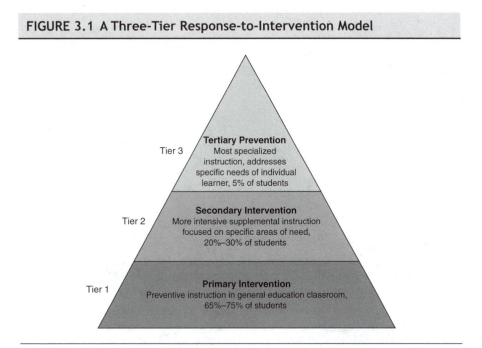

NOTE: Percentage of students participating at each level is approximate. Duration of intervention is approximate. Students may move between tiers as individual needs dictate.

While RTI may be used currently to identify students with intellectual disability, it is increasingly being used as a pre-referral strategy in a school's **child find system**. Students with more moderate and severe intellectual disability are very likely to have been identified before reaching formal K–12 education and hence would already be receiving special education services.

Positive behavioral interventions and supports are similar to RTI in that they are associated with three tiers and are focused on prevention, such as by recognizing positive behavior. However, PBIS address school climate and behavioral challenges in students (Bradshaw, Koth, Bevans, Ialongo, & Leaf, 2008). The first of the three tiers of PBIS involves universal or schoolwide interventions as well as ones in the classroom. Students who need additional support receive interventions in Tier 2, also known as secondary prevention. Finally, Tier 3 offers supports to students who need specialized or individualized interventions focused on their behavior, such as individualized behavior plans or self-monitoring (Gargiulo, 2015; Sailor, 2015). PBIS are considered evidence-based practices and are used for all learners, including those with an intellectual disability (Sailor, Wolf, Choi, & Roger, 2009; Sugai & Horner, 2009). (See Figure 3.2 for a visual depiction of PBIS.)

FIGURE 3.2 A Three-Tier Model of Positive Behavior Interventions and Supports

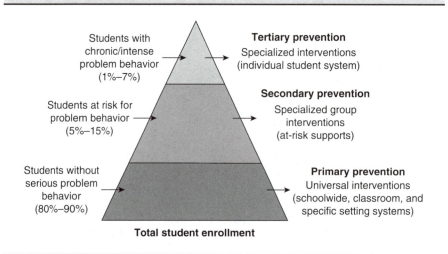

SOURCE: Adapted from G. Sugai, R. Horner, G. Dunlap, M. Hieneman, T. Lewis, C. Nelson, et al., *Applying Positive Behavior Support and Functional Assessment in Schools* (Washington, DC: Office of Special Education Programs, Center on Positive Behavioral Interventions and Supports, 1999), p. 11.

UNIVERSAL DESIGN FOR LEARNING

Universal design for learning (UDL) is an educational framework derived from a principle of architecture referred to as universal design. Universal design in architecture was premised on the belief that if structures (for example, buildings, sidewalks) were designed to be accessible from the beginning, then not only could everyone use them, but it would cost less and be more aesthetically appealing. Examples of universal design in architecture are curb cuts, Braille in elevators, and closed-captioning television. While these examples benefit individuals with specific disabilities (for example, individuals with mobility challenges, visual impairments, and hearing impairments), they also benefit others, such as individuals pushing strollers, transporting luggage, and sitting in noisy places like an airport or workout facility.

UDL applies the idea of accessibility from the start to education; UDL applies accessibility to teaching and learning and focuses on the removal of barriers for learning (Hitchcock, Meyer, Rose, & Jackson, 2002; Rose, Hasselbring, Stahl, & Zabala, 2005; Rose & Meyer, 2002). Despite the term *universal*, UDL does not mean "one size fits all" but suggests teaching and learning can be designed with options to allow everyone to access and succeed. UDL consists of seven features (see Table 3.5) and three principles (see Figure 3.3). The three principles of UDL include multiple means of representation or presentation, multiple means of engagement, and multiple means of expression (Council for Exceptional Children, 2005). To engage in multiple means of presentation or

TABLE 3.5 Features of UDL

FEATURES	DESCRIPTION
Equitability	The needs of all students are met.
Flexibility	The diversity students bring to learning is embraced.
Simple and intuitive	Teaching and learning are accessible and adjustable.
Multiple means of presentation	Educators use different ways to teach.
Success-oriented	Barriers are removed, and student learning is supported.
Appropriate level of student effort	Educators adjust their teaching and assessing.
Appropriate environment for learning	The environment is accessible and encourages learning for all.

SOURCE: E. Bouck, *Assistive Technology* (Thousand Oaks, CA: Sage, 2015), p. 18.

FIGURE 3.3 The Essential Elements of UDL

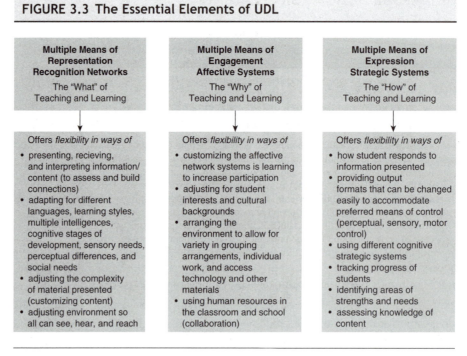

Multiple Means of Representation Recognition Networks The "What" of Teaching and Learning	**Multiple Means of Engagement Affective Systems** The "Why" of Teaching and Learning	**Multiple Means of Expression Strategic Systems** The "How" of Teaching and Learning
Offers *flexibility in ways of*	Offers *flexibility in ways of*	Offers *flexibility in ways of*
• presenting, recieving, and interpreting information/content (to assess and build connections) • adapting for different languages, learning styles, multiple intelligences, cognitive stages of development, sensory needs, perceptual differences, and social needs • adjusting the complexity of material presented (customizing content) • adjusting environment so all can see, hear, and reach	• customizing the affective network systems is learning to increase participation • adjusting for student interests and cultural backgrounds • arranging the environment to allow for variety in grouping arrangements, individual work, and access technology and other materials • using human resources in the classroom and school (collaboration)	• how student responds to information presented • providing output formats that can be changed easily to accommodate preferred means of control (perceptual, sensory, motor control) • using different cognitive strategic systems • tracking progress of students • identifying areas of strengths and needs • assessing knowledge of content

SOURCE: R. Gargiulo and D. Metcalf, *Teaching in Today's Inclusive Classrooms*, 3rd ed. © (Boston, MA; Cengage Learning, 2017), p. 44. Reproduced by permission. www.cengage .com/permissions.

representation, an educator presents information in multiple formats, including, for example, speaking (that is, auditory representation) and writing (that is, verbal representation). Students choosing how they participate in or engage with the content they are learning reflects multiple means of engagement. For example, teachers can make concrete and virtual manipulatives available during mathematics instruction and allow students to individually select; teachers can also allow choice in individual, partner, or small-group work. Finally, when students are given choice and flexibility in their expression of their learning, the principle of multiple means of expression is being evoked. Rather than all students writing a paper, students can choose, for example, to write a paper, create a poster, make a video, or give an oral response.

UDL supports all students, including those with intellectual disability. UDL implementation can result in fewer individual accommodations, as the

TABLE 3.6 Examples of Ways Educators Can Implement UDL in Practice

AUDITORY	VISUAL	TACTILE/KINESTHETIC	AFFECTIVE	TECHNOLOGY OPTIONS

Multiple ways to present information to students

AUDITORY	VISUAL	TACTILE/KINESTHETIC	AFFECTIVE	TECHNOLOGY OPTIONS
• Lecture • Discussion or questioning • Song • Read-aloud	• Videos • Sign language • Watching a play • Book • Graphs, tables, or charts • Slide show • Whiteboard	• Field trip • Drawing • Braille books • Demonstration • Manipulatives • Dance • Games	• Small-group work • Peer-mediated instruction • Cross-age tutoring • Role-playing	• Mobile devices • Videoconferencing • Electronic discussion boards • eBooks or eText • Smartboards

Multiple ways to engage students

AUDITORY	VISUAL	TACTILE/KINESTHETIC	AFFECTIVE	TECHNOLOGY OPTIONS
• Listening to text read aloud • Debating • Discussing • Giving verbal prompts • Talking through steps • Using songs/raps • Oral storytelling	• Adding novelty with props • Posting goals • Charting progress • Outlining steps to solving a problem • Using visual schedules • Designing posters • Illustrating/taking pictures	• Using manipulatives • Building a model • Using response cards • Using a game format • Working outside • Building movement into lessons • Role-playing	• Working in areas of student interest with some choice • Working alone, with peer, or in cooperative group • Using positive behavior support • Increasing self-regulation • Developing coping skills • Providing feedback • Adding mentors	• Recording on mobile device • Word processing • Charting data with spreadsheets • Creating a video • Blogging, text messaging

(Continued)

TABLE 3.6 (Continued)

Multiple ways students can express their learning

AUDITORY	VISUAL	TACTILE/ KINESTHETIC	AFFECTIVE	TECHNOLOGY OPTIONS
• Oral report • Speech/debate • Song/rap • Storytelling • Interview	• Visual demonstration using a chart, graph • Written report • Drawing/poster • Portfolio • Journal/diary • Mural	• Demonstration of an experiment • Dance • Written report • Pointing or gazing at answers • Puppet show	• Group presentation or response • Drama/play production • Role-play demonstration	• Multimedia productions • Podcast • Electronic book production • Photographic essay • Typed report • Electronic assessment

SOURCE: Adapted from R. Gargiulo and D. Metcalf, *Teaching in Today's Inclusive Classrooms*, 3rd ed. (Boston, MA: Cengage Learning, 2017).

accessibility features are built into the teaching and learning. For learners with intellectual disability who require accommodations, UDL creates access points that are offered to all students, thus potentially reducing the number of individual accommodations (see Table 3.6).

EVIDENCE-BASED PRACTICES

As found in NCLB, IDEA, and RTI, schools are to be using **evidence-based practices** in the education of *all* students with disabilities. Evidence-based education is "the integration of professional wisdom with the best available empirical evidence in making decisions about how to deliver instruction" (U.S. Department of Education, 2002). Empirical evidence refers to empirical data (for example, research with intervention and control groups); professional wisdom is information obtained through a professional's (that is, a teacher's) own experiences or through a consensus of professionals (U.S. Department of Education, 2002). A variety of different organizations have defined evidence-based practice as well as provided resources for both evaluating evidence-based practices and labeling practices as evidence-based (West, McCollow, Kidwell, Umbarger, & Cote, 2013). For example, the What Works Clearinghouse (see http://ies.ed.gov/ncee/wwc/) provides reviews of interventions and practices in education to help teachers understand what works in education.

However, responsibility also falls on educators to determine effective practices for teaching students, including pupils with intellectual disability. West and colleagues (2013) provided a five-step model for helping teachers incorporate evidence-based practice. Step 1 involves "defining the disorder"; in other words, teachers must understand the student's disability and what general impacts it has on learning as well as how each student is individually educationally affected by his or her disability. Step 2 involves "searching the literature for the evidence." West and colleagues (2013) suggested systematic reviews and meta-analyses can help teachers determine effective, research-based practices. See Table 3.7 for examples of systematic reviews or meta-analyses for educational practices for students with intellectual disability. In Step 3, teachers conduct "critical evaluation of the evidence," which is challenging. To truly evaluate the evidence of educational practices, teachers need to understand research methods as well as the statistics researchers report regarding the effectiveness, or lack thereof, of such practices. Step 4 involves teachers "choosing and applying the evidence." Here the teachers take the effective intervention and apply it to their particular student(s) and program. A key element of implementation

TABLE 3.7 Examples of Reviews or Meta-Analyses About Evidence-Based Practices for Students With Intellectual Disability

SOURCE	EDUCATIONAL PRACTICES
Spooner, F., Knight, V. F., Browder, D. M., & Smith, B. R. (2012). Evidence-based practice for teaching academics to students with severe developmental disabilities. *Remedial and Special Education, 33*(6), 374-387.	Task-analytic instruction and discrete response are evidence-based practices for teaching academics to students with severe developmental disabilities.
Browder, D., Ahlgrim-Delzell, L., Spooner, F., Mims, P. J., & Baker, J. N. (2009). Using time delay to teach literacy to students with severe developmental disabilities. *Exceptional Children, 75*(3), 343-364.	Time delay is an evidence-based practice for learners with severe developmental disabilities with respect to teaching word and picture recognition.
Hudson, M. E., Browder, D. M., & Wood, L. A. (2012). Review of experimental research on academic learning by students with moderate and severe intellectual disability in general education. *Research & Practice for Persons With Severe Disabilities, 38*(1), 17-29.	Embedded trial instruction in conjunction with constant time delay is an evidence-based practice for teaching academics to pupils with moderate and severe intellectual disability.

is fidelity; an evidence-based practice can be effective to the degree a teacher implements it as closely as it was designed. Finally, Step 5 concludes the process with "evaluating the outcomes." Teachers need to evaluate what they implement and determine if it works as well as whether it is worth the cost, including resources or time (West et al., 2013, p. 450).

COMMON CORE STATE STANDARDS

The **Common Core State Standards (CCSS)** are academic standards for education (see www.corestandards.org; Council of Chief State School Officers, 2010). The CCSS provide literacy and mathematics standards for students in Grades K–12 as well as standards for literacy in history/social studies, science, and technical subjects for pupils in secondary education (Common Core State Standards Initiative, 2015). The CCSS focus on college and career readiness (Council of Chief State School Officers, 2010). As of September 2016, 43 states and the District of Columbia had adopted the Common Core State Standards.

All students, including students with intellectual disability, are expected to have access to the CCSS; access can involve the use of accommodations or

TABLE 3.8 Resources on the CCSS and Students With Intellectual Disability

Jimenez, B., Courtade, G., & Browder, D. (2013). *Six successful strategies for teaching Common Core State Standards to students with moderate to severe disabilities*. Verona, WI: Attainment Company.	Book that provides strategies for teachers to teach the CCSS to learners with moderate to severe disabilities
http://ec.ncpublicschools.gov/disability-resources/significant-cognitive-disabilities/nc-extended-content-standards/ela/3-5.pdf	Example of Extended CCSS from North Carolina
http://education.ohio.gov/getattachment/Topics/Special-Education/Students-with-Disabilities/Students-With-Disabilities-(1)/OACS-E-Mathematics.pdf.aspx	Ohio's Extended CCSS in mathematics

other supports (Common Core State Standards Initiative, 2015). However, concerns exist regarding the CCSS and learners with more severe disabilities, such as students with intellectual disability (Saunders, Spooner, Browder, Wakeman, & Lee, 2013). In response, states developed extended standards for pupils with severe disabilities who take an alternate assessment (Courtade & Browder, 2011). (See, for example, North Carolina's Extended CCSS [http://ec.ncpublicschools.gov/disability-resources/significant-cognitive-disabilities/nc-extended-content-standards] or Ohio's [http://education.ohio.gov/Topics/Special-Education/Ohios-Learning-Standards-Extended]). Specifically, two primary options exist for alternate standards for students who take the alternate achievement test based on alternate achievement standards: the Extended Common Core State Standards (e.g., Public Schools of North Carolina, 2016) or Essential Elements of the Common Core (Dynamic Learning Maps, 2016). These alternate standards provide a connection to the academic standards for students with more severe needs, including students with moderate and/or severe intellectual disability. See Table 3.8 for additional information on the CCSS and students with intellectual disability.

ACCOUNTABILITY

As indicated previously, under NCLB and IDEA 2004, all students with disabilities are to participate in each state's accountability system. In other words, learners with disabilities must participate in the statewide assessment system required under NCLB and IDEA, in which students are assessed yearly in Grades 3–8 and once again in high school. Learners with disabilities can participate in the accountability system through multiple means, including taking the general large-scale assessment that pupils without disabilities take, taking the general large-scale assessment with accommodations, or taking an alternate assessment (Perner, 2007; Yell & Drasgow, 2005).

An alternate assessment is "an assessment designed for a small group of students with disabilities who are unable to participate in the regular state assessment, even with appropriate accommodations" (U.S. Department of Education, 2003, p. 68699). Alternate assessments, although not explicitly stated in the law, are typically used for only pupils with more severe disabilities, given the government cap of 1 percent of a school's student body to take an alternate assessment based on alternate achievement standards (AA-AAS) and have it count toward the school's AYP. More students can take an alternate assessment, but their scores would not count toward achieving AYP (Branstad et al., 2002; NCLB, 2002; Perner, 2007; Yell & Drasgow, 2005).

The federal government recognized the limiting nature of the 1 percent cap and in 2007 allowed states to develop alternate assessments based on modified achievement standards (AA-MAS) for an additional 2 percent of the student body population, for whom the general large-scale assessment, even with accommodations, was not appropriate (Burling, 2007; Council for Exceptional Children, 2008; Lazarus, Thurlow, Christensen, & Cormier, 2007; U.S. Department of Education, 2007). The additional 2 percent would support learners beyond those with moderate or severe intellectual disability, such as pupils with mild intellectual disability.

However, the government removed approval for the AA-MAS for the additional 2 percent, with states to phase out the assessments by the 2014–2015 academic school year (Center on Standards and Assessment Implementation & National Center on Educational Outcomes, 2014). The rationale for the regulation rollback was that new assessments were being developed that were more inclusive and would accommodate students who previously took the AA-MAS. These high-quality, inclusive assessments include the one from the Partnership for Assessment of Readiness for College and Careers and the one from the Smarter Balanced Assessment Consortium (National Center on Educational Outcomes, 2014).

The accountability system, including the type of alternate assessments, affects the education of students with intellectual disability. The assessment a student is taking can, to some degree, drive what a pupil is learning—in other words, the notion of teaching to the test. For learners with intellectual disability to have an opportunity to be successful on a general large-scale assessment, including the newly designed assessments, these students need access to the general education curriculum (Bouck, 2009). It is unfair to test pupils on material they have not had an opportunity to learn. For additional and more in-depth information regarding accountability, assessment, and alternate assessments, see Chapter 4.

WHAT TO TEACH STUDENTS WITH INTELLECTUAL DISABILITY

The most challenging question to answer in terms of the education of students with intellectual disability may be what to teach—that is, curriculum. There is no easy answer, although many individuals will try to tell you what to do. What to teach learners with intellectual disability is controversial and complicated, particularly for students in secondary education (Bouck, 2012).

Throughout the history of teaching students with disabilities, different curricular approaches have been used, including the two most discussed options: an academic or standards-based curriculum and a **functional curriculum** (Bouck, Taber-Doughty, & Savage, 2015; Pugach & Warger, 2001). A functional—or life-skills or real-world—curriculum has historically been used to teach learners with intellectual disability (Cronin & Patton, 1993; Kolstoe, 1970). The peak time for use of a functional curriculum was the late 1970s and early 1980s, after which attention increasingly turned to an **academic curriculum** and students with intellectual disability being educated in general education settings (Billingsley & Albertson, 1999; Cronin & Patton, 1993).

A functional curriculum is focused on preparing students for the skills deemed necessary or important for daily living post-school or in adult life; it often includes components related to functional academics, daily living skills, community access, vocational education, financial skills, independent living skills, social/relationships skills, transportation skills, and self-determination (Browder et al., 2004; Brown et al., 1979; Patton, Cronin, & Jairrels, 1997). Important within the conceptualization of a functional skill is that the skills targeted are authentic rather than artificial. Functional instruction should translate into real-life activities one may perform in adult life (Bouck et al., 2015; Storey & Miner, 2011). An academic curriculum is focused on teaching academic content (for example, language arts and mathematics) and typically focused on teaching to content standards (Bouck, 2012). Students with disabilities can access an academic curriculum with or without accommodations (Wehmeyer,

Lattin, & Agran, 2001) or participate in a general education curriculum via modification or augmentation, such as educating a learner in a secondary algebra class but focusing his or her instruction on a subskill within algebra, such as addition (Giangreco, Clonigner, & Iverson, 1998).

Current discussions of curriculum for students with intellectual disability often paint academic and functional curricula as opposites and highlight the tension between opposing views. Concerns about privileging one curricular approach over the other come to light in terms of making sure pupils with intellectual disability acquire real-world skills to be successful post-school while simultaneously holding high expectations for these students and maintaining a commitment to meaningful inclusion (Ayres, Lowrey, Douglas, & Sievers, 2011; Bouck, 2012; Collins, 2013; Courtade, Spooner, Browder, & Jimenez, 2012). However, the two curricular approaches do not need to be mutually exclusive, including, but not limited to, infusing a functional curriculum into an academic curriculum or an academic curriculum into a functional curriculum (Bouck et al., 2015; Browder & Cooper-Duffy, 2003; Courtade, Spooner, & Browder, 2007).

Issues relative to providing students with intellectual disability a functional curriculum and an academic curriculum, as well as aspects of behavioral interventions, will be discussed in depth in subsequent chapters, exploring these instructional domains and support across the three main school phases: early childhood education, the elementary school years, and the secondary school years (see Chapters 7–12).

WHERE TO TEACH STUDENTS WITH INTELLECTUAL DISABILITY

Closely related to what to teach (that is, curriculum) is where to teach, or the instructional environments in which students are educated. Technically, learners with intellectual disability, regardless of curriculum, can receive instruction in any of the options along the continuum of the least restrictive environment and, according to IDEA, are to be educated in the least restrictive environment possible. Historically, however, students with intellectual disability have been more likely to be educated in restrictive environments. According to the most recent data available on the educational placements of students with intellectual disability from the 2013–2014 school year, the most frequent placement for pupils with intellectual disability enrolled in public schools was a separate class (i.e., self-contained; 46.2%), and the next frequent was a resource room (26.6%) (see Figure 3.4).

FIGURE 3.4 Educational Placements of Students With Intellectual Disability

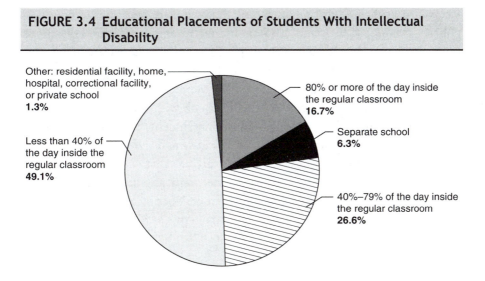

Other: residential facility, home, hospital, correctional facility, or private school
1.3%

Less than 40% of the day inside the regular classroom
49.1%

80% or more of the day inside the regular classroom
16.7%

Separate school
6.3%

40%–79% of the day inside the regular classroom
26.6%

SOURCE: U.S. Department of Education. (2015). *Thirty-seventh annual report to Congress on the implementation of the Individuals with Disabilities Education Act, 2014.* Washington, DC: Office of Special Education and Rehabilitative Services. Retrieved September 5, 2016, from http://www2.ed.gov/about/reports/annual/osep/2015/parts-b-c/37th-arc-for-idea.pdf

Where to educate students with intellectual disability can be as controversial as what curriculum they should receive. While pupils with intellectual disability legally and ethically should be included with their peers without disabilities to the maximum extent possible in general education settings, the general education setting may not always be the most appropriate educational setting for each learner. Decisions about educational placement, like all decisions affecting the education of students with intellectual disability, should be made on an individualized basis per the IEP team. Some pupils with intellectual disability benefit from instruction in a separate classroom or separate school. The appropriate setting for instruction for some students with intellectual disability, especially at the secondary level, may be in the community. Learners with intellectual disability can benefit from **community-based instruction**, which focuses on the instruction and practice of skills in natural settings (for example, a grocery store) rather than the simulated or artificial setting of a classroom.

CONCLUSION

Students with intellectual disability are a heterogeneous population with unique needs and strengths. However, like all learners with disabilities, multiple facets impact their education, including the various implications of education policies (that is, IDEA and ESSA). Indirectly or directly, the educational programs of pupils with intellectual disability are also impacted by contemporary educational issues that affect education in general, including the Common Core State Standards, the current accountability system, and response to intervention. The remainder of this textbook will provide evidence-based or research-supported practices for educating students with intellectual disability from early childhood through adolescence and transition to adulthood. In addition to considering functional life skills instruction, academic instruction, and behavioral interventions for learners with intellectual disability, the textbook will provide information relative to conducting assessments, helping students transition, and using assistive technology.

Chapter Summary

- Federal laws like Every Student Succeeds Act (ESSA), the Individuals with Disabilities Education Improvement Act (IDEA 2004), and Section 504 of the Rehabilitation Act of 1973 impact the education of students with intellectual disability.

- An individualized education program (IEP) is a legal document that states the educational programming of all students with disabilities, including pupils with intellectual disability.

- Prior to IDEA 1975, litigation involving students with intellectual disability resulted in rulings supporting free appropriate public education

(FAPE) for learners with intellectual disability.

- Response to intervention (RTI) can impact students with intellectual disability as RTI is being increasingly used as a child find or pre-referral technique.

- Positive behavior interventions and supports (PBIS) impact pupils with intellectual disability like all pupils with disabilities; PBIS are used to focus on prevention by recognizing positive behavior.

- Universal design for learning (UDL) supports learners with intellectual disability similarly to how it supports all learners;

UDL offers built-in accessibility that can reduce many individualized accommodations.

- Evidence-based practices should be used for all students, including students with intellectual disability. Teachers of pupils with intellectual disability need to take responsibility for implementing evidence-based practices.

- Learners with intellectual disability are expected to access the Common Core State Standards, including, as a possibility, Extended Common Core State Standards.

- Students with intellectual disability participate in the accountability system through the general large-scale assessment, general large-scale assessment with accommodations, or an alternate assessment.

- Pupils with intellectual disability can be taught by a variety of curricula; the two most common are a functional curriculum or an academic or standards-based curriculum.

- Like all learners with disabilities, learners with intellectual disability can be educated in a variety of instructional environments, although it should be the least restrictive environment (LRE). Data suggest the most frequent instructional environment for learners with intellectual disability is a self-contained class.

Review Questions

1. Describe the major provisions of IDEA 2004 and how each of these provisions impacts students with intellectual disability.

2. Explain how the following contemporary education issues directly or indirectly impact the education of students with intellectual disability: response to intervention, positive behavior interventions and supports, the accountability system, the Common Core State Standards, universal design for learning, and use of evidence-based practices.

3. What is the difference between a functional curriculum and an academic or standards-based curriculum?

Key Terms

adequate yearly progress (AYP)
(page 51)

scientifically based (page 51)

free appropriate public education
(FAPE) (page 53)

least restrictive environment (LRE)
(page 53)

individualized education program
(IEP) (page 53)

accommodations (page 55)

multi-tiered systems of support
(MTSS) (page 58)

response to intervention (RTI)
(page 58)

positive behavior interventions and
supports (PBIS) (page 58)

child find system (page 60)

universal design for learning (UDL)
(page 61)

evidence-based practices (page 65)

Common Core State Standards
(CCSS) (page 66)

functional curriculum (page 69)

academic curriculum (page 69)

community-based instruction
(page 71)

Organizations Concerned With Education

Center on Response to Intervention

www.rti4success.org

Common Core State Standards Initiative

www.corestandards.org

National Alternate Assessment Center

www.naacpartners.org

U.S. Department of Education— Building the Legacy: IDEA 2004

http://idea.ed.gov

What Works Clearinghouse

http://ies.ed.gov/ncee/wwc/

PART II

Educational Concerns Across the School Years for Students With Intellectual Disability

CHAPTER 4

Assessing and Evaluating Students With Intellectual Disability

Ginevra R. Courtade and Robert C. Pennington

Learning Objectives

After reading Chapter 4, you should be able to:

- Describe the roles of assessment in the educational programming for students with intellectual disability.
- Discriminate the roles of assessment in the educational programming for students with intellectual disability.
- Identify data collection procedures to record a range of student responses.
- Explain appropriate use of accommodations and alternate assessment for students with intellectual disability.

Assessment is a critical component of the educational process for all students. Recently, there has been an increased emphasis on the role of assessment in school accountability. In this capacity, assessment can be used to identify districts, schools, and teachers that need support in improving educational programs. This important and highly politicized function of assessment must not overshadow the many roles that assessment serves in educating students with disabilities. The Individuals with Disabilities Education Improvement Act (PL 108–446), commonly called IDEA 2004, mandates that assessment drive eligibility, programming, and progress monitoring (Capizzi, 2008). That is, from the initial identification of a disability to everyday instructional practice, assessment is a key mechanism in promoting student success.

WHAT IS ASSESSMENT?

Assessment is a term that is used to describe the ways that educators gather, record, and interpret information about students in order to make instructional decisions (Cohen & Spenciner, 2015). Assessment generally involves the review of multiple sources of data. For instance, when using assessment to determine eligibility for services under a category of disability, educators are required to make decisions based on data collected from the use of multiple instruments (for example, intelligence tests, adaptive behavior scales, classroom performance data). Decisions cannot be made based on a single test score (Heward, 2013). At the classroom level, assessment is used to guide instruction and measure student progress toward academic and behavioral goals. Teachers must use multiple sources of data to develop individualized education programs

---

NONDISCRIMINATORY IDENTIFICATION AND EVALUATION: A KEY PRINCIPLE OF IDEA

Assessment plays a crucial role in the development of curriculum and instruction; therefore, it is critical that assessments used with students are inherently nonbiased. In order to facilitate this idea, one of the key principles of IDEA is *nondiscriminatory identification and evaluation*. To adhere to this principle, educators should consider the following:

- Nonbiased, multiple methods of evaluation must be used to determine eligibility and services.
- Tests and evaluation procedures must not discriminate on the basis of race, culture, or native language.
- All tests must be administered in the child's native language.
- Identification and placement decisions cannot be made on the basis of a single test score (Heward, 2013).

(IEPs) composed of strategies and specially designed instruction that are tailored to meet the needs of individual students. Because of the importance of assessment in the educational system for students with intellectual disability, teachers must thoroughly understand different methods of assessment and how to effectively use assessment in a way that benefits students.

NORM-REFERENCED TESTS

Norm-referenced tests are standardized assessments used to compare a student's performance to that of a normative sample of students. This sample is composed of individuals deemed representative of the targeted audience for the assessment. In determining if a sample is representative, the authors select individuals with characteristics relevant to the construct that will be assessed. These characteristics may include age, gender, grade in school, geography, intelligence, race and cultural identity, acculturation of parents, and socioeconomic status (Salvia, Ysseldyke, & Bolt, 2007). Educators typically use norm-referenced tests to measure intelligence, academic achievement, and adaptive behavior.

Norm-referenced intelligence tests are designed to assess cognitive ability and problem-solving processes. Often, they comprise subtests that measure verbal comprehension, perceptual reasoning, working memory, processing speed, quantitative reasoning, and general knowledge. Results from intelligence tests are often used as one source of data in the determination of eligibility for services under the category of intellectual disability.

Commonly used norm-referenced intelligence tests include the Stanford-Binet Intelligence Scales (5th ed.), or SB-V (Roid, 2003), and the Wechsler Intelligence Scale for Children (5th ed.), or WISC-V (Wechsler, 2014). Some students may have impairments in language that preclude effective administration of these assessments. Several nonverbal intelligence tests have been developed for use with these students. It is important to consider that some of these tests may measure different areas related to the construct of intelligence. For example, the Leiter International Performance Scale (3rd ed.), or Leiter-3 (Roid, Miller, Pomplun, & Koch, 2013), measures fluid intelligence, memory, and attention, and the Test of Nonverbal Intelligence (4th ed.), or TONI-4 (Brown, Sherbenou, & Johnsen, 2010), measures problem-solving ability. Fluid intelligence may be measured by having students sequentially order items, classify items, complete analogies, and match or repeat patterns. Memory can be assessed by having students recall a sequence of numbers in order or reverse order after they have been originally presented. Attention is typically measured as sustained (attention to one task) or divided (attention to multiple tasks). Problem solving, as measured by the TONI-4, involves matching or completing patterns of figures that incorporate characteristics of shape, position, direction, rotation, contiguity, shading, size, and movement.

Norm-referenced academic achievement tests are also commonly used as a part of an assessment battery to determine eligibility for services for students with an intellectual disability. These tests are designed to measure what skills a student has learned. Academic achievement tests are composed of subtests that assess performance in a particular area of content. Subtests typically address the areas of reading, math, written language, and oral language. The Woodcock-Johnson Tests of Achievement (4th ed.), or WJ-IV (Woodcock, Schrank, McGrew, & Mather, 2014), and the Kaufman Test of Educational Achievement (3rd ed.), or KTEA-3 (Kaufman & Kaufman, 2014), are commonly used academic achievement tests.

Finally, norm-referenced assessments of adaptive behavior are critical in the determination of eligibility for services for students with intellectual disability. Adaptive behavior is "the collection of conceptual, social, and practical skills that are learned and performed by people in their everyday lives" (American Association on Intellectual and Developmental Disabilities, 2013, para. 4). Adaptive behavior assessment can be used to determine an individual's level of functioning in the areas of language and literacy, basic mathematical concepts, interpersonal skills, social problem solving, and daily living activities (for example, grooming, personal hygiene, travel). Commonly used adaptive behavior assessments are the Vineland Adaptive Behavior Scales (2nd ed.), or VABS-II (Sparrow, Balla, & Cicchetti, 2007), and the Adaptive Behavior Assessment System (3rd ed.), or ABAS-III (Harrison & Oakland, 2015).

Despite their value in helping to determine educational eligibility for services and the design of those services, it is important to understand the limitations of norm-referenced tests. First, the interpretation of test results is limited if the individual tested does not share characteristics with the sample to which the test was normed. Teachers can use the test manual to identify the sample on which the instrument was normed and then make decisions concerning its appropriateness for a particular student. Second, the title of tests and subtests might not clearly depict what is actually assessed. It is important that teachers understand the assessment tasks in order to interpret how students might perform on related tasks in a classroom setting. Finally, the results from the tests are subject to influence by the context in which the test was administered. Although protocols and recommendations are provided for administering these assessments, adherence to them cannot always be guaranteed. In light of these limitations, it is important that results from norm-referenced tests are viewed in the context of other data on student performance.

CRITERION-REFERENCED TESTS

In contrast to norm-referenced tests, **criterion-referenced tests** compare student performance to a criterion or goal (Cohen & Spenciner, 2015). Results of criterion-referenced tests indicate what a student can or cannot do, rather than how the student's performance compares to that of other students (Salvia et al., 2007). Criterion-referenced tests also differ from norm-referenced tests in the depth of coverage of content. Typically, norm-referenced tests broadly assess a domain, whereas criterion-referenced tests assess fewer domains in greater depth—that is, more test items in each domain (Cohen & Spenciner, 2015). When teachers use well-designed criterion-referenced tests, they can construct a picture of student performance across a range of relevant skills and develop instructional programs that target students' areas of need with precision.

Criterion-referenced tests can be developed by teachers or purchased as commercially available test batteries. Teacher-made criterion-referenced tests often draw content items from IEPs, objectives within a curriculum, or standards from published tests (Overton, 2016). Although it is common practice for teachers to develop criterion-referenced tests, some teachers may struggle to establish an exact criterion for whether a student has mastered a skill (Overton, 2016). It is recommended that teachers consider attending to what performance looks like among peers who have mastered the skill, determine their performance level, and take that level as a standard for mastery (Taylor, 2009). In addition, teachers of students with intellectual disability should consider whether a passing score on a test is an indicator of fluency, maintenance, or generalization of the skill and consider the phase of learning to make additional instructional decisions (Collins, 2007). Teachers who have constructed valid and meaningful IEPs may already have goals and objectives with criteria established that meet these recommendations.

In addition to teacher-made criterion-referenced tests, there is a broad range of published tests for use with students with intellectual disability. The BRIGANCE® series of criterion-referenced tests are used to determine student performance in specific areas of skill including developmental skills, readiness activities, academic skills, and transition skills. Results from the BRIGANCE® series (Brigance, 2004, 2010a, 2010b) may be useful for teachers as they determine present levels of performance for IEPs, as well as write IEP goals and objectives. Assessments in the BRIGANCE® series can be used to measure a range of specific skills across multiple areas (for example, identifying parts of the body, reading numerals, computing totals for purchases, reading employment signs, ordering pairs on a coordinate plane, constructing a Venn diagram).

The Verbal Behavior Milestones Assessment and Placement Program (VB-MAPP) (Sundberg, 2008) is a criterion-referenced test that has been used to assess the verbal and related skills of children with developmental disabilities. The assessment consists of five interrelated components: (1) a language milestones assessment, (2) a learning barriers assessment, (3) a transition assessment, (4) task analysis and skills tracking tools, and (5) guide placement and the development of IEP goals. The language milestones assessment comprises 170 measurable milestones that address specific communication skills across three developmental levels (0–18 months, 18–30 months, 30–48 months). Teachers can use the VB-MAPP to develop instructional programs to improve students' communication functioning.

The Choosing Outcomes and Accommodations for Children (3rd ed.), or COACH-3 (Giangreco, Cloninger, & Iverson, 2011), is designed to help collaborative teams determine components of appropriate IEPs for students ages 3–21 with intense support needs (individuals often characterized as having moderate or severe disabilities). The COACH-3 is divided into two main components (Determining a Student's Educational Program, and Translating the Family-Identified Priorities Into Goals and Objectives) and offers criteria in the following goal areas: communication, socialization, personal management, recreation, access academics, applied academics, school, community, vocation, and general curriculum areas. The collaborative team could include the student, family members, a special educator, general education teachers, related service providers, therapists, and psychologists. Typically, the team comes together in a meeting/interview format held at a mutually agreed upon location. The special education teacher or a psychologist generally facilitates the meeting, recording input provided by the team about student progress related to the goal criteria. The COACH-3 results are often used when developing IEPs or completing reevaluations to address current performance levels in the goal areas. The results will help drive planning and instruction in order for the student to reach educational goals and objectives as determined by the team.

FORMATIVE AND SUMMATIVE ASSESSMENTS

A requirement of IDEA 2004 related to the IEP is that a team determines how students' progress toward annual goals will be measured (Etscheidt, 2006). In order to appropriately monitor progress, a team should first develop relevant, clear, and measureable goals and, as appropriate, objectives and then develop a plan that includes methods to monitor progress both formatively and summatively. (Under IDEA 2004, short-term objectives are only required in an IEP for students who take alternate assessments aligned with alternate achievement standards.) **Formative assessment** "is a process used by teachers and students during instruction that provides feedback to adjust ongoing teaching and learning to improve students' achievement of intended instructional outcomes" (Council of Chief State School Officers, 2008, p. 3). Teachers should use formative assessment as a means to continuously gauge students' understanding of the content and use that information to make adjustments to instruction as necessary. Formative assessments can involve a range of procedures including direct questioning, teacher–student conferencing, post-instruction exit slips, quizzes, active student responding strategies (for example, choral responding, response cards), and student self-assessments. In 2008, the Council of Chief State School Officers (CCSSO) prescribed attributes of effective formative assessment (see Table 4.1).

In contrast, **summative assessment** is the final assessment of progress used to evaluate student learning at the end of a period of instruction. Results of summative assessments should indicate how many skills or concepts a student has retained over a period of time (Spinelli, 2006). The goal of summative assessment is to compare student learning against a standard or benchmark. For students with intellectual disability, this might be the assessment of an annual goal or an end-of-grade/course assessment. Summative assessments may include teacher-made end-of-unit tests, performance tasks, portfolios, student projects, and standardized achievement tests. The CCSSO also developed high-quality summative assessment principles to guide the design of assessments aligned to College and Career Readiness (CCR) standards. Although these principles were developed with CCR standards in mind, the principles can be applied to all student goals and objectives and used as a guideline for teachers as they are developing summative assessments for students with intellectual disability (see Table 4.1).

CURRICULUM-BASED EVALUATIONS

Curriculum-based evaluation measures are short-duration measures that monitor growth on relevant classroom skills. Curriculum-based evaluation

---

TABLE 4.1 Attributes of Effective Formative Assessment and Summative Assessment Principles

ATTRIBUTES OF EFFECTIVE FORMATIVE ASSESSMENT	SUMMATIVE ASSESSMENT PRINCIPLES
1. Learning Progressions: Learning progressions should clearly articulate the subgoals of the ultimate learning goal. *Teachers understand the overall goals of what students are to learn as well as short-term objectives.*	1. Align assessments to state standards or student IEP goals or objectives. *Focus on content needed for success on later standards/goals. Require a range of cognitive demand.*
2. Learning Goals and Criteria for Success: Learning goals and criteria for success should be clearly identified and communicated to students. *Students are aware of learning goals and expected criteria for success.*	2. Yield valuable reports on student progress. *Results of the assessments should be reported in ways that are instructionally valuable, easy to understand, and useful to all stakeholders (i.e., students, parents, teachers).*
3. Descriptive Feedback: Students should be provided with evidence-based feedback linked to the intended instructional outcomes and criteria for success. *Specific, timely feedback should be given to the students.*	3. Adhere to best practices in testing administration. *Assessments are valid (measure what they purport to), reliable (accurately evaluate across contexts and scorers), and unbiased.*
4. Self- and Peer Assessment: Both self- and peer assessment are important for providing students an opportunity to think metacognitively about their learning. *Students and peers should be involved in giving and receiving feedback.*	4. Provide accessibility to all students. *Follow principles of universal design for learning, and offer appropriate modifications and accommodations.*
5. Collaboration: A classroom culture in which teachers and students are partners in learning should be established. *Students should be partners in the learning process.*	

SOURCE: Adapted from *Attributes of Effective Formative Assessment* (Washington, DC: Council of Chief State School Officers, 2008); *High Quality Summative Assessment Principles* (Washington, DC: Council of Chief State School Officers, 2013).

---

measures can generally be classified as curriculum-based assessments or curriculum-based measurements. Curriculum-based assessments are typically used to measure short-term objectives while curriculum-based measurements are used to determine growth on annual goals (Spinelli, 2006).

CURRICULUM-BASED ASSESSMENTS

Curriculum-based assessment (CBA) is a method used to determine how a student is performing by employing the actual content of the curriculum within frequent and direct measures of student performance (Spinelli, 2006). CBA directly ties classroom instruction to assessment and can be useful in determining eligibility, developing goals for IEPs and instruction, and evaluating student progress in the classroom curriculum (Cohen & Spenciner, 2015). Teachers typically create these assessments in order to match what is taught in the classroom. For students with intellectual disability, teachers often make modifications to the curriculum, altering a grade-level curriculum goal and performance criteria (Janney & Snell, 2011). For example, if a first-grade-level goal is to correctly read 30 sight words, a modified goal could be that a student would correctly read 20 sight words with picture symbol supports. Thus, a CBA may need to be developed in lieu of a formal assessment that has been developed to measure the grade-level goal. The creation of a CBA requires more than just the development of test questions. A well-developed CBA should clearly integrate the curriculum, assessment, and analysis of results. Cohen and Spenciner (2015) recommend the following steps to construct a CBA instrument:

1. Identify the purpose of the assessment (eligibility, developing instructional goals, evaluating student progress). Note that some instruments may be used for multiple purposes.

2. Analyze the curriculum. (Consider what tasks the student should be learning.)

3. Develop performance objectives. (Consider what behaviors the student should demonstrate in order to indicate progress in the curriculum.)

4. Develop the assessment procedures. (Develop test items that correspond to the performance objectives and maintain validity of the assessment by having close correspondence with the curriculum. Scoring procedures must also be created.)

5. Implement the assessment procedures. (Test the test by administering the CBA according to the prescribed procedures to determine if any changes need to be made. Then administer the finalized test and collect student data.)

6. Organize the information. (Summarize the data.)

7. Interpret and integrate the results. (Results of the CBA should be used to inform instruction.)

For example, a teacher may decide to evaluate her student's progress on a reading comprehension goal written in the student's IEP. The teacher will analyze the IEP to determine what short-term objectives and/or benchmarks should be measured and at what level the student needs to perform in order to show mastery of those objectives. She will then develop assessments that directly measure the reading comprehension objectives (for example, develop 10 comprehension questions related to informational text the student has read; create an activity in which the student must identify elements of a story that was read; ask the student to identify the author's purpose of five short passages). The teacher will then pilot the assessments (with a different student, or using different reading passages), then administer the finalized CBAs and collect data. After the data have been collected, the teacher will graph results and use the results to determine if and what type of changes should be made to instruction.

CURRICULUM-BASED MEASUREMENT

Curriculum-based measurement (CBM) is characterized by research-validated indicators of student performance with standardized administration and scoring procedures used to assess performance over an extended period of time (Fuchs & Fuchs, 2000). CBMs involve the repeated administration of the same measure until a student reaches a level of mastery. Subsequently, the measure (probe) is changed to reflect a more difficult goal within the same domain (for example, a higher-grade-level reading passage in a reading fluency probe) (Spinelli, 2006). CBM procedures exist for monitoring basic skills in reading, mathematics, spelling, and writing. Teachers can generate their own CBMs using free Internet sources (for example, www.interventioncentral.org). CBMs may be used to monitor student progress, determine eligibility for services, and make instructional decisions. See Figure 4.1 for an example of a CBM fluency probe, accompanying administration procedures, and scoring procedures.

FIGURE 4.1 Example of Directions for a Curriculum-Based Measurement Administration

Oral Reading Fluency: Directions for Administration

1. The examiner and the student sit across the table from each other. The examiner hands the student the unnumbered copy of the CBM reading passage. The examiner takes the numbered copy of the passage, shielding it from the student's view.

2. The examiner says to the student, "When I say, 'Begin,' start reading aloud at the top of this page. Read across the page [demonstrate by pointing]. Try to read each word. If you come to a word you don't know, I'll tell it to you. Be sure to do your best reading. Are there any questions? [Pause.] Begin."

3. The examiner starts the stopwatch when the student says the first word. If the student does not say the initial word within three seconds, the examiner says the word and starts the stopwatch.

4. As the student reads along in the text, the examiner records any errors by marking a slash (/) through the incorrectly read word. If the student hesitates for three seconds on any word, the examiner says the word and marks it as an error.

5. At the end of one minute, the examiner says, "Stop," and marks the student's concluding place in the text with a bracket ( ]).

6. Initial assessment: If the examiner is assessing the student for the first time, the examiner administers a total of three reading passages during the session using the above procedures and takes the median (middle) score as the best estimate of the student's oral reading fluency.

7. Progress monitoring: If the examiner is monitoring student growth in oral reading fluency (and has previously collected oral reading fluency data), only one reading passage is given in the session.

SOURCE: Adapted from J. Wright, *How To: Assess Reading Speed With CBM: Oral Reading Fluency Passages*. (2013). Available at http://www.jimwrightonline.com/mixed_files/lansing_IL/_Lansing_IL_Aug_2013/2_CBA_ORF_Directions.pdf

Some CBMs should be administered individually (for example, oral reading fluency, letter naming fluency), while others can be administered individually or to a group (for example, maze, spelling, writing, math). The frequency of CBM administration depends on purpose, but general recommendations are as follows:

- Screening/benchmarking for all students in the classroom, three to four times per school year

- Progress monitoring for students in the bottom 25 percent of the class based on screening, one to two times per week

- Monthly progress monitoring of all students to maintain effectiveness of classroom instruction (Hosp, Hosp, & Howell, 2007)

ECOLOGICAL ASSESSMENT

Ecological assessment is a process that involves the consideration of skills needed for individuals to be competent in a range of personally relevant environments (Cooper, Heron, & Heward, 2007). For example, ecological assessment might indicate that an individual in New York requires instruction in riding the subway, whereas another, in New Orleans, must learn to hop on a trolley. Brown et al. (1979) introduced the **ecological inventory** as a method for the identification of meaningful instructional targets for learners with severe intellectual disability. When conducting an ecological inventory, teachers must first consider an individual's current and future environments across major domain areas (for example, domestic, education, community, employment, recreation/leisure). Once the relevant environments have been identified, the teachers then list sub-environments within each setting. For example, if a pool is identified as an important environment for a learner within the recreation domain, the teacher must identify the smaller contexts within the pool setting (for example, entry area, snack bar, changing room, diving pool). Next, teachers must identify activities within each area and list the skills required to participate in those activities. Finally, teachers can use the inventory to identify common skills required across settings to prioritize for instruction. It is important to note that the ecological inventory process can be applied at multiple levels of complexity. An IEP team might conduct a comprehensive ecological inventory to assist in person-centered planning for an individual entering high school or conduct a focused ecological inventory of a cafeteria setting for a preschooler with intellectual disability, transitioning to shifting demands of an elementary school setting. The ecological inventory is an invaluable tool for educators as it helps to promote the inclusion of curricular items that are immediately relevant to individuals with intellectual disability and their families. Table 4.2 is an example of a focused ecological inventory that might be used to identify instructional targets for a student in a preschool setting.

Once teachers identify the skills required of a specific environment, they may conduct a **situational assessment** to determine which of the identified skills will require instruction. When conducting a situational assessment, a student is presented with an opportunity to attempt activities in the natural environment (Spooner, Browder, & Richter, 2011). The teacher then records those skills that the student performs with and without supports. For example, a teacher might present an opportunity for a young adult to order food at a local chain restaurant. She notices that the student maneuvers and waits in line, but

TABLE 4.2 Example of Using an Ecological Inventory for a Preschool-Age Student

Domain	Recreation/Leisure
Environment	Playground
Sub-environment	Jungle Gym
Activity	Using the climbing wall
Skills	Waiting, turn taking, asking for help, climbing

does not accurately respond to several questions concerning choices of condiments posed by restaurant workers. Situational assessments are unique in that they provide an opportunity to assess student performance in the presence of naturally occurring stimuli. They also may help teachers to identify unforeseen features of novel environments.

ASSESSMENT OF STUDENT PREFERENCES

The assessment of student preferences is critical in the development of programming for all learners. Through **preference assessment**, teachers may identify powerful reinforcers that can be delivered during instruction and in the treatment of challenging behavior. There are three general methods for identifying student preferences. First, teachers may indirectly assess preferences by asking students and caregivers to report their preference for particular stimuli (for example, foods, activities, books). Teachers gather these data by directly interviewing respondents or by asking them to complete preference surveys. Interviews concerning student preferences are relatively easy to conduct, and a range of premade preference surveys are widely available. Unfortunately, data suggest that respondents often fail to identify stimuli that actually serve as effective reinforcers (Northup, 2000; Northup, George, Jones, Broussard, & Vollmer, 1996). A second method, free operant assessment, involves watching students within their natural environments and recording the duration in which they interact with particular stimuli. When conducting a free operant assessment, teachers can observe the student in the environment "as is," or they may salt the environment with potentially reinforcing stimuli. For example, Sautter, LeBlanc, and Gillet (2008) placed several toys within close proximity of six young children with developmental disabilities. They recorded the duration of the children's interactions with each toy during four 5-minute sessions, calculated the total percentage of engagement with each toy, and determined high- and low-preference toys. Although free operant assessments may be more effective in identifying potential reinforcers in an individual's natural environment, they may be difficult to conduct in a typical classroom arrangement and require a substantial amount of time spent in observation. A third method, trial-based assessment, involves presenting stimuli and observing students' response to those stimuli. Researchers have demonstrated the effectiveness of several trial-based preference assessments in the identification of reinforcers for a range of individuals (Cannella-Malone, Sabielny, Jimenez, & Miller, 2013).

In the **single-stimulus presentation assessment** method (Pace, Ivancic, Edwards, Iwata, & Page, 1985), multiple stimuli are presented to an individual, one at a time and in random order. Each stimulus is presented multiple times, and the observer records a specified dimension of an individual's response (for example, duration of interaction, latency to approach, frequency of contact). This procedure may be useful for students with a limited skill repertoire, as it does not require scanning or making a selection between multiple stimuli. Unfortunately, it is generally considered time consuming and tends to overestimate preference as individuals may approach items, independent of preference, because they are novel. Another procedure, referred to as the **paired-stimulus or forced-choice assessment**, requires individuals to select from two stimuli that are presented simultaneously (Fisher et al., 1992). Multiple stimuli are paired such that each one is presented with every other stimulus multiple times. Once the assessment is completed, stimuli can be rank ordered by the number of selections, from high to low preference. Data suggest that the paired-stimulus assessment may be more effective in identifying reinforcers than the single-stimulus assessment. Unfortunately, it requires the presentation of many trials and therefore also may be considered time consuming. A third type of procedure involves the simultaneous presentation of multiple stimuli, reducing the amount of time required to administer an assessment. In the **multiple-stimulus-with-replacement assessment**, a selected item is replaced, and the array is rearranged at the onset of each trial. In the **multiple-stimulus-without-replacement assessment**, the selected item is not replaced, and the remaining stimuli are rearranged and presented during the next trial (DeLeon & Iwata, 1996). An advantage of the multiple-stimulus-without-replacement assessment procedure is that it requires minimal time to conduct and has been shown to accurately

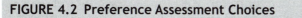

FIGURE 4.2 Preference Assessment Choices

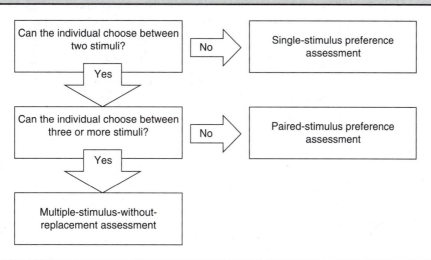

SOURCE: Adapted from H. Cannella-Malone, L. Sabielny, E. Jimenez, & M. Miller, "Pick One! Conducting Preference Assessments With Students With Significant Disabilities," *Teaching Exceptional Children, 45*(6), 2013, pp. 16-23.

identify stimuli that serve as reinforcers (Higbee, Carr, & Harrison, 1999). See Figure 4.2 as a guide for determining appropriate preference assessments for students.

It is important to note that preference assessment procedures are limited in that they can only identify student preferences in the context of assessment. That is, they may fail to identify stimuli that will serve as reinforcers in instructional contexts. The effectiveness of a reinforcer is observed when its contingent presentation following a response produces future responding. For example, a teacher may observe a sudden decrease in responding in the absence of any instructional change, or a consistently high rate of problem behavior despite the application of a token economy. In both instances, undesirable patterns of responding may have resulted from the delivery of stimuli with little or no reinforcing value.

ASSESSMENT FOR EFFECTIVE INSTRUCTION

Another function of assessment is to ensure that students are not exposed to ineffective instruction. Despite common perceptions that teaching is synonymous with the artful presentation of information, any accurate description of teaching must include an observed effect on student performance (Vargas, 2013). That is, teaching only occurs when students are observed to have learned. Teachers of students with intellectual disability should use a range of assessment procedures to determine the effectiveness of their teaching practices. The accurate application of these procedures cannot proceed without a teacher's basic understanding of the measurement of behavior and data collection.

MEASURING STUDENT BEHAVIOR

When developing any type of measurement system, it is important that teachers first determine the characteristic of student performance that is expected to change following instruction. Often teachers are interested in how frequently a student performs a particular response. These responses of interest may occur in the absence (for example, talk-outs, making requests) or the presence of programmed instructional stimuli (for example, saying the name of the main character after hearing a passage). Some teachers may be interested in the temporal features of a response such as how long a response lasts (duration) or how long it takes for a student to respond following a teacher directive or natural environmental cue (latency). Once a teacher decides on the most critical dimension of a response to measure, he or she must select an appropriate procedure for collecting data. This process of matching the measure of interest to the method for data collection is paramount as it ensures the usability of data. When teachers collect data using inappropriate collection procedures, they help create **artifacts** in measurement. Artifacts are results or response patterns that appear to exist but do not reflect actual performance (Cooper et al., 2007). Below we have provided descriptions of several important measures and the procedures used to obtain them.

Number/count. This measure involves a simple count of the number of each occurrence of a response within a given time period. To make comparisons over time, teachers must ensure that students have an equal number of opportunities to respond across sessions. When collecting number/count data, teachers use **event recording**, which entails a range of methods for recording the occurrence of each response. Teachers can employ a variety of methods to record responses including writing tally marks, moving pennies from one pocket to another, clicking an analog counter, or touching a digital counter on a smartphone. A critical derivative measure that can be obtained from number/counting is percentage. Teachers can obtain the percentage of responses that occur in the presence of a particular stimulus by dividing the number of responses by the total number of opportunities. Again, it is important that students are presented with an equal number of opportunities when comparing performance over time. Consider a student who solves two math problems correctly across two consecutive sessions, but on day 1 the teacher presents five problems, and on day 2 she presents ten. The resulting data would inaccurately reflect a drop in performance from 40 to 20 percent.

Rate. Teachers use rate to determine how many responses occur within a specified period of time. Rate is calculated by dividing the number of responses by the period of time observed and is obtained using event recording. When teachers calculate rate, they gather additional information about a student's performance. For example, they can learn how quickly a child reads, answers math problems, or writes words. These data are critical to assessing the fluency at which students can employ skills to complete increasingly complex tasks. Rate also is used to measure the occurrence of challenging behaviors that are short in duration, and can be used to compare levels of responding across observation periods that differ in length.

Duration. Teachers use duration measures when they are interested in the length of time that a response occurs. For instance, a teacher may want to know how long a student engages in a particular task or persists in emitting a challenging behavior. There are two recording procedures for collecting duration data. **Total duration recording** involves starting a recording device (for example, a timer) at the onset of each occurrence of a target behavior and stopping it when it ceases. When using this method, the timer is reset at the end of the observation period but not between occurrences. This method provides the observer with the total duration that a behavior occurs within a specified period of time and permits the calculation of the percentage of total time that an individual is engaged in a specific behavior. Another method, **duration per occurrence (DPO) recording**, requires the observer to record the length of each occurrence by resetting the timer between instances. When using DPO recording, teachers can obtain data related to the number of occurrences, the average duration of each occurrence, and the total amount of time engaged in the target behavior.

Latency. Latency is defined as the amount of time between a particular environmental cue and the onset of a response (Kazdin, 2011). For example, a teacher may be interested in how quickly a student starts an assignment following a directive or asks for assistance following a change in routine. Teachers collect these important data through **latency recording** or starting a timer when the cue is presented and stopping the timer when the desired response occurs.

Time sampling. Time sampling involves a set of procedures for estimating the actual occurrence of a behavior. Teachers may choose to use one of these procedures when the behavior occurs at a rate that is difficult to measure or when the behavior cannot be observed continuously. When using time sampling, an observation period is divided into equal short intervals (5–120 seconds), and behavior is recorded if it occurs throughout an entire interval, anytime during the interval, or at the end of an interval. **Whole-interval recording (WIR)** is best applied when an observer is interested in behaviors that are expected to occur for long durations (for example, staying in one's seat, long vocalizations). When using WIR, a response is recorded as occurring only if it persists through an entire interval. This method may underestimate the occurrence of a behavior, as any cessation of the response, no matter how brief, precludes recording of its occurrence.

Partial-interval recording (PIR) involves recording whether or not a response occurs at any point during an interval. Since PIR requires a behavior to occur only once and for a brief duration, PIR provides a crude measure, as it tends to overestimate the actual duration of a response and underestimate the number of times a response occurs. PIR is advantageous in that it does not require the continuous observation of a response during each interval and may allow the observer to record the occurrence of multiple behaviors. Finally, **momentary time sampling (MTS)** requires an observer to record whether or not a response is occurring at the end of an interval. For example, a teacher sets a timer for two-minute intervals and at the end of each interval looks to see if his student is engaged in "on task" behavior (for example, looking at the teacher or instructional materials, pencil to paper). MTS is best suited for behaviors that occur at high rates or for long durations, and it is recommended that observers only use intervals that are less than two minutes in length (Cooper et al., 2007). Despite their potential advantages, practitioners should carefully consider whether time sampling procedures are necessary to collect meaningful data on a behavior of interest. Again, these procedures are only estimations of the actual occurrence of responses and have been repeatedly shown to be prone to measurement errors (Lane & Ledford, 2014; Powell, Martindale, & Kulp, 1975).

GRAPHING STUDENT DATA

Once teachers identify appropriate measures and commence data collection, they should regularly plot those data on a graph. Teachers can use a variety of graphs to display data (for example, line graphs, cumulative). The simple line graph is most commonly used in educational settings to display student data (see Figure 4.3). When using a line graph, data are plotted at the intersection of two perpendicular lines. The vertical lines across the horizontal axis (abscissa) represent the passing of time (for example, days, sessions), whereas the lines across the vertical axis (ordinate) represent the quantifiable level of the behavior measured. Graphing data permits teachers to continuously evaluate student performance and adjust instructional practice in response to patterns of responding (level, trend, and variability). If a student's pattern of responding does not change in a desirable direction, the teacher can adjust the delivery of instruction. Instructional changes are noted on the graph by the insertion of a vertical line prior to plotting data following introduction of the instructional change.

Interpreting student data to make instructional decisions. Once teachers become proficient in collecting and displaying data, they must proceed in using those data to make decisions about their instructional practice; data collected in the absence of evaluation are meaningless. Browder and colleagues provided

FIGURE 4.3 Simple Line Graph Depicting Instructional Changes

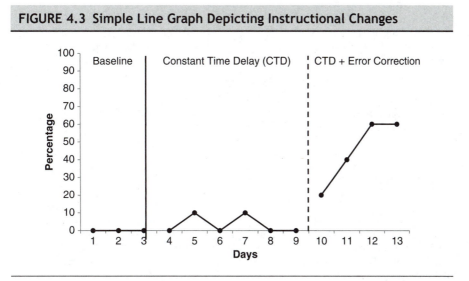

guidelines to help practitioners use graphed data to make decisions about instruction (Browder, Liberty, Heller, & D'Huyvetters, 1986). In this system, data are collected at least three days a week, and decisions about instruction are considered every two weeks. At the end of each two-week period, teachers apply a set of decision rules to the data (see Figure 4.4). First, if a student meets criterion levels of performance during the two-week period, develop a plan for extending performance through the promotion of fluency, generalization, and maintenance. Second, if the student makes no progress and it is the first two weeks of instruction, continue for two additional weeks. If it is not the first two weeks of instruction, then consider identifying a simpler skill. Third, if the

FIGURE 4.4 Data-Based Decision Rules

Basic Data-Based Decision Rules

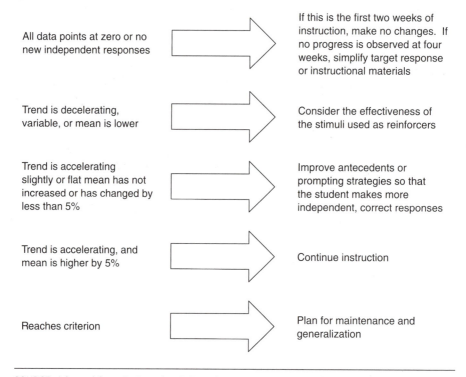

All data points at zero or no new independent responses	If this is the first two weeks of instruction, make no changes. If no progress is observed at four weeks, simplify target response or instructional materials
Trend is decelerating, variable, or mean is lower	Consider the effectiveness of the stimuli used as reinforcers
Trend is accelerating slightly or flat mean has not increased or has changed by less than 5%	Improve antecedents or prompting strategies so that the student makes more independent, correct responses
Trend is accelerating, and mean is higher by 5%	Continue instruction
Reaches criterion	Plan for maintenance and generalization

SOURCE: Adapted from D. Browder, F. Spooner, & B. Jimenez. (2011). "Standards-Based Individualized Education Plans and Progress Monitoring," in D. Browder & F. Spooner (Eds.), *Teaching Students With Moderate to Severe Disabilities* (pp. 42-91). New York, NY: Guilford Press.

data depict an accelerating (increasing) trend and the mean is at least 5 percent higher than the previous two-week period, continue instruction. Fourth, if data reflect a flat or slight accelerating trend and the mean has increased by less than 5 percent, consider adjusting the prompting strategies to help students make more independent correct responses. Fifth, if a decelerating (decreasing) trend or a mean lower than the previous two weeks is observed, consider the effectiveness of the stimuli used as reinforcers during instruction.

Another strategy for evaluating students' progress is to compare their pattern of actual performance against a projected pattern of performance. This projected pattern of responding is referred to as an aim line and extends from a student's initial level of performance to a criterion level of performance set at a projected date in the future (see Figure 4.5). When drawing an aim line, a teacher starts at the intersection of the mid-rate (the median data value of the data when arranged from lowest to highest value) and mid-date (for example, day 3 of a five-data-point baseline condition) of the last three days of baseline and ends the line at the intersection of criterion-level performance and the projected date for meeting that criterion (Brown & Snell, 2011). When setting an aim date, it is important to consider that it may be difficult to predict how quickly a student will respond to intervention on particular skills. One should consider students' performance during the acquisition of similar skills in the past. It is also important to note that often student progress will only approximate projected patterns of responding and that decisions about instruction should be made only after a pattern of discrepant performance is observed.

FIGURE 4.5 Example of Student Data With Projected Aim Line

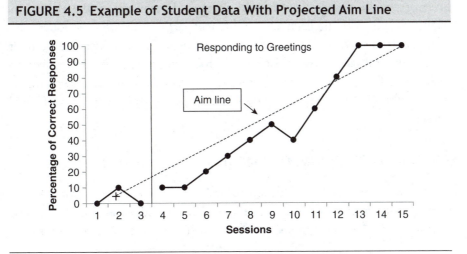

PARTICIPATION IN ACCOUNTABILITY SYSTEMS

In order to create an equitable curricular framework for students with disabilities, IDEA 1997 and 2004 mandate that students have access to and make progress in the general curriculum. The No Child Left Behind Act of 2001 (PL 107–110) mandates accountability in this area by requiring that all students (regardless of ability) be assessed in the academic areas of reading, mathematics, and science. In turn, large-scale, high-stakes accountability systems have become the norm across the country. Administrators, teachers, and even students are now held responsible for performance on these high-stakes assessments. For administrators, this could mean a positive reputation for the school (for example, School of Excellence) or sanctions if the students do not meet certain criteria. For teachers, student performance may be directly tied to evaluations and, ultimately, decisions regarding future employment and compensation. For students, promotion or retention to the next grade may be at stake. Although high-stakes accountability systems may be considered controversial, particularly when testing students with intellectual disability, some researchers suggest they may positively impact students. Quenemoen, Lehr, Thurlow, and Massanari (2001) reported that emphasis on standards and assessment had positive effects for students with disabilities, including an increased focus of IEPs on instruction and curriculum, more inclusion of students with disabilities in general education classes, and the perception of shared responsibility for students with disabilities among special and general educators.

All students with intellectual disability participate in standardized assessments, but may require differing levels of support as determined by the IEP team. Many students with intellectual disability will participate with no accommodations, but some may require accommodations, or alternate assessment methods for meaningful participation. Each state has determined specific regulations related to inclusion of students in state-required assessments and accountability systems; however, these regulations are similar as they are based on federal regulations.

ASSESSMENT ACCOMMODATIONS

Accommodations are intended to provide individualized support for students during both instruction and assessment. **Accommodations** should support learning during instruction and give students the opportunity to demonstrate achievement during assessment. Accommodations do not serve as a substitute for high-quality instruction and should not limit expectations for student success. The IEP team determines accommodations needed for instruction and assessment. When making decisions concerning accommodations, the team should consider the impact of disability on a student's learning, multiple sources of evaluation data, and the types of supports used during daily instruction.

State regulations that guide the use of accommodations not only provide a list of accommodations that can be used and the test still considered valid (that is, standard accommodations), but also provide general guidelines for their use. An example of general state guidelines is as follows:

Accommodations shall meet the following conditions:

- Be student initiated—School staff will make the accommodation available to the student during routine instruction and assessment, and may ask the student if he or she would like to use the accommodation, but may not instruct the student when to use the accommodation.

- Use of accommodations should be faded as appropriate.

- Accommodations should not impact the validity of the assessment.

- Accommodations should be age-appropriate and described in the IEP.

- Accommodations should be used to ensure student access to the curriculum; accommodations do not ensure a correct answer.

- Accommodations should be based on individual needs and not disability category.

- Accommodations do not substitute for high-quality instruction.

- The use of technology should be the first accommodation before any adult accommodation—for example, reader or scribe (Kentucky Department of Education, 2014).

Types of accommodations. Accommodations are selected based on an individual student's needs. Again, decisions to provide specific accommodations must be supported by evidence. Table 4.3 provides examples of accommodations. Note that some accommodations may not be used on specific areas of content tests (for example, the use of a reader during a reading fluency section of a test is considered a nonstandard accommodation).

TABLE 4.3 Representative State-Approved Accommodations

ACCOMMODATION	EXPLANATION/EXAMPLE
Use of assistive technology	May include amplification equipment, magnifying devices, communication boards or devices, computer/laptop, speech-to-text software, FM trainer, or word prediction.
Manipulatives	May be used by a student when the IEP team has determined that manipulatives will also be used by the student during instruction to complete a task or solve a problem. Manipulatives should be free of writing and used by the student to organize thoughts.
Calculator	May be used by a student when the IEP team has documentation of the disability's impact on mathematical calculations/reasoning and has determined that the student will use the calculator as part of routine instruction.
Paraphrasing	May include (and is limited to) breaking directions into parts or segments, using similar words or phrases in directions, and repeating or rephrasing directions.
Extended time	May be used as long as the student is demonstrating on-task efforts that allow the student to make constructive progress on completing his or her assessment responses.
Reinforcement and behavior modification	May include verbal, tangible, or tactile reinforcements for being on-task; use of technology to focus attention or reduce stress; or testing in a separate location outside the regular classroom.
Reader	The role of the reader is to read the directions, prompts, situations, and passages as written; re-read the directions, prompts, situations, and passages only if specifically requested by the student; and read individual words or abbreviations that are mispronounced by text or screen readers, if specifically requested by the student.
Scribe	The role of the scribe is to record what the student dictates word for word; format, capitalize, and punctuate as directed by the student; give the written product to the student to edit or revise; and not alter, edit, or revise a student's own ideas.
Interpreter for students with deafness	May be used when the student has a verified disability in the area of hearing to the degree that the student's development of language (receptive and expressive) is significantly impacted; the student uses sign language as the normal mode of communication due to his or her disability.

SOURCE: Kentucky Department of Education. (2014). *Inclusion of Special Populations in the State-Required Assessment and Accountability Programs: 703 KAR 5:070.* Available at http://education.ky.gov/districts/legal/Documents/5070%20doc.pdf

ALTERNATE ASSESSMENT

For some students, general education assessments, even with accommodations, are not appropriate measures for school accountability. Both IDEA and No Child Left Behind support the use of **alternate assessments based on alternate achievement standards (AA-AAS)** for these students, labeled as students with "significant cognitive disabilities." Although this regulatory label does not describe a category of disability identified under IDEA, students who are deemed eligible by state criteria to take these alternate assessments are primarily those with intellectual disability, autism spectrum disorder, and multiple disabilities. These students generally represent less than 1 percent of all students, or less than about 10 percent of students with disabilities. In order to avoid inappropriate inclusion of students in this type of assessment, a 1 percent regulatory cap was placed on the percentage of students whose scores on AA-AAS can be counted as proficient in school accountability systems (National Center on Education Outcomes, 2014).

WHAT ARE ALTERNATE ACHIEVEMENT STANDARDS?

As defined by the U.S. Department of Education (2005), alternate achievement standards must (a) be aligned with state academic content, (b) describe at least three levels of achievement, (c) include a description of competencies for each level of achievement, and (d) include assessment or cut scores that differentiate between achievement levels. Alternate achievement standards differ from grade-level standards in complexity and breadth and depth of coverage, but must still be aligned to grade-level content (Kleinert, Quenemoen, & Thurlow, 2010). As an example, North Carolina developed Extended Common Core State Standards to be used as alternate achievement standards for assessment of its students with the most significant cognitive disabilities. See Figure 4.6 to compare the differences in a portion of the sixth-grade English/language arts Common Core State Standards and the sixth-grade English/language arts Extended Common Core State Standards. Notice that while there is a difference in the complexity and depth of knowledge, the Extended Common Core State Standards are still closely aligned to the Common Core State Standards.

WHAT DO ALTERNATE ASSESSMENTS LOOK LIKE?

As recommended by the National Alternate Assessment Center, AA-AAS are typically developed in three different formats: portfolios, rating scales, and item-based tests. A portfolio is a collection of student work that measures a

FIGURE 4.6 Examples of Grade-Level State Standards and Aligned Alternate Achievement Standards

Sixth-Grade English/Language Arts Reading Standards for Literature		
Common Core State Standards	Essence	Extended Common Core
Key Ideas and Details	Use text to understand characters and themes	Key Ideas and Details
Cluster: 1. Cite textual evidence to support analysis of what the text says explicitly as well as inferences drawn from the text. 2. Determine a theme or central idea of a text and analyze its development over the course of the text; summarize the text. 3. Describe how a particular story or drama's plot unfolds in a series of episodes as well as how the characters respond or change as the plot moves toward resolution.		Cluster: 1. Analyze text to determine events or actions that are stated explicitly and those that must be inferred (e.g., *The text reads, "The boy jumped out of bed and ran to school."* Explicit = *boy jumping and running.* Inferred = *got dressed, ate breakfast*). 2. Determine the theme or central idea of a text. 3. Describe the ways that characters respond to a problem or event in a story.

SOURCE: Public Schools of North Carolina. (2016). North Carolina *Extended Common Core State Standards: English language arts 6-8*. Available at http://www.ncpublicschools.org/docs/acre/standards/extended/ela/6-8.pdf

limited number of benchmarks or objectives. Portfolios may be unstructured, or structured with fixed protocols for the collection of evidence. The portfolio tasks and activities are teacher-designed or modified from state protocols. Rating scales involve a teacher rating of performance on a list of skills based on classroom observation. Item-based tests consist of pre-scripted test items to which students respond in a one-on-one test administration setting (on demand). Items may include performance tasks, writing prompts, constructed-response items, or multiple-choice items (National Center on Education Outcomes, 2013). Regardless of the assessment format, alternate achievement standards addressed, and slight differences in eligibility criteria across states, the purpose of AA-AAS remains the same—to ensure educational accountability for *all* students.

CASE STUDY

Rachel is a fifth-grade student with a moderate intellectual disability. She was determined eligible for services under state guidelines when she was 6 years old. The assessment team used the results of the Wechsler Intelligence Scale for Children (5th ed.), or WISC-V; the Kaufman Test of Educational Achievement (3rd ed.), or KTEA-3; the Vineland Adaptive Behavior Scales (2nd ed.), or VABS-II; and classroom data to make the determination.

Each year, Rachel's IEP team determines her goals and objectives using information gathered from teacher-developed curriculum-based assessments and data obtained from the Choosing Outcomes and Accommodations for Children (3rd ed.), or COACH-3. Ecological assessments are used to determine skills that Rachel must be able to master to be successful in activities in her current and future environments. Rachel's teacher (Mrs. Larson) also periodically evaluates Rachel's preferences in order to determine the most effective reinforcers for use during instruction.

Mrs. Larson monitors Rachel's daily performance using a variety of data sheets depending on the skills being monitored. For example, Mrs. Larson uses event recording to track the number of sight words Rachel reads accurately and uses duration recording to monitor Rachel's time on task during her inclusive science lessons. Mrs. Larson graphs Rachel's data weekly and uses data-based decisions to adjust her instruction.

Because Rachel is in fifth grade, she is assessed in reading, mathematics, and science as part of the school district's large-scale accountability system. Rachel's IEP team has determined that she should be assessed using alternate assessments based on alternate achievement standards (AA-AAS). The state's current AA-AAS format is an on-demand, item-based administration.

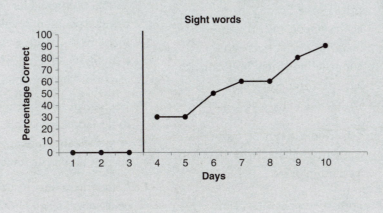

CONCLUSION

Assessment is a major thread that runs through the fabric of educational programming for students with and without disabilities. It is a complex construct involving the application of multiple strategies and instruments specifically designed to capture both an overall picture of a student's performance and precise indicators of skill level within particular contexts. To thoroughly understand and effectively implement the assessment process is to be cognizant of the individualized needs of every single student, despite their diverse and complex backgrounds. This process is empowering to teachers as it provides to them direct feedback on their performance and allows them to self-correct to improve their daily instructional practice. Most importantly, assessment helps ensure that every child is in receipt of educational programming that is personally relevant, addresses critical skills, and, most importantly, is effective.

Chapter Summary

- Assessment is used to determine eligibility, guide classroom and individualized instruction, and measure student progress.

- Norm-referenced tests have been developed to measure intelligence, academic achievement, and adaptive behavior of students and compare individual performance against a group of individuals with similar characteristics.

- Criterion-referenced tests compare student performance to a criterion or goal.

- Formative assessments are used to gauge student performance during instruction.

- Summative assessments are used to evaluate student progress at the end of a period of instruction.

- Curriculum-based measurements are research-validated measures that focus on long-term or annual progress. Curriculum-based assessments typically measure short-term objectives that are directly linked to classroom instruction.

- Ecological assessments are used to develop individualized goals/objectives for students based on current and future environments.

- Preference assessments can be used to identify potential reinforcers for use during educational programming.

- In order to determine if instruction is effective, teachers must frequently measure student progress. Examples of data collection methods include event recording, duration recording, latency recording, and interval recording. To ensure students are making adequate progress, student data should be graphed, and instructional decisions should be based on specific data patterns.

- All students with disabilities are required to participate in large-scale assessments for accountability. Students may participate with accommodations. Alternate assessments can be administered to students for whom general assessments, even with accommodations and modifications, are not appropriate.

Review Questions

1. What are the limitations of norm-referenced assessments in the design of daily instructional programming for students with intellectual disability?

2. Which assessment strategies can be employed to ensure that instruction is relevant to the personal lives of students with intellectual disability?

3. How can teachers ensure that students are not exposed to ineffective instructional practices for extended periods of time?

4. When is alternate assessment used with students with intellectual disability, and how does it promote access to the general education curriculum?

Key Terms

assessment (page 78)
norm-referenced tests (page 79)
criterion-referenced tests (page 81)
formative assessment (page 83)
summative assessment (page 83)
curriculum-based assessment(s) (CBA) (page 85)
curriculum-based measurement(s) (CBM) (page 86)

ecological inventory (page 88)
situational assessment (page 88)
preference assessments (page 89)
single-stimulus presentation assessment (page 90)
paired-stimulus (forced-choice) assessment (page 90)
multiple-stimulus-with-replacement assessment (page 90)

multiple-stimulus-without-
replacement assessment
(page 90)
artifacts (page 92)
event recording (page 92)
total-duration recording
(page 93)
duration per occurrence (DPO)
recording (page 93)
latency recording (page 94)

whole-interval recording (WIR)
(page 94)
partial-interval recording (PIR)
(page 94)
momentary time sampling (MTS)
(page 94)
accommodations (page 98)
alternate assessment based on
alternate achievement standards
(AA-AAS) (page 101)

Professional Organizations/ Associations Concerned With Assessment

Center on Response to Intervention at American Institutes for Research

www.rti4success.org

Intervention Central

www.interventioncentral.org

National Alternate Assessment Center

www.naacpartners.org

National Center on Educational Outcomes

http://nceo.info

National Center on Student Progress Monitoring

www.studentprogress.org

Positive Behavioral Interventions & Supports

www.pbis.org

CHAPTER 5

Behavioral Interventions for Students With Intellectual Disability

E. Amanda Boutot, Kylan Turner,
and Samuel A. DiGangi

Learning Objectives

After reading Chapter 5, you should be able to:

- Describe the functional behavior needs of students with intellectual disability across the life span.

- List and describe the approaches to assess the function of challenging behavior for students with intellectual disability.

- Explain the intervention approaches that address the behavioral needs of and decrease challenging behavior in students with intellectual disability.

Overview of Behavioral Challenges and Approaches for Students With Intellectual Disability: Preschool Through Secondary

PRESCHOOL STUDENTS

The preschool years are a time of increasingly heightened expectations across all areas of development. Preschoolers experience an increase in social demands, as this is often the first time that children are required to interact with greater frequency, duration, and complexity with same-aged peers. Additionally, preschoolers are expected to be able to engage in developmentally appropriate play behavior, share with peers, and follow routines (Paulus & Moore, 2014). Preschool activities also become more intellectually demanding for learners, which may increase fatigue and contribute to the likelihood of behavioral challenges. Young children with mild, moderate, or severe intellectual disability may require specialized instruction to successfully and fully engage in this environment. Behavioral challenges may occur with greater frequency at this stage in development due to the co-occurrence of heightened demands and deficits associated with the diagnosed intellectual disability. It is critical, therefore, that practitioners and educators consider time-efficient and effective interventions to prevent the occurrence of behavioral challenges before they occur.

ELEMENTARY STUDENTS

As children progress from preschool into elementary school, they continue to face new academic and social demands, while also being provided less direct support and held to greater expectations for independence by their parents, teachers, and other caregivers (McClelland, Acock, & Morrison, 2006). Although similar patterns of steadily increased expectations are seen during children's preschool years, the stakes are higher during the elementary school years, there is often less explicit or programmed support, and the results of academic assessment and behavioral outcomes have the potential to influence students' progression through the grade levels. For individuals with mild, moderate, or severe intellectual disability, failing to receive adequate support in the educational environment can result in school failure as well as behavioral challenges (McIntyre, Blacher, & Baker, 2006). It is imperative that practitioners and instructors explore and become trained in the best practices of instructional strategies for elementary school–aged children with any degree of intellectual disability.

SECONDARY STUDENTS

The transition from elementary to secondary school is marked by a variety of physical, developmental, emotional, social, academic, and behavioral needs for all students, including those with intellectual disability. While the stakes are higher for elementary students than for preschool students due to increasing academic demands, with secondary students, the need for strategic, specialized supports is at its greatest. Secondary students face a number of challenges, most notably preparation for the future beyond school. While the Individuals with Disabilities Education Improvement Act (PL 108–446) ensures students with intellectual disability may remain in school until their twenty-second birthday, extended time in school does not guarantee their postsecondary success. For individuals with mild, moderate, or severe intellectual disability, failing to receive adequate support in the educational environment can result in failure to find employment, failure to participate successfully in postsecondary education and vocational training options, failure to develop social relationships, and inability to access independent living and community supports. To complicate matters even further, in adolescence, students begin to experience sexuality needs, which, if they go unaddressed, can lead to significant behavioral challenges (Travers, Whitby, Tincani, & Boutot, 2014). Behavioral supports in secondary school are needed to promote students' success academically, vocationally, socially, and in the community after high school, and to allow students to be as independent as possible in those environments. As is true for preschool and elementary students, the principles of applied behavior analysis are effective at improving behaviors that will allow secondary students to become as independent as possible, which provides opportunities for success upon leaving high school.

APPLIED BEHAVIOR ANALYSIS

Applied behavior analysis (ABA) is defined as the application of behavioral principles to change socially important behaviors, while making data-based decisions as to effectiveness of the interventions (Boutot & Hume, 2012). Often thought of as an intervention exclusively for children on the autism spectrum (Boutot & Hume, 2012), ABA was designed as an applied, ethically responsible response to the challenges associated with behavior modification in the late 1960s and the 1970s (Bailey & Burch, 2011). The applied nature of ABA implicitly means that it is used to address behaviors that are in need of change (socially important). Further, the use of ongoing data collection and analysis to identify areas in need of change and ensure effectiveness is a hallmark of ABA. Although ABA can be used to teach a variety of skills to children with intellectual disability of all functioning levels, for the purposes of this chapter, we will focus on the use of ABA to address behavioral challenges for preschool, elementary, and secondary students with intellectual disability.

The primary principles of behavior used in ABA to treat challenging behavior include **reinforcement** and **punishment**. Reinforcement is defined as anything that maintains or increases a behavior. Punishment, by contrast, is anything that decreases a behavior (Alberto & Troutman, 2013). These definitions are dependent not on the intent of the intervention, but on its impact on the behavior. If a behavior continues or increases following the application of an intervention or stimulus, that intervention or stimulus is said to be reinforcing. Conversely, if a behavior decreases following the application of an intervention or stimulus, that intervention or stimulus is said to be punishing. Reinforcement and punishment can further be broken down as either negative or positive, depending on whether stimuli are presented or removed following a given behavior and the subsequent impact on that behavior. **Negative reinforcement** is the removal of an aversive stimulus following a given behavior that results in an increase in that behavior. **Positive reinforcement** is the presentation of a preferred stimulus following a given behavior that results in an increase in that behavior. The key to the application of any of these behavioral principles is that they are applied contingently and immediately. Contingent presentation means that the application of the behavioral principle occurs based on a particular behavior. To be most effective, this application must also immediately follow the behavior.

Figure 5.1 presents negative and positive reinforcement and punishment visually. The use of punishing procedures should be considered with caution. A more appropriate, proactive approach is to consider preventative techniques through the use of positive behavior interventions and supports in addition to **antecedent** interventions, which will be discussed in the next sections.

In addition to these principles of behavior, ethical and responsible use of ABA requires the use of a **functional behavior assessment** to determine what is

FIGURE 5.1 Negative and Positive Reinforcement and Punishment

Negative reinforcement: removal of an aversive stimulus that results in an increase in targeted behavior	Positive reinforcement: presentation of a preferred stimulus that results in an increase in targeted behavior
Negative punishment: removal of a preferred stimulus that results in a decrease in targeted behavior	Positive punishment: presentation of an aversive stimulus that results in a decrease in targeted behavior

currently acting as reinforcement for a challenging behavior. Behavior analysts do not attempt to change a behavior without identifying its function. Another way to think about a behavior's function is to think about what is reinforcing it. If a challenging behavior is occurring at a rate requiring intervention, it must, according to the principles of behavior, be reinforced in some way. The next section will briefly discuss the process of functional behavior assessment as it relates to preschoolers with intellectual disability.

FUNCTIONAL BEHAVIOR ASSESSMENT

Functional behavior assessment is the process of defining a target behavior, identifying its antecedent (that is, what occurs immediately prior to the behavior) and **consequence** (that is, what occurs immediately following the behavior), and determining its function (Alberto & Troutman, 2013). Identifying the function a behavior serves for a particular learner will allow practitioners to design interventions to effectively change the behavior. For much of its history, behavior analysis focused predominantly on the study of consequence variables and response–consequence relations associated with challenging and disruptive behaviors. Although consequence-based interventions (for example, time-out) hold potential to quickly and radically alter behavior, when properly implemented, function-based antecedent (that is, preventative) interventions can be used successfully to offset the occurrence of challenging behaviors or decrease their eventual frequency, intensity, or duration (for example, give fewer tasks to complete, thus eliminating a need for escape) (Alberto & Troutman, 2013). Although the functional behavior assessment process has been a mainstay in the field of behavior analysis for decades, components of the procedure have been refined continuously over time and now include comprehensive antecedent assessment to best inform the selection of antecedent interventions.

Antecedent assessment is a critical step in the process of identifying which variables evoke the target behavior and, ultimately, how they might be modified, in simple ways, to prevent the target behavior from occurring. As stated previously, because antecedent and consequence relations are inextricably and temporally tied to one another, the analysis of both types of variables must occur simultaneously and in the context of those contingencies to confidently conclude information about the behavior's function.

Students with mild, moderate, or severe intellectual disability present a variety of instructional challenges and may require time-intensive interventions to decrease challenging behaviors, learn replacement behaviors, and acquire new skills (Mancil, Conroy, Nakao, & Alter, 2006). It is therefore necessary, after concluding the behavior's function and clearly defining antecedent variables, to explore which antecedent interventions may assist in preventing challenging behavior from occurring in the first place in order to optimize time spent in instruction. Practitioners and teachers working with students with intellectual disability of any severity, or in any age group, may significantly improve the efficacy of their instructional approach by paying close attention to antecedent variables, systematically evaluating them, and considering how they may be manipulated to evoke desired target behaviors. **Positive behavior interventions and supports (PBIS)** offer an opportunity to apply the results of the functional behavior assessment in the development of an individualized behavior support plan that specifically includes antecedent interventions.

POSITIVE BEHAVIOR INTERVENTIONS AND SUPPORTS

Positive behavior interventions and supports make up a comprehensive, systemic assessment and intervention framework for prevention of problem behaviors. PBIS take a proactive approach toward identifying and managing challenging behaviors, supporting instructors' management of behaviors, and ensuring challenging behaviors do not impede learning. Prevention and intervention are approached from the perspective of a three-tiered model—providing a continuum of general to more intensive and specialized support (Benedict, Horner, & Squires, 2007). A PBIS system is established at the school level, as well as within each classroom at the preschool, elementary, and secondary levels. A clear explanation of classroom rules and structured activities is communicated along with procedures for ensuring that students are acknowledged for performing appropriate behaviors (Kelm, McIntosh, & Cooley, 2014). There are three tiers of intervention in a PBIS model (see Figure 5.2). The primary tier of supports is structured for the benefit of the majority of students in the school and classroom. The primary tier consists of general considerations to promote clear expectations for all students. At the preschool level, these behavioral expectations can be made clear with explicit explanation of these rules, as well as visual representations of the classroom rules and consequences (Benedict, Horner, & Squires, 2007). For preschool-aged students, teachers may include visual supports and visual schedules that provide some structure for the children; they may also include choices for center time in the form of visual cues. For teachers of elementary students with intellectual disability, this may include classroom structure and rules that are impactful for all students, such as a daily schedule or the use of a timer to designate transitions. Secondary students also benefit from rules, as well as from more self-management

FIGURE 5.2 Positive Behavior Interventions and Supports Model

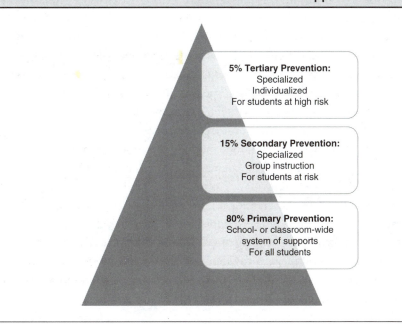

5% Tertiary Prevention:
Specialized
Individualized
For students at high risk

15% Secondary Prevention:
Specialized
Group instruction
For students at risk

80% Primary Prevention:
School- or classroom-wide
system of supports
For all students

strategies and vocationally relevant management systems, including rules for being on time and working independently.

The second tier on the PBIS continuum in the school environment consists of providing more focused interventions for students requiring additional support. Students receiving this level of support may be identified as "at risk," benefiting from targeted interventions to more fully access the educational curriculum. Preschool students needing support at this level could be placed in small groups for certain activities or paired with a peer buddy to assist in following the routine. For teachers of elementary students with intellectual disability, this may mean using an individual schedule for some children or providing a token system for others in an inclusive classroom. In the secondary school environment, second-tier PBIS strategies often include group interventions, such as social skills groups, which place the onus of responsibility for progress monitoring on students to check their own behavior after scheduled prompting (Carter, Carter, Johnson, & Pool, 2013).

The third tier on the PBIS continuum includes the implementation of interventions designed to address specific developmental deficits and more intense challenging behaviors. Third-tier strategies are composed of intensive individualized intervention plans. These interventions may be delivered outside of the school classroom in an individualized setting or with the support of a paraprofessional. For teachers of students with intellectual disability at any age, this involves a **behavior intervention plan (BIP)** developed following a functional behavior assessment, which targets challenging behaviors in a more systematic way including data collection and instructional goals. At all age levels, a BIP should be implemented that specifically targets skill deficits through direct instruction, along with antecedent interventions to prevent challenging behaviors and specific behavioral protocols to follow in the event that problem behaviors occur. Younger children may require more visual supports that include drawings or photographs, whereas older students may be able to read and thus benefit from written rules or other supports. The age of the student should be considered in the creation of the materials so that older students do not have materials that are age inappropriate; however, the strategies used at this tier are applicable to all age groups. An example of a BIP for a student with an intellectual disability is provided in Figure 5.3. The remainder of this chapter will focus on strategies and interventions that can be used at each of these tiers, with a focus on those used for the third tier.

FIGURE 5.3 Sample Behavior Intervention Plan

Student: Cooper, age 8, with Down syndrome and intellectual disability

Behaviors to Target:

1. Screaming—When a preferred activity is interrupted, Cooper will scream (high-pitched, lasting two seconds or longer). This behavior may result in a tantrum (multiple screams, crying, throwing objects, and body-on-ground behavior). Most recently, Cooper has been screaming when taken to the bathroom to urinate in the toilet. Perceived function—access to preferred task/activity, escape from nonpreferred task/activity.

2. Tantrum—When a preferred activity is interrupted, Cooper will have a tantrum (multiple screams, crying, throwing objects, and throwing body on ground). This behavior occurs following screaming in 100 percent of the episodes, though not all screaming episodes result in a tantrum. Tantrums appear most frequently during transitions involving the computer or the iPad. Perceived function—access to preferred task/activity, escape from nonpreferred task/activity.

Goal/Objective:

1. During transitions to a nonpreferred task or away from a preferred task, Cooper will verbally request a break or "one more minute" without screaming or tantrums for five consecutive school days.

2. When he wants an item or activity (computer or iPad), Cooper will verbally request it without screaming or tantrums for five consecutive school days.

INSTRUCTIONAL STRATEGIES PLAN

Antecedent/ Preventative Strategies (Put in place before Cooper engages in problem behavior)	Teaching Strategies Functionally Equivalent Replacement Behavior	Reinforcement Strategies (Put in place when Cooper engages in desired behavior)	Consequence Strategies (Put in place when Cooper engages in problem behavior)
1. Create a visual schedule in order to provide structure and routine (set up the schedule prior to beginning the session and review it with Cooper when he arrives). 2. Create a social narrative to let Cooper know that he can use his words to get his needs met. The narrative should include the specific words Cooper will use instead	1. Teach Cooper to ask for a break or access to his preferred activities; teach him to ask for "one more minute" before transitioning to the next activity away from preferred activities.	1. Every time Cooper uses his words to ask for a break or "one more minute" or to gain access to a preferred item/ activity, reinforce this behavior (honor his request) until Cooper has been scream/tantrum free for five consecutive school days. At that point, begin to introduce a "first–then" procedure, honoring 90% of requests.	1. When Cooper engages in screaming behavior, provide a verbal prompt to "use your words," and provide immediate delivery of desired item and verbal praise for compliance; if Cooper continues to scream, wait until he stops (even for a second) and model again. 2. When Cooper begins to have a tantrum, make sure he is safe

(Continued)

FIGURE 5.3 (Continued)

Antecedent/ Preventative Strategies	Teaching Strategies	Reinforcement Strategies	Consequence Strategies
of screaming or tantrums (e.g., "one more minute"). Review the narrative four times throughout the day, reducing it to twice per day and then once per day as behaviors improve.		Following the same criteria (five consecutive school days scream/tantrum free), reduce the percentage of times honoring Cooper's request by 10% until 10% is reached and hold at that level.	and block him from injuring himself or others. Provide the visual support (the social narrative) in his view as a reminder to use his words. Calmly remind him verbally as he is quiet.

ANTECEDENT INTERVENTIONS

Antecedent interventions consist of a variety of environmental considerations and strategies to prevent a challenging behavior from occurring, or to promote skill acquisition.

VISUAL SCHEDULE FOR PREDICTABILITY

Visual schedules for predictability are a very straightforward and cost-effective antecedent intervention that consists of placing photographs or picture icons on a board to indicate a sequence of events. As time is an abstract concept for many students with intellectual disability, the provision of tangible visual stimuli can illustrate when one activity is beginning and one is ending. The use of visual schedules, and the resulting consistency and predictability, can promote improvements in challenging behaviors (Knight, Sartini, & Spriggs, 2015; Lequia, Machalicek, & Rispoli, 2012). This approach can effectively communicate current activities and expectations and outline what is coming next. See Figures 5.4, 5.5, and 5.6 for examples of types of visual schedules appropriate for students with intellectual disability at different ages.

Visual schedules for preschool and elementary students are useful for both independence and predictability as a lack of predictability can be a precursor to challenging behaviors. While this is also true for secondary students, visual schedules for this age group are also focused on developing students' ability to function as independent adults. Visual schedules are a natural part of many adults' lives; many of us have calendars and to-do lists on our phones,

FIGURE 5.4 Example Visual Schedule for a Preschool Student With Intellectual Disability

SOURCE: Preschool Plan It. Available at http://www.preschool-plan-it.com/separation-anxiety.html

FIGURE 5.5 Example Visual Schedule for an Elementary School Student With Intellectual Disability

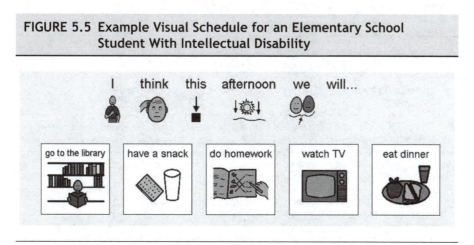

SOURCE: PrAACtical AAC. Available at http://praacticalaac.org/strategy/visual-schedules-411/

meeting agendas, or notes posted on our refrigerators. Secondary students with intellectual disability can and should be taught to use a visual schedule as a natural part of their day, and to independently create and follow their own visual schedule. The visual schedule can prevent challenging behaviors by providing the student with an overview of expectations, which will prevent

FIGURE 5.6 Example Visual Schedule for a Secondary Student With Intellectual Disability

Robert's Daily Schedule

☑ 9:00–9:30: Breakfast

☑ 9:30–9:40: Clean-up/Grooming

☑ 9:40–11:15: Work Stations/Work With Teacher

☐ 11:15–12:00: Office Aide

☐ 12:00–12:50: Lunch

☐ 12:50–1:00: Clean-up/Brush Teeth

☐ 1:00: Bus for Work

☐ 1:15–4:00: Work at Newspaper

☐ 4:00: Bus for School

☐ 4:15–4:30: Get Ready to Go Home

☐ 4:30: Bus Home

TABLE 5.1 Examples of Mobile Device Apps for Use as Visual Schedules/Reminders

- Visual Schedule Planner by Good Karma Applications: https://itunes.apple.com/us/app/visual-schedule-planner/id488646282?mt=8

- Choiceworks by Bee Visual: https://itunes.apple.com/us/app/choiceworks/id486210964?mt=8

- First Then Visual Schedule by Good Karma Applications: http://www.autismpluggedin.com/2011/05/visual-schedules-for-autism-apps-first-then-visual-schedule-review.html

- Visual Routine by Megan Holstein, Pufferfish Software: https://itunes.apple.com/us/app/visual-routine/id455706114?mt=8

- Picture Scheduler by Petr Jankuj: https://itunes.apple.com/us/app/picture-scheduler/id315050461?mt=8

- Stories2Learn by MDR: https://itunes.apple.com/us/app/stories2learn/id348576875?mt=8

- QuickCues by Fraser: https://itunes.apple.com/us/app/quickcues/id360381130

surprises and help to provide an understanding of the Premack Principle, which will be discussed in greater depth later in the chapter. The idea of "first work, then break" can be readily seen on a daily schedule that includes a mix of required tasks and opportunities for breaks. A number of commercially available applications (apps for mobile devices) are available to assist in developing a daily schedule, which can be taught to elementary or secondary students for use as their personal visual schedule. Table 5.1 provides a list of some of these apps.

SOCIAL NARRATIVES

Behavior challenges may arise due to deficits in social-emotional development in students with intellectual disability. An antecedent intervention of providing social narratives to students was found to be effective (Myles, Trautman, & Schelvan, 2004). **Social narratives** are short "stories" that clearly depict and explain the social subtext present in a variety of social interactions and typically occurring behavioral expectations. Social narratives need not be lengthy, and most often consist of a one-page symbolic depiction or a small book with photographs. Recognizing that students' needs and abilities vary, social narratives are written in a relatively standard format and at a language level that matches each individual student's receptive communication ability. Social narratives consist of summary and explanatory information about the social and environmental variables relating to a given social situation (Bledsoe, Myles, & Simpson, 2003). For example, a social narrative may remind a student that speaking softly while indoors will result in more conversations with peers (see Figure 5.7).

An additional element to note about social narratives is the style in which they are written. Social narratives often include "I" statements such as "I need to raise my hand before answering the teacher's question." By presenting these statements in first person, the social narrative provides student readers with a clear stimulus for what *they*, specifically and explicitly, should be doing. Additionally, social narratives include emotional statements about the reactions or perspectives of others around them when this behavior is exhibited, such as "My teacher likes it when I raise my hand and wait to be called on." Such statements give readers the reason and awareness that they may receive reinforcement if they engage in the appropriate behavior. Preschool and elementary school students may benefit from having visual stimuli, such as photographs, picture icons, or even drawings, to assist with their comprehension of the social narrative. For older secondary learners who may find the story to be less mature with visual stimuli included, it is important to ensure that the text of the story is written at the appropriate reading and comprehension level. Initially, the

FIGURE 5.7 Social Story for Using an Indoor Voice

Cover page text:
Inside voice

Page 1 text:
Sometimes I like to talk to my friends when we are inside.

Page 2 text:
I have noticed that when they are inside, my friends talk in a soft voice.
When they are inside, my friends do not yell, even if they are excited.
This makes it so others do not need to cover their ears or move away when having a
conversation.

Page 3 text:
I can use a soft voice when I am inside with my friends.
If I do this, my friends will want to talk to me when we are inside and will not need to
move away or cover their ears.

narrative should be read to young students, followed by discussion to ensure comprehension. For older students, depending on their intellectual ability, the narrative can be read to them, or may simply be given to them and supervised to ensure it is read and understood. After some amount of repetition, it is possible the students will begin to tell the story themselves, and reading the story will no longer be necessary.

Though not evaluated extensively with preschool students with intellectual disability, social narratives may be useful if the appropriate steps are taken to ensure the narrative suits the student's receptive communication ability (Kokina & Kern, 2010). For example, social narratives may need to be constructed to include less text and more visual representations in the form of pictures, as preschoolers with intellectual disability are unable to read. Ongoing data collection on progress following the use of social narratives is essential given this is an area of limited empirical evaluation.

Social narratives have been evaluated with elementary students with intellectual disability. Reynhout and Carter (2007) created a social narrative to address the repetitive tapping behavior displayed by an eight-year-old child with autism spectrum disorder, moderate intellectual disability, and associated language impairment. After several weeks of the social narrative being read to the student and the individual being provided access to the social narrative,

FIGURE 5.8 Sample "I Will" Card

> When I want a turn on the game, I will:
> - Ask for a turn
> - Wait for my turn

a decrease in the target behavior was observed, suggesting that the intervention was effective. The researchers indicated it is likely necessary to consider language skills when evaluating the appropriateness of this intervention for students with moderate intellectual disability, due to the inherent deficits in communication and cognitive skills. Ongoing monitoring of comprehension is a recommended practice when using social narratives with this population.

Secondary students can also benefit from use of social narratives. Secondary learners can be taught a variety of "I" statements that give them choices for behaviors in specific circumstances. For example, a ninth grader with a developmental disability was taught to use "I will" cards when confronted with situations that previously resulted in his exhibiting challenging behaviors, such as fighting (Boutot, 2009). The "I will" cards were carried by the student from class period to class period and were reviewed at the beginning and end of every day (see the "check-in/check-out" procedure in the following section). The card presented the individual with a situation (for example, "Someone looks at me funny") and appropriate choice options (for example, "Look away" or "Walk away"). To address common issues they face, students with intellectual disability may benefit from social narratives, which may include drawings or pictures if the student is not able to read. See Figure 5.8 for an example of an "I will" card.

VIDEO MODELING

A widely used antecedent intervention, **video modeling** is conducted by video recording a person performing a particular behavior or skill and showing the video to the individual (Wong et al., 2015). Video modeling is classified as an antecedent intervention as it demonstrates and instructs the individual how to perform the given behavior. Video modeling is considered an effective approach toward promoting skill acquisition in the areas of social development, communication, and daily living skills (Wong et al., 2015). Videos for use with video modeling can be found via public sources online, or can be created by parents or teachers by filming themselves engaging in the skill to be taught, or having the individual engage in the skill to be taught. In the video, it is important to indicate each step of the skill very clearly so the viewer may imitate the model precisely.

As is the case with other interventions, preschool students with intellectual disability may benefit from minor adaptations to the design of videos for use in video modeling. These adaptations might include ensuring the videos provided are brief in duration and communicate information at an appropriate level to match receptive communication ability. Providing reinforcement while the child is watching the video may also lead to greater efficacy of the intervention (Green et al., 2013).

Video modeling has been used to teach preschool and elementary students with intellectual disability a variety of skills from functional life skills to academics. Use of video modeling for improving challenging behaviors of this group has not been specifically examined in the literature to date. However, its efficacy for other skills is well documented. For example, Mechling and Swindle (2012) conducted a study to evaluate the effects of computer-based video self-modeling on fine and gross motor skills in a group of three elementary students with moderate intellectual disability and three students with autism spectrum disorder. The study evaluated the performance of all six participants across three sets of tasks to determine the effectiveness of self-modeling across fine and gross motor skills. Teaching critical adaptive skills such as fine and gross motor skills often reduces the occurrence of challenging behaviors related to skill deficits. Of particular interest to these researchers was whether the video modeling would produce different effects across the two groups of students. The results suggested an increase in the number of fine and gross motor tasks correctly performed following the introduction of video modeling for both groups; however, the change was more pronounced in the gross motor task set. Independently, students with moderate intellectual disability performed more tasks correctly than the group of students with autism spectrum disorder. These findings suggest that the use of video modeling may be useful to teach a variety of critical adaptive and academic tasks effectively, promoting functional skill development, and potentially reduce the occurrence of challenging behaviors.

The use of video modeling with adolescents and adults with intellectual disability gained considerable research support over the past several years. Positive effects were obtained using a variety of modeling techniques including typical video modeling where someone other than the target student is viewed performing a task as well as video self-modeling in which the target student is recorded while performing the appropriate skills or behavior (Mechling, Ayres, Bryant, & Foster, 2014). Further, researchers investigated whether performing the skill immediately following observation of the video, or after a delay, results in efficacy of video modeling (Taber-Doughty, Patton, & Brennan, 2008). A third type of video modeling—video prompting—involves reviewing steps of a task broken down into separate videos, each viewed separately from the others (Mechling et al., 2014). The use of video prompting produced positive results, particularly for teaching students daily life skills.

TOKEN ECONOMY

A **token economy** is a system that delivers reinforcement on a schedule that promotes the target behavior through motivating the learner to engage in the behavior (Cooper, Heron, & Heward, 2007). (See Figures 5.9 and 5.10.) A token economy system provides generalized reinforcers (tokens) to learners following occurrences of a target behavior. These generalized reinforcers are collected and then traded in for either primary or secondary backup reinforcers once the individual reaches a predetermined number of tokens (Alberto & Troutman, 2013). Tokens may be represented by a variety of different stimuli depending on the learner's receptive communication skills as well as his or her preferences. Tokens can range from check marks placed on a page visible to the student, to stickers, poker chips, or virtually any visual stimulus that represents a tangible token for the learner. The tokens serve as individual discriminative stimuli that indicate that reinforcement will be provided if the learner continues to display the target behavior.

Although typically developing preschool students have been taught to use a token economy in a whole-class approach to decrease disruptive behavior (Filcheck, McNeill, Greco, & Bernard, 2004), extensive research has not been conducted on the use of token economy systems with children with intellectual disability in this age group. Nevertheless, at the preschool level, it would be likely necessary to provide frequent explanation of the rules of the token economy (for example, the behaviors that will result in earning tokens and the reinforcers that may be received in exchange for the tokens).

FIGURE 5.9 Example Token Board for a Preschool or Elementary Student With Intellectual Disability

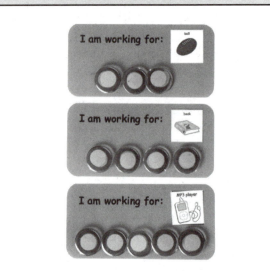

SOURCE: Pyramid Educational Consultants. Available at www.pecsproducts.com/catalog/product_info.php?cPath=25&products_id=181 ©Pyramid Educational Products, 2015.

FIGURE 5.10 Example Token System for a Secondary Student With Intellectual Disability

"I Am Earning Points for Friday Fun Day"	
Schedule	**Points Earned (circle)**
First Period	1 2 3 4 5
Second Period	1 2 3 4 5
Third Period	1 2 3 4 5
Fourth Period	1 2 3 4 5
Lunch	1 2 3 4 5
Vocational Trip	1 2 3 4 5

For older students, teachers and parents may find that using stickers and the like is less socially appropriate and may thus determine that tokens should no longer be used as a strategy. However, considering that all forms of money are effectively tokens, it is easy to see how the use of a token economy can be modified for older students to better suit their age level. For example, a teacher can use tally marks or coins instead of stickers; check marks may also be appropriate for older students. For older students, use of tokens becomes an opportunity to learn valuable life lessons about wages, savings, and money management. Paper tickets that can "buy" items needed or wanted can teach this same lesson. Many of the earliest studies on the use of token systems were conducted with adolescents and adults with intellectual disability, with a great deal of success (Tymchuk, 1971; Woods, 1971); however, more current research suggests the effectiveness of this technique for elementary students as well (Davis, Kurtz, Gardner, & Carman, 2006).

BEHAVIORAL MOMENTUM

At times, a target behavior or skill may not be displayed because behavioral momentum has not been established. **Behavioral momentum** is the propensity for individuals to be more likely to engage in a challenging task when provided several easy tasks in rapid succession prior to being prompted to engage in the challenging task (Cooper et al., 2007). The phenomenon of building behavioral momentum by prompting the learner to rapidly engage in easy tasks before engaging in more challenging tasks is known in applied behavior analytic terminology as the high-probability (high-p) request sequence. This phenomenon is activated through the presentation of a small number of easily mastered tasks (typically three to five) that the learner is known to be able to do quickly (the high-p requests). These tasks are prompted in rapid succession immediately prior to presenting the target (that is, more challenging) request known to be less probable to occur (the low-probability, or low-p, request) (Cooper et al., 2007).

For example, a preschool teacher could employ behavioral momentum to try to reduce tantrums and increase appropriate transitioning behavior by having a child demonstrate a number of quick and easy skills first. For example, the teacher could say, "Touch your nose. Touch your tummy. Where's your head?" followed by "Go check your schedule." Behavioral momentum in this case would set the child up to respond positively and compliantly to requests, and create a situation where he is more likely to comply with the target request of "Go check your schedule."

Behavioral momentum has been more widely studied in students with autism spectrum disorder, although in most cases the participants also had intellectual disability. For example, in a study of two elementary school–aged children, Zuluaga and Normand (2008) demonstrated the efficacy of high-p request sequencing on compliance behaviors with two young children with autism. When reinforcement was provided following the occurrence of high-p requests, the subsequent low-p requests were completed more frequently. Similarly, while not specifically examined in the literature for students with intellectual disability at the secondary level, the concept of behavioral momentum is the same for this group. For example, a teacher who knows that a student often engages in challenging behaviors when presented with a particular academic task may have the student do several easier tasks immediately prior to the less preferred task, to improve the likelihood that the student will comply. This may include having the student open a notebook, write his name, and read the day's date.

PREMACK PRINCIPLE

The **Premack Principle** consists of programming activities in sequence—prompting the individual that first one event will occur and next another event will occur. In elementary schools, this is also shown as a "first–then" visual support (see Figure 5.11 for an example). Although this may appear to be quite similar to the visual schedule for predictability, the Premack Principle involves systematic programming—arranging activities such that the first activity is less preferred and the second activity is highly preferred. Colloquially, this principle is often referred to as Grandma's law—"You need to eat your vegetables before you can eat dessert." To optimize effectiveness, the visual stimulus or spoken directive should be provided to the individual before the activity. In the example in Figure 5.11, the teacher would show the student the visual and then direct him or her to first complete a "work" task and then access the computer.

This is a useful and effective strategy in preschools, since providing the "first–then" sequence verbally to students can occur in any environment, rather spontaneously. Additionally, the receptive communication ability required from students is minimal. Because the visual support can be made relatively easily and

FIGURE 5.11 Sample "First-Then" Board

SOURCE: B. Cralte, *First/Then Boards: Simple & Effective.* Available at http://spectrumpediatrics.com/blog/2015/04/firstthen-boards-simple-effective/

is transferable to multiple environments, it is a commonly used strategy by many teachers.

In secondary schools, a "first–then" schedule may be used to increase independence and self-sufficiency. Because many job and community tasks are required of adults that may not be highly preferred (for example, going to the bank or drugstore), students at the secondary level need to be taught to arrange their own daily schedule such that they can receive natural reinforcement for the completion of one task through access to a second. In some cases, secondary students may be taught to complete a short list of less preferred activities, followed by a longer break for something more fun. Adults do this frequently; we clean house and pay bills on Saturday morning so that we can go to a movie with friends on Saturday afternoon. Because one of the primary goals of secondary school is to prepare students to be as independent as possible after high school, teaching them to develop and reinforce their own task completion is critical.

CHECK-IN/CHECK-OUT PROCEDURE

The **check-in/check-out procedure** was successfully used with elementary students for a number of years, and recently found effective for secondary students as well (Filter et al., 2007). This procedure is well known as a second-tier intervention under the positive behavior interventions and supports model (Boden, Ennis, & Jolivette, 2012). The procedure involves specific steps, which allow the student and adults to check progress toward school-wide or individual behavior goals (Boden et al., 2012). The steps to check in/check out include the following:

- Checking in with a trusted adult at the beginning of the day to go over behavioral expectations

- Receiving feedback throughout the day from other teachers (and/or monitoring one's own behavior through self-management)

- Checking out with the same or another trusted adult to review the day's behaviors and receive reinforcement for meeting goals (Boden et al., 2012; Boutot, 2009)

The procedure is relatively easy to implement, but requires commitment on the part of the adults who perform the check-in and check-out contact with the student. The check-in/check-out procedure can easily be combined with other procedures including token systems, social narratives, or video modeling for a complete package to prevent challenging behaviors.

CHOICES

Providing choices to students can be a very simple yet effective strategy to prevent the occurrence of behavioral challenges. Described by Dunlap and Liso (2004) as an evidence-based strategy for young children, **choice** involves allowing children to indicate their preference and giving them access to the items or activities they choose at various points throughout the day. Choice strategies include providing students the option to express their preference and providing access to the items or activities they choose. It is recommended that practitioners offer two or three choices verbally ("Would you like X or Y?") or provide a visual stimulus in the form of a choice menu (see Figure 5.12 for an example of potential activities a student may choose from). Research supports the use of choice in increasing compliance, independence, communication, and motivation, as well as decreasing acting out (Jolivette, Stichter, & McCormick, 2002; McCormick, Jolivette, & Ridgley, 2003). For example, a student may be offered the option of *where* to complete a work task, *which* work task to complete first, *what* materials to use to complete the task, and *what* activity to do on break when finished. Providing choices for less preferred tasks can create a sense of buy-in for such pupils, who may be more willing to complete a task without challenging behaviors if they have some autonomy. While more research has been conducted with young children, secondary students may benefit as well. Anytime students are provided with the opportunity to have autonomy in their environment, it has the potential to improve compliant behavior.

FIGURE 5.12 Sample Choice Board

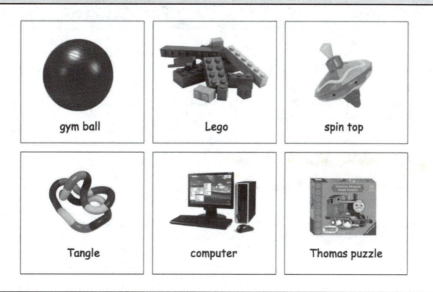

SOURCE: ASD Teacher. *Setting Up a Choice Board at Home to Aid Communication and Structure*. Available at http://asdteacher.com/picturechoiceboard/

See Table 5.2 for a summary of the various forms of antecedent interventions discussed in this section of the chapter.

TABLE 5.2 Summary of Antecedent Strategies and Interventions

STRATEGY	APPLICATION	EXAMPLE
Visual Schedule	Use of photographs or pictures indicating a sequence of events	A visual schedule can be used to map out a student's school day or individual steps for completing a task (e.g., brushing one's teeth).
Social Narratives	Short stories that explain components or elements of social or environmental situations with accompanying behavioral expectations	A social narrative can be used to explain how to respond to feedback from an employer or to ask a peer to play a game.
Video Modeling	Video portraying a person performing a specific skill or action; video shared with the individual	A video model can be used to support a student in learning how to independently prepare food (e.g., a smoothie), as well as to ask for help if lost in the community.

(Continued)

TABLE 5.2 (Continued)

STRATEGY	APPLICATION	EXAMPLE
Token Economy	A reinforcement strategy that provides a reinforcer (token) to a student upon satisfactory completion of a target behavior	A token economy can be used to support a student completing an academic task (e.g., solving a math problem) or greeting a peer appropriately in the morning.
Behavioral Momentum	Prompting a student to quickly complete several easy tasks prior to attempting a more difficult activity	Behavioral momentum can be used when a student becomes frustrated with writing a spelling word. The student is asked to clap his hands, touch his head, and then write the word.
Premack Principle	Completing a less preferred or desired activity prior to receiving access to a highly desired behavior (Grandma's law)	The Premack Principle can be used to set up a situation in which a student who solves five math problems can have two minutes on her iPad.
Check-In/ Check-Out Procedure	A behavioral strategy that assesses progress toward personal behavioral goals	The check-in/check-out procedure can be used at the beginning of the school day to go over expectations for the day and at the end of the day to review if the student met expectations.
Choices	Providing students with access to their preferred activities or items during the school day	Choices can be provided to students throughout the day, including "Would you like to do math or spelling first?," "Would you like pretzels or goldfish for lunch?," and "Would you like to play with Legos or the iPad during free time?"

ADDRESSING CHALLENGING BEHAVIORS IN THE CLASSROOM

Although the principal goal of any behavior plan for any learner is to prevent the occurrence of challenging behaviors before they start, consequence-based interventions must be put into place when challenging behaviors occur. Antecedent interventions can do a great service toward decreasing the frequency, duration, or intensity of a challenging behavior, but to implement longer-lasting and more significant behavior change, alternative behaviors should be taught using reinforcement. Alternative behaviors should be "functionally equivalent" in that they are more appropriate behaviors that serve the same function as the challenging behavior. As an example, we can determine through functional behavior assessment that Carlos bites his teacher to gain attention. Because we know that Carlos is engaging in biting behavior to gain his teacher's attention, we would teach and reinforce a more appropriate, alternative way for Carlos to gain his teacher's attention, such as tapping her shoulder.

FUNCTIONAL COMMUNICATION TRAINING

Providing students with functionally equivalent replacement behaviors is used in the approach known as **functional communication training (FCT)**. FCT is a strategy supported by a plethora of research involving students with intellectual disability or developmental disability. For example, Durand (1999) studied the effects of FCT on improving behaviors of five students with intellectual disability aged 3.5–15 years in both school and community settings. Students were taught to use an alternative communication device to gain access to the identified reinforcer (for example, attention, escape), as determined by a functional behavior assessment prior to study implementation. All participants' behaviors improved, as did their use of assistive technology in the form of alternative communication devices. The study demonstrates that FCT can be used for a variety of behaviors in various settings (Durand, 1999). As students with intellectual or developmental disability often display communication deficits in the form of language delays, much of their challenging behavior may be the result of communication deficits.

FCT provides learners with critical skills to appropriately make requests. Requests can address all functions of behavior, including to escape a task or activity, to obtain attention, or to obtain tangible items, such as food or activities. When functional communication training is properly implemented, it offers great potential to reduce challenging behaviors, since learners are taught a more appropriate behavior or skill to address their needs. As with all applied behavior analysis procedures, the process of FCT begins with the identification of the function of the behavior. Then, the teacher will identify a more appropriate behavior to serve the same function and then teach it to the learner through the provision of reinforcement. To use the example of Carlos, who bites his teacher to gain attention, we would need to identify a more appropriate behavior that Carlos could engage in to gain his teacher's attention. If Carlos were in a preschool environment, it would be appropriate to teach him to tap his teacher on the shoulder instead of biting. Once he progressed into the elementary or secondary school classroom, Carlos might be taught to raise his hand to gain his teacher's attention. In any setting, his teacher would need to work with him to learn this skill. The teaching procedure may consist of first waiting for Carlos to seek attention from his teacher, then prompting him to tap her shoulder or raise his hand, and then quickly providing him with high-quality attention (for example, turning to face Carlos, looking him in the eyes, and responding verbally to his request for attention) as an immediate response to him for engaging in the appropriate behavior. Because, initially, Carlos needs to learn this new behavior, raising his hand needs to be reinforced as often (at the same frequency) as the biting behavior was being reinforced in order for FCT to be effective.

Researchers consistently demonstrated the effectiveness of functional communication training in reducing challenging behaviors as well as increasing functionally equivalent communicative behaviors (Schieltz et al., 2011). In a classic study, Carr and Durand (1985) demonstrated its use with four elementary school–aged children with developmental disabilities. In their study, the children's behavior was determined to be maintained by negative reinforcement; thus, the children were taught to ask for a break instead of engaging in destructive behaviors. Further, these researchers demonstrated that relevant phrases (those that specifically addressed the behavioral function) were more effective than irrelevant phrases at decreasing the destructive behaviors (Carr & Durand, 1985). In another example, one child with a severe disability was taught to sign "please" to gain access to preferred items, which subsequently decreased destructive and self-injurious behaviors (Wacker et al., 1990). Similarly, other studies demonstrated that microswitches (that is, electronic switches that can be operated with relatively small movements) could be used as the functional communication mode and were effective at reducing challenging behaviors (Winborn, Wacker, Richman, Asmus, & Geier, 2002; Winborn-Kemmerer, Ringdahl, Wacker, & Kitsukawa, 2009).

A growing body of research suggests FCT can reduce challenging behaviors in older students and adults with intellectual disability, even at the lower functioning levels (Durand, 1990; Keen, Sigafoos, & Woodyatt, 2001). In a recent study, Byiers, Dimian, and Symons (2014) investigated the efficacy of functional communication training with adolescents and adults with Rett syndrome. Following a functional behavior assessment, three young women (ages 15–27) were taught to use switches to communicate wants and needs, resulting in a decrease in challenging behavior for all three participants (Byiers et al., 2014). The use of FCT is common for adolescents with intellectual and developmental disabilities. In their review of 32 studies, Matson and colleagues found that one of the most commonly used treatments for aggression in adolescents was FCT (Matson, Dixon, & Matson, 2005). Certainly of concern in functional communication training is the type of communication the student will use to request reinforcement. Teachers must ensure that the device or system the student uses to communicate is either one with which the student is already familiar, or one that can be easily taught to the student. The success of FCT is tied to the student's ability to effectively use the alternative communication system.

GUIDED COMPLIANCE

Guided compliance can be an effective technique with learners who demonstrate difficulty carrying out requests from adults. This approach is implemented to increase the frequency and consistency of learners' compliance with adult demands by providing a sequence of prompts with progressively greater intrusiveness to help the learner to comply. For example, a child who is not complying with a request that he or she put down a toy he or she is playing with would first be verbally prompted to put down the toy, then be physically prompted to do so (Wilder et al., 2012). For older students, guided compliance may include guiding the hand of a student who is attempting to hit his own head or clapping to reduce the opportunity to self-hit.

DIFFERENTIAL REINFORCEMENT

Differential reinforcement is another behavioral principle that is used as a strategy to address behavioral challenges and consists of providing varying amounts of reinforcement to different types of behaviors in relation to the target behavior. First, in the case of **differential reinforcement of alternative behaviors (DRA)**, reinforcement is provided for behaviors that serve the same function as the challenging behavior (for example, functional communication training). **Differential reinforcement of incompatible behaviors (DRI)** consists of identifying a behavior that is incompatible with the challenging behavior (for example, putting one's hands in one's pockets is incompatible with loudly and repetitively tapping one's fingers on a desk) and then reinforcing the incompatible behavior at higher rates than the challenging behavior. To implement **differential reinforcement of low rates of behavior (DRL)**, the behavior would be reinforced when it occurs at lower rates (for example, reinforcing a student for taking less time to clock in at a job site each day until the student is able to clock in within an appropriate amount of time). Finally, in the case of **differential reinforcement of other behaviors (DRO)**, a behavior other than the target behavior is differentially reinforced, typically on a specific time interval (for example, providing reinforcement to a student at each two-minute interval during a period in which he has engaged in any appropriate behavior) (Alberto & Troutman, 2013).

To choose an effective differential reinforcement procedure, teachers first need to identify the behavior's function. If it is possible to identify an alternative behavior that serves the same function, DRA would be the option of choice. When DRA procedures include teaching the learner how to communicate to address his or her needs, the procedure is considered functional communication training. A classic example of DRA would be if a child were tired of a task, he or she would be taught to request a break instead of engaging in aggression. If it is possible to identify an incompatible behavior but it does not serve the same function as the problem behavior, then DRI could be effective. DRI would be shown if a teacher asked a student who was running around the room to sit in a chair and provided reinforcement to the student for doing so.

When differential reinforcement of low rates of behavior is used, it is typically because the goal (terminal) behavior is not yet in the learner's skill set. As an example, imagine a preschool student who independently communicates two requests but has the goal of independently communicating twenty; the pupil is a long way from reaching his or her goal behavior. In this example, reinforcement may be provided when the child is communicating four requests, then five and six until the goal behavior is reached. DRL may also be indicated when the behavioral challenge is mainly a problem due to its frequency. Perhaps an elementary school pupil is very interested in sharing with others, to the point where he or she is simply obtaining items in order to give them to others. The student's teacher may be heartened by the fact that the student would like to share, but the behavior has become disruptive and is hindering the learner's time engaging in the activity. Instead of completely eliminating this behavior through extinction, the teacher could use DRL and only reinforce the individual when he or she engages in low rates of this behavior.

Lastly, differential reinforcement of other behaviors is implemented to provide reinforcement when the challenging behavior is not displayed. When DRO is used, reinforcement is provided regardless of whether another alternative or incompatible behavior is being displayed. DRO is most often implemented when the behavioral function is automatic or when there may be multiple functions of the behavior. As an example, consider an adolescent who engages in loud self-stimulatory vocalizations at a high frequency (for up to 30 minutes of every hour). This pupil could be reinforced for every 5 minutes that the vocalizations are *not* displayed (meaning that every 5 minutes, if he is not engaging in loud vocalizations, he is reinforced, regardless of what else he is doing). Regardless of the variation of differential reinforcement used, over 20 years of research support suggesting that as long as the function of the behavior is properly identified and the appropriate type of differential reinforcement is implemented, there is a high likelihood of effectively addressing challenging behaviors in individuals with intellectual disability (Matson et al., 2005).

PUNISHMENT PROCEDURES

Although reinforcement strategies should be provided as often as possible, at times, educators and parents could require the use of punishment procedures to decrease the frequency, duration, or intensity of behavioral challenges. Punishment should *never* be the first step in any behavior change plan, but it may be used when reinforcement does not result in sufficient behavior change. It is critical to note that punishment does *not* teach new behavior or skills. This is an essential consideration if punishment is used. A possible use of punishment may be when elementary school–aged students are engaging in aggressive behavior toward others or themselves. Consider a preschooler who slaps his or her own face in order to gain attention from peers in the classroom. It may be challenging to identify a replacement behavior (for example, FCT or DRA) because at the time when this behavior is occurring, the class is focused on the lesson being taught by the teacher, and stopping the classroom instruction to provide attention to the child may not provide sufficient reinforcement to compete with that provided by the self-injurious behavior. When behaviors that need to be decreased rapidly occur but teaching and reinforcing an alternative behavior is not effective, the use of a punishment procedure should be explored to complement the use of a differential reinforcement procedure. When decreasing (punishing) strategies are deemed necessary, the least intrusive, least aversive punisher should be selected. In general, negative punishment may be less intrusive than some positive punishers, particularly corporal punishment. However, overcorrection strategies (which are positive punishers) may be less aversive than a time-out (negative punishment) procedure. The decision should be made by a team and should consider the individual student and situation. What is considered less aversive for one student (for example, time-out) may be extremely aversive to another. Thus, the decision should be made based on the individual student and situation. Further, the potential risks and benefits should be carefully evaluated prior to using procedures based on punishment (see Table 5.3).

Ethical use of punishment. The use of punishment procedures with children with and without disabilities drew the attention and consideration of various professional organizations and state agencies. The Behavior Analyst

TABLE 5.3 Risks and Benefits of Punishing Procedures

RISKS	BENEFITS
• May not generalize well	• May work quickly
• May not be long lasting	• May decrease inappropriate behaviors
• May be overused or misused	• May be relatively easy to use
• May lead to additional challenging behaviors	
• May cause challenging behaviors to escalate	
• May lead to negative associations with the punisher (for example, the adult)	
• Does not teach appropriate behaviors	

SOURCE: P. Alberto and A. Troutman, *Applied Behavior Analysis for Teachers*, 9th ed. (Upper Saddle River, NJ: Pearson Education, 2013).

TABLE 5.4 Conditions on the Ethical and Responsible Use of Punishment

- Recommend reinforcement rather than punishment whenever possible.
- If punishment is necessary, always include reinforcement procedures for alternative behavior in the behavior plan.
- Ensure that appropriate steps have been taken prior to implementation of punishment procedures that include implementation of reinforcement.
- Ensure that appropriate training and supervision is provided.
- Evaluate the effectiveness of punishment quickly and make changes to the plan if needed.
- Include a plan for the discontinuation of punishment when it is no longer necessary.

SOURCE: Adapted from *Professional and Ethical Compliance Code for Behavior Analysts*, Behavior Analyst Certification Board, 2014.

Certification Board© (BACB) developed and published several critical ethical guidelines relating to the use of punishment (see Table 5.4). In addition, a policy on the use of restraint and seclusion (only two examples of several types of punishment) was developed by the Council for Exceptional Children. The Association of Professional Behavior Analysts produced a similar policy to address the use of specific punishment procedures. Perhaps most notably, the U.S. Department of Education (2012) put forth specific guidelines on the use of restraint and seclusion in public schools. These guidelines list precautions, restrictions, and alternative considerations for using restraint (see Table 5.5).

TABLE 5.5 Principles on the Use of Restraint and Seclusion

1.	Every effort should be made to prevent the need for the use of restraint and the use of seclusion.
2.	Schools should never use mechanical restraints to restrict a child's freedom of movement, and schools should never use a drug or medication to control behavior or restrict freedom of movement (except as authorized by a licensed physician or other qualified health professional).
3.	Physical restraint or seclusion should not be used except in situations where the child's behavior poses imminent danger of serious physical harm to self or others and other interventions are ineffective and should be discontinued as soon as imminent danger of serious physical harm to self or others has dissipated.
4.	Policies restricting the use of restraint and seclusion should apply to all children, not just children with disabilities.
5.	Any behavioral intervention must be consistent with the child's rights to be treated with dignity and to be free from abuse.
6.	Restraint or seclusion should never be used as punishment or discipline (e.g., placing in seclusion for out-of-seat behavior), as a means of coercion or retaliation, or as a convenience.
7.	Restraint or seclusion should never be used in a manner that restricts a child's breathing or harms the child.
8.	The use of restraint or seclusion, particularly when there is repeated use for an individual child, multiple uses within the same classroom, or multiple uses by the same individual, should trigger a review and, if appropriate, revision of strategies currently in place to address dangerous behavior. If positive behavioral strategies are not in place, staff should consider developing them.
9.	Behavioral strategies to address dangerous behavior that results in the use of restraint or seclusion should address the underlying cause or purpose of the dangerous behavior.
10.	Teachers and other personnel should be trained regularly on the appropriate use of effective alternatives to physical restraint and seclusion, such as positive behavioral interventions and supports, and, only for cases involving imminent danger of serious physical harm, on the safe use of physical restraint and seclusion.
11.	Every instance in which restraint or seclusion is used should be carefully and continuously and visually monitored to ensure the appropriateness of its use and the safety of the child, other children, teachers, and other personnel.
12.	Parents should be informed of the policies on restraint and seclusion at their child's school or other educational setting, as well as applicable federal, state, or local laws.
13.	Parents should be notified as soon as possible following each instance in which restraint or seclusion is used with their child.
14.	Policies regarding the use of restraint and seclusion should be reviewed regularly and updated as appropriate.
15.	Policies regarding the use of restraint and seclusion should provide that each incident involving the use of restraint or seclusion should be documented in writing and provide for the collection of specific data that would enable teachers, staff, and other personnel to understand and implement the preceding principles. (pp. 12-13)

SOURCE: U.S. Department of Education, *Restraint and Seclusion: Resource Document* (Washington, DC: Author, 2012).

Although punishment is not advised unless special circumstances warrant it (only for the most dangerous behaviors), there are behavior change procedures designed to decrease behavior that present less aversion to learners. Less aversive approaches may be combined with antecedent and reinforcement strategies to create rapid reductions in challenging behaviors. These approaches are discussed in the following sections.

RESPONSE INTERRUPTION AND REDIRECTION

A natural response from adults when children indicate they may engage in a likely dangerous behavior is to block them from doing so. This might occur when an individual is likely to engage in an aggressive behavior (such as kicking a peer or destroying property) or a behavior that poses safety concerns (such as jumping from a significant height). In the methodology of applied behavior analysis, when a student is blocked from engaging in a behavior, this is an example of **response blocking**. Technically, response blocking is a punishment procedure since it blocks the learner from engaging in the particular response (behavior). Redirection is then provided to direct the student to engage in a different behavior. Martinez and Betz (2013) indicated response interruption and redirection is an intervention with mounting research support to address stereotypy in individuals with developmental disabilities, who often have a coexisting diagnosis of intellectual disability.

EXTINCTION

Another behavioral principle that is frequently employed in applied behavior analysis is extinction. **Extinction** consists of the removal or withdrawal of reinforcement from a behavior that was previously reinforced (Cooper et al., 2007). Put another way, extinction consists of completely removing reinforcement after the occurrence of a particular behavior, which, in essence, makes it a negative punishment procedure. In the case of Carlos, who was discussed previously due to his behavior of biting his teacher to obtain attention, if the preschool teacher suddenly blocked his biting behavior and did not provide him with attention, the teacher would be employing extinction. Extinction can occur naturally in classrooms, when teachers and students fail to provide reinforcement for specific behaviors. Despite this, for extinction to be used systematically, a careful analysis of the function of the challenging behavior needs to be conducted. Once this is done, the precise reinforcer that was maintaining the behavior can be identified and then withheld. As extinction is a behavioral intervention, data must be collected and analyzed to confirm the procedure is effective at reducing the challenging behavior. Because extinction is a broad behavioral principle and it is often used in concert with other behavioral interventions (such as differential reinforcement and response blocking), it is well represented in the literature as a particularly effective intervention for individuals with intellectual disability. Lancioni, Singh, O'Reilly, and Sigafoos (2009) conducted a systematic literature review and identified 41 studies that were published expounding on the efficacy of extinction for use in the reduction of hand-related stereotypical behavior in individuals with intellectual disability. Two studies focusing on elementary school children addressed eye-poking behaviors by providing goggles to the child (Lalli, Livezey, & Kates, 1996; McDonald, Wilder, & Dempsey, 2002). In an application of extinction to address hand/face hitting, Hanley and colleagues (Hanley, Piazza, Keeney, Blakely-Smith, & Worsdell, 1998) placed wrist weights on a child to prevent the individual from hitting himself. In another example of extinction, the reduction of handmouthing in elementary school children was reduced by presenting preferred stimuli and halting the provision of those stimuli when the behavior of putting one's hand on one's mouth occurred (Lancioni et al., 2007). A review of extinction efficacy with students with intellectual disability ages 2–18 was analyzed by Rooker, Jessel, Kurtz, and Hagopian (2013), who found that in 90 percent of the cases, extinction combined with functional communication training reduced and improved problem behaviors. Thus, evidence suggests that extinction, in conjunction with replacement behavior instruction, may be successful for students with intellectual disability across ages.

CONCLUSION

Students with intellectual disability frequently present behavioral challenges, across ages (Lee, Harrington, Chang, & Conners, 2008). These challenging behaviors may be associated with deficits in communication, receptive language, and social interaction (Emerson et al., 2001). The behaviors that result from these deficits present great difficulty to teachers as well as parents. When a behavioral challenge is identified, the first step to resolving the issue is a functional behavioral assessment (Crone, Hawken, & Horner, 2015). Interview forms and questionnaires such as the Functional Analysis Screening Tool (Iwata, DeLeon, & Roscoe, 2013) and the Functional Assessment

Interview (O'Neill et al., 1997) assist teachers and others to identify the key information to conduct a functional behavioral assessment. Once this assessment identifies the function of the behavior, an appropriate intervention can be implemented. To prevent challenging behaviors from occurring, antecedent interventions can be implemented (Luiselli, 2006). These may consist of teaching new skills using positive reinforcement and altering the environmental variables to prevent the challenging behavior from needing to occur (Bambara, & Knoster, 2009). The use of evidence-based strategies to prevent challenging behaviors from occurring and to address them once they do occur will assist in promoting effective instruction for individuals with mild, moderate, and severe intellectual disability (Smith, Polloway, Taber-Doughty, Patton, & Dowdy, 2016).

Chapter Summary

- Behavioral challenges can impact students with intellectual disability across the preschool through secondary education years.

- One evidence-based approach for preventing and addressing behavioral issues is applied behavior analysis (ABA), which is application of behavioral principles to change socially important behaviors, while making data-based decisions as to effectiveness of the interventions.

- A key element to being able to apply ABA is to conduct a functional behavior assessment to help educators identify the function (or purpose) of a student's behavior.

- ABA includes antecedent interventions, which work to prevent a challenging behavior from occurring, or to promote skill acquisition. Antecedent interventions include visual schedules, social narratives, video modeling, token economy, behavioral momentum, Premack Principle, check-in/check-out procedures, and choices.

- Antecedent interventions will not always work; alternative behaviors should be taught using reinforcement.

- Different approaches for teaching alternative behaviors include functional communication training, guided compliance, and differential reinforcement.

- Punishment may be used when reinforcement does not result in sufficient behavior change, but should *never* be the first step in any behavior change plan and should always be done following ethical principles.

Review Questions

1. What are the functional behavioral needs of students with intellectual disability?

2. How are functional behavior assessments conducted to determine the function a target behavior serves?

3. Why is it necessary to identify the function of a target behavior?

4. How can teachers assess the function of challenging behaviors of students with intellectual disability?

5. What interventions can teachers use to increase or decrease behaviors in their classroom?

Key Terms

reinforcement (page 110)

punishment (page 110)

negative reinforcement (page 110)

positive reinforcement (page 110)

antecedent (page 110)

functional behavior assessment (page 110)

consequence (page 111)

positive behavior interventions and supports (PBIS) (page 112)

behavior intervention plan (BIP) (page 114)

visual schedule (page 116)

social narratives (page 118)

video modeling (page 121)

token economy (page 123)

behavioral momentum (page 125)

Premack Principle (page 126)

check-in/check-out procedure (page 127)

choice (page 128)

functional communication training (FCT) (page 131)

guided compliance (page 133)

differential reinforcement of alternative behaviors (DRA) (page 134)

differential reinforcement of incompatible behaviors (DRI) (page 133)

differential reinforcement of low rates of behavior (DRL) (page 133)

differential reinforcement of other behaviors (DRO) (page 133)

response blocking (page 138)

extinction (page 138)

Organizations Concerned With Behavior or Applied Behavior Analysis

Association of Professional Behavior Analysts

www.apbahome.net

Behavior Analyst Certification Board

www.bacb.com

CHAPTER 6

Assistive Technology for Students With Intellectual Disability

Emily C. Bouck and Richard M. Gargiulo

Learning Objectives

After reading Chapter 6, you should be able to:

- Understand the legal and legislative aspects of assistive technology.
- Explain what makes a tool or device an assistive technology.
- List assistive technology to support students with intellectual disability in academics, life skills, and behavior.
- Explain how assistive technology can benefit students with intellectual disability.

Assistive technology is a related service, accommodation, or goal that is provided at no cost to students with disabilities, including students with intellectual disability, if it is written into their individualized education program (IEP) (Netherton & Deal, 2006). According to the Individuals with Disabilities Education Improvement Act of 2004 (IDEA 2004, PL 108–446), IEP or individualized family service plan (IFSP) teams are to consider assistive technology for *all* students with a disability (Lee & Templeton, 2008).

Assistive technology within IDEA, however, actually refers to two things: assistive technology devices and assistive technology services. An **assistive technology device** refers to "any item, piece of equipment, or product system, whether acquired commercially off the shelf, modified, or customized, that is used to increase, maintain, or improve the functional capabilities of a child with a disability" (IDEA 2004, Section 300.5). Examples of assistive technology devices include pencil grips, calculators, text-to-speech software, seat cushions, and augmentative and alternative communication devices. **Assistive technology services**, as defined in PL 100–407 (the 1988 Technology-Related Assistance for Individuals with Disabilities Act), and subsequently in IDEA, include "any service that directly assists an individual in the selection, acquisition, or use of an assistive technology device." Assistive technology services include selecting, acquiring, implementing, and maintaining devices (Parette, Peterson-Karlan, & Wojcik, 2005).

The goal of this chapter is to discuss assistive technology supports for students with intellectual disability. In this chapter, we will examine assistive technology to support individuals with intellectual disability across the school years (that is, early childhood through high school and transition) relative to academics, life skills, and behavior. While assistive technology supports individuals with disabilities across the life span, from birth until death, in this chapter we will be focused primarily on devices and supports for students ages 3–21 with intellectual disability.

ASSISTIVE TECHNOLOGY DECISION MAKING

Under IDEA 2004, assistive technology is to be considered for all students with disabilities, including students with mild, moderate, severe, or profound intellectual disability. It is the IEP team who makes the assistive technology decisions. Including the typical members of an IEP team (for example, parent, special education teacher, general education teacher, local education agency representative, and an individual to interpret any evaluations), when assistive technology might be needed or is already used by a student with an intellectual disability, additional IEP participants might include an **assistive technology specialist**. Although beneficial, assistive technology specialists may not be common or typically available in schools. In such cases, a speech–language pathologist, occupational therapist, or instructional technologist may assume the role of providing assistive technology services (Edyburn, 2004; Marino, Marino, & Shaw, 2006).

IEP teams can use a range of different decision-making frameworks, guides or tool kits, and assessments to assist with assistive technology consideration and decision making (Edyburn, 2001; Jones & Hinesman-Matthews, 2014). (See Table 6.1 for different assistive technology decision-making

TABLE 6.1 Resources for Assistive Technology Decision Making

DECISION-MAKING GUIDE/ FRAMEWORK/ASSESSMENTS	RESOURCES
Guides	
University of Kentucky Assistive Technology (UKAT) Toolkit	http://edsrc.coe.uky.edu/www/ukatii/; follows the Unifying Functional (Human Function) Model (Downloadable documents to assist in assistive technology decision making)
National Assistive Technology Research Institute, Assistive Technology Planner	http://natri.uky.edu/atPlannermenu.html; see also www.tamcec .org/publications/planning-tools/ (Downloadable kits, available for purchase, to help make assistive technology decisions)
Education Tech Points	www.educationtechpoints.org/manuals-materials/education-tech-points-manual (Downloadable manual for purchase)
Assessments	
Wisconsin Assistive Technology Initiative (WATI) Assessment and Decision-Making Guides	www.wati.org/?pageLoad=content/supports/free/index.php (Free documents to assist in assistive technology decision making and assessments from the WATI)
National Professional Resources Functional Evaluation for Assistive Technology (FEAT)	www.nprinc.com/the-feat-functional-evaluation-for-assistive-technology/ (Assessment for purchase)
Frameworks	
Student, Environment, Tasks, and Tools (SETT)	www.joyzabala.com/Documents.html (Downloadable documents to assist in implementing the SETT Framework)
Matching Person and Technology (MPT)	www.matchingpersonandtechnology.com/mptdesc.html (Online sample assessment items; complete form available for purchase)
Transportable, Available, Practical, and Engaging (TAPE)	Bouck, E. C., Jasper, A., Bassette, L., Shurr, J., & Miller, B. (2013). Applying TAPE: Rethinking assistive technology for students with physical disabilities, multiple disabilities, and other health impairment. *Physical Disabilities: Education and Related Services, 32*(1), 31-54. (Reproducible document for applying TAPE framework)

SOURCE: Adapted from *Assistive Technology* by E. C. Bouck, 2016. Copyright 2017 by Sage.

resources.) A good practice for IEP teams when making assistive technology decisions is to allow a student to try the device or tool prior to implementation. Assistive technology can be written into an IEP as a related service, an accommodation, or an annual goal or short-term objective (Netherton & Deal, 2006).

UNDERSTANDING ASSISTIVE TECHNOLOGY

Assistive technology devices are technologies—tools—to support students with disabilities specifically. Assistive technologies help learners with disabilities, for example, increase independence, access materials, and experience an improved quality of life (Blackhurst, 2005b). Assistive technologies represent one of the six types of technology within schools for students—in other words, one type of **educational technology**. The other types of educational technology include the technology of teaching, medical technology, productivity technology, information technology, and instructional technology (Blackhurst, 2005a, 2005b). (See Table 6.2 for examples of the six types of educational technology.)

Assistive technology devices, by their very definition in IDEA 2004, are ambiguous. In other words, according to the federal definition, assistive technology can be anything from a wheelchair to a pencil grip to a step stool to a text-to-speech program (Edyburn, 2004). Hence, often assistive technology is categorized by level or purpose. In terms of level of technology, assistive technology is often classified into one of three levels: low-tech, mid-tech, or high-tech (Blackhurst, 1997; Edyburn, 2005; Johnson, Beard, & Carpenter, 2007; Vanderheiden, 1984). However, some also include a category of no-tech (see Table 6.3). No-tech assistive technology is a teaching strategy or technique such as mnemonics (Behrmann & Jerome, 2002; Blackhurst, 1997). Low-tech assistive technology is generally technology that requires no power source, does not require much training, and is lower in cost (for example, pencil grips). Mid-tech or moderate-tech assistive technology includes devices that are more sophisticated, such as those that require a battery power source (for example, a calculator). Mid-tech assistive technology devices generally require more training than low-tech devices as well as come with an increased price tag. Finally, high-tech assistive technology devices are considered the most sophisticated technology and often are computer based (for example, text-to-speech, iPad **apps**). High-tech assistive

TABLE 6.2 Examples of Six Distinct Types of Educational Technology

TECHNOLOGY OF TEACHING	MEDICAL TECHNOLOGY	PRODUCTIVITY TECHNOLOGY	INFORMATION TECHNOLOGY	INSTRUCTIONAL TECHNOLOGY	ASSISTIVE TECHNOLOGY
• Direct instruction • Inquiry	• Cochlear implants • Feeding tubes	• Word processor • PowerPoint	• Internet	• Educational software • Smartboards	• Text-to-speech • Pencil grips

SOURCE: Adapted from A. Blackhurst, "Perspectives on Applications of Technology in the Field of Learning Disabilities," *Learning Disability Quarterly, 28*(2), 2005, pp. 175–178.

TABLE 6.3 Example Assistive Technology Devices by Category

NO-TECH	LOW-TECH	MID-TECH	HIGH-TECH
• Mnemonics (e.g., HOMES for remembering the Great Lakes' names) • Graphic organizers	• Pencil grips • Raised lined paper • Highlighter strips • Braille playing cards	• Calculator • Audio recorder • Switches	• Speech-to-text • iPad and iPad apps • Word prediction • Text-to-speech

SOURCE: Adapted from R. Gargiulo, *Special Education in Contemporary Society*, 5th ed. (Thousand Oaks, CA: Sage, 2015), p. 137.

technologies typically have the highest cost and require the most training (Behrmann & Schaff, 2001; Blackhurst, 1997; Edyburn, 2005; Johnson et al., 2007; Vanderheiden, 1984).

Another way to categorize assistive technology is by purpose. The Wisconsin Assistive Technology Initiative (WATI) suggested fourteen purposes of assistive technology: seating, positioning and mobility, communication, computer access, motor aspects of writing, composition of written material, reading, mathematics, organization, recreation and leisure, activities of daily living, vision, hearing, and multiple challenges (Gierach, 2009). In another classification, Bryant and Bryant (2012) suggested seven purposes: positioning, mobility, augmentative and alternative communication (AAC), computer access, adaptive toys and games, adaptive environments, and instructional aids. See Table 6.4 regarding examples of assistive technology devices by purpose.

For students with intellectual disability, assistive technology can support them across the school-aged years in a variety of areas, including—as focused on in this chapter—academic skills (for example, instructional aids—reading, writing, mathematics), life skills (for example, adaptive environments, recreation and leisure, communication), and behavior (for example, organization, self-management). Because assistive technology benefits and IEP recommendations are not—and should not be—made along disability category lines, many of the assistive technologies discussed in this chapter would also benefit students with other types of disabilities, such as learning disabilities and autism spectrum disorders, among others.

For students with intellectual disability, technology support for success within school can also occur through the implementation of **universal design for learning**, or **UDL** (Wehmeyer, Tassé, Davies, & Stock, 2012). UDL encourages multiple means of presentation, engagement, and expression so all learners can access and experience success (Council for Exceptional Children, 2005); involves building accessibility into teaching and curriculum; and allows students with intellectual disability who struggle to read to experience options for accessing printed text within their classroom, such as audio books, e-text, or picture symbols to support comprehension (Douglas, Ayres, Langone, Bell, & Meade, 2009). Likewise, for learners with intellectual disability who struggle with calculation, a calculator and manipulatives would be

TABLE 6.4 Example Assistive Technology Devices by Purpose

BRYANT & BRYANT PURPOSES	WATI PURPOSES	EXAMPLES
Positioning	Seating and positioning	Adjustable desks: either desks that adjust in height to allow a wheelchair to fit underneath or desks that convert from a sitting to standing position
Mobility	Mobility	Gait trainer: a mobility device with wheels that provides support for students who cannot bear their own weight when walking
Augmentative and alternative communication (AAC)	Communication	Proloquo2Go® app: an app where a student selects (primarily) prerecorded messages via icons arranged on a grid
Computer access	Computer access	Alternative keyboard: a keyboard that differs from the standard QWERTY keyboard, including alphabetical, Dvorak, or Maltron
Adaptive toys and games	Recreation and leisure	Switch-operated battery toys: battery-operated toys that a student can operate using a switch rather than interacting with the toy
Adaptive environments	Activities of daily living	Adapted utensils, bowls, and cups: dishes and utensils that are adapted, such as with a suction bottom or lip, or by being weighted or positioned at different angles
Instructional aids	Motor aspects of writing	Speech-to-text: when an individual's spoken words are translated into text on a computer (Word documents, e-mail, etc.)
	Composition of written material	Word prediction: when options for words appear when a student begins to type the word (e.g., when a user types *h-o*, *house*, *home*, and *hotel* appear as options)
	Reading	E-text or supported e-text: traditional print text translated to be read digitally (e.g., on a computer or mobile device) or including additional accessibility features (e.g., text-to-speech, contrast colors)
	Mathematics	Calculator: a tool that students use to calculate mathematical operations
	Organization	Picture schedule: a visual schedule that includes pictures or icons to tell a student what is going to happen next
	Vision	Text-to-speech: when the text that appears on a computer screen is read to the user (e.g., in Word documents, e-mails, and Internet pages)

(Continued)

TABLE 6.4 (Continued)

BRYANT & BRYANT PURPOSES	WATI PURPOSES	EXAMPLES
	Hearing	FM system: an assistive listening device operated by radio waves in which sound, such as a person's voice, is transported directly into a student's hearing aid or cochlear implants or played via speakers around the room

SOURCE: AssistiveWare® http:www.assistiveware.com; E. Bouck and S. Flanagan (2009), "Assistive Technology and Mathematics: What Is There and Where Can We Go in Special Education," in *Journal of Special Education Technology*, 24(2), pp. 17-30; D. Bryant and B. Bryant, *Assistive Technology for People With Disabilities* (Boston, MA: Allyn & Bacon, 2003); J. Gierach, *Assessing Students' Needs for Assistive Technology*, 5th ed. (Milton: Wisconsin Assistive Technology Initiative, 2009); L. Johnson, L. Beard, and L. Carpenter, *Assistive Technology: Access for All Students* (Upper Saddle River, NJ: Pearson Education, 2007); B. Loeding, "Assistive Technology for Visual and Dual Sensory Impairments," in O. Wendt, R. Quist, and L. Lloyd (Eds.), *Assistive Technology: Principles and Applications for Communication Disorders and Special Education* (pp. 267-412) (Bingley, UK: Emerald, 2011).

made available for students to select to use (Bouck, Bassette, Taber-Doughty, Flanagan, & Szwed, 2009).

ASSISTIVE TECHNOLOGY TO SUPPORT ACADEMIC SKILLS ACROSS THE SCHOOL YEARS

For students with intellectual disability, like other students with disabilities, assistive technology can support their access to and independence in academic areas, including literacy and mathematics. Educators can implement low-tech, mid-tech, and high-tech options to benefit pupils with intellectual disability in early childhood, elementary school, and secondary school (see Table 6.5 for examples of low-tech, mid-tech, and high-tech assistive technology devices to support students with intellectual disability in reading, writing, and mathematics).

READING

Multiple technologies can support students in reading, from low-tech to high-tech. Low-tech options to support students with intellectual disability in reading include highlighters (erasable or regular), nonpermanent highlighter tape, and highlighter strips (i.e., strips of colored transparency film laminated and cut to about the width of printed text). Learners

TABLE 6.5 Assistive Technology Examples for Content-Area Instruction

	LOW-TECH	MID-TECH	HIGH-TECH
Reading	Highlighter strips or tape: tape or strips can be applied to allow students to follow along or highlight ideas/words in a passage	Reading pen: reads printed text as students scan the pen along the words	Text-to-speech: programs that read text on a computer to students (e.g., Word document, webpage)
	Picture symbols: symbols added to reading passages to aid students in comprehension	Audiobooks: books that students can listen to on a tape recorder or CD player	E-books or e-text: books or textbooks delivered digitally to be read on a computer or mobile device
Writing	Pencil grips: small grips added to a pencil to provide stability and support	Handheld spell-checkers: battery-operated tools to provide the spelling of words	Speech-to-text: programs that translate students' spoken words into text (e.g., in a Word document)
	Raised lined paper: paper with raised lines to provide feedback to students about where the line is to support handwriting	Handheld dictionary: battery-operated tool that allows students to look up a word in an electronic dictionary (versus using a book-based dictionary)	Word prediction: programs that predict the word students are typing before they complete the word; lessens amount of typing as well as supports students with spelling challenges
Mathematics	Concrete manipulatives: objects (e.g., tiles, cubes, base 10 blocks) that can be manipulated to support students	Calculators (e.g., four-function, graphing): tools that support students with basic (e.g., multiplication) and more complex mathematical operations (e.g., exponents)	Virtual manipulatives: web- or app-based counterparts to concrete manipulatives; support students in understanding and solving math problems
	Number lines: lines with numbers marked at intervals to assist students in understanding addition and subtraction as well as magnitude	Coin-U-Lators: battery-operated calculator-like devices that add coins (e.g., dimes) and dollars	MyScript Calculator app: acts as a calculator but allows students to input problems via writing on the device with their finger

SOURCE: Adapted from R. Gargiulo, *Special Education in Contemporary Society*, 5th ed. (Thousand Oaks, CA: Sage, 2015), p. 140.

with intellectual disability can receive support in reading through the use of picture symbols to supplement text, especially grade-level text (Shurr & Taber-Doughty, 2012). Teachers can create their own adapted text or use for-purchase products that come with visual supports to aid text comprehension, such as News-2-You (n2y, 2016; www.n2y.com/news-2-you/). News-2-You is a newspaper that provides four different reading levels. Students might also benefit from Rewordify (2016; https://rewordify.com), a website that simplifies language pasted from another website (URL) or document.

In terms of more sophisticated (mid- to high-tech) technology, students with intellectual disability can use tools that read text. Assistive technology to read text to students (that is, **text-to-speech**) can occur via a stand-alone device, a computer, or a more **mobile device**, such as a tablet, smartphone, or MP3 player. One stand-alone device for reading printed text is the Quicktionary2 (www.wizcomtech.com/product-catalog/products-english), a handheld optical character recognition system (Higgins & Raskind, 2005; WizcomTech, 2014). To use the pen, students drag it along printed text, such as a book or document. Other stand-alone devices are products marketed to read specific books. For example, LeapFrog™ markets the LeapReader™ Reading and Writing System, a pen that reads specifically designed books from LeapFrog (www.leapfrog.com). The handheld pen, targeted for students ages 4–8, will read books at the word, sentence, or page level; the books are also equipped with comprehension or other literacy activities. Another handheld pen that reads books is the AnyBook personal reader from Franklin (www.anybookreader.com). Instead of having special books, individuals can record their own readings of any story at each page. Students then connect the pen to the stickers placed on the book to read. For individuals who use a **switch**, a similar product is Bookworm from AbleNet (www.ablenetinc.com/bookworm), which allows students to access a recorded book via a switch (see Figure 6.1).

Computer-based text-to-speech options can be both free or for purchase. Computer-based text-to-speech can read materials available on a computer, such as e-mails, websites, and documents (for example, Word and PDF), as well as digital books. An example of a free text-to-speech option, although one can also purchase additional features, is NaturalReader (see www.naturalreaders.com). NaturalReader works on both Windows and Mac operating systems and also comes as an app for mobile devices (NaturalSoft Limited, 2016). For-purchase

FIGURE 6.1 Bookworm, a Switch-Accessible Device to Play Recorded Books, by AbleNet

SOURCE: AbleNet. Reproduced with permission.

options also exist, such as the Kurzweil 3000 + firefly (Kurzweil Education, 2016; www.kurzweiledu.com/k3000-firefly/overview.html), Read&Write Gold (Texthelp, 2016; www.texthelp.com/en-us/products/read-and-write-family), and wordQ+speakQ (GoQ, 2016; www.goqsoftware.com/wordQspeakQ .php). Digital books for students include both free options (for example, Project Gutenberg; see www.gutenberg.org) and for-purchase options (for example, from Amazon, iTunes, and Barnes & Noble). Digital books can be accessed on a computer or mobile device, including tablets as well as specifically designed e-text (or digital text) readers (for example, Kindle, Nook). A more mid-tech alternative to digital text is audiobooks, such as the older books on tape or, a bit more recent, books on CD. Audiobooks on CD are often available at public libraries; public libraries are also increasingly making e-books available for checkout to library patrons.

WRITING

The low-tech, mid-tech, and high-tech options to support writing encompass the complex and multifaceted aspects of writing, such as handwriting, spelling, and composition (that is, the writing process of planning, organizing, generating and drafting text, editing, and revising) (Flower & Hayes, 1981; National Commission on Writing for America's Families, Schools, and Colleges, 2005). Low-tech options to support pupils with handwriting can include pencil grips as well as alternative pencils and pens (for example, thicker, thinner, ergonomic). Students might also benefit in terms of handwriting from raised lined paper, which provides tactile feedback about the lines, or writing on different media, such as gel boards or whiteboards, or writing on a slanted surface. A higher-tech means to support handwriting is for learners to type on a computer or mobile device, including a desktop, laptop, **Google Chromebook**, or tablet with an external or on-screen keyboard.

In terms of spelling, students can use the standard built-in spell-checker when typing on a computer. Other options can include downloading applications, such as Ginger (Ginger Software, 2016; www.gingersoftware.com), which not only checks spelling across multiple platforms (for example, documents, websites) but also checks grammar and understands context (for example, *meet* vs. *meat*).

Students can use paper-based graphic organizers (that is, advanced organizers, procedural facilitators, or think sheets) to support them in the writing process (Englert, Zhao, Dunsmore, Collings, & Wolbers, 2007). One option that provides think sheets to support the entire writing process is POWER, which stands for *planning, organizing, writing, editing,* and *reviewing* (Mariage, Englert, & Garmon, 2000). Another think sheet focused on just the organizing part of prewriting is the paragraph hamburger (see www.readingrockets.org/strategies/paragraph_hamburger for two downloadable templates) (Mariage & Bouck, 2004). Computer-based graphic organizers also exist, such as the for-purchase options of Inspiration (www.inspiration.com) and Kispiration (www.inspiration.com/Kidspiration) (Inspiration Software, 2016a, 2016b) to support students in planning their writing. Free computer-based concept mapping program options include Cmap software (Institute for Human & Machine Cognition, 2014; http://cmap.ihmc.us) and Visual Understanding Environment (Tufts University, 2015; http://vue.tufts.edu) for use on a computer and Popplet as an app-based option (Notion, 2014; http://popplet.com).

In terms of drafting text, students can use a scribe or a computer-based option, such as typing on a traditional keyboard, typing on an adaptive or alternative keyboard, or **speech-to-text**. Alternative or adaptive keyboards include those with layouts different from QWERTY (for example, alphabetical, Dvorak, and Maltron), larger keys, color-coding of keys, IntelliKeys, mini keyboards, on-screen keyboards, and keyboards compatible with mouth or head sticks (Burgstahler, 2012; Cook & Polgar, 2015; Dell, Newton, & Petroff, 2012; Parette, Blum, & Quesenberry, 2013; York & Fabrikant, 2011). (See Figure 6.2 for a picture of IntelliKeys, an alternative keyboard.) Speech-to-text involves spoken text being translated into words within a computer application, such as a document or e-mail (MacArthur, 2009). Free and for-purchase speech-to-text options exist. A popular for-purchase speech-to-text option is Dragon NaturallySpeaking (Nuance, 2016; www.nuance.com/dragon/index.htm). However, current operating systems for both Windows and Apple computers are equipped with free speech-to-text options, such as Windows Speech Recognition (Microsoft, 2016; https://support.microsoft.com/en-us/help/17208/windows-10-use-speech-recognition) and Dictation (Apple, 2016; https://support.apple.com/en-us/HT202584).

Another tool to support drafting text is **word prediction**. Word prediction predicts the word an individual is typing so she or he uses fewer keystrokes. With word prediction, word choices appear based on the first letters typed (that is, as one types *m-o*, a word prediction program might suggest *mouth*, *mouse*,

FIGURE 6.2 IntelliKeys, an Alternative Keyboard by AbleNet

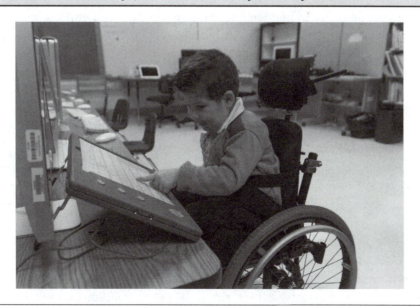

SOURCE: AbleNet. Reproduced with permission.

or *mole*) (MacArthur, 2009). For-purchase word prediction programs include Co:Writer 7 (Don Johnston, 2016; http://donjohnston.com/cowriter-7), SoothSayer (Applied Human Factors, 2016; http://newsite.ahf-net.com/soothsayer), wordQ+speakQ (goQ, 2016), and Read&Write Gold (texthelp, 2016). A few free computer-based word prediction programs exist, such as eType (eType, 2016; http://etype.com) and Turbo Type (Soft Grup Construct SRL, 2016; www.easytousetools.com/turbo_type), which are both compatible with computers using Windows operating systems. Of course, mobile devices, such as tablets and smartphones, are equipped with word prediction.

With postwriting (that is, editing and revising), students can use the spelling and grammar checks previously discussed (for example, Ginger Software, 2016). They can also use text-to-speech. Pupils are assisted in identifying errors to be fixed when they hear their own text read (Kelly, Kratcoski, & McClain, 2006; Madraso, 1993). While the student or someone else can read the printed text, text-to-speech programs can also read typed text, such as the free and for-purchase options discussed earlier (for example, NaturalReader [NaturalSoft Limited, 2016], Read&Write Gold [Texthelp, 2016]).

MATHEMATICS

Low-tech, mid-tech, and high-tech options can support students with intellectual disability in mathematics. In terms of low-tech options, the most common assistive technology may be **concrete manipulatives**, which are commonly used in mathematics classes to support all students in developing a conceptual understanding of mathematics. Concrete manipulatives are also considered an evidence-based practice for educating learners with disabilities, and are used to support students in learning a variety of different mathematical ideas, including algebra, integers, area and perimeter, fractions, and addition/subtraction (Maccini & Gagnon, 2000). A more high-tech take on concrete manipulatives is **virtual manipulatives**, which are similar to concrete manipulatives but accessed digitally, such as on a computer or mobile device. For example, the National Library of Virtual Manipulatives (Cannon, Dorward, Duffin, & Heal, 2004) is a website (http://nlvm.usu .edu) that provides virtual manipulatives to support students of all ages across the different areas of mathematics (for example, numbers and operations, algebra, measurement). Other websites include Illuminations by the National Council for Teachers of Mathematics (2016; http://illuminations.nctm.org) and Inter*activate* by Shodor (2016; www.shodor.org/interactivate) (Bouck &

Flanagan, 2010). Apps for virtual manipulatives also exist to support students on mobile devices, such as Base Ten Blocks, Color Tiles, and Fraction Tiles, all produced and distributed by Brainingcamp, LCC (https://www.brainingcamp.com/product/mobile.html).

Aside from manipulatives, low-tech assistive technologies include number lines, graph paper, and 100s charts. Number lines can be used to support price comparison by secondary students with intellectual disability. Number lines can also be delivered by technology, such as an app on a mobile device for greater portability, for example to support students with price comparison in a grocery store setting (Weng & Bouck, 2014).

Calculators are a mid-tech assistive technology to support pupils in mathematics. Calculators are one of the most common accommodations for students with disabilities (Maccini & Gagnon, 2000, 2006). Students with intellectual disability can successfully use calculators to assist them in solving computational problems, including word problems (Bouck et al., 2009; Yakubova & Bouck, 2014). In addition to basic, scientific, and graphing calculators, learners with intellectual disability can use a specifically designed calculator for money—a Coin-U-Lator, which, instead of numbers as buttons, includes dollars, quarters, dimes, nickels, and pennies.

ASSISTIVE TECHNOLOGY TO SUPPORT LIFE SKILLS ACROSS THE SCHOOL YEARS

COMMUNICATION

One important aspect of daily living or life skills is communication. "Communication is the exchange of ideas, information, thoughts, and feelings" (Gargiulo, 2015, p. 365). For students who struggle with communication, including students with intellectual disability, a specific type of assistive technology exists—**augmentative and alternative communication**, or **AAC**. AAC "includes all forms of communication (other than oral speech) that are used to express thoughts, needs, wants, and ideas" (American Speech-Language-Hearing Association, 2015). AAC supports (that is, augments) or serves as an alternative for individuals' communication (Hanline, Nunes, & Worthy, 2007).

In addition to low-tech, mid-tech, and high-tech, AAC is classified as unaided and aided. An unaided communication system is one not external to the individual. In other words, communication is what an individual can do with his or her body, such as hands (for example, sign language) and face (for example, facial expressions). Aided communication systems are external to an individual. Aided AAC can range from picture systems (that is, non-electronic) to stand-alone speech-generating devices to speech-generating apps on a mobile device (that is, electronic). Non-electronic (or low-tech) AAC includes communication books or boards, eye-gaze displays, and the Picture Exchange Communication System (PECS) (Bondy & Frost, 1994, 2001). See Table 6.6.

Many electronic AAC options exist for individuals. Electronic AAC involves devices that use digital speech (that is, an individual records a message; for example, GoTalk by Attainment Company, 2016) and synthesized speech (that is, computer-generated speech; for example, Accent by Prentke Romich Company) (Brownlee, 2015). Electronic AAC devices run the gamut from

TABLE 6.6 Augmentative and Alternative Communication Examples

UNAIDED	AIDED NON-ELECTRONIC	AIDED DIGITAL SPEECH	AIDED SYNTHESIZED SPEECH
Sign language: a language that involves making signs with one's hands; interpretation is combined with facial expressions and body posture	Communication book: a "book" that provides symbols or icons for a student to select to communicate	GoTalk by Attainment: an individual records messages for a student to select; options include GoTalks with 1-32 messages, which also play sequences	Accent series by Prentke Romich Company: a student selects prerecorded messages via icons
Fingerspelling: a student signs by spelling words using the signs associated with each of the 26 alphabetical letters	Eye-gaze board: typically, a transparent board that includes letters, numbers, or symbols a user selects by scanning and gazing with his or her eyes	QuickTalker family by AbleNet: an individual records messages for the student to select via icons	Proloquo2Go® app by AssistiveWare: a student selects (primarily) prerecorded messages via icons
Gesture or facial expression: a way of expressing one's face or body parts to communicate (e.g., shrugging, smiling)	Picture Exchange Communication System (PECS): a student exchanges a symbol with a communication partner	Scene Speak app: a visual scene display option, which presents language in the natural context of a photograph; an individual records the language connected to parts of the image	DynaWrite 2.0 by DynaVox: a student types in messages via a keyboard

FIGURE 6.3 SuperTalker Progressive Communicator

SOURCE: AbleNet. Used with permission.

devices that store one message to devices in which entire speeches can be delivered. (See Figure 6.3 for an example.) In addition to stand-alone electronic AAC devices, various apps for AAC exist, including those that display a grid (see Figure 6.3) or use a photograph or image (referred to as visual scene display, or VSD; Tuthill, 2014). AAC apps can also involve digital or synthesized speech and include options for students to type words versus selecting a symbol (that is, premade or customized). One of the most common AAC apps is Proloquo2Go® by AssistiveWare (2016; www.assistiveware.com/product/proloquo2go).

INDEPENDENT AND DAILY LIVING

Assistive technology can also support students with intellectual disability in terms of independent or daily living skills. Independent or daily living skills include, but are not limited to, hygiene, dressing, food preparation, eating, purchasing, money, and safety (Wehmeyer et al., 2012). Many aspects of independent or daily living for individuals with intellectual disability are supported through **self-operated prompting systems,** which support students through self-instruction (that is, antecedent cues) (Ayres, Mechling, & Sansosti, 2013; Savage, 2014; Taber-Doughty, 2005). Self-operated prompting systems exist in the form of pictures, audio, and video. Picture prompts involve photographs, icons, or drawings. Audio prompts involve aural prompts, delivered by such technology as MP3 players, smartphones, and audio recorders. Video prompts can be delivered by a computer, DVD player, tablet, or smartphone. (See Figure 6.4 depicting video prompting being delivered via an iPad.) Video-based self-operated prompting systems can include video prompting or video modeling. Video modeling involves a student watching an entire video before performing a task whereas video prompting involves a student watching each step of a task and then subsequently performing that step until the entire task is completed (Ayres et al., 2013). Self-operated prompting systems support pupils with intellectual disability with a variety of independent or daily living

FIGURE 6.4 Example of Video Prompting for Teaching Price Comparison

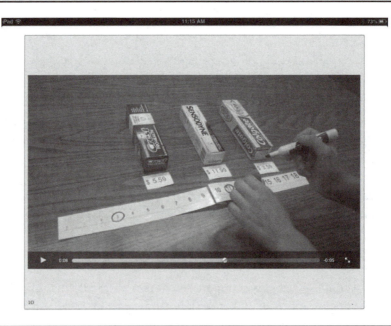

SOURCE: Reprinted from E. Bouck, T. Taber-Doughty, and M. Savage, *Footsteps Toward the Future: Implementing a Real-World Curriculum for Students With Disabilities* (Arlington, VA: Council for Exceptional Children, 2015) p. 34. Copyright 2015 by Council for Exceptional Children.

skills, including food preparation, grocery shopping, and obtaining money (Bouck, Satsangi, Bartlett, & Weng, 2012; Scott, Collins, Knight, & Kleinert, 2013; Taber-Doughty et al., 2011). See Table 6.7 for information about how to create each type of self-operated prompting system.

Outside of self-operated prompting systems, other assistive technologies support students with intellectual disability in daily living and independent living skills. For example, in terms of dressing, multiple low-tech options exist

TABLE 6.7 Steps for Developing a Self-Operated Picture, Auditory, and Video System

SELF-OPERATED PICTURE PROMPTING SYSTEM	SELF-OPERATED AUDITORY PROMPTING SYSTEM	SELF-OPERATED VIDEO SYSTEM
1. Identify the target task.		
2. Develop a task analysis.		
3. Determine types of pictures to use (drawings, photos, icons [e.g., Boardmaker by Mayer-Johnson]).	3. Determine a "script" of auditory prompts.	3. Determine if the student will use video prompting or video modeling.
4. Identify words (if any) that will accompany pictures.	4. Determine who will be the "voice" on the audio system (student, teacher, favorite paraeducator, parent) or whether a "tone" will be used to prompt the student to the next step.	4. Decide the video point of view. (Will it be from the student's perspective? Will it depict the student or a different known or unknown individual engaged in the task?)
5. Identify how pictures will be presented (e.g., communication notebook, paper, or an electronic system such as a tablet or smartphone).	5. Determine the system for delivering auditory prompts (e.g., audio recorder, tablet, smartphone, MP3 player) and if headphones are needed.	5. Identify the system for delivering videos (e.g., DVD player, computer, tablet, smartphone).
6. Develop a prompting system and ask two novel individuals to complete the task using the self-operated system. Make edits based on individuals' performance.		
7. Determine if students will use self-management skills when using the self-operated system. Will students self-monitor their progress using a checklist? Will they engage in self-evaluation?		
8. Evaluate students' performance as they use the self-operated system.		

SOURCE: Adapted from E. Bouck, T. Taber-Doughty, and M. Savage, *Footsteps Toward the Future: Implementing a Real-World Curriculum for Students With Disabilities* (Arlington, VA: Council for Exceptional Children, 2015), p. 35. Copyright 2015 by Council for Exceptional Children.

to support individuals, including extended shoe horns, zipper pulls, button hooks, and devices to aid in putting on one's socks or pulling up one's pants (Koehler, 2011). With hygiene, individuals can procure everyday items adapted or modified to support students with intellectual disability, including enlarged, elongated, weighted, or angled hands on hairbrushes, toothbrushes, or combs. With eating and food preparation, students might also benefit from adapted or modified everyday items, including dishes that can be stuck to a surface and dishes with food guards, partitions, or larger sides for easier scooping (Bryant, Seok, Ok, & Bryant, 2012). Likewise, utensils can be adapted to be enlarged, curved, weighted, flexible, and textured, and glasses can have easier grip handles or grasps, more stability, and options for flexible or elongated straws. Assistive technology devices to prepare food can include roller or rocker knives, angled measuring cups to more easily read the measurement, and picture-based cookbooks (see Figure 6.5). Finally, learners can use the Note Teller 2 by BryTech (2016; www.brytech.com/noteteller) or Money Reader iOS app by LookTel (2016; www.looktel.com/moneyreader) to identify paper money with audio

---

FIGURE 6.5 Picture-Based Cookbook: *Look 'n Cook* by Attainment Company

SOURCE: Attainment Company. Reproduced with permission.

output (that is, both the stand-alone device and the app scan bill money and provide an auditory output of the amount).

Technology can also support students with intellectual disability in terms of safety. Just as all individuals can be supported in terms of safety with cell phones, so can pupils with intellectual disability. Cell phones allow students with intellectual disability to alert someone that they are lost or may need assistance through calling, texting, or sending pictures. In addition to calling or texting, students with intellectual disability can use apps such as Google Maps to support their safety in terms of telling someone where they are or finding their way back home when lost. These apps can also support learners with intellectual disability in independently navigating public transportation.

LEISURE AND RECREATION

Assistive technology can support students with intellectual disability in participating in leisure and recreation. Low-tech options exist for games and crafts, including large game pieces (that is, dice), playing card holders, a switch-activated spinner (for example, All-Turn-It; see Figure 6.6) or other battery-operated toy, easy-to-grip

FIGURE 6.6 All-Turn-It Spinner

SOURCE: AbleNet.com. Reproduced with permission.

scissors, battery- (and switch-) operated scissors, and the Infila Needle Threader to automatically thread a needle by pushing a button. For students of all ages, but especially younger children, a variety of different crayons exist, including jumbo crayons, easy-to-grip crayons, triangular crayons, and egg-shaped crayons.

More sophisticated technology leisure opportunities also exist. For example, students with intellectual disability can use computers and/or computer-like devices (that is, mobile devices) for leisure. These leisure activities can involve texting, interactive online games, and social media (for example, Facebook, Twitter, Google+, and Instagram) (Bryant et al., 2012). However, to use a computer or mobile device, some individuals with intellectual disability may need specific assistive technology devices, including adaptive or alternative keyboards (for example, alternative layout, enlarged or mini, mouth or head stick compatible, or on-screen) and mouse alternatives (for example, trackballs, joysticks, no-hands mouse, eye gaze, touchscreen, voice recognition, or switches) (Cook & Polgar, 2015; Dell et al., 2012; Green, 2014; York & Fabrikant, 2011). See Figure 6.7 for an example of a trackball, an alternative means to a mouse to access a computer.

A variety of switches exist for students with disabilities, including ones that can be activated by any part of the body. While the most common switch is

FIGURE 6.7 Trackball and Alternative Keyboard for Computer Access

SOURCE: AbleNet.com. Reproduced with permission.

a mechanical switch activated by pushing with one's hand (for example, Jelly Bean or Big Beamer switches by AbleNet), switches can also be activated by pushing with any part of one's body, including foot, elbow, and head (for example, Pillow switch). Other mechanical switches are activated by moving a level, grasping, pulling (for example, string switch), gripping, or bending (for example, ribbon switch) (Drescher, 2009). Other switches can be activated without physically touching, such as the Candy Corn proximity sensor, which is activated when a body part moves close to the switch. Infrared switches are controlled with such body parts as the eyebrow, finger, or eye. Finally, switches can be activated by puffing, blowing, or sipping; these are referred to as pneumatic switches (Bornman, 2011; Cook & Polgar, 2015). See Table 6.8 for examples of switches.

TABLE 6.8 Examples of Switches

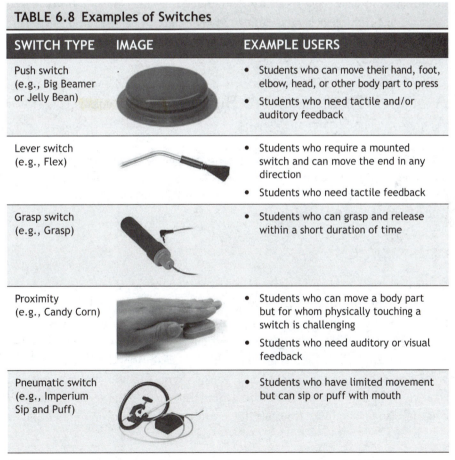

SWITCH TYPE	IMAGE	EXAMPLE USERS
Push switch (e.g., Big Beamer or Jelly Bean)		• Students who can move their hand, foot, elbow, head, or other body part to press • Students who need tactile and/or auditory feedback
Lever switch (e.g., Flex)		• Students who require a mounted switch and can move the end in any direction • Students who need tactile feedback
Grasp switch (e.g., Grasp)		• Students who can grasp and release within a short duration of time
Proximity (e.g., Candy Corn)		• Students who can move a body part but for whom physically touching a switch is challenging • Students who need auditory or visual feedback
Pneumatic switch (e.g., Imperium Sip and Puff)		• Students who have limited movement but can sip or puff with mouth

SOURCE: Adapted from *Assistive Technology* by E. C. Bouck, 2016. Copyright 2017 by Sage.

In terms of recreation, students with intellectual disability benefit from the increased attention to recreational activities, like walking. Similar to most individuals, students with intellectual disability increase their physical activity when using such wearable technology as a Fitbit (Ptomey et al., 2015). Other options for physical activity with socially accepted, popular technology include playing Nintendo Wii (for example, Wii Sports, Wii Sports Resort). Other recreation-based assistive technology devices include adaptive bikes, such as a Rifton adaptive tricycle or the different bike options from Freedom Concepts Inc. (for example, prone recumbent bikes or semi-recumbent bikes), as well as adaptations to such recreational activities as bowling (that is, ramp or plastic-coated foam balls) (Koehler, 2011). Finally, pupils with intellectual disability may need mobility-based assistive technology to participate in recreational activities. Students with intellectual disability who also have mobility challenges may use such mobility-based assistive technology as a gait trainer to participate in basketball or a specific sports wheelchair to participate in different sports (for example, basketball, tennis, football).

ASSISTIVE TECHNOLOGY TO SUPPORT BEHAVIOR ACROSS THE SCHOOL YEARS

Students with intellectual disability can benefit from assistive technology to support behavior across the school years. Assistive technology to support organization, monitoring, and social skills will be discussed in this section, as will sensory-based technology.

ORGANIZATION

Low-tech, mid-tech, and high-tech assistive technology can support organization for students with intellectual disability. In terms of low-tech support for organization, some learners with intellectual disability may benefit from planners to record their assignments and tasks, color-coded folders or work, and sticky notes. Some pupils with intellectual disability may also need visual or picture schedules that allow them to see their schedule across a day and remove the picture or symbol icon when they have completed an activity (that is, visual schedules are typically secured to a board or laminated paper via Velcro).

Students with intellectual disability, or their educators, may also elect to use more sophisticated technology to support their organization. For example, rather than using a physical visual schedule, apps exist for mobile devices to provide visual schedules (for example, Choiceworks, available from www.beevisual.com [Bee Visual, 2016]) Similarly, instead of using a paper-based planner, individuals with mobile devices (for example, smartphones, tablets) can use apps to record their assignments and activities as well as organize their time (that is, iHomework 2 [Paul Pilone, 2016; http://ihomeworkapp.com], Studious [2016; www.studiousapp.com/planner], What's Today [Love Learning, 2015; www.whatstodayapp.com].

Another aspect of organization is note taking. While students can take notes via paper and pencil or a scribe (that is, another individual who takes notes for a student), students can also use technology. A mid-tech approach to support note taking is using an audio recorder. While audio recorders are inexpensive, they only record aural notes (that is, not what a teacher might write on the board), and a student may need to listen to the whole recording. However, technology such as the stand-alone Livescribe smartpen (www.livescribe.com) allows students to write notes on special paper while simultaneously recording the audio. To access the audio, the learner needs to tap on the paper where he or she wrote something connected to that portion of the class, and the audio for that sequence of time is played. Hence, a student with an intellectual disability could write key words and then listen to the audio notes from that time in class by later clicking on each key word. Rather than a stand-alone device, pupils who have mobile devices can take advantage of apps with similar features. For example, Notability (Ginger Labs, 2016; http://gingerlabs.com) allows students to handwrite notes on their mobile device as well as record audio, which is linked to the written notes. Notes taken on Notability can also be shared with others.

MONITORING

Both teachers and students can monitor a student's behavior. Teachers can monitor through a variety of means, including the low-tech options of paper and pencil. Technology is also available to support monitoring of student behavior. For example, educators can use the free **Web 2.0** or app technology ClassDojo (www.classdojo.com). With ClassDojo, teachers can record students' positive and negative (that is, needs work) behaviors through the day for their own records and/or IEP goal monitoring. Each student's daily and weekly behavior reports are also available to parents via an app. Other technology teachers can use to help monitor students' behavior, as well as allow learners to monitor their own behavior as a whole, includes apps that measure and visually depict the noise in a classroom (for example, Too Noisy [Walsall Academy, 2016; http://toonoisyapp.com]) or provide a countdown or timer (for example, Timer for Kids [Idea4e, 2015; www.idea4e.com] and Kids Timer [Skywise, 2016; www.apkplz.com/board/kids-timer]).

Students can also **self-monitor** their behavior, typically through low-tech paper-and-pencil means. Self-monitoring refers to identifying, recording, and regulating one's behavior, typically performance (for example, productivity or accuracy) or attention (for example, being on task) (Ackerman & Sharipo, 1984; Agran, 1997; Rafferty & Raimondi, 2009; Reid, 1996; Reid, Trout, & Schartz, 2005). (See Figure 6.8.) Technologies for self-monitoring include technology to prompt students to record and technology on which the behavior is recorded. In terms of technology to prompt the self-monitoring, a common method is by teachers raising their hands or showing a symbol or sign. However, teachers may also use audio signals (for example, beep, tone, or voice) or tactile prompts (for example, vibration through a specific device [for example, MotivAider or WatchMinder] or mobile device) (Bedesem & Dieker, 2014; McDougall, Morrison, & Awana, 2011). Technology for recording self-monitoring is typically paper-and-pencil, although more sophisticated technology can be used, such as recording on mobile device apps (see Figure 6.8). Educators and pupils can repurpose everyday apps, such as UPAD 3 (PockeySoft, 2016; www.youtube.com/watch?v=d2c5sdXu91s) TickTick (Appest Limited, 2016; https://ticktick.com/home), Remember the Milk (2016; www.rememberthemilk.com), Do It (Tomorrow) (Adylitica, 2014; www.tomorrow.do), and Wunderlist (6 Wunderkinder, 2016; www.wunderlist.com), to support behavior or performance self-monitoring.

SOCIAL SKILLS

Social skills represent another dimension of behavior, such as understanding how to interact with others, making good decisions, and regulating emotions (Reid et al., 2011). Technology can support social skills intervention and instruction. Aside from self-monitoring and video modeling to support social

FIGURE 6.8 Paper-and-Pencil and iPad Cooking Self-Monitoring Checklist Examples

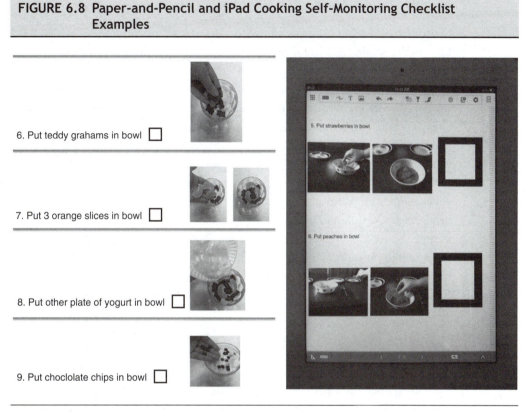

NOTE: The figure on the left shows paper-and-pencil self-monitoring of task completion of a cooking activity; the figure on the right shows using an app (that is, UPAD) on a tablet to self-monitor task completion of a cooking activity.

SOURCE: Reprinted from E. Bouck, T. Taber-Doughty, and M. Savage, *Footsteps Toward the Future: Implementing a Real-World Curriculum for Students With Disabilities* (Arlington, VA: Council for Exceptional Children, 2015), p. 38. Copyright 2015 by Council for Exceptional Children.

skills, the low-tech option of social stories or social narratives can also be used (Gray & Garand, 1993). With social stories, a first-person point-of-view story is written and supplemented with images, such as icons or pictures. Learners and educators can go through the story and role-play or answer questions using the skill presented (Kassardjian et al., 2014). Apps now also exist to support social stories, such as StoryMaker for Social Stories (Handhold Adaptive, 2016; www.handholdadaptive.com/StoryMaker.html), I Create ... Social Skills Stories (I Get It, 2016; http://igetitapps.com), and Stories About Me (Limited Cue, 2016; www.limitedcue.com).

SENSORY-BASED TECHNOLOGY

Sensory-based technology, while without a strong research base, is also used to support students with intellectual disability in education. Sensory-based technology includes devices or objects that provide sensory input or sensory stimulation. Low-tech sensory-based assistive technologies include Silly Putty, weighted vests or blankets, and different seating options. Silly Putty, Koosh balls, squeeze balls, and tactile rings, as examples, can serve as fidget toys, or handheld objects to provide sensory stimulation. Other students might use weighted vests, weighted lap blankets, therapressure brushes, swings, or bubble panels as sensory-based assistive technology. Instead of typical classroom chairs, some pupils might benefit from the use of seat cushions filled with air, beads, beans, or foam or a therapy or exercise ball as a seat. Despite the interest in and use of sensory-based assistive technologies, a recent meta-analysis of the research on sensory integration therapy concluded the evidence suggested the effect of such interventions was weak for students with disabilities (Barton, Reichow, Schnitz, Smith, & Sherlock, 2015; Leong, Carter, & Stephenson, 2015).

CONCLUSION

Individuals with intellectual disability can use and benefit from a variety of assistive technology throughout their lives. Older research suggested common assistive technology for individuals with intellectual disability across the life span included technology for vision and hearing (for example, enlarged print, hearing aids), wheelchairs and associated technology (for example, ramps), adaptations to home living (for example, adaptive utensils), and computers (Wehmeyer, 1988). More recently, Bryant and colleagues (2012) found service providers to individuals with intellectual disability reported the following technology being used: adaptive utensils, picture-based cookbooks, computers, electronic organizers, audiobooks, augmentative and alternative communication, and cell phones. However, the majority of service providers reported their clients, including school-aged students with intellectual disability, used no assistive technology, suggesting a continual lack of assistive technology use by individuals with intellectual disability (Bryant et al., 2012; Wehmeyer, 1988, 1999).

Assistive technology for all students with disabilities, including pupils with intellectual disability, is likely to not only continue but also increase. Technology in general is becoming more standard in society, and technology, including assistive technology, is also becoming more affordable. However, it is predicted that future assistive technology trends will likely follow those of technology in general: becoming more mobile, personalized, smaller, and faster (Bolkan, 2012). While mobile devices and their apps are already used in multiple ways for learners with intellectual disability (for example, video modeling/prompting, AAC), this trend is likely to continue. With apps, as with other stand-alone assistive technology devices, educators need to carefully select those that are appropriate and address the particular task, skill, or support the student needs. Educators are encouraged to carefully evaluate apps, which can range in price from free to upwards of $200. Different apps to support students with intellectual disability across academics, life skills, and behavior were discussed throughout the chapter. Table 6.9 provides additional apps to consider.

TABLE 6.9 Apps to Consider for Students With Intellectual Disability

TOPIC	APP	INFORMATION
Writing	Popplet (http://popplet.com)	Allows students to create mind maps for planning and organizing writing projects
Mathematics	MyScript Calculator (www.myscript.com/calculator)	Recognizes handwriting and computes, for example, basic operations, powers, roots, and trigonometry
Daily living/ independent skills	Number Line (http://catalog.mathlearningcenter .org/apps/number-line)	Can be used to support cost comparison; students can circle numbers in two different colors
Communication	GoTalk Now (www.attainmentcompany.com/ gotalk-now)	Customizable app (i.e., choose layout) modeled after Attainment's GoTalk devices; students can use symbols or insert own images
Social-emotional development	Daniel Tiger's Grr-ific Feelings (http://pbskids.org/apps/daniel-tigers-grr-ific-feelings.html)	Addresses social-emotional development through learning, playing, and singing about feelings

Chapter Summary

- Assistive technology devices are *anything* that can benefit a student with a disability.

- Assistive technology services are services that support the selection, acquisition, implementation, and maintenance of assistive technology tools and devices.

- Different frameworks, guides, and assessments guide individualized education program (IEP) teams in making assistive technology decisions for students with intellectual disability.

- Assistive technology devices range in terms of level of technology (for example, low-tech and high-tech) as well as purpose (for example, instructional aids, positioning and mobility, augmentative and alternative communication).

- Assistive technologies exist to support students with intellectual disability in preschool through Grade 12 in terms of reading, writing, and mathematics.

- Students with intellectual disability in preschool through Grade 12 are supported by assistive technologies in terms of life skills, including communication, independent and daily living, and leisure and recreation.

- Students with intellectual disability in preschool through Grade 12 are supported in terms of behavior, including organization, monitoring, social skills, and sensory integration through assistive technologies.

- Stand-alone devices as well as apps for use on mobile devices support students with intellectual disability in academics, life skills, and behavior.

Review Questions

1. What is the difference between assistive technology devices and assistive technology services?

2. Describe the different levels of assistive technology and provide an example of each that would benefit a student with an intellectual disability.

3. Name at least three assistive technology devices to support students with intellectual disability in academics and

explain how each device can support or benefit students.

4. Identify at least three assistive technology devices to support students with intellectual disability in life skills and explain how each device can support or benefit students.

5. Describe at least three assistive technology devices to support students with intellectual disability in behavior and explain how each device can support or benefit students.

Key Terms

assistive technology device (page 144)

assistive technology service (page 144)

assistive technology specialist (page 144)

educational technology (page 146)

app (page 146)

universal design for learning (UDL) (page 148)

text-to-speech (page 152)

mobile device (page 152)

switch (page 152)

Google Chromebook (page 154)

speech-to-text (page 154)

word prediction (page 155)

concrete manipulatives (page 156)

virtual manipulatives (page 156)

augmentative and alternative communication (AAC) (page 157)

self-operated prompting systems (page 159)

Web 2.0 (page 167)

self-monitor (page 168)

Organizations Concerned With Assistive Technology

Assistive Technology Industry Association (ATIA)

www.atia.org

Center for Applied Special Technology (CAST)

www.cast.org

Rehabilitation Engineering and Assistive Technology Society of North America (RESNA)

www.resna.org

Technology and Media Division, Council for Exceptional Children

www.tamcec.org

PART III

Preschool Students With Intellectual Disability

CHAPTER 7

Teaching Academic Skills to Preschool Students With Intellectual Disability

David F. Cihak and Joan Grim

Learning Objectives

After reading Chapter 7, you should be able to:

- Summarize key features of instructional practices that enhance academic skills for preschool students with intellectual disability.

- Describe how teachers can support emerging literacy, writing, math, and science for preschoolers with intellectual disability.

- Compare the different developmental levels of literacy-related skills and accompanying instructional strategies.

OVERVIEW OF PRESCHOOL STUDENTS WITH INTELLECTUAL DISABILITY

This chapter is written for teachers of young children with intellectual disability. Educators may use this chapter as a road map for setting up quality academic experiences for preschool students with intellectual disability. The material resources and instructional features recommended in this chapter are derived from research-based preschool curricula, environmental assessments, everyday routines, and play-based activities that sustain purposeful and engaging academic instruction. Since young children spend most of their early lives in the care of their families, parents' active involvement in assessment, planning, and interventions for their child is an important factor for designing and implementing programs (Gargiulo & Kilgo, 2014). Families and practitioners have a shared interest in developing academic skills for their child. Thus, families have the right and responsibility to share in the decision making regarding their child's instructional program. This chapter's premise is that all young children with intellectual disability can begin academic instruction in their homes, childcare programs, or preschools when these environments are designed to target academic skills. No longer is the question asked, "Should we teach academic skills to children with intellectual disability?" Rather, practitioners ask, "How will we teach them?" The purpose of this chapter is to describe the characteristics of quality academic instructional approaches for preschool students with intellectual disability in literacy, mathematics, and science within developmentally appropriate contexts. The practices presented in this chapter expand the definition of academics to include broader contexts in which academic concepts take place; the primary focus will be adapting instruction and incorporating strategies into typical preschool curriculum experiences.

CHARACTERISTICS OF PRESCHOOL STUDENTS WITH INTELLECTUAL DISABILITY

Preschool children with intellectual disability represent a heterogeneous group. These students exhibit a broad range of development in communication, emotional, motor, cognitive, and social-adaptive domains. Their progression through these developmental domains is often sequential; however, some skills may appear out of sequence, earlier or later than predicted, and in some instances not at all. From this perspective, the learning environment must be skillfully structured, and teachers must be attentive to what children are doing so they can design interventions that foster positive developmental outcomes (Gargiulo & Kilgo, 2014).

Typically, interventions in preschool programs target more developmentally advanced outcomes than those for infants and toddlers (Schertz, Reichow, Tan, Vaiouli, & Yildirim, 2012). One of the challenges in teaching academic skills to preschoolers with intellectual disability is their delayed and uneven developmental trajectory. Opportunities to explore and manipulate objects may be limited by motor delay while in other instances neurological feeding problems associated with deficits in oral-motor skills can inhibit the give-and-take of mealtime conversations. Children's combined cognitive and social deficits may also diminish playtime initiations and responses to peers (Gargiulo & Kilgo, 2014; Odom, Buysse, & Soukakou, 2011). Consequently, teachers must decide not only when to begin instruction given inconsistent or nonexistent prerequisite skills but also what skills to teach (Goldstein, 2011; Wolery & Hemmeter, 2011). In order to meet the needs of preschool students with intellectual disability, it is important to know how young children with and without disabilities learn as well as how to customize teaching strategies to meet specific learning needs.

AN INSTRUCTIONAL STRATEGY MODEL FOR PRESCHOOL STUDENTS WITH INTELLECTUAL DISABILITY

The Division for Early Childhood (2014) recommends that early childhood special educators develop educationally and developmentally significant goals. Appropriate goals offer direction for designing and implementing programs for young learners with delays or disabilities. Goals should be determined by the child's strengths and challenges. Assessments should be used to determine individualized program plans that specify where teachers should begin instruction by accurately pinpointing the child's entry-level behaviors and outcome behaviors. Careful and appropriate assessment is necessary to determine and prioritize goals for targeted academic skills. Assessments should be conducted by a skilled team of professionals including the child's parents or primary caregivers before embarking on instruction.

Once assessments are completed, teachers are ready to begin teaching. A general instructional model is useful for teaching specific academic skills. The role of the teacher is to encourage active engagement in each step of instruction by embedding, prompting, and using reinforcement throughout each instructional session. Preschoolers with intellectual disability tend to need repeated and consistent feedback on their behavior. For example, teachers can give children social reinforcement (it's more natural), such as praise, hugs, or other signs of affection, throughout or pair social reinforcement with tangible or edible items. Some children may need to hold a toy or a preferred object to help them maintain attention to the activity. Other children may need very brief sessions with regular reinforcement and feedback in order to learn important behaviors such as staying in the designated space, attending to the correct stimulus, following simple teacher instructions, or handling materials appropriately. There is also a tendency for young children with intellectual disability to need extra time to respond to teacher instruction, particularly when the task is unfamiliar. Educators need to give young children with intellectual disability adequate time to think and formulate a response before prompting. Preschool children who do not have several opportunities to respond independently and receive positive feedback for their efforts may become passive or disengage from the activity.

Teachers need to preplan all materials, as well as embedded supports and prompts, in advance so the pace of instruction flows naturally without interruption. A general instructional model is suggested as one way to facilitate efficient and effective teaching sessions. This model includes the following steps:

1. Identify and specify the goal.

2. Observe the child performing the skill.

3. Collect data on performance in the normal environment at least three or four times before beginning instruction and six to ten times during instruction.

4. Teach skill steps by giving support or prompts only where the child needs them.

5. Watch and wait for the child to perform the skill steps, and provide the least level of assistance.

6. Systematically fade prompts.

7. Check for maintenance and collect data.

8. Check for generalization and collect data.

9. Evaluate outcomes data.

10. Probe regularly for maintenance and generalization of the skill.

ARRANGING THE LEARNING ENVIRONMENT

Teachers often organize classroom space into specific interest areas such as sand and water play, painting and drawing, building blocks, dress-up, reading and writing centers, and musical as well as quiet areas. The spaces are usually filled with interesting and engaging materials as well as an assortment of accessible items from which the student may choose to engage. The teacher's role is to support learning opportunities that enable children to demonstrate active exploration of materials and guide them in initiating interactions with their typical peers (Gargiulo & Kilgo, 2014).

Classroom areas should have clear boundaries so children know when they are in a designated space. Activity areas need ample room for pupils to move and play freely with the materials. In Figure 7.1, notice the areas are divided up according to specific interests. Theme materials, books, and dress-up clothes can be rotated in and out of the areas regularly so students can engage with new and varied items. Favorite toys such as baby dolls, cars, blocks, and sensory toys like Play-Doh and sand should also be available for those children who are interested in these types of activities.

NATURALISTIC INSTRUCTION

It is generally recognized that learning develops in the context of a young child's positive experiences in everyday classroom activities (Robyak, Masiello, Trivette, Roper, & Dunst, 2007). Naturalistic instruction is based on the

FIGURE 7.1 Preschool Classroom Arrangement

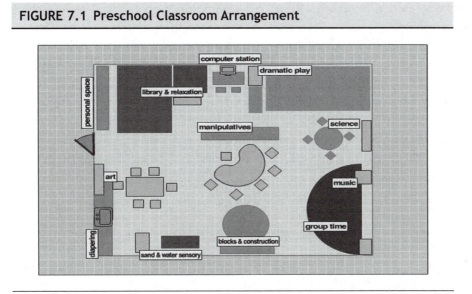

ways people normally interact with young children. In naturalistic environments, teaching opportunities are often spontaneous or on-the-spot happenings. Snack times, for example, are often overlooked everyday activities when teachers can model academic skills such as counting or reading product labels. **Naturalistic instruction** grew out of PL 105–17, which mandated that early intervention services be provided in the **natural environments**, defined as any "setting that is natural or typical for the child's age peers who have no disabilities" (34 C.F.R. 303.18). Although the preponderance of work in naturalistic approaches has been done in the domains of communication and language, Noonan and McCormick (2006) proposed an extension of these approaches to broader curriculum goals. They believe that "the naturalistic curriculum is a process model of curriculum, with content derived through environmental assessment, and instruction using behavioral techniques" (p. 82). Natural environments are the "sources and contexts" of intervention (Dunst, Hamby, Trivette, Raab, & Bruder, 2000). Preschool teachers create natural learning opportunities by planning their classrooms around child interests and themes. Interest promotes motivation, and motivation drives learning.

Preschool classrooms enhance a naturalistic approach when teachers construct child-centered themes and classroom learning centers that are aligned with student interests. Students with intellectual disability, like all preschool children, are fascinated by novelty. They enjoy hands-on learning. They explore by touching and tasting. Emergent science experiments and mathematic concepts are all around thoughtfully prepared classrooms when children begin making categorizations and comparisons. For example, after a teacher reads *The Very Hungry Caterpillar* (Carle, 1969), he takes his students outside to find caterpillars. They dig in the dirt and search leaves on plants. He talks about the shape and size of caterpillars ("fat" or "thin"; "big" or "little"). He looks quizzically at the children and asks, "Do caterpillars have legs?" He observes carefully how the child with intellectual disability responds to the question. For a child with intellectual disability, providing pictures of bugs with legs and without legs helps them visually distinguish bug characteristics during this search-and-find mission. Teachers can easily observe the things children want to touch and what they do when they search for answers.

ACTIVITY-BASED INTERVENTION

Naturalistic instructional delivery serves as a catalyst for **activity-based instruction** (Gargiulo & Kilgo, 2014; Pretti-Frontczak & Bricker, 2004).

Activity-based instruction takes advantage of daily transactions between teachers and students by embedding a pupil's goals from the beginning to the end of an activity. An activity-based model is guided by the practical philosophy of anytime, anywhere learning (Dunst, Trivette, & Raab, 2013). Teachers can coordinate learning opportunities for preschool students within everyday routines and activities. There are four major elements in activity-based instruction (Pretti-Frontczak & Bricker, 2004): (1) child-initiated transactions; (2) goals and objectives embedded in routine, planned, or child-initiated activities; (3) logically occurring antecedents and consequences; and (4) development of functional and generative skills.

Child-initiated transactions. The foundation of an activity-based model is the use of student interests in intrinsically motivating activities as a way to promote unprompted initiations. When children initiate actions, they show what kinds of things motivate them into action as well as their likes and dislikes. Learners with an intellectual disability may become mere passive observers if teachers do not make an effort to identify their interests. One helpful method of identifying student interests is through systematic observation. Teachers observe the choices pupils with intellectual disability make during the course of the day and note on their preferences, as illustrated in the box below.

SPOTLIGHT

Lauren is a 4-year-old child with Down syndrome and mild motor delays who attends her community pre-kindergarten program. One day, Lauren's teacher observed Lauren run to the art area and eagerly grab the paintbrushes and paint at the painting table where several other students were painting. Lauren observed the other students' paintings and copied similar figures on her paper. Her teacher decided to turn Lauren's highly preferred painting activity into a literacy event. She made a simple word picture table, as shown in Figure 7.2, and placed one copy on the paint cabinet and another on the paint table area. Whenever Lauren wanted to paint, she could point to the picture and color words to indicate the items she wanted. The teacher responded to her request by setting up a painting activity for Lauren. Her teacher noticed that Lauren was beginning to use more vocalizations while painting, and she started to initiate pointing at color words in the book-reading activity.

FIGURE 7.2 Lauren's Picture Words for Painting

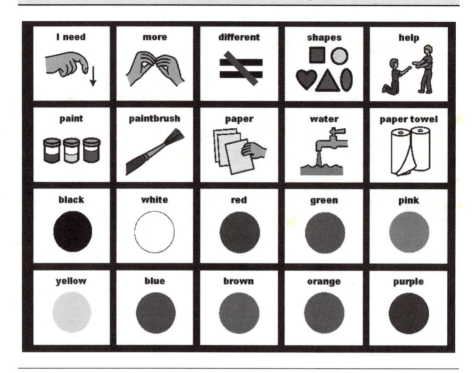

Embedding goals and objectives. Embedding a child's goals and objectives into the daily curriculum is a critical component of an activity-based approach (Gargiulo & Kilgo, 2014; Pretti-Frontczak & Bricker, 2004). Wolery (2005) defines **embedding** as

> identifying times and activities when a child's goals and the instructional procedures for those goals can be inserted into children's ongoing activities, routines and transitions in a way that relates to the context. It involves distributing opportunities to learn goals and apply instructional procedures for those goals across different activities, routines, and transitions of the day. (p. 94)

(Under IDEA 2004, short-term objectives are only required in an individualized education program [IEP] for students who take alternate assessments aligned with alternate achievement standards.) IEP goals are often embedded into routine and planned activities. **Routine activities** are those that occur as regular events during the school day such as arrival and dismissal, nap time, and recess. **Planned activities**, however, are those events that will not happen without a teacher's direction. Examples of these activities include involvement and engagement in various learning center activities like the reading center, computer center, or science corner.

Teachers can use an **activity demands** matrix to prepare the classroom areas and adapt or expand materials at varied levels of complexity. Demand dimensions should be considered when trying to alter and adapt classroom areas or activities for a student's particular need. For example, if the demand requires the learner follow a verbal directive, be sure the directive is depicted in a different format, such as providing the same message in visual or gestural forms. Because teachers aim to see meaningful outcomes from student participation, providing clarity will help the child perform the appropriate task requirements. A sample activity demands matrix completed for an entire preschool day is shown in Table 7.1.

Logically occurring antecedents and consequences. The third element of activity-based instruction is the use of logically occurring antecedents and consequences. **Logically occurring antecedents** are those events that elicit the student's desired response and are directly meaningful to the activity. Stimulus materials, objects, pictures, words and gestures, and physical assistance are often combined to ensure errorless responses. Name labels are an example of a visual stimulus that is so common in many classrooms that it becomes part of the learning environment. Engaging a child's attention to his name in print is an example of a logical antecedent when the name card serves a function that is immediately meaningful to the student.

Logical consequences are outcomes that follow a child's response in a meaningful way. The consequence comes as the result of completing a task or accomplishing a goal. A pupil points to the picture of a toy, and the adult gives her the toy. A child counts as he stacks ten blocks and then knocks over the tower. **Artificial reinforcers** (such as food, candy, or trinkets) are often paired with **natural reinforcers** like verbal praise or a smile, but then the artificial reinforcers are systematically faded. From the example in the box on page 183, the typical morning routine provides a meaningful situation to teach Benjamin his IEP goal, which is to identify his name in print. Each step of this

TABLE 7.1 Embedded Concepts and Activity Demands Matrix

CLASSROOM ROUTINES/ ACTIVITIES AND LOCATION	EMBEDDED CONCEPTS	ACTIVITY DEMANDS	MATERIALS	PARTICIPATION STYLE/ MEANS OF ENGAGEMENT
Arrival/ Departure Cubby	• Print awareness • Distinguish shapes	• Put personal items in closet/cubby	• Picture activity schedules • Monthly or weekly pictograph calendar of events (send home) • Name in print on an animal shape	• Send home daily/weekly calendar of school and class events and activities • Find name in an array of name shapes • Point to word, picture, object • Eye gaze at word, picture, object • Say word, picture, object
Breakfast/Snack/ Lunch Kitchen or group tables	• Rational counting • Rote counting • 1:1 correspondence • Environmental print • Science vocabulary	• Set table • Hand out utensils, cups, plates, napkins • Pass meal items family style • Pour • Scoop to self-serve • Social conversation • Clean-up	• Utensils, bowls, cups, placemats with print, pictures, topics of interest • Food containers • Milk cartons • Clean-up checklist	• Read daily menu; count and distribute spoons, forks, napkins • Read daily snack menu • Read container instructions (e.g., "Open here") • Read clean-up list • Distribute items • Read followed by a food choice • Perform clean-up according to checklist of clean-up procedures

Area/Location	Skills	Routines/Activities	Materials	Activities
Playtime/Sensory Activities/Artistic Expression Play centers	• Writing • Prewriting • Shared writing • Matching	• Inside/outside toys/equipment • Building blocks • Water/sand/sensory tables • Paint/draw/writing utensils • Puzzles • Dress-up	• Variety of high-interest picture books • Paper, cloth, plastic, and texture books • Variety of artistic media and drawing utensils (crayons, markers, pens, paintbrushes, sponges, paper, paint) • Computer drawing programs • CD player, music • Play-Doh • Stamps and stamp pads, stickers, etc. • Pictures and word labels posted • Routines in routine pictures	• Explore books • Turn pages, point to colorful pictures • Activate noise making computer program • Paint with fingers, hands, or feet on large paper • Make shapes, letters, or numbers out of Play-Doh, or stamp letters or numbers with a stamp pad • Finger paint or trace letters or name • Tear, cut, and paste pictures • Find plastic numbers, letters, objects in water or sand • Teach turn taking by trading pictures
Circle Time Carpet or group area	• Identifying words • Picture recognition • Pretend play story sequence	• Greeting a friend • Dialogic reading with pictures or objects • Singing with pictures and objects	• Printed names, photo, on shape • Storybooks • Music/nursery rhymes • Daily schedule • Attendance board with removable name/picture cards • Story props • Computer	• Select friend's name shape, give to friend and greet • Greet friend by activating AAC device or with a phrase • Picture card exchange to peers • Child uses props that represent story characters
Hand Washing Bathroom sink area	• Science vocabulary (cold/hot) • Reading left to right	• Clean hands	• Hand washing action checklist	• Teacher and child share read

One of 3-year-old Benjamin's IEP goals is to begin to understand that printed labels represent his name and the names of his peers. At arrival time, Benjamin practices his recently acquired skill of removing his jacket and hanging up his backpack. Arrival is also a logical time to begin directing attention to his printed name shape. The classroom cubby or closet area is a useful hub for introducing him to his printed name and to practice recently acquired skills for putting his personal items away. Benjamin's day at school begins with stop at his cubby to remove his jacket and deposit his backpack. He is eager to begin playing with his favorite toy train in the play area and runs into the play area without putting his belongings away. The teaching assistant quietly directs him to the cubby immediately as he enters the classroom. She directs Benjamin's attention to the name tag on his cubby, models reading his name, and prompts him to do the same. She points to his name and says, "Benjamin, look! The cubby has your name." She taps her finger across his name from left to right and says, "I see 'Benjamin.' Say 'Benjamin.'" He replies, "Benjamin." She points to the cubby. Benjamin responds by putting his backpack and coat in his cubby. He's accomplished his first literacy event and goes running to play with the train.

routine sets the stage for teaching and practicing reading when he goes to his cubby. His use or lack of use of the target skill in these situations gives teachers information on deciding the kinds of supports he needs. In this case, the teaching assistant prompted his focus of attention first to his name tag and second to watch her model read his name beginning from left to right.

Functional and generative skills. Functional skills refer to skills a child needs to negotiate his or her environment as independently as possible (Pretti-Frontczak & Bricker, 2004). Children with an intellectual disability often require explicit instruction in basic skills. If students are learning to count, they will need to learn to rote count and touch real objects by counting them in real situations. Acquiring **generative skills** is equally important as learning functional skills. *Generative* refers to a student's use of a skill in a variety of real or authentic situations under different conditions from where the skills were taught. If a pupil learns to sort round and square block shapes, a generative skill would be his ability to sort several different shapes of different sizes and dimensions. If a child identifies a photograph of the family cat, she can identify cats in a variety of pictures, books, and real life. Likewise, if a child claps rhythms to nursery rhymes, she can clap a vocabulary word into syllables (for example, ca-ter-pil-lar).

SPOTLIGHT

Benjamin's teacher makes the effort to model functional and generative use of her students' name labels. Each child's name is printed on a shape that begins with the same first letter as the child's name. For example, Benjamin's name is printed on a cutout of a ball (see Figure 7.3). She uses the name labels on the attendance flannel board. She gives students a basket of the class name labels and has them find their own names from the array to place on the attendance board. The students read the names of their friends who are at school. Before center activities, the teacher plans a Find-a-Friend game for Benjamin. She asks him to pick a friend to play with. Benjamin chooses a name by selecting a name shape, handing the shape to the friend, and inviting her to play. During art activities, the teacher writes the children's names on their artwork and concurrently emphasizes the sound of the first letter of the name and the name shape card. She prompts each student to look at his or her name on the paper and sound it out to ensure that there is a connection to their name and the print.

FIGURE 7.3 Student Name Shapes: Find-a-Friend!

Teaching Academic Skills to Children With Intellectual Disability

LITERACY

Literacy is the ability to obtain information from the environment with which to make decisions, alter the environment, or gain pleasure. It is defined as a combination of reading- and writing-related skills guided by some explicit practices of when, where, and why we read and write (Robyak et al., 2007). Preschool students with intellectual disability need special considerations and specifically tailored adaptations to enhance their literacy outcomes.

Create an inviting reading environment. The first step toward successful literacy instruction begins when the teacher prepares inviting literacy spaces in the preschool classroom. Thoughtful preparation of literacy spaces benefits children at every developmental age level. Some children with intellectual disability may come from impoverished families who cannot afford to purchase books while other pupils may live in communities without public libraries; consequently, these students enter preschool with little or no experiences with books. Such children will need to have time and classroom space dedicated to making book reading part of their daily routine. The classroom needs a clearly defined carpeted space with minimal distractions for quiet reading. Comfortable seating on beanbag chairs or large pillows makes this area a natural place for children to relax. Adult- and child-sized rocking chairs can also be frequently found in the reading area. Children who are fidgety may prefer to sit in a child-sized rocking chair or sit on an adult's lap to share book reading. Experimenting with books that have interactive features such as textures and sounds are effective in accommodating young children who have difficulties showing interest in books or attending when adults read books with them.

According to Dunst, Trivette, Masiello, Roper, and Robyak (2006), there are three phases of literacy development—preliteracy, emergent literacy, and early literacy. Because literacy skills begin to develop from birth until a child is an independent reader and writer, children with intellectual disability exhibit disparate learning characteristics (Cook, Klein, & Chen, 2016; Dunst et al., 2006; Linder, 2008). Children with intellectual disability often experience delays in basic communication, memory, and attending behaviors necessary for learning to read (Cook et al., 2016). The majority of preschool-age students with intellectual disability begin formal instruction at preliteracy or emergent literacy levels. Due to these characteristics, brief scripted examples of teacher responses and practice strategies are presented later in this chapter for each phase of literacy development.

Children's **entry-level skills** and characteristics and their interest in reading are related to positive learning outcomes (Raab & Dunst, 2006). Dunst et al. (2006) asserted child interest is one of the most important entry characteristics. Learning to read begins when teachers identify and observe child interests. Experiencing pleasure early in their lives learning from books makes it easier for students to experience later academic success (Massaro, 2004).

Preliteracy. Preliteracy represents the earliest stage of development from birth to age 15 months. Preliteracy development is grounded in early social communication skills and concept development that begins very early after birth (Cook et al., 2016). Behavioral precursors to literacy competency begin with a child's earliest social interactive skills. Formal reading has its beginnings in communication behaviors such as the ability to listen and respond to people, react to environmental sounds, coo and babble, take turns, and initiate using simple gestures (for example, pointing, showing, giving, or reaching).

Appropriate planning for teaching literacy skills to preschoolers with intellectual disability must take into consideration characteristic delays in referential language skills that support literacy. Students with significant delay experience delays in language that may be below their mental age (Cook et al., 2016). In light of research showing language competency is predictive of future literacy outcomes (Koppenhaver & Yoder, 1993), receptive and expressive communication is a major priority for students with intellectual disability (Gargiulo, 2015). For students with intellectual disability, their communicative behaviors come in varied forms and abilities. Some students with intellectual disability have limited or no communication skills while others have a wide range of communicative competencies.

Preschool students with intellectual disability are dependent on the presence of real objects and actions to make sense of them. The academic demands of literacy require students with intellectual disability to interpret and extrapolate meaning from language, pictures, printed words, and numerals. Playing with toys gives students background experiences in realizing their function. **Responsive teaching** means talking to students about toys as they explore them. A teacher's direct comments about a child's toy choice are critical for building a comprehensive literacy-rich environment.

SCRIPTED EXAMPLE: RESPONSIVE TEACHING

Child: Grabs a squeaky plastic book, waves it in the air, and bangs it on the floor.

Teacher: Observes the child waving and banging the book.

Teacher: Responds smiling and pleasant, "You want the book! Let's read together." Gently positions the book in the child's hands, right side up, pages turning front to back.

Teacher: Models turning the page and activating a squeaky "cat" noise. Pauses and waits for the child's response.

Child: Smiles and pats the page.

Teacher: Says, "The cat says meow," which helps the child activate the squeak by giving the least amount of assistance.

Teacher and Child: Together turn the page. Repeat.

NOTE: It is not necessary to finish the entire book at this time. As the child's interest wanes, close the book and say, "We're all done reading."

Responding to children with intellectual disability with objects, toys, books, or sensory activities is the optimal time for teachers to talk to children about their immediate interest. Mere exposure to experiences and literacy materials is not enough. According to Massaro (2004), it is the adult–child interaction around the early communicative event that is important. Responsive teaching practice means the teacher pays attention to the child's attempts to interact with literacy materials. A quick response to the child's attempts reinforces and strengthens new behaviors. Teachers can make any child attempt a pleasant experience by expanding on the child's interest in literacy materials. Dunst et al. (2006) maintained that young children must experience the pleasure of reading before reading for other purposes.

Since students with intellectual disability enter preschool at various developmental levels, it is critical that teachers begin instruction at the child's level of comprehension while considering his or her strengths and needs. It's important to remember that later literacy skills do not develop out of a vacuum but are built on much earlier behaviors. Activities such as adult–child lap games, singing to the child, adult–child word play, reciprocal imitation games, and touching and talking are foundational events. Looking at photos, recognizing pictures, and book handling are skills critical to later literacy performance.

Emergent literacy. Emergent literacy represents a wide range of behaviors in the developmental age range of 12 to 42 months. Students at this level attend to and interact with print in the environment. (See the scripted example below.) They engage in exploration but begin to show preferences for some books or toys over others. They understand familiar routines and categorize objects and related verbal language within those routines. For example, asked if he wants to have a drink, a young child hands his cup to the adult. Children at this age are beginning to intentionally communicate with gestures, speak in single words or phrases, attend to and label pictures, follow along with and comprehend story sequences, and attend to short video. Within this age range, children are beginning to make connections between gestures, spoken words, and print.

SCRIPTED EXAMPLE: SHARED READING

Child: Chooses a favorite book from an array of his favorite books. (The teacher or another child may help pick a book.)

Teacher: Sitting at the child's eye level, points to each word in the title and says, "The Very Busy Spider." Encourages the child to repeat the title or point to the word *spider*. Pauses and waits for a response.

Child: Says "pidaw" (attempt to pronounce *spider*).

Teacher: Says "Yes! Spider." As she speaks, she helps the child point to the word *spider* and moves his finger from left to right.

Child: Says, "Da pidaw."

Teacher: Points to the title and says, "Yes! The Very Busy Spider." Pause.

Child: Points to the word *spider* (with or without assistance).

NOTE: In shared reading, the teacher and child turn taking is balanced. The child and teacher have an equal number of turns to respond to the story.

Preschool students with and without intellectual disability benefit from instruction that gives them the ability to read and write in varied natural environments. This idea of **authentic literacy** capitalizes on students' interests and preferences. When adults share literacy events with children in meaningful contexts, they readily acquire the foundations of reading for personal and shared knowledge. Cook et al. (2016) referred to these contexts as **literacy events**. This shift in conceptualizing literacy as built in to all environments validates the role it plays in enhancing the quality of life for all learners. Examples of literacy events include finding product labels in daily living activities for cooking or shopping, reading TV or screen titles for entertainment, finding religious symbols at church, or reading and writing birthday cards for friends. For classrooms to have impact on literacy, the teacher needs deep knowledge of a student's competencies in communication, motor development, imitation, and play skills in order to match child strengths to the environmental adaptations (Guo, Sawyer, Justice, & Kadervek, 2013). Early behaviors that support the emergence of literacy are children's abilities to respond to questions and comments by teachers or other adults. Young children participate in interactive games, imitate rhythms and rhymes, repeat parts of songs and finger plays, or recall characters in familiar stories (Bruns & Pierce, 2007; Dunst, Gorman, & Hamby, 2010; Dunst, Jones, Johnson, Raab, & Hamby, 2011; Linder, 2008).

As students become exposed to printed materials in the natural events of daily activities, they begin to show interest in print such as product logos, fast-food symbols, favorite movie titles, or character names. Playing with rhyming words and the rhythm of poetry and music is a precursor to **phonological awareness**. Phonological awareness is hearing and understanding the sounds and rhythms in spoken language (for example, a child can separate and hear each word and syllable in the sentence "Daddy is home"). Teachers build phonological awareness by having children perform finger plays, imitate simple word play, follow rhythm in language and music, and discriminate the first letter sound in their name or in other familiar words. Sounds, rhythm, and word play emerge when pupils listen to music, songs, and rhymes. To get the most benefit out of rhythm and dance activities, students should be allowed to act out simple nursery rhymes with toys as props.

The following represents an example of emerging literacy practice for preschool-age students relative to phonological awareness. To address the connection between sounds and words, the teacher is using the nursery rhyme Humpty Dumpty. At story time, the teacher says, "We're going to play and say our Humpty Dumpty rhyme," as she shows a picture of Humpty Dumpty. To engage the children, the teacher demonstrates and engages the children by both saying and acting out the parts of the rhyme relative to sitting on and falling time. The teacher's goal is that the children connect their actions to the words in the nursery rhyme. As the teacher is reading, she emphasizes the rhythm in each phrase. After an initial reading or two, the teacher reads again, but leaves the last word of each line blank and allows the children to provide the missing rhyming words. The teacher then follows up with the children's understanding of rhyming words by asking such prompts as "What rhymes with *wall?*" The teacher can support students who are struggling by having them engage in the actions they used throughout the first few readings (for example, falling like Humpty Dumpty).

Early literacy. Early literacy is the time from approximately 30 months up to 5 years of age. As students progress from emergent to early literacy levels, they begin to bridge concrete concepts to more abstract symbols such as language, pictures, and print. Teachers make printed words and phrases directly relevant to what they see, hear, taste, smell, or touch. Early literacy behaviors are evident when children know words are separate from pictures, know which words go with pictures, pretend to read words, and later actually read the words (Linder, 2008).

Early writing develops at the same time as early literacy skills emerge. Children begin trying to read and write. They identify some letter names and attempt to copy shapes or letters in their name. Writing by children with intellectual disability can begin with writing through art. For example, a teacher can give children thick finger paint and wax paper and have them use their fingers to write their names or draw pictures. Similarly, students can trace letters in shaving cream or sand. Teachers can also give children who have weak grip strength an intensified writing experience by placing paper over rough materials like window screening or sandpaper. For example, a piece of window screening can be mounted on a 9- by 12-inch wood frame, and a piece of paper placed on top of the screened frame. Young children can then be allowed to write or scribble with a crayon. By feeling their scribble, children make the connection between holding a crayon and making marks on paper. More purposeful writing emerges when children attempt to copy simple lines and shapes or write their names on their work. Providing several choices of writing instruments gives children with unusual or delayed grip patterns opportunities to experiment with a comfortable writing grip. Positioning the paper upright on an easel and taping it in place will promote use of a three-finger grip for writing shapes and letters with precision.

Literacy is not simply an accumulation of reading and writing skills. Concepts related to later reading achievement emerge gradually when students make sense of, categorize, organize, and interact with the constant flow of visual, auditory, and sensory experiences (McGhee & Richgels, 2014; National

Early Literacy Panel, 2008). Teachers need to allow children to read and write throughout the day by having a center dedicated to just that in the preschool setting. Teachers can place an easel in the center of the room and write a different shape on it every day. Children can then attempt to copy it. Teachers can also create picture word sequences in each center area that has a "story" about using toys or other items in the center while also providing magnet letters so children can build their own words.

Another example that teachers of young children with intellectual disability can use to support writing is the use of shared writing involving a grocery list. Teachers can set up a play kitchen area in their classroom, including artificial food (or empty boxes of real food) and providing matching word cards available for labeling. The children can be encouraged and taught to decide what they want to purchase at the grocery store, such as through selecting the food and the matching word cards. Providing students with writing tools such as blank or lined paper and writing utensils encourages them to write their own shopping list. Teachers can easily differentiate this activity, such as by beginning to write the words for students who struggle more or providing multiple pictures that students can use to form the list with Velcro rather than writing.

In summary, Table 7.2 presents examples of classroom adaptations appropriate for students with intellectual disability across the three levels of early literacy.

EMERGENT MATH AND SCIENCE SKILLS

Early math and science skills have a big impact on students' successful school readiness. According to Zero to Three (2016), a strong set of early math skills predicts later math skills and later literacy skills. Math and science skills can be taught together by embedding math goals into science activities—or vice versa—since both math and science originate from inquiry and exploration. Preschool children enjoy exploring and experimenting with the elements in their world. Water, air, plants, and animals make fascinating topics for children with and without disabilities.

Special education teachers can draw from early language instructional strategies to prepare children for learning math and science. Classroom daily routines can be "math rich" and support "math talk" and "science talk." Just as in literacy, emerging math and science skills can be taught within daily routines and activities. **Seriation**, a math skill, can be taught by having students line

TABLE 7.2 Literacy Behaviors and Adaptations

LITERACY LEVELS	ENTRY-LEVEL CHILD BEHAVIORS	SUGGESTED TOYS/MATERIALS	ADAPTATIONS
Preliteracy	• Uses gestures for communication • Little or no interest in people around him or her • Passive or disengages in preschool activities • Little or no experience with books, rhythm activities, or literacy events • Identifies photo of self with one object distractor	• Music and singing songs • Colorful toys/materials that make sound • Toys/materials with shapes and textures • Toys/materials that can be shaken and mouthed • Photographs • Finger games/finger play with music • Books with textures, sounds, or mirrors • Computer programs with visuals and sounds • Blocks, balls of different weights and sizes • Labels on all materials/classroom areas • Puppets	• Headphones • Mobiles or switch-activated toys/CD player • Laminated photos • Large mirror mounted or positioned on carpet • Magnetic letters with grips • Page fluffers • Textured symbols • Wedges • Tabletop easel
Emergent Literacy	• Attends to communicative partner • Takes turn with prompt • Attends to objects/photos/pictures in familiar routines • Imitates a few simple gestures or finger plays • Begins to use signs or objects for communication • Begins to understand people and objects have names/signs/labels • Shows interest in books and writing materials • Uses markers to scribble, not always confined to paper boundaries • Identifies first name in print isolated • Recalls events immediately after occurrence with little detail	• Action schedules in print and pictures • Schedules with simple icons or photographs • Recorded books and stories • Watching and talking about video or computerized stories • Matching object to video representations • Paint, markers, crayons, easels • Play-Doh, cutters, molds • Shaving cream • E-paint computer programs • Tear paper for confetti • Books with 1-2 rhythmic phrases per page • Picture books • Labels on all materials/classroom areas	• Model reading and writing • Textured words, names, letters • Pictures paired with words • Page fluffers • Switch-adapted books, CDs, video stories • Touch-activated screens • Hand, head, or foot pointer • Light box • Large pencil/paintbrush grip • Positioning switches or toys at feet • Wedges • Tabletop easel

(Continued)

TABLE 7.2 (Continued)

LITERACY LEVELS	ENTRY-LEVEL CHILD BEHAVIORS	SUGGESTED TOYS/MATERIALS	ADAPTATIONS
Early Literacy	• Holds, carries, turns book pages • Takes/waits turn • Lets someone know he or she wants to look at a book • Searches for favorite picture • Participates in story reading • Interest in print/experiments with writing and drawing • Repeats familiar parts of stories/ songs/nursery rhymes • Points to or names signs • Understands text/pictures convey meaning • Makes connection between language and print • Recognizes or reads familiar words/ signs • Finds first name in print • Sorts two objects by color or shape attributes • Identifies name in print from an array • Identifies name and friends' names in print • Recalls events immediately after occurrence/some detail	• Books with 3–6 words, rhythmic phrases, or sentences per page • Books about routines/bath/bedtime/pets/ family • Cut, tear, color, paint, glue, and create a model alone or with peer • Role-play in dress-up • Variety of narrative and expository books • Touch screen or smartboard • ABC blocks/pattern blocks • Communication boards • Pretends to write notes • Makes identifiable figures in Play-Doh or with pens, pencils, markers • Attempts to copy name/shapes/letters • Shaving cream writing • Picture/word schedules • Action checklists words/sentences/pictures • Visual and auditory timers • Interactive computer programs • Sorting toys/games • Labels on all materials/classroom areas	• Model reading and writing • Textured words, names, letters • Pictures paired with words • Page fluffers • Switch-adapted books, CDs, video stories • Touch-activated screens • Hand, head, or foot pointer • Light box • Large pencil/paintbrush grip • Headphones • Mobile or switch-activated toys/ CD player • Laminated photos • Large mirror mounted or positioned on carpet • Magnetic letters with grips • Textured symbols • Puzzles with knobs • Wedges • Tabletop easel

up or be *first* or *last* to do something, like washing their hands after recess or going to the library.

While playing, children often realize that sorting objects, like toy cars or colored blocks, involves focusing on similarities and differences. Preschoolers will frequently place the item in some kind of ordered series. One-to-one correspondence develops when children match numbers to an equivalent number of objects. Prior to developing one-to-one correspondence, children should be able to compare numbers of things by recognizing differences or similarities in groupings. A key learning experience is having children visually compare sets. See the scripted example for one possible activity.

SCRIPTED EXAMPLE: COMPARING SETS OF DIFFERENT OBJECTS

Child: Makes a collage with leaves and sticks found on a nature walk.

Teacher: Says, "You have *more* sticks than leaves. Count the sticks."

Child: With the least level of help, counts five sticks.

Teacher: Asks, "How *many* leaves?"

Teacher and Child: Count the leaves together. The teacher prompts the child to touch each item as he says the corresponding number.

Teacher: Looks at student quizzically and says, "You have how many leaves?"

Child: Counts, "1, 2."

Teacher: Pointing to each item, says, "You have *more* sticks than leaves."

NOTE: For children with intellectual disability, emphasize the key concept words. Encourage the child to repeat them in his or her responses.

Likewise, a creative teacher can often find many ways to embed math and literacy goals into a science activity.

This science lesson is an engaging activity for children to experiment with different forces that move objects. It involves children moving different weighted objects by blowing them with their mouths and with straws. Cause and effect, distance, force, air, and movement are some of the science concepts children will experience in this lesson.

1. **Science Lesson Objective:** Recognize the basic concept that forces can move objects.

2. Visual supports like a picture sequence can be used to list the "Experimental Procedures." Posting the steps offers opportunities for children with and without intellectual disability to repeat the experiment in the future with other objects and to make predictions.

Concepts: air, force, distance, comparison, measurement

Vocabulary: far, move, high, low, air, blow, still

Large Group: Students will have an opportunity to blow a small pom-pom with their mouth first and then through a straw to see how much they can cause it to move. After everyone has a turn, the teacher will hold a blow dryer up to the pom-pom and let the children observe how far the pom-pom moves. The teacher will record the distances on a bar graph.

Small-Group Centers: Three different centers will be set up to give the students the opportunity to explore the concept that blowing air causes objects to move.

Children will rotate in small groups and experiment blowing a ping-pong ball, golf ball, and softball with their mouths, and how far each ball goes will be recorded in bar graph form.

Center 1: mouth blowing only

Center 2: straw blowing only

Center 3: blow dryer only

After the children have blown each of the three balls, an adult will record the distances of the mouth, straw, and blow dryer conditions on the bar graph. The teacher facilitates science and math relations by asking questions: "Which one moved farthest?" "How far did the ping-pong ball go with the blow dryer/straw/mouth"?

Students with intellectual disability can easily participate in all phases of this activity. Questions can be individualized according to their language and math comprehension skills—for example, "How many ping-pong balls did you blow?"

Just like their peers, preschoolers with intellectual disability enjoy hands-on exploration and problem solving. Teachers should use explicit labels when teaching math and science ideas. Math concepts emerge when students sort similar objects into groups. Teachers can draw students' attention to the interesting characteristics by using math talk to point out critical features such as quantity (for example, "one," "one more," "many," "big," "small"); shape (for example, "round," "square"); order (for example, "first, second, third,"); and time (for example, "begin," "all done," "yesterday").

Chapter Summary

- Preschool is typically the first school experience for many students with intellectual disability.

- Preschool teachers and school staff share the responsibility for ensuring that students with intellectual disability fully participate and engage in learning experiences that are available to their typical peers, including academics and emergent academic skills.

- Giving pupils the freedom to explore and learn from trial and error is one defining feature of an engaging and interesting learning environment.

- Cognitive development in children with intellectual disability varies widely, and this diversity can pose a challenge for educators.

- Effective instructional strategies often enhance academic learning outcomes for young children.

- Giving children a firm foundation in literacy, math, and science is vital for their future success in school.

Review Questions

1. Explain how a math lesson can be embedded into a typical classroom routine.

2. What is the definition of a logical antecedent? Logical consequences? Give examples.

3. Describe the ten steps of the general instructional model.

4. Why does a preschool teacher need to understand the relationship between early communications in a child with intellectual disability before beginning academic instruction?

5. Compare and contrast preliteracy, emergent literacy, and early literacy.

6. Discuss the key features of activity-based instruction.

7. A child with intellectual disability in your classroom does not identify her name in print. What types of activities and possible adaptations could you use to teach a child to identify her name? How will you know if she generalizes that skill?

8. How might you teach a child with the entry-level skill of looking at pictures in favorite books to read the words in that book?

Key Terms

naturalistic instruction (page 182)

natural environments (page 182)

activity-based instruction (page 182)

embedding (page 184)

routine activities (page 185)

planned activities (page 185)

activity demands (page 185)

logically occurring antecedents (page 185)

logical consequences (page 185)

artificial reinforcers (page 185)

natural reinforcers (page 185)

functional skills (page 188)

generative skills (page 188)

entry-level skills (page 191)

preliteracy (page 191)

responsive teaching (page 191)

emergent literacy (page 193)

authentic literacy (page 193)

literacy events (page 193)

phonological awareness (page 194)

early literacy (page 195)

seriation (page 196)

Professional Organizations/Associations Concerned With Young Children

Center for Early Literacy Learning

www.earlyliteracylearning.org

Council for Exceptional Children

www.cec.sped.org

Division for Early Childhood, Council for Exceptional Children

www.dec-sped.org

High Scope

www.highscope.org

National Association for the Education of Young Children

www.naeyc.org

CHAPTER 8

Life Skills for Preschool Students With Intellectual Disability

Megan Purcell and Teresa Taber Doughty

Learning Objectives

After reading Chapter 8, you should be able to:

- Describe preschool models and the theoretical framework for differing programs.

- Define the life skill domains that are the focus in preschool programming.

- Discuss how instructional objectives are prioritized for preschool students with intellectual disability.

- Identify the least restrictive instructional settings for preschool students with intellectual disability.

- Summarize evidence-based instructional strategies when teaching preschool students with intellectual disability.

- Describe key components of a life skills curriculum for preschoolers with an intellectual disability.

Preschool is the time before kindergarten when young children learn the basic skills for success in subsequent years. Here they learn a little about everything—social and emotional skills; the foundations of language, literacy, and communication; mathematics, science, technology, and social studies; and the arts. These skills prepare them for the increasing academic and social demands of kindergarten and beyond while encouraging the development of creativity, problem solving, cooperation, and independence skills. In this chapter, we will examine the historical foundation for preschool education, various curricula and approaches to teaching preschoolers, what and where to teach young children with intellectual disability, the general instructional and intervention frameworks, and how to specifically plan and prepare for life skill development in early childhood environments.

Overview of Preschool Students and Early Educational Options

Since there is no federal expectation for formal education for typically developing children at the preschool age, communities approach this early education in a variety of ways. Several types of preschool programs exist that may be private, federally funded, or state funded. Examples of private preschool programs include Montessori schools, Primrose Schools, KinderCare, faith-based preschool programs, and small community-based preschools. Federally funded pre-kindergarten programs include Title I–funded programs (Part A of the Elementary and Secondary Education Act), Head Start, Promise Neighborhoods, and Race to the Top–Early Learning Challenge programs. State-funded preschool programs are available in forty-two states plus the District of Columbia and are offered through both community-based organizations and school districts (Barnett et al., 2016). Private programs follow their own curriculum whereas federally and state-funded programs follow defined curricular standards. Table 8.1 provides a brief description of several preschool models.

Most preschool programs and curricula are based on a theoretical framework to promote early learning such as developmental learning theory (Piaget), sociocultural learning theory (Vygotsky), discovery learning (Bruner), social learning theory (Bandura), and behaviorism (Skinner) to name a few. Parents generally select their preferred preschool based on a number of factors including interpersonal teacher characteristics, safety, ability to meet their child's needs, location, cost, teacher–child ratio, hours, curriculum, cleanliness of environment, and quality of personnel (Glenn-Applegate, 2011).

Two prevalent private early learning models include the **Montessori approach** and the **HighScope curriculum**. In 1907, Italian physician and educator Maria

TABLE 8.1 Preschool Models

Bank Street Developmental-Interaction Approach	Developmental approach focusing on child's mental, social, emotional, and physical growth. Active learning through experience. Self-paced with teacher as a guide. Teaches lessons through hands-on activities.
Montessori	Developmental approach emphasizing nature, creativity, and hands-on learning. Teachers provide guidance.
HighScope Curriculum	Developmental approach. Participatory learning with hands-on experiences and supported through daily routines and well-organized classrooms. Provides planned experiences with basic academics: mathematics, reading, and science.
Direct Instruction Model	Behavioral approach that focuses on academics. Teachers lead small groups of children in planned lessons in language, mathematics, and reading. Minimal environmental distractors. Teacher-centered approach to learning.
Waldorf	Hands-on learning with a focus on rhythmic repetition in a supportive environment. Strives to generate a strong inner enthusiasm for learning. Instruction is teacher directed.
Reggio Emilia	Encourages exploration and focuses on community and self-expression. Students learn through art, projects, and activities of interest. No formal curriculum, but teachers will plan according to child interest.

Montessori designed an educational model that focused on a child-centered, natural learning approach. Heavily influenced by special education pioneers Jean-Marc Gaspard Itard and Edouard Seguin, she developed an education method that involved placing children in multiage groupings where they were able to learn from their older peers while concurrently emphasizing uninterrupted work time and guided work activities (American Montessori Society, 2015; Gutek, 2004). Today, these programs are available internationally and across the United States in mostly private programs but include some public schools. The costs of these private programs vary greatly (North American Montessori Teachers' Association, 2015).

The HighScope curriculum (Hohmann, Banet, & Weikart, 1979; Hohmann & Weikart, 1995; Weikart, Rogers, Adcock, & McClelland, 1971) is based on Piagetian developmental and constructivist theory where children plan, engage in, and evaluate their experiences while adults structure classrooms in a manner that facilitates active learning in areas of interest. It is an active participatory learning curriculum with an emphasis on interactions between children and adults and a "Plan-Do-Review" process (Georgeson & Payler, 2013). Preschool programs that use the HighScope curriculum allow children to have hands-on experiences and construct their own knowledge while engaging in activities. The adults support and expand children's thinking and reasoning.

In addition to private preschool programs, federally funded preschool programming is available. With the amendments to the Elementary and Secondary Education Act of 1965 (PL 89–10), legislators recognized the need for high-quality education for all individuals and especially targeted children living in poverty. Title I preschool programs were the result that provided for local education agencies and/or public schools to use federal funds to serve eligible children below the grade at which free public elementary education is provided (U.S. Department of Education, 2012). The curricula in these programs focus on improving children's social-emotional, cognitive, and health outcomes so that they may benefit from later school experiences. Their purpose is to prepare children in the prerequisite skills and dispositions they need for later success in school (U.S. Department of Education, 2012).

Head Start is a federally funded program of the U.S. Department of Health and Human Services that serves low-income children and their families. A child must be at least 3 years of age and the family must meet income eligibility requirements of being at or below the poverty line to be served through Head Start. (The Economic Opportunity Amendments of 1972 [PL 92–424] require that no less than 10 percent of Head Start enrollment be reserved for children with disabilities without regard to family income.) Head Start approaches curriculum from a framework based in the practices of ongoing child assessment, engaging interactions and environments, research-based curricula and teaching practices, and highly individualized teaching and learning. These tenets then align with Head Start outcomes that include approaches to learning, social and emotional development, language and communication, literacy, mathematics development, scientific reasoning, and perceptual, motor, and physical development (U.S. Department of Health and Human Services, 2015).

Increasingly, preschool education is provided in the public schools. According to Barnett et al. (2016), forty-two states plus the District of Columbia serve 4-year-olds, while twenty-five states plus the District of Columbia offer 3-year-olds public preschool programming. While not all states do so, some states require that children be deemed at risk to be considered eligible for public preschool programming. This includes children from low-income families, from single-parent families, and with identified disabilities who are likely to experience academic failure without intervention (Robbins, Stagman, & Smith, 2012). For children with a disability, legislation guarantees access to early childhood programming.

Finally, Title III of the Americans with Disabilities Act (ADA) (PL 101–336) ensures that most child care centers make reasonable accommodations to their policies and practices to include children with disabilities in their programs and may not exclude these children unless their presence poses a threat to the health and safety of others. As with general ADA requirements, the exception is child care centers run by religious entities or organizations that are exempt from meeting the ADA regulations. Since some state-funded preschool programs are served via community-based child care organizations, meeting ADA requirements is particularly impactful when these programs also serve young children with disabilities and developmental delays.

PRESCHOOL STUDENTS WITH INTELLECTUAL DISABILITY

Preschool children with intellectual disability are often labeled as having an intellectual disability or a developmental delay. While an intellectual disability may be identified early as a result of an existing condition such as Down syndrome, a **developmental delay** may be recognized as a child develops and exhibits challenges in meeting developmental milestones. Generally, a developmental delay encompasses language, speech, motor, social, emotional, or cognitive delays and is an all-inclusive term used to describe a child who is not meeting developmental milestones according to his or her age (U.S. Department of Education, 1999). The label is often used with young children from birth to 9 years of age to identify that the child is experiencing delays in one or more of the developmental domains but a specific diagnosis is not yet determined. These children are afforded access to special education services and may continue to receive these services under this label into their school career.

While preschool programming for children who are typically developing tends to be based on experiential learning with a schedule focused on child choice and less structured activities, a more direct instructional approach is used for early childhood special education programs where teachers can ensure the individual needs of children and their families are being met and **individualized education program (IEP)** goals and outcomes are being achieved. Yet, preschool experiences for children with and without a disability can be blended to allow all students access to an experiential early childhood environment while concurrently meeting specialized learning needs. The IEP often serves to facilitate this success.

An IEP is written for students age 3 to 21; however, for children from birth through age 2, a different document is used. Although outside the scope of this chapter, an individualized family service plan (IFSP) is a legally mandated written treatment plan for children with a disability from birth through 2 years of age. It is a family-based intervention plan that identifies the major outcomes for a child and family and includes details about how instruction will occur and learning will be measured (Pacer Center, 2011). Decisions are made based on assessment results that highlight a child's strengths and areas for growth. Specific developmental outcomes and goal statements are included in the IFSP, and data are recorded to determine the specific instructional strategies and approaches that will ensure the most positive outcomes for the child and family. The goals outlined in the IFSP build on developing skills that assist in each child's smooth and successful transition to preschool programming.

PRESCHOOL READINESS

Locally developed or nationally published assessment instruments are often used to determine a child's readiness for school. These instruments evaluate a child in comparison to the academic and behavior expectations of the local kindergarten program. In addition to the pre-academic and developmental skills in which young children will progress, teachers report a variety of skills that are even more important in improving the transition to and achievement in kindergarten (Ackerman & Barnett, 2005; Connors-Tadros, Dunn, Martella, & McCauley, 2015). These additional skills include communication, refraining from being disruptive, following directions, attending, turn taking and sharing, empathy toward others, and maintaining overall good health.

While readiness for preschool education is important to facilitate continued growth and development as children transition from home or infant and toddler programs, for children with intellectual and developmental disability, access to early childhood programming is essential. Eligibility for preschool special education is determined through Part B of the Individuals with Disabilities Education Improvement Act (IDEA 2004, PL 108–446) where children must meet the criteria established by federal and state rules and regulations. Federal eligibility criteria require that children be identified with a disability defined under Part B of IDEA. Most states require quantitative testing results and/or professional judgment of a disability to be deemed eligible for preschool special education while eight states (Illinois, Iowa, Kansas, Maine, Nebraska, New Hampshire, Texas, and Virginia) set their own guidelines or allow local education agencies to establish their own criteria (Danaher, 2011).

Preschool Programs for Students With Intellectual Disability

DETERMINING WHAT TO TEACH

Once eligibility for preschool special education services is determined, the approaches to and location of services will be determined, and an intervention program will be developed. Young children with special needs may receive educational services at home, in community centers, and/or in schools. Regardless of placement, preschoolers with a disability must have access to instruction that meets their individual learning needs. Generally speaking, homebound instruction focuses on speech/language development, motor skills, and self-help skills while public schools typically emphasize cognitive skills. Team members including the child's family, teachers, and related service professionals must document all programming and placement decisions in the IEP.

IEP team members may use a variety of informal techniques to determine the most appropriate instructional strategies and approaches for serving preschoolers with an intellectual disability. Informal approaches include naturalistic observation, transdisciplinary play-based measures, routines-based interviewing, functional assessment, and family outcomes evaluation. These informal strategies are used to determine the needs of the child and preferences of the family within the context of the environments where the child will work toward independence.

Naturalistic observation takes place under regularly occurring conditions and provides professionals an opportunity to observe a child's unaltered behaviors in his or her typical environments. Subsequent data will reveal a child's strengths and challenges and assist IEP team members in determining the exact tasks in which a child needs assistance as well as the possible strategies to provide for instruction. Understanding the environments in which a child will be learning and using new skills will improve the likelihood of future independence in the environment.

Transdisciplinary play-based assessment assesses a child's functioning in four developmental domains: cognitive, sensorimotor, social-emotional, and communication (Linder, 2008). Here, a facilitator engages the child in play while observers watch the child for the skills he or she possesses and those he or she still needs to develop or the supports required to perform. This assessment allows for observation of the child in self-directed and guided play rather than a formal assessment. The child's responses are more natural, and a factual picture of his or her skills is provided.

Conducting a **routines-based interview** allows service providers to understand the context of a family's daily activities and the strengths and challenges of the child's skills and behaviors within those activities (McWilliam, Casey, & Sims, 2009; Woods & Lindeman, 2008). This offers more information about the environments where the child engages and expectations within those environments than a formal assessment. Family members can identify the areas of greatest need for them to function more efficiently while concurrently building a positive relationship with education professionals. For example, a formal assessment finds that a child needs to work on eye–hand coordination; however, the family identifies self-feeding as an area of greatest need. Thus, formal assessment and a routines-based interview will provide the context for IEP goals and outcomes that address self-feeding as the focus of eye–hand coordination. Table 8.2 provides a sample set of questions that might be used during a routines-based interview.

TABLE 8.2 Sample Routines-Based Interview Questions

- Who lives in the house with your child?
- If there are other children, what are their ages?
- Why was your child referred for early intervention?
- What are the main concerns for your child and family?
- How does your day begin, and what is each person doing during this time?
- How does your child begin his or her day? How does your child participate in each activity? How much does he or she do autonomously? How does your child interact with others at this time?
- Is there a typical event or activity of concern? What about on weekends?
- If you could change anything about your life, what would it be?
- Which tasks/behaviors/skills would you like to be the focus of instruction?
- From the list of tasks/behaviors/skills, what is their order of importance?

SOURCE: Adapted from R. McWilliam, *Protocol for the Routines-Based Interview* (Chattanooga, TN: Siskin Children's Institute, 2009).

Functional behavioral assessment is typically used to determine the function that undesirable or ineffective behaviors serve for an individual. When conducted with a young child, this evaluation determines if a child is seeking attention, escape from a demand or setting, sensory stimulation, or tangibles by demonstrating a specific behavior (Alberto & Troutman, 2013). Once a behavior's function is identified, target interventions may be designed to specifically address the child's needs. For preschool-age children, a functional assessment is often used to determine their psychosocial functioning (psychological and social aspects of functioning) in the areas of role performance (fulfilling specific childhood roles across environments), thinking and communication, behavior toward others, moods and emotions, and self-injurious behaviors (Murphy et al., 1999). Questions that might be asked include "What are some of the child's favorite activities at home and preschool?" "What are his or her emerging skills?" "What behaviors need to be developed for success in future learning environments?"

Another means to determine educational programming is to consider family outcomes. Singularly focusing on child outcomes may not address all of the family needs. Since the child does not live in isolation, family needs may influence his or her growth and development. Thus, a family-centered approach to intervention recognizes that a child achieving his or her goals and outcomes may be directly impacted by family support and growth. Consequently, the IEP team may wish to consider family goals when constructing the IEP, although this is not a requirement.

Family needs may be determined through assessment results previously mentioned. One additional strategy to determine family needs is through the development of an **eco-map**. The eco-map process develops a visual representation of the social systems and relationships in the life of the family. This process allows for a true family-centered approach because individual family strengths, support systems, resources, and needs are specifically identified. McCormick, Stricklin, Nowak, and Rous (2008) identified the advantages of this approach as

> (a) establishing rapport with families to build a foundation for the provision of family-centered services, (b) appropriateness for families of culturally diverse backgrounds and families with limited literacy, (c) organizing information and facts and linking to the IFSP, (d) facilitating services in natural environments, and (e) maximizing utilization of informal resource. (p. 24)

TABLE 8.3 Steps in Developing an Eco-Map

STEP	PROCESS
Identifying Informal Supports	• Define informal supports • Determine family, friends, church members, neighborhood members, etc., who could provide support if needed to child and family • Describe what type of support may be provided and how often it is provided

Identifying Strengths of Relationships	• Draw lines between the informal supports and the child and family
	  ○ Thicker lines to indicate stronger relationships
	  ○ Dashed lines for more tenuous relationships
	  ○ Arrows to show directionality of relationship

Identifying Formal Supports	• Determine the physicians, therapists, child care providers, housing/financial assistance, etc., child and family receive

SOURCE: Adapted from K. McCormick, S. Stricklin, T. Nowak, and B. Rous, "Using Eco-mapping to Understand Family Strengths and Resources," *Young Exceptional Children, 11*(2), 2008, pp. 17-28.

While this process is aimed at infants and toddlers, this same approach would be beneficial to preschool and even K–12 programs. Table 8.3 describes the steps involved in developing an eco-map while Figure 8.1 illustrates an example of an eco-map.

In addition to the various assessments described previously and the development of an eco-map to determine IEP goals and outcomes, a final tool may be helpful for prioritizing the learning goals and writing those goals for a preschooler with an intellectual disability. The Goal Functionality Scale III (McWilliam, 2009a) was designed to measure whether targeted goals are functional as well as provide guidance to IEP teams as they develop instructional goals and objectives. This seven-question scale evaluates a child's participation in routines, desired behaviors, skill importance, and quality of criteria for acquisition, generalization, and time frame (McWilliam, 2009a). Using a Likert-like scale, this instrument allows professionals to determine the functional nature of skills for children as well as prioritize those that are critical. If additional goals are written, they may be evaluated using this scale and scored for their usefulness for a child. For example, the goal "Jane will use three- and four-word phrases to request assistance when dressing" would be scored for importance to the child. A score of 1 would indicate the goal is not important while a score of 4 reflects a very important goal. Figure 8.2 illustrates the questions that are used to determine the importance of a particular goal identified by team members.

FIGURE 8.1 Example of an Eco-Map

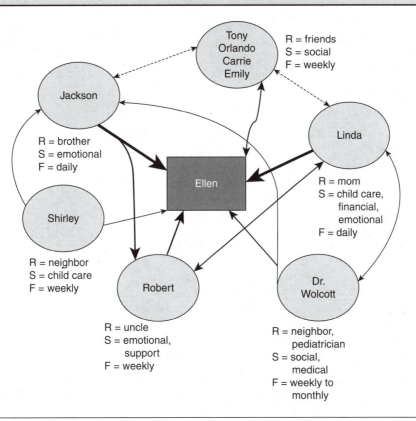

NOTE: R = relationship, S = support type, F = frequency.

SOURCE: Adapted from K. McCormick, S. Stricklin, T. Nowak, and B. Rous, "Using Eco-mapping to Understand Family Strengths and Resources," *Young Exceptional Children, 11*(2), 2008, p. 21.

DETERMINING WHERE TO TEACH

As with school-age students who receive special education services, the same expectation for a continuum of service options applies to young children with intellectual disability. Options may include the general education classroom, a special education class, special schools, home instruction, or instruction in hospitals or institutions. To meet the IDEA requirement and be considered a "general education" early childhood program, the majority (over 50%) of children enrolled must be typically developing (U.S. Department of Education, 2012). Since there is not consistently "general education" early childhood programming available in local education agencies, the continuum of options for young children may include the home, early childhood special education

FIGURE 8.2 Goal Functionality Scale III

Goal Functionality Scale III
R. A. McWilliam
TElOS—*Plus* Study
Siskin Children 's Institute
2009

Child ID:	IFSP Date:	District:
Rater:		

Outcome 1

To what extent does the goal/outcome	Not at all	Some—what	Much	Very much
1. Emphasize the Child's *Participation* in a routine (i.e., activity)? (*Child will participate in outside play time* not *child will participate in running*)	1	2	3	4
2. State specifically (i.e., in an observable and measurable manner) what the child will do?	1	2	3	4
3. Address a skill that is either *necessary or useful* for participation in home, "school," or community routines?	1	2	3	4
4. State an acquisition criterion (i.e., an indicator of when the child can do the skill)?	1	2	3	4
5. Have a meaningful acquisition criterion (i.e., one that shows improvement in functional behavior)? (We will know he can do this when he holds a spoon for 2 minutes not ...when he holds a spoon on 5 out of 7 trials)	1	2	3	4
6. Have a generalization criterion (i.e .. using the skill across routines, people, places, materials, etc.)? (...when he holds a spoon for 2 minutes at lunch and dinner)	1	2	3	4
7. Have a criterion lor the timeframe? (...when he holds a spoon for 2 minutes at lunch and dinner on three consecutive days or ...at lunch and dinner on 3 days in 1 week)	1	2	3	4

SOURCE: Adapted from R. McWilliam, Protocol for the Routines-Based Interview (Chattanooga, TN: Siskin Children's Institute, 2009).

classrooms, Head Start, state-funded preschool, private preschool, and community-based child care (U.S. Department of Education, 2012).

Once the IEP team determines the instructional needs and best approaches for positive child and family outcomes, the most appropriate location of services will be determined. Young children with intellectual disability may receive their services through home-, center-, or school-based settings. The determination of the location of services may also lead to the discussion of the child receiving his or her services in an inclusive or a self-contained setting.

Some young children with an intellectual disability may receive services in their natural environment—that is, their home. Thus, the home may be considered the least restrictive environment for a particular child. When providing **home-based services** for a child, professionals will come to the home for a designated period of time per week or per month to provide education and/or related services to the child and family. While in the home, these individuals will serve as a coach to the family in how to address the needs of the child within the family's daily routines.

While some youngsters receive early childhood special education services in their home, other children may be served in community-based early care and education programs. Although options for **center-based/school-based services** are typical settings for children 3 to 5 years of age, other preschoolers may receive services in community-based programs such as a private preschool or child care agency. These programs are often designed for children who are typically developing. Some private programs, however, are designed specifically for young children with a disability. These children may receive services in classrooms housed in local schools in programs designed for children with and without a disability.

The decision-making process for determining where to teach youngsters with intellectual disability is grounded in both the child's needs and the family's needs (see Figure 8.3). While traditional preschool settings may be the most effective for meeting the needs of some children, less inclusive and more family-based settings may be more appropriate. For example, if a child requires intensive medical and physical therapies, these may best be provided in a home-based or private child care setting. However, a combination of traditional child care and home-based settings may provide the strongest mix of settings to achieve learning and development goals. Here, a child would interact with his or her typically developing peers part of each week while concurrently receiving individualized services at home. Thus, when determining which settings are the best for serving a preschool child with an intellectual disability, professionals should first ask whether a particular setting will address the overall needs of the family as well as meet the learning needs of the child. As with older students with a disability, consideration should always be given to the child's access to the general education curriculum and his or her typically developing peers. A service provision process that incorporates a focus on current needs while simultaneously exposing young children to integrated learning environments will better prepare them for their eventual transition to inclusive kindergarten settings.

FIGURE 8.3 Decision-Making Model for Where to Teach Preschool Students With Intellectual Disability

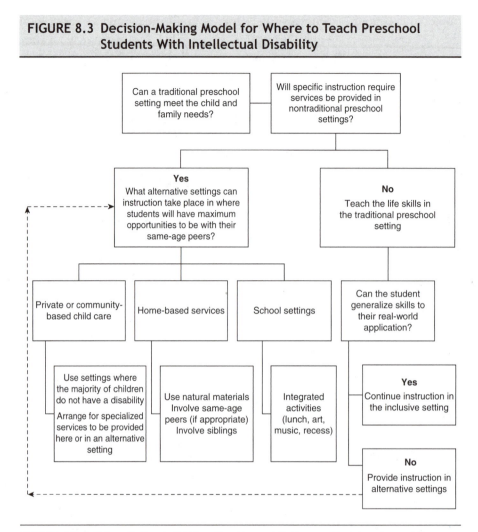

SOURCE: Adapted from E. Bouck, T. Taber-Doughty, and M. Savage, *Footsteps toward the future: Implementing a real-world curriculum for students with developmental disabilities* (Arlington, VA: Council for Exceptional Children, 2015), p. 30.

GENERAL INSTRUCTIONAL APPROACHES

When planning for and implementing classroom- or home-based services for preschoolers, developmentally appropriate instruction should be considered. **Developmentally appropriate practice (DAP)** requires providers to meet a child's age and developmental needs while simultaneously challenging a child to achieve increasingly complex goals (National Association for the Education of Young Children, 2009). DAP is the foundation for planning and preparing for children to develop and meet developmental outcomes at their own pace and in their own way. A program based in DAP possesses a strong understanding of how children learn. Teachers can generally predict the developmental process of children to plan appropriately for an increasingly complex sequence of skills. Specific DAP strategies include acknowledging children's actions and words, encouraging their efforts, providing feedback, modeling problem solving, challenging skills through increasingly difficult tasks, asking questions, providing assistance and information, and giving directions (National Association for the Education of Young Children, 2015). Together, these strategies facilitate flexibility in providing a challenging and stimulating learning environment that assists young children in developing skills across learning domains.

Following the early learning guidelines in each state is also important to ensure that young children are exposed to content areas that lead to mastery of skills in kindergarten. Every state has early learning guidelines, and nearly half include infants and toddlers in the expectations (Daily, Burkhauser, & Halle, 2010). Early learning guidelines are based in developmental areas that align with K–12 academic standards in areas such as language and literacy, early mathematics, early science, creative arts, social studies, and physical health/motor skills. Since quality interaction and play skills along with a strong foundation in social and emotional development are vital for young children to have positive outcomes in academics and life skills, these guidelines often include additional developmental areas of social-emotional skills and approaches to learning that K–12 academic standards may not contain. These guidelines offer a framework for teacher professional development and improvement in teaching and learning in early childhood programs and inform families of the expectations that early care and education programs will have on child progress and development.

For children with intellectual disability, the Division for Early Childhood (DEC) of the Council for Exceptional Children offers guidance on how to meet the needs of children from birth through 5 years of age who need additional supports to improve in learning goals and general development. These specialized strategies build on developmentally appropriate practices and the use of early learning guidelines to enhance a program to more fully engage and meet the needs of children with developmental delays, with identified disabilities, or at risk for disabilities. The DEC Recommended Practices are organized in topic areas that address how a provider plans and prepares for positive child outcomes including assessment, environment, family, instruction, interaction, teaming and collaboration, and transition (Division for Early Childhood, 2014). These guidelines are the added supports when planning according to developmentally appropriate practices and following the early learning guidelines is not enough to meet the individual needs of a child. Table 8.4 provides an example of the recommended practices in the environment area for youngsters with a disability.

SYSTEMATIC TEACHING STRATEGIES

Systematic teaching strategies facilitate a child's ability to learn and actively participate across a variety of instructional settings, tasks, and daily routines (Division for Early Childhood, 2015). Specific strategies a provider may use include those based on (a) designing the environment to encourage a child to state wants and needs, (b) embedding intervention strategies within the routines of the day, and (c) incorporating prompting strategies to encourage skills to be demonstrated. Each increases the likelihood of increasing a child's learning success.

A setting's **environmental design** focuses on ensuring that children and their families are at ease, a teacher's ability is maximized to manage the setting, and a child's ability to learn is supported (Klein, 2008). Design elements can include another teacher in a classroom or the intervention strategies that team

TABLE 8.4 DEC Recommended Practices: Environment

E1. Practitioners provide services and supports in natural and inclusive environments during daily routines and activities to promote the child's access to and participation in learning experiences.

E2. Practitioners consider Universal Design for Learning principles to create accessible environments.

E3. Practitioners work with the family and other adults to modify and adapt the physical, social, and temporal environments to promote each child's access to and participation in learning experiences.

E4. Practitioners work with families and other adults to identify each child's needs for assistive technology to promote access to and participation in learning experiences.

E5. Practitioners work with families and other adults to acquire or create appropriate assistive technology to promote each child's access to and participation in learning experiences.

E6. Practitioners create environments that provide opportunities for movement and regular physical activity to maintain or improve fitness, wellness, and development across domains.

SOURCE: Division for Early Childhood, *DEC Recommended Practices in Early Intervention/Early Childhood Special Education, 2014.* Available at http://www.dec-sped.org/recommendedpractices

members are targeting for the child in the home environment. For example, a child who needs to work on maneuvering his feet up and down stairs at home could cross a "bridge" to go between centers in a classroom. A child will have multiple opportunities throughout the day to cross that bridge and practice the skill leading to a more rapid achievement. Or, a caregiver at home could place a desired toy slightly out of reach so that a child must crawl to the toy to access it. This can occur several times throughout a day to encourage practice of the skill. In these cases, a well-designed environment becomes an integral part of learning and growth since the child is practicing the behavior in a contextually relevant circumstance and has multiple times to practice; achievement and generalization of the skill greatly increase.

Embedding intervention strategies within daily routines also facilitates a child's goal achievement and generalization (Dunst, Bruder, Trivette, Raab, & McLean, 2001). This strategy refers to instruction that is deliberately inserted into and distributed throughout the regular activities or routines of a child's day. Here, a child practices a skill when it is necessary so it has contextual relevance. For example, a child who is learning to follow one- and two-step directions might retrieve items for playing a game or articles of clothing when dressing. In the community, a child who needs to learn specific motor skills might learn to turn on a faucet to wash his or her hands in a restroom. Caregivers and instructional professionals can plan to embed instruction throughout the day so that the child experiences multiple opportunities to practice, learn, and generalize those that are priorities.

Finally, **prompting strategies** provide a child the assistance he or she needs to perform a task correctly so that reinforcement can occur. Prompting strategies (see Table 8.5) can involve antecedent stimuli and/or response prompts and include various cues such as verbal directives, physical gestures, picture models, or environmental design that occasion a behavior or those that are delivered after the behavior to reinforce the likelihood of the behavior being repeated (such as the system of least prompts and system of most prompts) (Alberto & Troutman, 2013). (Please see Chapter 5 on behavioral intervention for a more in-depth discussion of antecedent interventions for students with intellectual disability across the age ranges.) Providers and caregivers should strategically plan prompting strategies so that they are consistently used across environments and adults in the child's life. The more consistently prompts are used, the more quickly they can be removed as the child grows in independence of performing the skill and overall accomplishment of the goal.

TABLE 8.5 Antecedent and Response Prompt Strategies

ANTECEDENT STRATEGIES	RESPONSE STRATEGIES
Expanded and relevant feature prompts— 1. Providing additional elements to the natural cue 2. Highlighting natural cues that gain the student's attention	**Natural cues**—stimuli currently within an environment that may be experienced by the student while engaged in the target activity
Natural context prompts—teaching skills within the context in which they will be used	**Instructional cues**—initial directive provided by the instructor occurring before prompts are delivered (e.g., "Class, sit on your carpet square for circle time")
Associative prompts—pairing a concrete representation with an abstract concept	**Verbal prompts**—a verbal follow-up to the instructional cue (e.g., "Cindy, remember to raise your hand")
Antecedent modeling—demonstrating how to complete a task prior to asking the student to do so	**Gestures**—a slight physical hint for occasioning the correct response (e.g., point to the cabinet where a toy is stored)
Proximity prompts—physically arranging materials on the instructional plane to increase the likelihood the student will make the correct selection	**Response modeling**—demonstrating how to complete a task after the student demonstrates an inability to do so correctly **Physical prompts**—partially or fully physically assisting a student in completing a task

SOURCE: Adapted from E. Bouck, T. Taber-Doughty, and M. Savage, *Footsteps toward the future: Implementing a real-world curriculum for students with developmental disabilities* (Arlington, VA: Council for Exceptional Children, 2015), p. 32.

LIFE SKILLS FOR PRESCHOOL STUDENTS

To facilitate the movement toward kindergarten, preschoolers with intellectual disability should not only participate in educational programming alongside their typically developing peers to benefit from the curriculum in place but also experience enhanced instruction in life skills. For these children, particular attention is paid to growth and development in the domains of cognitive, communication, motor, self-help/adaptive behavior, and social-emotional skills. Interestingly, these skills are the same as those for preschoolers who are typically developing. When planning for and improving life skills in early childhood, providers are preparing the child for future success in which these skills serve as the foundation for further growth. Competency in and across developmental domains is vital for a child to be successful both academically and in life. Table 8.6 describes each of the life skill domains for preschool children.

TABLE 8.6 Developmental Life Skill Domains

DOMAIN	DESCRIPTION
Cognitive	These skills are often based on pre-academics such as early literacy, math, and science. Although this domain is often used to reference these pre-academic skills, consideration is given to more basic life skills such as understanding and following directions or understanding routines and schedules as well as foundational skills on which the more advanced pre-academic skills will build.
Communication	Children will express themselves in a variety of ways starting at birth. Infants cry, coo, whimper, and whine in order to get their needs met. As children develop, their communication strategies become more complex. Understanding what is communicated and expressed is clearly a life skill. Children must understand what is being communicated to accurately follow instructions, know when they are endangering themselves, know when it is time to switch activities in a classroom, and so on. As well, children must express themselves for basic needs to be met.
Motor	Motor skills (both fine and gross) are necessary for general health and physical growth and development. Strong motor skills are vital if a child is to become mobile and independent in tasks such as toileting, hygiene, feeding, and play skills.
Self-help/ adaptive	Children are expected to understand and care for their own needs, manage stress, have persistence to complete tasks, and demonstrate problem-solving skills.
Social- emotional	These skills include play skills, relationship skills, recognizing and labeling emotions, and managing one's own emotions.

SOURCE: Adapted from S. Odom, C. Peck, M. Hanson, P. Beckman, A. Kaiser, J. Lieber, W. Brown, E. Horn, and I. Schwartz, *Inclusion at the preschool level: An ecological systems analysis.* Available at http://education.jhu.edu/PD/newhorizons/Exceptional%20Learners/Inclusion/General%20Information/inclusion_preschool.htm

While the five developmental domains are functional in nature, to be meaningful for preschoolers with an intellectual disability, they should be embedded within the typical routines of their day (see Table 8.7). In doing so, individual skill achievement and generalization are greatly improved as the child focuses on target skills in the context in which they are needed. Three characteristics of functional skills that are part of a life skills curriculum are (a) the skills are matched to the early childhood curriculum to ensure multiple opportunities for practice, (b) natural cues are identified and used to occasion target behaviors and skills, and (c) natural consequences to behavior occur without the need for external reinforcement. An example of these characteristics is approaching peers to engage in play during free choice or outside time. The natural cue for this behavior might be the teacher dismissing children for recess, and a natural consequence is that the child is incorporated into play with his peers after successfully approaching and engaging them.

TABLE 8.7 Embedded Life Skills Across Daily Activities

	COGNITIVE	COMMUNICATION	MOTOR	SELF-HELP	SOCIAL
Story time	Answers questions	Contributes to the story, makes comments	Sits in chair or on carpet square	Uses tissue for runny nose	Takes turns, uses "inside" voice
Center time	Completes activities	Asks for help, interacts with peer	Grasps materials	Washes hands after handling messy materials	Assists peer, works cooperatively
Reading	Identifies letters, recalls details	Answers and asks questions	Turns pages	Covers mouth when coughing or sneezing	Takes turns, shares books
Outside play	Keeps score	Talks with peers and adults	Walks, runs, bounces ball	Dresses self for weather	Takes turns, shares
Meal/ snack	Identifies food items	Asks for food items or materials	Feeds self	Wipes mouth with napkin	Stands in lunch line, interacts with peers

Ensuring that cognitive, communication, motor, self-help, and social life skills are embedded throughout the curriculum and daily routines is fairly easy to implement when planning instruction for a preschooler with an intellectual disability. Planning should include a review of the child's IEP to determine instructional goals, alignment of the child's goals with daily activities, and identification of the materials and environments in which instruction will occur. For example, when addressing expressive communication skills, a teacher might ask children to name the characters in the story they are reading, answer questions about holidays during calendar time, or request white or chocolate milk at lunch. When fine motor skills are targeted for instruction, opportunities to button or zip a coat, use a pencil or crayon, or use a pincer grasp to select materials during arts and crafts may be provided. Cognitive skills may be taught across all activities. A child may be asked to identify numbers on a clock or practice one-to-one correspondence when setting the table for snack time (each child gets one napkin, one cup, and one box of raisins). Self-help skills beyond hand washing before meals or after using the bathroom might include using a tissue to cover one's mouth when sneezing or coughing, using utensils during meal and snack times, and putting on a hat and gloves when it is cold outside. Finally, social skills may include taking turns and sharing materials during play time, working with a classmate to build a block tower (cooperative play), or responding positively to demands, frustration, or criticism during any activity in which these challenges are encountered. Fortunately, each of these functional activities is age-appropriate for all preschoolers and serves as the foundation for much of the preschool curriculum.

To effectively engage children with exceptional learning needs in a classroom curriculum and achieve their goals, adaptations may need to be considered. These should be implemented systematically to support a child just enough to accomplish his or her goals and then be faded or removed so that the child will begin to perform the necessary skills independently. Milbourne and Campbell (2007) offer a continuum of these adaptations in *CARA's Kit: Creating Adaptations for Routines and Activities*. This continuum provides guidelines for developing adaptations that evolve from least to most intrusive. For example, providing adaptations to the learning environment such as labeling cabinets with pictures to facilitate room clean-up would be considered the least intrusive whereas adjusting how instruction is provided (for example, physical guidance to put toys away) would be most intrusive. Figure 8.4 illustrates this continuum of adaptations, and Table 8.8 describes the steps for consideration when creating and implementing adaptations.

For preschool children with intellectual disability and their typically developing peers, the focus of curriculum is often based on social-emotional development and basic skills such as hygiene, toileting, self-feeding, and engaging appropriately in play. However, life skills exist in and across all developmental areas: cognitive, communication, motor, self-help/adaptive, and social-emotional. Table 8.9 illustrates some of the life skills per developmental domain that are important to

FIGURE 8.4 Adaptation Continuum

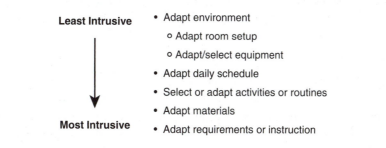

Least Intrusive

- Adapt environment
  - Adapt room setup
  - Adapt/select equipment
- Adapt daily schedule
- Select or adapt activities or routines
- Adapt materials

Most Intrusive
- Adapt requirements or instruction

SOURCE: Adapted from S. Milbourne and P. Campbell, *CARA's Kit: Creating Adaptations for Routines and Activities* (Philadelphia, PA: Child and Family Studies Research Programs, Thomas Jefferson University, 2007), p. 4.

TABLE 8.8 Adaptation Steps for Consideration

STEP	TASK	PROCESS
1	Understand the Children's Needs	• Understand performance so you can select adaptations
2	Decide What You Want to Happen, and Ask Yourself:	• What would you like to see happen? • What would the child/children be doing? • What would the adults be doing? • How would the environment look? • What would you like to hear happen?
3	Consider Adaptations	• Brainstorm possible adaptations
4	Select Adaptations You Will Use	• Record the adaptations to be used
5	Plan for Implementation, and to Ensure Success Ask:	• Why am I making the adaptation? • How will the adaptation improve the activity or routine? • What steps will I take to make the adaptation? • How will I know if the adaptation is working? What will I see and hear that will tell me the adaptation has improved or changed the situation?
6	Try the Adaptation	• Try the adaptation for at least one week and then reflect on previous questions • If any answer to the questions in Step 5 are "no," return to Step 3 and repeat the process

SOURCE: Adapted from S. Milbourne and P. Campbell, *CARA's Kit: Creating Adaptations for Routines and Activities* (Philadelphia, PA: Child and Family Studies Research Programs, Thomas Jefferson University, 2007), p. 5.

teach and will establish a strong foundation for later life and academic success. Life skills can also be embedded across preschool content activities and routines. Examples of skills taught in classroom routines are presented in Table 8.10.

CONCLUSION

Educational activities and instruction for preschool-age children with intellectual disability are almost identical to those taught to typically developing peers. Children at this age are learning basic life skills in academics, motor, communication, self-help, and social-emotional skills. What differs is that youngsters with an intellectual disability also have an IEP that specifically targets individualized instructional and developmental learning needs while concurrently considering family needs. As well, a range of early childhood special education service delivery

TABLE 8.9 Preschool Life Skills Per Developmental Domain

DOMAIN	SKILLS
Cognitive	• Grasp basic academics such as counting, letter recognition, and name recognition. • Hold writing tools appropriately, hold a book and turn pages, draw with tools, and identify basic shapes and matches. • Demonstrate attention, perception, and memory skills.
Communication	• Develop a communication system through spoken language or an alternative format such as sign language. • Build general vocabulary for use in play and around the learning environment. • Understand what is said (receptive communication) to complete tasks such as following directions. • Express wants and needs.
Motor	• Develop motor skills for play and self-care such as putting on a coat to go outside and play, caring for one's clothing during toileting, or using a spoon to self-feed. • Develop motor skills to engage with the environment (e.g., move from one center in the classroom to another, sit with peers at large- and small-group times).
Self-help/adaptive	• Understand and care for one's own hygiene needs. • Use self-feeding skills. • Demonstrate basic awareness of safety and safe behaviors to be safe in the classroom environment and less structured places. • Develop general awareness of how to lead a healthy lifestyle (e.g., making good food choices and being physically active).
Social-emotional	• Develop vocabulary for emotions such as happy, sad, mad, scared, and frustrated to label one's own emotions and understand them in others. • Self-regulate/understand consequences for behavior. • Understand turn taking during large group activities or play. • Understand and follow simple directions. • Understand routines of the day and the predictable order of activities. • Engage in play with peers during center time/free choice and outside play. • Demonstrate persistence in completing difficult tasks. • Make choices.

SOURCE: Adapted from R. Cook, M. Klein, and D. Chen, *Adapting Early Childhood Curricula for Children With Special Needs*, 9th ed. (Boston, MA: Pearson Education, 2016).

options and placements are available to preschoolers with an intellectual disability that include center-based programs, private preschool programs, home-based programs, and those provided within the local school system. The educational goal for all children at this age is to master the foundational life skills presented in the preschool curriculum to prepare them for success at the elementary level.

TABLE 8.10 Preschool Activities and Life Skill Domains Targeted During Daily Routines

DAILY ROUTINE	ACTIVITIES	LIFE SKILL DOMAIN
Large-group activities (calendar, story time)	• Turn taking • Following directions and rules • Vocabulary and concept development • Understanding the weather, current events • Classroom safety • Listening comprehension • Beginning literacy	• Cognitive, communication, social-emotional
Center time/free-choice activities	• Independent play • Sharing and turn taking • Academically based activities (block center: problem solving; sand/water: sensory exploration; math and manipulatives: problem solving, eye-hand coordination; emergent literacy: reading, writing, expressing ideas)	• Cognitive, social-emotional, communication
Small-group activities	• Arts and crafts (cutting with scissors, holding a writing utensil) • Emergent reading (expressive, receptive communication) • Individual skill development (IEP based)	• Cognitive, communication, motor, social-emotional, self-help
Outside play	• Engaging peers • Turn taking and sharing • Physical activities (running, biking, climbing stairs for the slide, playing with a ball, balancing on a beam) • Dressing for the weather	• Social-emotional, communication, self-help, motor
Meals and snacks	• Self-feeding (picking up small pieces of food, using a napkin) • Following instructions • Using utensils (fork, spoon, opening a milk carton) • Interacting with peers and adults • Choosing healthy foods • Setting a table (understand 1:1 correspondence, counting)	• Self-help, motor, communication, cognitive
Hand washing and toileting	• Using the toilet (flushing, wiping) • Washing hands with soap and drying hands	• Motor, self-care

DAILY ROUTINE	ACTIVITIES	LIFE SKILL DOMAIN
Activity transitions	• Following directions • Waiting in line • Activities while waiting for transition (standing on a particular number, letter, or color; counting; lining up by height) • Climbing stairs	• Cognitive, motor, social-emotional

SOURCE: Adapted from P. Deiner, *Inclusive Early Childhood Education: Development, Resources, and Practice*, 6th ed. (Belmont, CA: Wadsworth Cengage Learning, 2013).

Chapter Summary

- Programming for preschool-age children with intellectual disability is almost identical to that for typically developing peers.

- Preschoolers at this level may receive special education services under an intellectual disability or developmental disability category.

- Students may receive life skill instruction in a combination of settings including the home, public school, neighborhood center, or private school program.

- Families are directly involved in the planning and implementation of preschool service provision.

- Youngsters with an intellectual or developmental disability have an individualized education program (IEP) that guides their instructional service provision.

- Life skills for preschoolers with a disability are found in the domains of cognitive, communication, motor, self-help, and social-emotional.

Review Questions

1. What are some preschool models available to children? How do they differ from one another?

2. What assessment methods might be used to prioritize instructional programming for youngsters with intellectual or developmental disability?

3. What is a developmental delay?

4. What are the five developmental domains and some examples of life skills found in each?

Key Terms

Montessori approach (page 204)

HighScope curriculum
(page 204)

developmental delay (page 207)

individualized education program
(IEP) (page 207)

naturalistic observation (page 209)

transdisciplinary play-based
assessment (page 210)

routines-based interview (page 210)

functional behavioral assessment
(page 211)

eco-map (page 211)

home-based services (page 215)

center-based/school-based services
(page 215)

developmentally appropriate practice
(DAP) (page 216)

environmental design (page 218)

prompting strategies (page 219)

Organizations Concerned With Young Children With Intellectual Disability

**American Association on
Intellectual and Developmental
Disabilities**

https://aaidd.org

**Division on Autism and
Developmental Disabilities,
Council for Exceptional
Children**

www.daddcec.org

**Division for Early Childhood,
Council for Exceptional Children**

www.dec-sped.org

**National Association for the
Education of Young Children**

www.naeyc.org/yc

National Head Start Association

www.nhsa.org

PART IV

Elementary-Age Students With Intellectual Disability

Teaching Academic Skills to Elementary-Age Students With Intellectual Disability

David F. Cihak and Cate C. Smith

Learning Objectives

After reading Chapter 9, you should be able to:

- Understand how standards guide educational planning for elementary-aged students with intellectual disability.

- Identify academic instructional procedures across content areas.

- Summarize instructional prompting procedures.

- Discuss evidence-based practice for teaching academics to elementary-aged students with intellectual disability.

ELEMENTARY SCHOOL

For children with intellectual disability, the elementary school years are critical for developing a variety of skills including academic, social, and functional life skills. The years spent in elementary school allow children to connect with others, learn about the world, and imagine possibilities for the future. For the purposes of this chapter, we will define elementary school as kindergarten through eighth grade. Although instructional strategies and content presented will differ across grade levels, elementary school is a time in the life of each child that is highlighted by opportunities to learn, grow, and develop lifelong skills. Unique to elementary school are opportunities for students with intellectual disability to learn a variety of skills across different settings, such as team building during physical education, choice making in the cafeteria, and developing social skills in the general education classroom and during recess.

ACCESS TO THE GENERAL EDUCATION CURRICULUM AND ENVIRONMENT

The Individuals with Disabilities Education Improvement Act of 2004 (IDEA 2004, PL 108–446) mandates participation in the general education curriculum for all students with disabilities. While exposure to this curriculum is required, regardless of where services are provided, there are at least two specific reasons for considering the extent to which students with intellectual disability participate in general education classes. Participation in general education classes is an evidence-based practice directly related to academic outcomes for elementary students with disabilities. Students with intellectual disability who are educated in inclusive settings perform much better on measures of both social and adaptive behavior than similar students in self-contained settings (that is, separate classes or special schools). Students with mild, moderate, and even severe intellectual disability should be educated with peers without disabilities, to some extent, in order to access a teacher with expertise in the academic core content subject, learning materials and tools specific to that subject, and opportunities for learning alongside typical peers who can provide natural supports (Carter, Sisco, Brown, Brickham, & Al-Khabbaz, 2009; Hunt, McDonnell, & Crockett, 2012; Jimenez, Browder, Spooner, & DiBiase, 2012; Ryndak, Jackson, & White, 2013).

The general education classroom provides specific contextual factors, including "features of the physical setting, the activities, roles and contributions of the participants, the timing of events, and the interpersonal relationships" not often present or easily replicated in more segregated settings (Jackson, Ryndak, & Wehmeyer, 2009, p. 179). Moreover, Jackson and his colleagues (2009) observed increased opportunities for incidental and imitative learning as well as the inherent difficulties of providing general education curriculum instruction explicitly linked to grade-level academic content standards in self-contained classrooms, where special educators typically have simultaneous teaching responsibilities for students across multiple grades or age levels.

The importance of access to general education classrooms for elementary students with intellectual disability was also accentuated by the earlier work of Fisher and Meyer (2002). Fisher and Meyer found significantly higher gains for students in inclusive settings in both adaptive behavior and social competence than for their counterparts in self-contained settings. Although this study did not target academic achievement per se, the social competence measure included skills such as initiating interactions, self-managing one's own behavior, making choices among alternatives, and obtaining relevant cues—all essential skills for accessing the general education curriculum, regardless of the setting in which that curriculum is taught.

OVERVIEW OF ACADEMIC SKILLS FOR ELEMENTARY-AGE STUDENTS

When determining which academic skills are important for elementary students with intellectual disability, there are several factors to consider. First, the individualized education program (IEP) outlines the specific long-term goals and short-term objectives for each child who receives special education services. (Note, under IDEA 2004, short-term objectives are only required in an IEP for students who take alternate assessments aligned with alternate achievement standards.) Created by a collaborative team of stakeholders, the IEP is reflective of all skill areas, including academics, needed for the learner to be successful and receive a free appropriate public education. After considering the unique needs of the student, the IEP team should recommend the programmatic inclusion of relevant and important academic skills for the individual child. These academic skills include those appropriate for both current and future settings. It is important for IEP teams to think about possible future environments and careers for the elementary student with intellectual disability in order to fill any gaps that may be present in his or her education. It is with the future in mind that special educators design and develop programming to reflect independent living and adult life goals for all children with intellectual disability.

In addition to the IEP goals and objectives, there are other considerations when choosing academic skills and content. Specifically, academic content for all students must relate to general education content standards. The **Common Core State Standards (CCSS)** are standards that outline the English/language arts and mathematics skills that all children in kindergarten through twelfth grade should know at the end of each grade level, for states that adopted these standards (refer to Chapter 3 for additional information regarding the CCSS as well as www.corestandards.org). Note many states also have implemented content standards in other areas such as science and social studies. Students in kindergarten through eighth grade in general education classes work toward these grade-by-grade content standards. Content standards—including the CCSS—are critical for students in elementary settings with intellectual disability, as they serve as indicators of developmentally appropriate content. Teachers of individuals with intellectual disability should refer to the CCSS when adapting content to meet the unique needs of each learner. Once special educators have analyzed the CCSS—or appropriate state standards for those states that did not adopt the CCSS—to determine age- and grade-level-appropriate standards, the IEP team can determine which standards are important to include for the individual learner. It is also noteworthy that IEP goals should reflect back to a grade-level-appropriate content standard (Yell, 2016).

The CCSS were designed to facilitate consistency for students across schools nationwide regardless of factors such as socioeconomic status or school system resources. There are advantages and disadvantages to implementing the CCSS or other standards-based curricula for all children, including those with intellectual disability (see Table 9.1 for some of the advantages and disadvantages). In spite of the disadvantages, the majority of states require all students to have access to the content of the CCSS, regardless of ability or disability.

In order to provide access to grade-level content for students with intellectual disability, teachers have access to alternative and extended standards. All states have alternate assessments based on alternate achievement standards for students with the most significant disabilities (Browder & Spooner, 2011). Most students with moderate to severe intellectual disability (up to 1% of the students in a school district according to federal law) will qualify for an alternate assessment (Yell, 2016). Refer to Chapter 4 for a more in-depth discussion of assessments for students with intellectual disability. However, even students who complete an alternate assessment must have access to the general education curriculum.

TABLE 9.1 Advantages and Disadvantages of the Common Core State Standards

ADVANTAGES	DISADVANTAGES
• Evidence and research based	• Do not match developmental or cognitive abilities of all students
• Based on rigorous content that holds schools and teachers accountable	• Do not address the functional/adaptive skill areas of need
• Assume all students are competent and able to learn	• Cannot meet the individualized needs of all students
• Allow special educators access to grade- and age-appropriate content and standards	• May cause stress for students and teachers
• Prepare students for college and career readiness	• Are unrealistic for some students with severe or profound disabilities

It is important for educators of students with intellectual disability to be familiar with standards—state general standards (for example, the CCSS) and/or alternate (or extended) standards, as appropriate. Teachers are often tasked with creating IEP goals relative to content standards, which can be referred to as a standards-based IEP approach. Part of the challenge of providing access to the general education curriculum for students with intellectual disability is determining how to make it meaningful. Students may need reduced breadth (number of topics or objectives to learn), depth (the levels of understanding expected for each topic/objective), or complexity (the time, steps, and memory involved) compared to peers without disabilities. In addition to planning for inclusion of standards-based content, there are critical curricular components that must be included in a well-rounded academic curriculum. The following sections outline the literacy, mathematics, science, and social studies skills needed for all elementary students with intellectual disability.

LITERACY

Literacy may be defined as the ability to read, write, and communicate (Armbruster, Lehr, & Osborn, 2003). It is critical to teach literacy skills to elementary students with intellectual disability for a variety of reasons. First, literacy provides opportunities to have the same life experiences as peers without disabilities. Second, literacy allows these students to access a larger sphere of life including social relationships, employment, and recreation activities. A third justification is that literacy improves the quality of life for every literate individual. As educators of elementary students with intellectual disability, it is imperative to focus on literacy instruction for these and other reasons.

For practical purposes, literacy involves reading and writing to understand and communicate ideas in order to participate in society. In order to learn literacy skills, students must first demonstrate early skills known as **emergent literacy skills** (Browder, Ahlgrim-Delzell, Flowers, & Baker, 2012; Browder & Spooner, 2011). Emergent literacy skills include language awareness and understanding the conventions, functions, and purpose of print, in addition to phonological awareness. Language awareness encompasses not only oral language, but also a general understanding or awareness of written language (Browder, Hudson, & Wood, 2013). In order to understand the conventions of print, students must know that the presentation of the print (left to right, top to bottom) follows the same structure regardless of where the print appears. Functions of print involve awareness of the multiple uses of print (such as newspapers, menus, web pages, signs). Purpose of print refers to the fact that words have meaning and are used for multiple reasons. Finally, phonological awareness encompasses the broad skills needed to learn the sound structure of language including phonemic awareness by hearing and manipulating individual phonemes, rhyming, syllabication, onset (beginning sound), and rime (ending sound). Children with phonological awareness skills are able to identify oral rhymes, clap out syllables in words, and recognize initial and ending sounds. Many students without disabilities will enter school demonstrating some emergent literacy skills; however, most students with intellectual disability will not (Browder, Gibbs, Ahlgrim-Delzell, Courtade, & Lee, 2007). However, each child—including those with intellectual disability—may not follow the same sequential path of skill acquisition and may create his or her own path to literacy. One such literacy path was suggested by Chall (1996), which starts with emergent literacy and goes through reading to learn; reading to learn is typically a skill developed in later elementary school and focuses on content-area learning. See Table 9.2 for the stages and corresponding skills that develop within each stage.

One challenge with teaching literacy skills to elementary students with intellectual disability is the lack of books that are appropriate and engaging. Most traditional books are too difficult for learners with intellectual disability to read independently. Although some teachers choose to read these texts aloud to their students, this is not always an appropriate accommodation as many

TABLE 9.2 Stages of Literacy Skill Development

STAGE	SKILLS DEVELOPED IN THIS STAGE	HOW TO TEACH THESE SKILLS
Prereading	Emergent literacy skills	Discuss conventions of print such as reading left to right and top to bottom when reading a new book
Stage 1: Learning to Read	Initial reading skills including relationship between letters and sounds	Use word-building cards to allow students to combine beginning and ending sounds to make words
Stage 2: Learning to Read	Basic decoding skills and use of sight vocabulary	Play a sight word game where students read as many sight word cards as possible in 30 seconds
Stage 3: Reading to Learn	Reading to gain new ideas and knowledge	Allow students to choose their own book based on a favorite topic and read aloud together
Stage 4: Reading to Learn	Reading to understand multiple viewpoints	Provide books from different viewpoints in classroom library and read aloud together
Stage 5: Reading to Learn	Reading for construction and reconstruction of knowledge	Incorporate a variety of nonfiction books in classroom library to assist students with research projects

SOURCE: Adapted from J. Chall, *Stages of Reading Development* (New York, NY: Harcourt Brace, 1996).

children are still unable to comprehend the text when presented orally (Mims, Hudson, & Browder, 2012). Instead, teachers need to provide access to engaging and appropriate books for students with intellectual disability.

In order to provide access, special educators must provide physical and cognitive access to appropriate books. Providing physical access to books means that students must be able to hold and physically manipulate the book and pages. Books must be in an accessible place with time each day for reading. Classroom libraries must include a variety of genres and themes that are engaging for all students in the classroom. Books should also reflect the students in the class by including relevant family-, culture-, and disability-related themes. Children should be able to identify elements of their own lives in their classroom books. The books may be adapted to provide access for students with physical disabilities or fine motor impairments. Page fluffers (that is, low-tech devices designed by attaching a small object to the side of the page) may be added to the pages to allow students to turn the pages more easily (Bryant & Bryant,

2012). Page fluffers may be made of paper clips, Velcro, Popsicle sticks, or other materials and are attached to the edges of each page to allow students to grasp and turn individual pages.

In addition to physical access to books, students must have cognitive access to the books they read. The most important consideration in providing cognitive access is readability of the text. Many books for young children feature colorful pictures that represent key concepts and illustrate repeated story lines and thematic sentences that explain the theme (for example, *Brown Bear, Brown Bear, What Do You See?* by Bill Martin). Special educators can capitalize on these engaging features by using strategies such as repeated story lines, pictures, and main idea identification to support comprehension in elementary students with intellectual disability. For example, when reading *Brown Bear*, teachers can point to the colorful illustrations, read the words aloud, and allow students to turn the pages independently using tools such as page fluffers.

In addition to these strategies, there are other ways to adapt books to make them easier to understand for children with intellectual disability. Strategies such as adding picture symbol cards or three-dimensional objects for key words to each page help to enhance comprehension of main themes. For books with no thematic sentence (one that describes the main idea), teachers can create their own and place it in the book. For example, in *The Cat in the Hat* by Dr. Seuss, teachers could write the sentence "The cat is playing games and making a mess" and add it to each page. Seeing this repeated thematic sentence will help students understand there is a recurring theme of a mischievous and messy cat. Of course, educators can use alternative means to provide access to books, such as using books on tape or e-books to be played on a computer or tablet device (for example, an iPad). See Chapter 6 for additional examples of technology to support literacy for students with intellectual disability.

After adapting books, there are many approaches to teaching associated content. One approach to consider is the **story-based lesson** (Browder, Gibbs et al., 2007). Derived from shared story experiences known as read-alouds, story-based lessons use a structured process to deliver important literacy skills and content to elementary students with intellectual disability. This approach incorporates the use of engaging, grade-level picture books or adapted chapter books that have already been modified to provide physical access. Next, up to five key vocabulary terms are identified from the text using paired pictures when possible. Highlight the words in the text if needed. After identifying vocabulary, a repeated main thematic sentence is created to represent the main idea. Table 9.3 features the stage and corresponding implementation steps. Through incorporating strategies such as the story-based lesson, book adaptations for physical access, and creating cognitive access, educators of elementary students with intellectual disability can provide a meaningful and engaging reading curriculum.

MATHEMATICS

In addition to literacy skills, elementary students with intellectual disability must have access to high-quality mathematics instruction. To choose appropriate math skills for instruction, educators must consider the unique needs of the child, recommendations of the IEP team, and the mathematics content standards for the specific state. The National Council of Teachers of Mathematics (2000) believes all students should be held to high expectations, individuals with disabilities should have opportunities to learn new skills across their time in school, and learning experiences should be personally relevant and important

TABLE 9.3 Story-Based Lesson Format

STAGE	STEPS OF EACH STAGE
1. Anticipatory set	Offer student a picture or object to connect to content of book
2. Read title	Point to book title and read aloud
3. Identify author	Point to author and read aloud; discuss the author is the person who wrote the book
4. Prediction	Ask student to look at pictures or cover and predict the topic or content of the book
5. Open book	Model opening the book; allow student to open the book
6. Point to text	Allow student to point to words as you read aloud
7. Identify vocabulary	Identify five preselected vocabulary words
8. Repeated story line	Identify the repeated story line (either teacher created or embedded within text)
9. Turn page	Let student turn pages
10. Comprehension question/ review prediction	During or after reading the book, ask comprehension questions; review the prediction made by the student earlier

SOURCE: D. Browder, S. Gibbs, L. Ahlgrim-Delzell, G. Courtade, and A. Lee, *Early Literacy Skills Builder* (Verona, WI: Attainment Co., 2007).

to the student. According to the National Council of Teachers of Mathematics, there are five content areas that must be included in math instruction for all students. These five areas along with a sample skill and related activity are identified in Table 9.4.

There are basic concepts and skills within each of the five areas that must be included for fundamental understanding of mathematical concepts. Critical skills include counting words in sequence, demonstrating one-to-one correspondence, understanding the order irrelevance principle (the order in which objects are counted is unimportant), comparing quantities of objects, and basic addition and subtraction skills (Browder & Spooner, 2011). In addition to these basic skills, students must learn basic number sense and functional mathematics skills for independence. Basic number sense skills include understanding the meaning and relationship of numbers and understanding symbolic relationships (National Council of Teachers of Mathematics, 2000).

TABLE 9.4 National Council of Teachers of Mathematics Content Areas of Mathematics

CONTENT AREA	SAMPLE SKILL	RELATED ACTIVITY FOR ELEMENTARY STUDENT WITH INTELLECTUAL DISABILITY
Algebra: the study of patterns and relationships	Identify and create patterns (e.g., blue, blue, red)	Use counting manipulatives (concrete or virtual) to allow for pattern creation
Geometry: understanding spatial organizations	Match and identify shapes in the environment	Provide shape manipulatives for students to compare against objects in the environment
Data analysis: organizing and interpreting facts and data	Record observations on a chart	Ask classmates to vote for favorite meal and record answers on table
Measurement: defining attributes in standard format	Record volume, weight, and size of different objects	Use different-shaped objects and measurement tools such as scales, graduated cylinder, and ruler to compare
Number and operations: understanding quantity and number sense	Represent greater than, less than	Illustrate these concepts using objects or picture symbols that first are obviously different from one another and then have more subtle differences

SOURCE: National Council of Teachers of Mathematics, *Principles and Standards for School Mathematics* (Reston, VA: Author, 2000).

To improve number sense skills in elementary students with intellectual disability, teachers can solve mathematics problems together and then discuss the answer. Asking students if an answer "makes sense" encourages them to evaluate the answer and determine if the calculations were correct, or if the student should try to solve the problem again. For example, when adding 20 + 10, if the student solves for a sum of 400, the teacher should ask the student if the sum "makes sense" followed by a discussion. Mathematics skills that are both academic and functional, meaning they impact one's daily life, include money and purchasing skills, time management, and using a schedule or planner for task completion. Functional mathematics skills should be incorporated in daily instruction to assist elementary students with intellectual disability with generalization and maintenance of skills. To incorporate functional mathematics skills, special educators can implement daily practices such as reviewing a whole-class picture schedule each morning at group time, allowing students to pay for purchases in the cafeteria using coins and bills, and providing opportunities for students to use the calendar to identify important dates. (See Chapter 10 for further discussion of functional skills for elementary-aged students with intellectual disability.)

A key mathematical skill for all students, particularly as they increase in their elementary career, is problem solving—the goal of mathematics education. Browder, Trela et al. (2012) indicated the usefulness of incorporating story-based problems during mathematics instruction for students with intellectual disability. When designing a story-based problem, one strategy is to use the actual name of the student along with details from his or her life such as the name of a favorite cartoon character or pet. For example, when writing a math addition problem for a student named Kai, you may write the story-based problem as follows: "Kai is ready to go to the movies with his best friend Seth. It costs $9.25 to get into the movie. Kai has $7.00. How much more money does Kai need to go to the movie?" By incorporating a literacy-based approach, such as story-based problems, and using real elements such as names and favorite activities, students will have a personal context to understand and apply math facts and problems to real-life situations (Pugalee, 2004).

One of the most beneficial mathematics strategies for many elementary students with intellectual disability is using visual prompts and/or concrete objects. Potential visual prompts and/or concrete objects to teach math include manipulatives, picture cards, TouchMath (2015), number lines, and multiplication charts. TouchMath incorporates a series of "TouchPoints" that are added to corresponding numerals 1–9. For example, the number 1 features one TouchPoint at the top of the line. The number 2 features two TouchPoints (one at each end of the number). Numbers 6 through 9 feature double Touch-Points. **Manipulatives** are easy to purchase or create and are used to represent numbers of objects in a set or alone to represent one-to-one correspondence. Manipulatives may be any small (safe) objects that the child can use to count. Ideas include counting bears, Popsicle sticks, cardboard dice, or buttons. Again, objects should be chosen with the individual student in mind and be safe and age appropriate. Other useful tools include five and ten frames to represent numbers in a visual format and number lines to provide support for students.

SCIENCE

In addition to fundamental literacy and mathematics skills, elementary students with intellectual disability must have access to science concepts and skill development. Science concepts are often more difficult for students with intellectual disability as they require abstract thinking and skills such as hypothesizing, theorizing, and predicting. Previously, science instruction for students with intellectual disability focused on identifying plants or animals or other less functionally relevant academic skills (Browder & Spooner, 2011). Recently, educators have taken a different approach to teaching science. Instead of focusing on memorizing terms or identifying features of plants and animals, science instruction should focus on teaching students to be aware of their surroundings, develop their own methods of problem solving, and apply science concepts to their own lives. Additionally, science curriculum for students with intellectual disability should include functional academic skills such as personal hygiene, health and safety, and nutrition. (See Chapter 10 for further discussion of functional skills for elementary-aged students with intellectual disability.)

According to the Next Generation Science Standards (2013), the current science standards are for all students, including students with disabilities. The Next Generation Science Standards' motto is "All Standards, All Students"; these standards focus on performance expectations for all students. The performance expectations connect to scientific and engineering practices (for example, using mathematics and computational thinking, engaging in argument from evidence), crosscutting concepts (for example, cause and effect, systems and system models), and disciplinary core ideas (that is, physical science [for example, energy]; life sciences [for example, biological evolution]; earth and space sciences [for example, earth's system]; and engineering, technology, and applications of science [for example, engineering design]; National Research Council, 2012). Table 9.5 provides representative examples of performance expectations and related activities when considering elementary students with intellectual disability.

To assist students in developing science concepts and skills, special educators can choose from a variety of evidence-based practices and supports. For students learning basic vocabulary and concepts, texts should first be adapted (see the "Literacy" section on page 235). After adapting texts, teachers can incorporate the use of visual aids including picture symbols, models, and demonstration of concepts or scientific processes (for example, the water cycle or seasonal weather). In laboratory settings, teachers can combine instructional methods such as systematic instruction and task analysis along with visual aids to provide access to higher-order thinking skills such as predicting and analyzing results. For example, when teaching students about the chemical reaction between two elements, teachers can create a task analysis of each step of the experiment accompanied by a picture of each step (Courtade, Browder, Spooner, & DiBiase, 2010). To provide further opportunities for practice or review, teachers can use virtual experiment software applications (apps) for

TABLE 9.5 Next Generation Science Standards and Related Activities

PERFORMANCE EXPECTATIONS	RELATED ACTIVITY FOR ELEMENTARY STUDENT WITH INTELLECTUAL DISABILITY
• Use and share observations of local weather conditions to describe patterns over time (K-ESS2-1)	Record temperatures over a two-week period using an outdoor thermometer; compare and look for changes
• Make observations of plants and animals to compare the diversity of life in different habitats (2-LS4-1)	Examine the classification system used for plants and animals with visual aid
• Use evidence to construct an explanation for how the variations in characteristics among individuals of the same species may provide advantages in surviving, finding mates, and reproducing (2-LS4-2)	Compare features of organisms such as body parts, function, and environment
• Use observations to describe patterns of what plants and animals need to survive (K-LS1-1)	Create model of Monarch butterfly life cycle

SOURCE: Adapted from the National Research Council, *A Framework for K-12 Science Education* (Washington, DC: National Academies Press, 2012).

tablet computers, online video demonstrations, or web-based modules. (Refer to Chapter 6 for a discussion on assistive technology to support students with intellectual disability.)

SOCIAL STUDIES

Social studies is the fourth major curricular area in which elementary students with intellectual disability, like all pupils, must have access to content from the general education curriculum. Social studies curriculum includes five discipline areas: history, geography, civics and government, economics, and psychology. According to the National Council for the Social Studies (2002), there are ten themes that should be addressed in the instruction of social studies. Table 9.6 depicts the themes, a sample skill, and a related activity for each area.

In the past, typical instruction in the areas of social studies for elementary students with intellectual disability focused on tasks such as reading simple maps or understanding the purpose of agencies such as the post office (Browder & Spooner, 2011). Students had access to basic social studies concepts, but were unable to apply this knowledge to their own lives. However, educators are now making academic social studies content more relevant and meaningful to elementary students with intellectual disability by helping them connect to their home, school, and communities.

To support social studies skill development, there are a variety of strategies and supports. Again, texts must first be adapted using the strategies mentioned in the preceding "Literacy" section. Once texts are adapted, educators should focus on making the content meaningful for individual students by examining their needs and areas of strength. Tools such as visual supports and technology should be used to teach critical skills to students. Social studies content allows students to engage with their communities and environments and provides numerous opportunities for community-based instruction. Community-based instruction involves creating learning and skill practice opportunities in locations within the community for students with disabilities (McDonnell, 2011). Community-based instruction is different from a field trip in that the desired outcome is providing students with an opportunity to practice and apply the same skills (academic and/or functional) from the classroom in a community setting, whereas a field trip is designed to provide a fun and engaging activity for students. Researchers indicate it is best to transfer academic skills to real-world skills in actual community locations. (Refer to Chapter 10 for additional

TABLE 9.6 National Council for Social Studies Instructional Themes

THEME	SAMPLE SKILL	RELATED ACTIVITY FOR ELEMENTARY STUDENT WITH INTELLECTUAL DISABILITY
1. Culture	Identify one's own culture	Create a poster of holidays that are unique to the American culture
2. Time, continuity, and change	Understand changes in one's community over time	Interview a community member who has lived in the area for many years and ask about changes
3. People, places, and environments	Understand the roles of community members	Create a graphic organizer that shows the duties of five community members
4. Individual development and identity	Understand how identity is developed	Create a drawing showing what is important to the individual student
5. Individuals, groups, and institutions	Understand the development of individual responsibilities	Read a story about a child who took responsibility in an emergency
6. Power, authority, and governance	Know the roles of authority figures	Visit a law enforcement agency and ask questions about law enforcement
7. Production, distribution, and consumption	Describe the consumption of goods and services	Take a trip to a local store or distribution plant to discover how goods are provided to others
8. Science, technology, and society	Understand advances in technology	Use the smartboard in a lesson
9. Global connections	Connect to other cultures worldwide	Call students in another country on Skype
10. Civic ideals and practices	Understand civic ideals	Ask students to draw a picture of "freedom" and explain their design

SOURCE: National Council for the Social Studies, *National Standards for Social Studies* Teachers (Washington, DC: Author, 2002). Available at http://www.socialstudies.org/standards/teacherstandards

information regarding life skills for elementary students with intellectual disability.)

ACADEMIC INSTRUCTION

In order to maximize learning opportunities with their peers without disabilities, it is important for students with intellectual disability to be provided with access to grade-level content, needed accommodations (see Table 9.7 for sample instructional accommodations for students with intellectual disability across academic areas), and systematic evidence-based instruction. Elementary students with intellectual disability need access to instructional materials and activities that are age appropriate and that allow them to progress with their peers. Shared learning experiences with same-age peers provide opportunities to develop necessary social skills and to practice essential communication skills. The principles of **universal design for learning (UDL)** provide a framework for educators to (1) use multiple approaches to teach the content, (2) allow students to demonstrate knowledge in a variety of ways, and (3) use multiple techniques to engage all learners (CAST, 2015). Individualization, including any additional accommodations, is built into grade-level lessons. Adopting the principles of UDL is one way for teachers to individualize learning as well as

TABLE 9.7 Example of Common Instructional Accommodations

ACCOMMODATION TYPE	ACCOMMODATION
Presentation	• Guided notes or recorded notes • Larger print/font • Fewer items on a page
Response	• Scribe • Responding orally, as opposed to in writing • Calculators
Setting	• Preferential seating • Taking tests in another room
Timing	• Frequent breaks • Extended time

SOURCE: Adapted from E. Strom, *Common Modifications and Accommodations*. Available at https://www.understood.org/en/learning-attention-issues/treatments-approaches/educational-strategies/common-modifications-and-accommodations

maximize learning opportunities for elementary students with intellectual disability (Gargiulo & Metcalf, 2017). See Chapter 3 for a more in-depth discussion regarding UDL.

Individualized curricula should reflect the individual needs of the student, functional skills, age and grade appropriateness, and access to the general content standards. The current literature regarding best practices for teaching academic content to students with intellectual disability include systematic instruction, task analysis, providing opportunities for student response, in vivo instruction, adapted text, graphic organizers, and peer-mediated supports (Browder, Spooner, Ahlgrim-Delzell, Harris, & Wakeman, 2008; Courtade, Test, & Cook, 2015; Hudson, Browder, & Jimenez, 2014; Hudson, Browder, & Wood, 2013; Knight, Spooner, Browder, Smith, & Wood, 2013; Spooner, Knight, Browder, Jimenez, & DiBiase, 2011; Spooner, Knight, Browder, & Smith, 2012). Table 9.8 displays these best practices for teaching students with intellectual disability and examples of how they might be applied across specific content areas.

SYSTEMATIC DIRECT INSTRUCTION

In order for elementary students with intellectual disability to be most successful at learning, teachers must use **systematic instruction** (Collins, 2012). This is a very structured form of instruction that incorporates prompting systems that ensure a high level of success for the student. Systematic instruction often leads to **errorless learning** because the prompts that are used increase the likelihood of student success. Errorless learning refers to the design of the instruction in order to allow the learner to succeed at the task without error. As students become more successful in their responding, prompts are gradually faded so the student demonstrates the skill as independently as possible.

Critical features of systematic **direct instruction (DI)** lessons include highly sequenced instruction, clear and concise directions, teacher guidance, active student participation, and assessment probes in order to practice and master new knowledge and skills (Carnine, Silbert, Kame´enui, Traver, & Juongjohann, 2006). There are seven sequential parts to a DI lesson: (a) gain learner's attention, (b) review prerequisites, (c) present new content, (d) probe learning, (e) provide independent practice, (f) assess performance and provide feedback, and (g) provide distributed practice and review. Further explanations for each

TABLE 9.8 Evidence-Based Practices for Teaching Elementary Students With Intellectual Disability

PRACTICE	PROCEDURE	MATHEMATICS EXAMPLE	LITERACY EXAMPLE	SCIENCE EXAMPLE	SOCIAL STUDIES EXAMPLE
Systematic Instruction (Browder, Spooner et al., 2008; Courtade et al., 2015; Hudson et al., 2013; Knight et al., 2013; Spooner et al., 2011; Spooner et al., 2012)	Using defined, explicit, consistent prompting and feedback with fading to teach a defined academic response	Using time-delay or hierarchical prompts to teach math facts	Using time-delay or hierarchical prompts to teach academic language and vocabulary	Using time-delay or hierarchical prompts to teach parts of the body	Using time-delay or hierarchical prompts to teach map components
Task Analysis (Browder, Spooner et al., 2008; Courtade et al., 2015; Hudson et al., 2013; Knight et al., 2013; Spooner et al., 2011; Spooner et al., 2012)	The process of breaking a skill down into smaller, more manageable components	1. Use objects/pictures to add within 20. 2. Use symbols (+, =) to add within 20. 3. Solve addition/word problems using objects/pictures for sums within 20. 4. Solve addition word problems using symbols (+, =). 5. Solve addition word problems with an unknown number in any position using a symbol.	1. Define concept of main idea. 2. Identify main idea in text. 3. Define concept of detail. 4. Identify details in text. 5. Explain how details support the main idea. 6. Explain in writing how details support the main idea.	1. Communicate a scientifically oriented question. 2. Review evidence when responding. 3. Communicate explanation using evidence. 4. Connect explanations to scientific evidence. 5. Communicate and justify explanation using the evidence.	1. Identify the purpose of the map. 2. Identify the symbols used in the legend. 3. Use the grid to find examples of absolute location (latitude and longitude). 4. Determine the purpose or use for this map.

Opportunities to Respond (Browder, Spooner et al., 2008; Courtade et al., 2015; Hudson et al., 2013; Knight et al., 2013; Spooner et al., 2011; Spooner, et al., 2012)	Providing various opportunities for the student to practice new skills	Teacher identifies a geometric shape, then student identifies a geometric shape, then all students identify geometric shapes in the classroom.	Teacher reads a vocabulary word, then student reads the word, then all students read the word in unison.	Teacher reads a part of the body. Students say the part of the body and then point to it on a figure labeling the body part.	Teacher points to a latitude on the map, then student points to the latitude on the map, then all students point to the latitude on the map in unison.
In Vivo (Browder, Spooner et al., 2008; Courtade et al., 2015; Spooner et al., 2012)	Teaching a real-life application for the concept or skill to be learned; teaching in real-life settings using real-life materials	Using money to make a purchase and comparing prices while shopping	Teaching environment to navigate and make choices while in the community	Using laboratory materials to conduct experiments	Using the school map to identify locations
Adapted Text (Hudson et al., 2013; Knight et al., 2013)	Modifying or augmenting the text for accessibility, such as shortening the text, reducing the number of words, rewriting text to lessen text complexity, adding definitions, adding pictures and visual aids, and adding predictable structure	Teacher inserts pictures within a word problem.	Teacher rewrites a story and inserts the main idea throughout the story.	Teacher rewrites science text to reduce text complexity.	Teacher reduces the amount of text per page.

(Continued)

TABLE 9.8 (Continued)

PRACTICE	PROCEDURE	MATHEMATICS EXAMPLE	LITERACY EXAMPLE	SCIENCE EXAMPLE	SOCIAL STUDIES EXAMPLE
Graphic Organizers (Knight et al., 2013; Spooner et al., 2011; Spooner et al., 2012)	Visual representation of knowledge that structures information by arranging important aspects of a concept or topic into a pattern using labels	Student uses a sequential organizer to illustrate a series of steps or events in a chronological order to complete a math word problem.	Student uses a hierarchical organizer to present main ideas and supporting details of a story.	Student uses a two-column graphic organizer to list examples and non-examples of illustrated science concepts.	Student uses a comparative organizer to depict similarities among key concepts.
Peer-Mediated Supports (Courtade et al., 2015; Hudson et al., 2014; Hudson et al., 2013; Jimenez et al., 2008)	One or more trained peers providing assistance to their classmates	Peer reads a math word problem, and the classmate rereads the word problem.	Peer supports the classmate with unknown vocabulary as the student reads a story.	Peer supports the classmate with conducting a science experiment using systematic instruction.	Peer supports the classmate with completing a graphic organizer using systematic instruction.

SOURCE: Adapted from D. Browder, F. Spooner, L. Ahlgrim-Delzell, A. Harris, and S. Wakeman, "A meta-analysis on teaching mathematics to students with significant cognitive disabilities," *Exceptional Children, 74*(4), 2008, pp. 407-432.

step in a systematic lesson are presented within the framework of developing scripted lessons in the following section (Slavin, 1994).

Systematic instruction can also involve **explicit instruction**. Explicit instruction follows a structure of modeling, guiding, and then independent practice (Doabler & Fien, 2013). In the modeling portion of explicit instruction, a teacher demonstrates as well as uses think-alouds. For example, in using explicit instruction to teach subtraction with regrouping, the teacher would model how to solve a problem—such as with the use of base ten blocks and a place value chart—while verbally explaining (i.e., thinking aloud) this process. After the teacher models how to approach a few problems (in math, for example), the teacher moves on to guiding. In the guiding portion, the student is trying to solve or complete the task him- or herself, but the teacher is there to provide prompts and cues; corrective feedback is provided during the guiding portion. Finally, the student moves onto the independent practice phase where he or she does the work independently (Doabler & Fien, 2013).

SCRIPTED LESSONS

Systematic instructional lessons are important for student achievement and teacher accountability. Over the course of the year, teachers engage in a variety of routinized schedules and activities. Frequently, these routines drive the structure of the day regardless of whether students are actively learning new knowledge and skills. Developing "scripted" lessons is a straightforward task that educators can do by themselves and that can apply to virtually all course content, with all levels of students.

Typically, **scripted lessons** are planned for teaching academic skills that comprise a series of chained behaviors (that is, behaviors that have multiple steps to complete) such as spelling words and math computation, as well as discrete behaviors such as sight vocabulary and math facts. (Table 9.9 provides an example of a scripted lesson.) In essence, a teacher would plan a scripted lesson for acquisition of knowledge and skills where there are definitive steps to completing the academic task. Scripted lessons are based on clearly stated objectives that are communicated to students. These objectives specify what the students should be able to do or say after the lesson. However, scripted lessons should not be limited to academic tasks that teach concrete skills. Bloom (1956) identified six levels of learning within a hierarchy beginning with knowledge (basic recall) and progressing through comprehension, application,

TABLE 9.9 A Scripted Lesson for Teaching Two-Digit Addition With and Without Regrouping

STEP	SCRIPT
1	*Up to now we have been adding one number to another. Today we are going to learn how to add two-digit numbers together. Two-digit numbers have two values: a ones value and a tens value. In the number 34, the ones value is 4, and the tens value is 3. What is the ones value in the number 47?* (Choral response followed by praise.) *What is the tens value?* (Choral response.) *Good! The first thing we have to do when adding two 2-digit numbers together is to make sure that the two numbers are arranged so that the ones value of the first number is right above the ones value of the second number, and the tens value of the first is also right above the tens value of the second. When we copy a problem, where should the ones values of the two numbers be? Where should the tens values be?* (Choral response.) *Good.* *After we write the two numbers, we draw a horizontal line under the bottom number. Where does the horizontal line go?* (Choral response.) *That's right, under the bottom number. Copy this problem so the numbers are positioned for us to add them together: 16 + 22.* (Check each student's work.)
2	*Once we have copied the problem, we first add the two ones value numbers. What do we add together first, the ones value numbers or the tens value numbers?* (Choral response.) *Right, we add the ones values first.* *If the sum of the ones values is 9 or less, we write the sum under the ones place below the horizontal line. The sum of 6 plus 2 is . . . ?* (Choral response.) *Correct, it is 8. Write the number 8 below the horizontal line under the 6 and 2.* (Teacher models the step and checks each student's work.)
3	*If the sum of the ones value numbers is more than 10, we have to write the ones value sum below the horizontal line and write the tens value above the two tens value numbers that are above the horizontal line. If the sum of the ones values is more than 9, what do we do? Yes, we write the ones value of the sum below the horizontal line, and carry the tens value to the tens column.*
4	*Once we have added both the ones values together and written their sum below the horizontal line, we add the two tens value numbers together and write their sum below the horizontal line. What is the sum of 1 and 2?* (Choral response.) *Right, it is 3. Watch where I write the sum of the tens values.* (Teacher models.) *Now you write the sum on your paper.* (Teacher checks each student's work.) *Now I am going to write another problem on the board. Copy it and add the values together.* (Teacher gives several problems without regrouping; after checking answers, gives several problems requiring regrouping.)

NOTE: Italics represents teacher voice.

analysis, synthesis, and evaluation. Teachers can prepare scripted lessons that reflect advanced levels of learning. In the following sections, the procedures for scripting will be integrated into an explicit instructional plan.

Presenting new content. A primary defining characteristic of scripted lessons is that new content is presented through a bottom-up approach with new information presented in small steps. Before introducing new content, teachers should revisit pertinent skills and knowledge previously taught through use of a review. Using a review allows teachers to focus learner attention on the task, probe student understanding of content, provide review opportunities for students, and present corrective or positive feedback to students. Formats for reviewing previous content can take many shapes. For example, teachers may plan a series of higher-order thinking questions that are sequenced based on the Bloom (1956) taxonomy in order to review and assess previous learning. Teachers could divide the class into teams, and the students could devise questions for the other team to answer based on previously learned material. A commonly used review strategy is having students check homework assignments. The overall goal is to review previous content, check for student acquisition, and determine whether re-teaching is required for content necessary to work with the new information or procedures to be presented.

Next, instructional objectives should clearly state what the students are to say or do rather than employing ambiguous terms such as *to know* or *to understand*. For example, if a teacher's goal is for students to learn how to add two 2-digit numbers, the objective could be "After the lesson on addition, when given a set of ten problems, students will correctly hand-compute two 2-digit addition problems with regrouping with 90 percent accuracy in thirty minutes or less." This objective follows the format of conditions ("After the lesson on addition, when given a set of ten problems"), behavior ("students will correctly hand-compute two 2-digit addition problems with regrouping"), and criteria ("with 90 percent accuracy in thirty minutes or less").

After developing objectives, the next step is creating an explicit lesson plan that involves identifying the step-by-step progression for successfully completing the academic task. This is formally called a **task analysis** (Browder, Trela, & Jimenez, 2007). A complex activity can be broken down into subcomponent behaviors that are placed within a sequential order. The key is to ensure that each subcomponent identifies an observable action that the students must perform. To create a task analysis, simply list the first step in completing the skill, the second, the third, and so on until the complex action stated in the objective is completed. Table 9.10 outlines the task-analyzed steps for a special educator to use when teaching a student to write the name *Tyler*. The most common mistakes in creating task analysis activities include (a) skipping steps, (b) not specifying an overt action at each step, and (c) not having sufficient steps. Ideally, each task analysis sequence should have three to fifteen steps.

Teachers generally are masters of their content and have no trouble understanding the concepts. Since it is so easy for teachers to do complex activities, it is a good idea to double-check the sequence of your academic content to ensure that certain steps have not been skipped. Specifying an observable action at each step is critical because it provides the teacher and learner with an objective reference point to monitor progress. No one can objectively "know" if a person has actually acquired a skill until the individual demonstrates it. Teachers should continue breaking down the objective's activity until the first step is a behavior that everyone in the class can do without training. Table 9.11 highlights an example of how to delineate the steps of adding two-digit numbers with and without regrouping. This forms the basis for the scripted lesson that is to be followed to teach students the series of discrete behaviors identified in the complex action specified by an objective.

TABLE 9.10 Task Analysis Example for Writing the Name *Tyler*

STEP	ACTION
1	Pick up pencil
2	Move pencil to paper
3	Draw long vertical line in capital *T*
4	Draw shorter horizontal line for top of capital *T*
5	Draw small slanted line for left side of lowercase *y*
6	Draw longer slanted line for right side of lowercase *y*
7	Draw vertical line for lowercase *l*
8	Draw lowercase *e* in one stroke starting with vertical line in middle of letter and then curving around the top to the bottom to complete the *e*
9	Draw the small vertical line in the lowercase *r*
10	Draw the small curve at the top of the lowercase *r*

TABLE 9.11 Identifying the Subcomponents of Teaching Two-Digit Addition With and Without Regrouping

STEP	SUBCOMPONENT
1	Copy the problem (if not already on a provided sheet), making certain that one of the numbers is above the other, the ones and tens place values for both numbers are aligned, and the bottom number is underlined.
2	Add the ones place values together, and if the sum is less than 10, write the sum below the horizontal line aligned with the ones place of the original numbers.
3	If the sum is greater than 10, write the ones value of the sum below the line and carry the tens value by writing that value above the two-digit numbers of the problem.
4	Add the tens place values including any carryover from the ones sum to the left of the ones sum and below the tens values of the original numbers.

Guided practice. For each step of scripted lessons, the teacher provides clear instruction and explanation and models the step in order to provide guided practice to students. When learning is occurring at an accuracy rate of 80 percent or higher, teachers should transition to providing practice at the independent level.

INSTRUCTIONAL PROMPTING

Instructional prompting procedures are useful for teaching new behaviors. Instructional prompts may be defined as any teacher behaviors that cause the student to know how to do a behavior correctly (Wolery, 1994). Prompting is intended to help the student make correct responses in the presence of a particular discriminative stimulus so that reinforcement can occur. Although several forms of prompts may be used, it is critical to keep in mind that prompts assist the student in initial acquisition of the skill or behavior; they should be faded or reduced to less intrusive or more naturally occurring stimuli as the student's learning improves over time. Educators should choose the level of beginning prompt by collecting baseline data to determine the present level of skill performance for each individual learner. The following sections outline specific examples of prompts.

Modeling. Imitation is a natural form of learning, and using **modeling** allows teachers to capitalize on this natural inclination. For example, a teacher attempting to teach a student to write his or her name might model the behavior at the start of the lesson to show the student a demonstration. Many students easily imitate the behavior of the model. For example, the teacher asks the student, "Can you write your name?" Contingent on a student's incorrect response or no response, the teacher prompts the student, saying "Do it like this," and models the behavior of writing the student's name. The teacher models/demonstrates the correct sequence of behaviors required for successful completion of the academic task. Teachers should select a model based on the needs of the student and the academic task. Typical models include verbal (verbally stating each letter of a word in sequential order), written (writing steps to complete the problem at the top of the page), pictorial (picture cue demonstrating an action), or physical demonstration (demonstrating the physical actions required to complete the appropriate step). Instructional models should ensure student responding and be individualized to the needs of the student.

Verbal prompts. The use of specific verbal statements or feedback that tells a student what to do and how to do it, as opposed to simply directing the student to do something, is a **verbal prompt**. For example, the teacher may ask, "What comes after Thursday?" Contingent on a student's incorrect response or no response, the teacher verbally prompts the student by stating "Friday." Wolery (1994) noted that there are five types of verbal prompts: (a) those that tell how to do a behavior, (b) those that tell how to do part of a behavior, (c) those that give rules to follow, (d) those that give a hint, and (e) those that provide options. When a verbal prompt is given, it must be clear and effective. That is, the student must be able to respond correctly to the prompt. However, some elementary students with intellectual disability may not have acquired a level of receptive language sufficient to allow them to respond to verbal prompts. Therefore, the teacher must use other forms of prompts with the verbal prompt until the individual responds correctly to the verbal response.

Gesture. Some behaviors may be prompted with hand motions, pointing, head nodding, or another action that students can watch their teacher complete. **Gestures** are intended to provide specific feedback to the students so that they will perform the behavior accurately. For example, the teacher asks, "Who is the main character of the story?" Contingent on a student's incorrect response or no response, the teacher prompts the student by pointing to a picture or to the name of the main character of the story.

Physical prompts. A **physical prompt** is where the teacher provides physical contact to guide the student through the entire requested behavior, skill, or activity. When the student does not respond to less restrictive prompts (for example, modeling, gesture, verbal), physical prompts may be used to teach the student how to respond. These prompts may be a full physical or partial physical prompt. Full physical prompt is the teacher leading a student through the task by providing full physical assistance (hand-over-hand) to ensure correct use of the target skill. For example, the teacher may place his or her hand over the student's hand and guide the student to grasp a pencil, pick up the pencil, write his or her name, and put the pencil back on the desk. As the student starts to use the skills, the physical prompts are withdrawn but quickly reinstated if the student regresses or stops using the skills. Partial physical prompt is when the teacher provides minimal physical assistance to help the student demonstrate the target skill correctly. Minimal physical prompts might be assisting the student's wrist, arm, or elbow, as well as touching the student's hand to initiate the response and providing minimal physical guidance to achieve the desired response.

Visual prompts. The terms *visual prompts*, *visual supports*, *visual strategies*, and *visual cues* are used synonymously. **Visual prompts** might include, but are not limited to, pictures, photos, graphic representations, written words, schedules, or videos used to prompt a student regarding a specific behavior, rule, routine, task, or social response. Visual prompts are any tools presented visually that support student learning across educational settings (Knight, Sartini, & Spriggs, 2015; National Research Council, 2001).

Many teaching strategies involve some form of visual prompting. Illustrations in children's books are designed to aid students in identifying the printed word. Teachers may give examples of correctly completed math problems or allow a student to use a number line when learning computational skills. Picture prompts include any two-dimensional image (for example, a line drawing or picture of an actual object) that is used to prompt the learner or assist in task completion. Picture prompts have been widely used in teaching sight words to elementary students with intellectual disabilities (Browder & Minarovic, 2000), warning labels (Collins & Stinson, 1994), mathematics (Browder, Spooner et al., 2008), and computer use (Frank, Wacker, Berg, & McMahon, 1985). Several studies have taught students with intellectual disability to independently use picture activity schedules to complete tasks (Hume, Plavnick, & Odom, 2012). A picture activity schedule incorporates pictures (visual representations, line drawings, or photos of actual objects) listed in order of the corresponding schedule for the day. For example, a student who followed a schedule of art class, math, and then lunch may use a picture activity schedule with a photo of a paintbrush, a calculator, and a lunch tray. Knight et al. (2015) found picture prompts were an evidence-based instructional method for increasing on-task, on-schedule, and transition behaviors in children with intellectual disability.

The use of visual prompts offers some advantages for both teachers and learners. First, this strategy offers the potential for students to exert control over their behavior, diminishing the degree to which direct instructor supervision is needed. In addition, students may be more motivated to perform a task over which they have greater control (Koegel & Koegel, 1995). The transition of elementary students with intellectual disability to less restrictive environments is often hindered by difficulties in managing their behavior in the absence of external controls. Pictures may serve as a form of external control, which can assist students in accessing normalized learning environments.

Time delay. There is a strong evidence base for using **time delay**, a system in which the prompt is concurrently presented with the target stimulus and then faded with small increments of time over successive trials. Time-delay strategies are response-prompting strategies that are considered to be nearly errorless (Doyle, Wolery, Ault, & Gast, 1990; Walker, 2008). In a review of time delay and recognition of it as an evidence-based practice, Browder, Ahlgrim-Delzell et al. (2009) defined the essential features of time delay as

> initial zero-delay trials with an opportunity for the student to make prompted correct responses followed by subsequent trials in which the teacher delays the prompt by a small increment of time (seconds), so that the student may either anticipate the correct answer before the prompt or wait for the prompt. (p. 357)

There are two types of time-delay procedures: progressive and constant. Each of these two types uses a controlling prompt, zero-second trials, and delay trials (Wolery, 1994). A controlling prompt is any type of support provided by the teacher to ensure that the learner consistently produces the correct target behavior (Riesen, McDonnell, Johnson, Polychronis, & Jameson, 2003; Walker, 2008; Wolery, 1994). The controlling prompt will always elicit the correct response from the student and should be chosen by analyzing baseline data. For example, some elementary students with intellectual disability may only require a verbal prompt to complete each step of a task, but others may need a partial physical prompt. Zero-second trials are presented at the beginning sessions during some predetermined number of initial trials. During zero-second trials, the controlling prompt is delivered immediately after the target stimulus is introduced and task directions have been presented (Neitzel & Wolery, 2009). After the student has consistently demonstrated correct responses with zero-second delays, trials using a fixed delay (three to five seconds) or a progressively increasing delay (from one to two, then two to three seconds) are implemented. During delay trials, the target stimulus and task direction are presented followed by the delay interval (waiting three seconds), the controlling prompt, and another delay interval. While progressive and constant time delays are similar, there are important differences in the two strategies. With progressive time delay, the delay interval between the task direction and the controlling prompt is incrementally increased over a number of trials. For example, the teacher may begin with zero-second-delay trials, followed by one-second-delay trials. After the student has met a criterion for mastery with the one-second-delay trials, the teacher increases the delay to two seconds. The two-second-delay trials would continue until the student has met the criterion, and then the teacher would implement three-second-delay trials. With constant time delay, "the delay interval is increased for a specified and fixed number of seconds and remains at that duration throughout the instructional program" (Wolery et al., 1992, p. 240).

The basic procedure for constant time delay involves gaining the child's attention, presenting the target stimulus and task direction, waiting during the delay interval, and providing the appropriate consequences (Wolery, 1994). The presentation of the target stimulus and task direction indicates to the student that the target behavior should be exhibited. The delay interval allows the individual an opportunity to respond independently before assistance is provided by the teacher. If a student responds correctly after the task direction and before the controlling prompt, then the prompt is not delivered, but positive and descriptive feedback is provided. Use of highly positive and descriptive feedback (for example, "I like how you found the red bird!") is critical because it tells the student exactly what he or she did that was correct, thereby increasing the probability that the pupil will demonstrate the target behavior again. If the student does not respond, or responds incorrectly after the task direction and before the controlling prompt, then the controlling prompt is delivered, and a second delay interval is provided. Table 9.12 displays different student responses and time-delay procedures, according to Wolery, Anthony, Caldwell, Snyder, and Morgante (2002).

The following illustration describes techniques to teach students how to identify key words related to a story, specifically how to identify the title of a book.

TABLE 9.12 Constant Time-Delay Student Responses

STUDENT RESPONSE	DESCRIPTION OF RESPONSE
Unprompted correct response	Student demonstrates the target skill correctly without prompts within the time delay interval.
Prompted correct response	Student demonstrates the target skill correctly after being prompted.
Unprompted incorrect response	Student attempts to demonstrate the target skill without prompts within the time-delay interval, but performs it incorrectly.
Prompted incorrect response	Student attempts to demonstrate the target skill after being prompted, but performs it incorrectly.
No response	Student does not initiate the target skill during the time-delay interval.

The teacher would place the book in front of the student and gain his or her attention by using an attention-getting strategy (for example, saying the child's name or "Look") and presenting the cue or directive, "Find the title of the book." Pupils can respond verbally, gesturally (pointing to the title), or by using an alternative or augmented communication device. The teacher might gesture or point at the book's title and say, "Find the title of the book." When initially teaching the skill, the teacher would provide a series of trials at a fixed zero-second delay in order to ensure that the student demonstrates the correct response or skill (points to or says the book's title). There is no wait time between the cue ("Find the title of the book") and delivery of the controlling prompt (partial physical prompt). (The controlling prompt will be different for each student and is chosen using baseline data.) After the student imitates the correct response consistently, the teacher increases the delay between the cue and controlling prompt. Keep in mind that some individuals may need a more intrusive controlling prompt level (for example, modeling, partial or full physical prompt) in order to imitate the response. Additionally, the teacher should provide descriptive feedback and reinforcement for correct responses.

When the student has imitated accurately and consistently the correct response at the zero-second delay, the teacher increases the delay of time between the cue and the controlling prompt, allowing the individual to respond with greater independence. In most cases, the teacher implements a constant delay of four seconds between the cue and controlling prompt, if needed. The delay is dependent on the amount of time the student needs to process the teacher's cue and demonstrate the expected response. While some students may only require a short delay of four seconds, others may require a longer delay to process and respond to the teacher's instruction. The delay provides an opportunity for the student to perform the target skill independently before being offered the controlling prompt or support from the teacher. For example, the teacher may present the cue to the student ("Find the title of the book") and wait four seconds for the child to perform the target skill (student says or points to book's title). If the student's response is correct, then the teacher provides immediate positive feedback or reinforcement stating what the student did ("Good! The book's title is . . ."). However, if the response is incorrect, or if the student does not respond to the cue, then the teacher can provide the cue again and wait four seconds, or implement the controlling prompt (the prompt that will always elicit the correct response) to help the student perform the target skill.

Systems of hierarchical prompts. Another prompting alternative with a strong evidence base is the **system of least prompts**—an instructional strategy that delivers prompts only as needed to teach discrete or chained tasks. In a system of least prompts, the teacher may begin with a verbal prompt, followed by a gesture, a model, and then a physical prompt (Aykut, 2012; Neitzel & Wolery, 2009). In this system, the teacher only provides the prompt needed for the student to produce the response. Sometimes, however, the safety or motoric demands of a task suggest the need to begin with a more intrusive prompt such as physical guidance (Aykut, 2012; Neitzel & Wolery, 2009). An example of this is teaching handwriting. In this case, the instructor initially uses physical guidance and then fades the physical prompts over time to less intrusive prompts such as partial physical, modeling, gesturing, or verbal. Figure 9.1 identifies the types of hierarchical prompts from least to most and most to least supportive.

MONITORING LEARNING

Monitoring student progress is essential because it allows the teacher to adapt instructional procedures as the learner becomes more proficient or if the student needs assistance at using target skills. Teachers typically begin data collection as the teaching activity is implemented. Many of the practice opportunities provided to students involve questions that require either choral answers (probes) or individual answers (checks). Because content and skills are taught in small steps, student responses are almost always correct and can trigger positive feedback from the teacher. Incorrect responses trigger nonpunitive corrective feedback and are easier to rectify because the "failure" is associated

FIGURE 9.1 Systems of Hierarchical Prompts

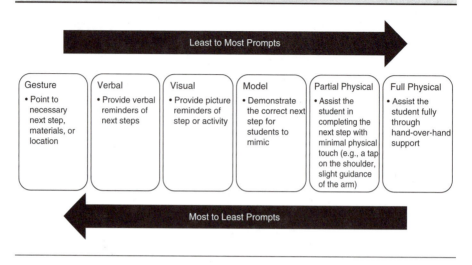

Least to Most Prompts

Gesture	Verbal	Visual	Model	Partial Physical	Full Physical
• Point to necessary next step, materials, or location	• Provide verbal reminders of next steps	• Provide picture reminders of step or activity	• Demonstrate the correct next step for students to mimic	• Assist the student in completing the next step with minimal physical touch (e.g., a tap on the shoulder, slight guidance of the arm)	• Assist the student fully through hand-over-hand support

Most to Least Prompts

with the most recently modeled step. After the choral response, the teacher can either model the next step or probe with a check by asking an individual student a follow-up question related to the step to ensure that all students are engaged with the material. After presenting the first two steps, it facilitates the learning process to model these steps together, and as additional steps are modeled, teachers should precede each new step by modeling and probing the previous steps done in series. One technique is to place clipboards with data collection sheets near the activity so teachers can easily record learner responses. Table 9.13 illustrates a data sheet for monitoring students' performance. Teachers should record the number of correct and incorrect student responses during the teaching activity.

GUIDED AND INDEPENDENT PRACTICE

After modeling/prompting/probing/checking all the steps in the lesson, the teacher should provide opportunities for guided and independent practice on previously acquired knowledge. These practice opportunities can be done individually or in small groups. In guided practice opportunities, the teacher monitors the work as it is being done in order to provide prompts to ensure success. In independent practice, the students work independently to practice the skills as the teacher observes and records data. Written exercises and cooperative

TABLE 9.13 Sample Data Sheet Recording Students' Performance Adding Two-Digit Addition With and Without Regrouping

Directions: Next to each step, record if the student performed the step independently and correctly (I) or with an instructional prompt: V = verbal, G = gesture, M = modeling, PP = partial physical assistance, FP = full physical assistance.

STEP	STUDENT PERFORMANCE				
	MON	TUES	WED	THURS	FRI
1. Copy the problem.	I	I	I	I	I
2. Ensure one of the numbers is above the other, the ones and tens place values for both numbers are aligned, and the bottom number is underlined.	I	I	I	I	I
3. Add the ones place values together, and if the sum is less than 10, write the sum below the horizontal line aligned with the ones place of the original numbers.	V	I	I	I	I
4. If the sum is greater than 10, write the ones value of the sum below the line and carry the tens value by writing that value above the two-digit numbers of the problem.	V	V	I	I	I
5. Add the tens place values including any carryover from the ones sum to the left of the ones sum and below the tens values of the original numbers.	M	M	V	I	I
Number of steps completed independently and correctly	2/5	3/5	4/5	5/5	5/5

learning activities are designed to help students review previously learned content and may be used in guided or independent practice.

CONCLUSION

IDEA 2004 calls for students with disabilities to have access to language arts, mathematics, science, and social studies content. Across the nation, many states are adopting the Common Core State Standards or standards promoted by professional associations. By giving elementary students with intellectual disability access to general education content, settings, and educators, we are providing the best learning experience for our students. It is crucial to continue advocating for these opportunities. In conjunction with the teaching methods and strategies explored in this chapter, special educators can provide access to rigorous content for all students regardless of disability. The ultimate goal for teachers is to target academic skills that will decrease dependency, increase independence, and improve the student's quality of life.

Chapter Summary

- The Common Core State Standards (CCSS) assist special educators in choosing, adapting, and delivering content to elementary students with intellectual disability.

- All students regardless of disability must have access to the general education curriculum.

- Academic instruction for elementary students should be designed with long-term outcomes such as employability and independence in mind and include academic and functional skill components.

- Using a standards-based individualized education program (IEP) approach helps ensure students have access to general education content.

- There are critical curricular components that must be included in curriculum for elementary students with intellectual disability including literacy, mathematics, science, and social studies skills.

- There are a variety of evidence-based teaching methods available for delivering content to students with intellectual disability. Systematic instruction, for example, featuring the use of direct instruction is a research-based method appropriate for these learners. Likewise, scripted lessons are another effective planning and instructional approach.

- Instructional prompting allows teachers of students with intellectual disability to offer the customized level of prompting and support needed for each individual student. Time delay is another research-based method to deliver instruction.

Review Questions

1. How can educators of elementary students with intellectual disability provide access to general education content and standards for their students?

2. What academic content should be included in a well-rounded curriculum for learners with intellectual disability?

3. What is a scripted lesson?

4. How would you design a task analysis for an academic skill such as adding one-digit numbers or writing a first name?

5. What are three evidence-based approaches for delivering instruction to students with intellectual disability?

Key Terms

Common Core State Standards (CCSS) (page 234)

literacy (page 235)

emergent literacy skills (page 236)

story-based lesson (page 238)

manipulatives (page 242)

universal design for learning (UDL) (page 246)

systematic instruction (page 247)

errorless learning (page 247)

direct instruction (DI) (page 247)

explicit instruction (page 251)

scripted lessons (page 251)

task analysis (page 253)

modeling (page 255)

verbal prompt (page 256)

gestures (page 256)

physical prompt (page 256)

visual prompt (page 257)

time delay (page 258)

system of least prompts (page 261)

Organizations Concerned With Curriculum Standards

Common Core State Standards

www.corestandards.org

National Council for the Social Studies

www.socialstudies.org

National Council of Teachers of Mathematics

www.nctm.org

Next Generation Science Standards

www.nextgenscience.org

CHAPTER 10

Life Skills for Elementary-Age Students With Intellectual Disability

Teresa Taber Doughty

Learning Objectives

After reading Chapter 10, you should be able to:

- Describe the functional learning needs of elementary-age students with intellectual disability.

- Define life skills and why they are important to include in an instructional curriculum for elementary students with intellectual disability.

- Explain how instructional skills are prioritized and the specific areas for consideration.

- Identify curricular content areas in which life skills instruction may be provided for elementary-age students.

Planning for and providing life skills instruction to elementary students with an intellectual disability is an important curricular focus in preparing them for autonomous functioning in current and future environments. In this chapter, we will examine the learning needs of elementary-age students and those with an intellectual disability, review the steps for prioritizing instruction, identify strategies for how to embed life skills instruction into the elementary curriculum, illustrate how and when to develop and use adaptations and accommodations for instruction, and describe the specific life skill domains for instruction.

OVERVIEW OF LIFE SKILLS FOR ELEMENTARY STUDENTS WITH INTELLECTUAL DISABILITY

During the 2012–2013 academic year, there were over 26 million students (kindergarten through sixth grade) attending public schools in the United States (National Center for Education Statistics, 2014b). Of these, approximately 7 percent were children with an intellectual disability (National Center for Education Statistics, 2014a). Many of these students were served in neighborhood schools, yet fewer than one out of five learners spent the majority (at least 80%) of their day in grade-level classrooms. Most students with intellectual disability spent less than 40 percent of their school day in inclusive settings (National Center for Education Statistics, 2014b). For these pupils, instruction typically occurred in resource and self-contained classrooms or other educational settings.

As noted in Chapter 3, the shift in instructional models for students with intellectual disability from academic mainstreaming and functional curriculum approaches of the 1970s and 1980s to inclusive education with a focus on the general education curriculum resulted in an expansion of the instructional placement options we see today. Students with intellectual disability are effectively taught in all settings, including grade-level classrooms where they may actively access the general education curriculum and life skills instruction they need for current and future environments. Today, a growing number of elementary students with intellectual disability are able to learn basic academic skills alongside their peers while also having their individualized educational needs met.

Elementary school represents each child's first opportunity for organized academic learning. Here, students move from more play-based learning in child care and preschool to learning basic skills filled with symbols and concepts. The general education curriculum is focused on introducing and building on learning in the areas of language and literacy, mathematics, science, and social studies. As students progress through each grade level, they interact with increasingly challenging concepts and their application to complex situations. By the time they enter secondary settings, students have a solid foundation in each content area and are ready to build on their knowledge and skills across a content-specific secondary curriculum. Yet, for elementary students with mild, moderate, and severe intellectual disability, teachers often see a considerable academic lag behind their grade-level peers in reading and basic mathematics skills as they progress through the grade-level curriculum (Taylor, Richards, & Brady, 2005). While this delay is common, studies indicate that these students can learn basic literacy and mathematics skills (Hudson, Browder, & Wood, 2013) and, with strategic instruction, numerous complex and abstract skills across academic areas (Browder, Jimenez, & Trela, 2012; Miller & Taber-Doughty, 2014; Riggs, Collins, Kleinert, & Knight, 2013; Spooner, Knight, Browder, Jimenez, & DiBiase, 2011; Wakeman, Karvonen, & Ahumada, 2013).

Though students with intellectual disability may demonstrate success in acquiring complex subject matter, they may still struggle with the skills needed for self-directed and independent functioning in home, school, and community settings. These students often require specific instruction in the locally and culturally relevant competencies that allow them to actively participate in daily activities across multiple settings (Cronin, Patton, & Wood, 2007; Wehman, Targett, & Richardson, 2012). Consequently, an expanded curricular focus on traditional academics as well as life skills is appropriate.

Life skills are those skills that enable students with mild, moderate, and severe intellectual disability to access and participate in everyday activities in their current and future environments (Wehman et al., 2012). A curriculum focused on life skills is synonymous with functional or real-world curricula and engages students in skills required for working, living, and recreating in integrated and inclusive school and community environments (Bouck, Taber-Doughty, & Savage, 2015; Brown et al., 1979). Students learn skills grounded in the **instructional domains** of daily living, recreation and leisure, community functioning, and employment. Embedded throughout a life skills curriculum are functional academics, communication skills, motor skills, and personal/social skills (Brown et al., 1979). Figure 10.1 illustrates the linkage between life skill instructional domains and **embedded skills**. Rather than teaching embedded skills in isolation, a life skills approach ensures that these skills are taught across each of the instructional domains. Together, life skills instruction facilitates opportunities for personal growth, social acceptance, and active participation across environments (see Table 10.1 for examples).

As illustrated in Figure 10.2, embedded skills are used and can be taught within and across settings and activities. Here, an elementary-age student might be

FIGURE 10.1 Instructional Domains and Embedded Skills in a Life Skills Curriculum

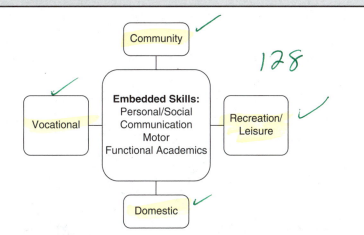

SOURCE: Adapted from E. Bouck, T. Taber-Doughty, and M. Savage (2015), *Footsteps toward the future: Implementing a real-world curriculum for students with developmental disabilities* (Arlington, VA: Council for Exceptional Children), p. 3.

TABLE 10.1 Example Skills per Instructional Domain

DOMAIN	SAMPLE SKILLS
Daily living—instructional	Self-advocacy; self-help; cleaning or picking up one's room; getting oneself a snack from the cupboard, pantry, or fridge
Recreation and leisure—instructional	Activities to do alone or with a group, social and communication skills (e.g., puzzles, board games)
Community functioning—instructional	Following directions, using community recreational facilities
Employment—instructional	Taking messages/notes to the office, cleaning up one's work space in the classroom
Functional academics—embedded	Identifying survival words, counting change, telling time
Communication skills—embedded	Writing a thank-you note, writing an e-mail
Motor skills—embedded	Walking to the school cafeteria, participating in physical education, joining in a group activity at recess
Personal/social skills—embedded	Using socially appropriate greetings, following social rules for differing occasions, dressing appropriately for various events

FIGURE 10.2 Embedded Skills Taught Within a Life Skills Activity

Life Skill Domain: Recreation/Leisure
Setting: Water park
Activity: Day at the water park

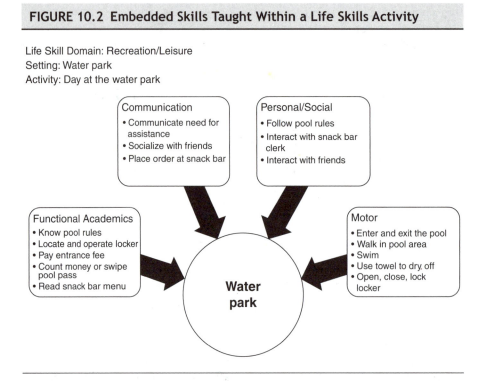

spending the day at a water park (recreation/leisure domain). While there, she would engage in a variety of activities that require the use of embedded life skills related to academic, communication, motor, and personal/social skills. She might purchase a drink at the snack bar or socialize with her friends while playing in the water. She might also need to store or retrieve her personal items in a locker. Thus, the need to prepare a student to use a variety of embedded skills in instructional domains is important. As well, providing multiple opportunities to practice these skills across domains will ultimately facilitate generalization.

For elementary students with intellectual disability, their introduction to the general education curriculum begins with the basic academic skills introduced in kindergarten and the first grade. This early curriculum focuses on academic skills considered foundational or even functional in nature. Basic literacy (learning letters and letter sounds; reading sight words, rhymes, and patterned stories), writing (formulating letters, writing one's name, invented spelling), mathematics (time, money, meaning of numbers, simple calculations), science (early steps of science inquiry; exploration of water, weather, plants, and animals), and social studies (following rules; being self-sufficient; discriminating between the ideas of past, present, and future) serve as the building blocks for more abstract academic concepts introduced in subsequent years. If students with intellectual disability are going to learn academic skills, this is where they begin. As children progress through the elementary grade levels and emphasis is placed on applying these foundational skills, academic delays are often observed for students with intellectual disability. It is at this point that academic remediation becomes a focus for those skills not yet acquired (Cronin et al., 2007) and life skills are introduced as an integral part of instruction. Individualized education program (IEP) goals are developed to enable students to progress through the general education curriculum while concurrently meeting individualized and functional learning needs (Wehman et al., 2012).

The overall educational goal for students at the elementary level is to master the academic building blocks on which future academic and functional skills may be built (Wehman et al., 2012). This is balanced with the individualized instructional needs for each student. For example, a student with a mild intellectual disability would participate in the general education curriculum across all content areas and may receive instruction to support her behavioral and social skill needs. She may require instruction in the use of organizational tools, learning playground social skills, and skills for solving problems. A learner with a moderate or severe intellectual disability would also receive instruction across all general education curriculum areas but may also receive instruction in using assistive technology to communicate his needs, instructional adaptations that include using picture prompts to complete task transitions, and self-help supports in the school cafeteria. However, simply because a student may require individualized instructional needs does not imply that he or she is excluded from the traditional academic instruction. Rather, the general curriculum and the student's daily functioning needs are supplemented by the individualized supports and instruction.

WHAT TO TEACH ELEMENTARY STUDENTS WITH INTELLECTUAL DISABILITY

When determining what to teach elementary students with intellectual disability, careful consideration should be given to the age of the student; his or her current and future learning needs; the pupil's present learning strengths and challenges; the preferences of the student, family, and teacher; whether a

FIGURE 10.3 Life Skills Instructional Considerations for Elementary Students

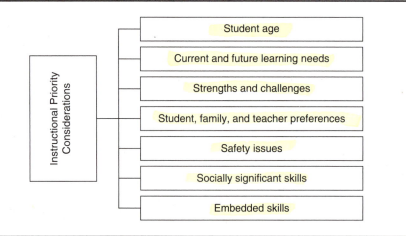

SOURCE: Adapted from L. Brown, J. Nietupski, & S. Hamre-Nietupski. The criterion of ultimate functioning. In M. Thomas (Ed.), *Hey, don't forget about me! Education's investment in the severely, profoundly, and multiply handicapped* (Reston, VA: Council for Exceptional Children, 1976), pp. 2-15.

skill is socially significant and will lead to increased access in future environments; if there are any safety issues for the learner; and if there are any embedded skills related to personal/social, motor, communication, and functional academic skills that should be taught (Brown, Nietupski, & Hamre-Nietupski, 1976). Each factor is critical for facilitating students' academic and functional achievement as they progress through each grade level as well as increasing the likelihood for successful social integration in current and future environments. Figure 10.3 illustrates what should be considered when determining the life skills instructional content and focus for individuals with intellectual disability.

STUDENT AGE

The first factor to consider in determining what to teach is a student's age. Priority should be given to the same or similar skills in which the student's same-age peers are performing. If suggested skills and activities are the same as those for their typically developing peers, then these also would be appropriate for pupils with intellectual disability. For example, most first graders are able to follow three-step directives, use the restroom with little to no help, open a milk carton at lunch with minimal assistance, and button or snap their own jackets. If a student with an intellectual disability were unable to engage in these skills at the same level as his peers, these skills would be targeted for instruction. Specific instruction and supports could be integrated into the regular school day for targeted tasks as they occur naturally. What should be avoided is introducing skills required of a much older child. For instance, you would not expect a 6-year-old to navigate his way through a grocery store and shop independently from a grocery list. This would be appropriate for a secondary-level student. An age-appropriate grocery shopping skill to expect from a 6-year-old would be to remain with an adult and to identify community helpers within a grocery setting. However, you would expect a 6-year-old to say and write her name and address, identify her parents' names, and describe her favorite activities to do for fun. Table 10.2 presents some sample general curriculum skills considered age appropriate for learners in early, middle, and late elementary levels.

CURRENT AND FUTURE LEARNING NEEDS

Determining what skills a student needs to function successfully in current and future environments is a critical factor to consider when planning for instruction. As discussed in Chapter 4, completing an ecological inventory for a pupil may be helpful in pinpointing functional skills needed across environments. For example, consider whether the learner is in the early elementary grades or nearing the time when he will transition to the middle school level. At the early elementary level, the skills required for greater independent participation might include learning to stand in line, selecting a desired book from the library and checking it out, making one-to-one correspondence when setting the table for snack time, and storing personal items on the shelf labeled with his name. As older elementary students prepare for the transition to middle school, functional skills instruction should center on the skills needed for that environment. These skills might include learning how to open a combination locker, changing clothes for physical education class, and selecting a seat with friends for lunch in the cafeteria.

ACADEMIC STRENGTHS AND CHALLENGES

Because the elementary curriculum introduces the fundamentals for academic learning that are often functional in nature, teachers should emphasize and reinforce individual students' learning strengths and successes and introduce

TABLE 10.2 Representative Age-Appropriate Skills for Elementary Students

DOMAIN/ SKILL	EARLY ELEMENTARY AGES 6-8	MIDDLE ELEMENTARY AGES 8-10	LATE ELEMENTARY AGES 10-12
Domestic—Health and Nutrition	Identify ways to promote health and wellness—for example, exercising, getting good sleep	Identify a healthy choice when making a decision—for example, riding a bike versus playing a video game	Choose a healthy option when making a decision—for example, selecting a healthy snack
Recreation/ Leisure—Movement Skills	Perform fundamental rhythmic skills alone, with a partner, or in a group—for example, dancing	Describe critical elements of correct movement pattern for fundamental movement skills—for example, dribbling a ball	Identify and participate in activities that can contribute to an active lifestyle—for example, playing on a soccer team
Community—Safety Skills	Repeat rules that promote personal health—for example, not talking to strangers	Identify possible consequences of not being safe—for example, getting lost	Describe procedures for seeking help when safety is an issue—for example, how to use a cell phone to call for assistance
Prevocational—Career Exploration	Identify different kinds of workers and jobs—for example, nurse, police, cashier	Identify why people work—for example, to earn money, to practice their skills	Identify how different academic classes relate to various jobs—for example, an awareness that additional training is needed to become an auto mechanic

accommodations or modifications when they experience learning challenges. This is accomplished through regular assessment of student performance and making ongoing decisions about instruction and curricular focus. When an academic strength is observed, instruction should continue in that content area alongside typically developing peers. For example, if an individual with an intellectual disability is acquiring elementary literacy skills following the prescribed curriculum in which his classmates are a part, then that student should continue to follow that same instruction. Yet, continuous monitoring of the student's progress as well as that of his peers should be ongoing. Assessment will reveal when learning challenges exist. Should a student struggle with content and demonstrate performance lags, accommodations or modifications to the curriculum should be introduced.

Accommodations are changes made to how material is presented or instruction is provided. They may be made to instructional content (what the student should learn), process (instructional activities), products (final assignments that demonstrate learning), or the learning environment (how the instructional setting is organized) (Olinghouse, 2008) but do not lower the standard or expectations for learning (Wright, 2003). Students who receive instructional accommodations are expected to acquire the same content as outlined in the curriculum. For example, a pupil who struggles with mathematical computations might be provided a calculator to solve problems. Yet, the student must still acquire the concepts and provide correct responses. Alternatively, modifications might be introduced to the curriculum when other instructional outcomes are needed for a student. **Modifications** are changes in the target task that result in an alternative performance standard for the student. For instance, if third graders are identifying the common structures of a plant (roots, pistil, stamen) and their functions, the student requiring modifications may be only required to identify the roots during a planting activity. In general, modifications may include alternative curriculum goals and expectations, completion of only part of the content requirements, and alternate assessments. Figure 10.4 highlights the decision-making questions to consider for providing accommodations or modifications.

PREFERENCES

When considering the instructional curriculum for individuals with intellectual disability, student, family, and teacher preferences should be considered. Families and teachers who seek to increase student participation and autonomy across settings and situations will certainly identify skills they want for their students. For example, teachers may prefer to focus on the specific skills identified through an ecological inventory (skills for current and future environments) while family members may want to increase their student's ability to demonstrate acceptable social and behavioral skills in public settings (for example, chew with mouth closed or use socially acceptable vocal levels according to the environment). The preferred skills identified by families and teachers may be easily incorporated into the daily curriculum. However, students also may demonstrate a desire to learn specific skills (for example, video games, cell phones, social media, e-mail). When student

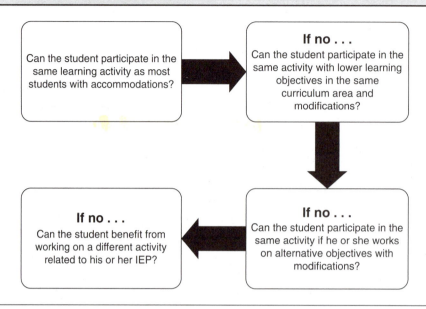

Can the student participate in the same learning activity as most students with accommodations?

If no . . .
Can the student participate in the same activity with lower learning objectives in the same curriculum area and modifications?

If no . . .
Can the student benefit from working on a different activity related to his or her IEP?

If no . . .
Can the student participate in the same activity if he or she works on alternative objectives with modifications?

SOURCE: Adapted from Florida Diagnostic and Learning Resources System, *Instructional Designs: A Resource Guide for Teachers of Students With Significant Cognitive Disabilities* (Fort Lauderdale, FL: Broward County Public Schools, 2010).

preferences are considered in determining what to teach, students acquire skills sooner, demonstrate greater focus on tasks, and complete tasks in less duration than when engaged in nonpreferred tasks (Bambara, Ager, & Koper, 1994; Bambara, Koger, Katzer, & Davenport, 1995; Killu, Clare, & Im, 1999; Stafford, Alberto, Fredrick, Heflin, & Heller, 2002; Taber-Doughty, 2005). Teachers can assess student preferences through observation, formal and informal assessments, and simply asking students what they want to learn and how they want to learn it. Skills that are socially acceptable and contribute to a student's ability to engage with peers in current and future environments should be considered.

SAFETY ISSUES

As students progress through the elementary curriculum, the number and type of learning environments increase. Any skill that addresses the health and security of a student in and across these settings is critical. If students are

TABLE 10.3 Examples of Safety Skills Taught or Emphasized

- Crossing busy streets

- Locating a police officer

- Using a cell phone when lost

- First aid—applying bandages, recognizing an emergency, first aid for choking

- Responding to dangerous situations—removing and discarding broken materials

- Reading product warning labels and demonstrating knowledge of their meanings

- Fire safety skills—extinguishing fires

- Social safety skills—saying "No" to an adult and moving away from that adult

taught in school and community settings, safety skills related to those environments must be considered. For example, in school settings, pupils should learn where and how to locate assistance, how to respond to emergency drills, and how to safely board and disembark the school bus. They might also learn how to use basic first-aid skills and how to read product warning labels. When in the community, learners should be taught what to do should they become lost, how to safely cross a street or parking lot, how to respond to dangerous weather (lightning, storms), and how to use escalators. Because students with intellectual disability often lack social, intellectual, and judgment skills, personal safety skills should be considered critical and taught across all settings. These skills include avoiding abduction and lures of strangers and sexual abuse (Mechling, 2008). Table 10.3 provides examples of safety skills typically taught to students with intellectual disability.

SOCIAL SIGNIFICANCE

When considering the social significance of a skill, educators must consider whether it is an acceptable and valued skill to consumers and others and whether it will lead to greater access in other settings. Socially valid skills are those considered important by individuals who are being taught the skills. In elementary settings, students with intellectual disability should be taught the same skills as their typically developing peers. However, when accommodations are used, they should be universal to the greatest extent possible. For example, a pupil with a mild intellectual disability might struggle with spelling. Allowing this student (and others) to use the spell-check function on the computer would be unobtrusive and socially appropriate. As well, an individual with a more severe intellectual disability might use audio prompts delivered via an iPhone to receive assistance in completing a learning task. In each instance, students with intellectual disability participate with their typically developing peers, the focus on their intellectual disability is decreased, and the skills they are learning are considered socially valid.

GENERAL INSTRUCTIONAL APPROACHES

Frequently used evidence-based instructional strategies for teaching life skills include the use of a task analysis approach; group instruction; system of least/most prompts; simulation and **in vivo**, community-based instruction; and technology-based instruction. Each incorporates systematic planning for delivering instruction that facilitates learning. In addition, each can be effectively used to teach students both traditional academic and life skills.

TASK ANALYSIS APPROACH

The task analysis approach requires teachers to breakdown an activity into teachable units or steps so that a student may learn each individual step or chain of steps for completing an activity. Students use either forward or backward chaining (such as teaching skills in sequential order [forward] or guiding the student through each step and teaching the last step first [backward]) to learn an activity. For example, when teaching a student to put on and zip a coat using forward chaining, the teacher would develop a task analysis and teach the first step to take the coat off the hanger, until it is learned. Then the second step of the student putting her right arm into the coat would be taught to mastery before subsequent steps are taught. An advantage of this approach is that students learn each step before moving to the next. A disadvantage is that instruction in the complete task will not occur until all steps are mastered. In backward chaining, the reverse is true. Here, a student would be guided through all steps of putting on her coat and receive direct instruction in the last step first (zipping it up). For this dressing skill, the student has the opportunity to experience all of the steps for putting on her coat before being required to perform them. When using a task analysis approach, teachers acquire a clear understanding of the activity and are able to easily gather student performance data as each student progresses through each step (Storey & Miner, 2011). A sample task analysis for teaching an elementary student with an intellectual

TABLE 10.4 Task Analysis for Using a Calculator for Adding Single Digits

	STEPS
1	Turn on calculator
2	Press first digit
3	Press "+"
4	Press second digit
5	Press "="
6	Read answer display
7	Write answer on paper

disability to use a four-function calculator to solve single-digit addition problems is presented in Table 10.4.

GROUP INSTRUCTION APPROACH

Both whole- and small-group instruction are effective instructional groupings for teaching elementary students with intellectual disability. In whole-group instruction, the teacher leads an entire class in the introduction or review of a lesson. The benefits of this format for learners with intellectual disability include exposure to the entire lesson and its concepts alongside their peers as well as opportunities to review previously learned material without removal from the instructional setting. Yet, differentiation of instruction for individual learning needs can be minimal. Alternatively, small-group instruction provides a smaller student–teacher ratio where the teacher works with two to four students to provide instruction. Teachers are able to match instruction to meet individual learning needs through direct instruction, increased opportunities for reinforcement, and checks for understanding. An example of how teachers might use both instructional formats for their class is for reading instruction. Teachers would build a sense of community during a whole-group instruction activity that would provide all students with access to authentic texts, opportunities to learn alongside peers with mixed abilities, and activities that introduce the topic and possible vocabulary to all students simultaneously (McLaughlin & Allen, 2009). This would be followed by small-group instruction where individual accommodations or modifications may be introduced. Students might engage in vocabulary development, individual reading, or comprehension activities.

SYSTEM OF LEAST/MOST PROMPTS

The systems of least to most or most to least prompts are considered to be foundational strategies that incorporate increasing or decreasing prompts following a student's incorrect response to a task cue. Either increasing assistance (system of least prompts) or decreasing assistance (system of most prompts) might be used to support a pupil's learning. For example, in using the system of least prompts after a student's incorrect response when following the printed directions for hand washing, the teacher would provide a verbal prompt, "Try it again." If the student continues to respond incorrectly, the teacher might point to the first step (gesture) on the page and provide a verbal prompt (such as "Pick the red one"). Continued incorrect responses would be followed by a verbal prompt plus modeling and then physical guidance. An example when using the system of most prompts might include providing full physical guidance (hand-over-hand) to teach a student to zip a pouch. When the pupil reaches the last step of the task, he would receive decreasing assistance until that final step is mastered (a model or gesture for pulling the zipper tab to open or close the pouch).

SIMULATION AND IN VIVO INSTRUCTION

Simulation and in vivo approaches involve the location in which instruction takes place. For simulation, students are taught a skill in a setting where it is not typically performed. Simulation involves previewing or reviewing the steps of a skill or task that is completed in another setting. For example, learners may discuss the physical tasks they will complete when participating in the school field day in which they complete a series of individual and team physical challenges. They may practice how they will line up and how they will listen to the coaches. They may also discuss how they will throw a ball, jump rope, and participate in the potato sack race. However, for elementary students with an intellectual disability, simulated instruction in a classroom cannot replace the instruction in the setting in which the skills must be performed (community or natural settings). To promote skill generalization, students should experience instruction in the actual setting in which they will encounter target skills and activities. For the school field day, learners would use the authentic materials and participate in the actual activities in the natural setting that would incorporate the sounds, people, sights, and motor demands expected in the gymnasium or outdoor

TABLE 10.5 Recommended CBI Frequency and Duration for Elementary Students

GRADE	FREQUENCY	DURATION
Grades K-3	1 day per week	1 hour per day
Grades 4-5	2 days per week	1 hour per day

SOURCE: Adapted from P. Alberto, N. Elliott, T. Taber, N. Houser, and P. Andrews, "Vocational content for students with moderate and severe disabilities in elementary and middle grades," *Focus on Exceptional Children, 25*(9), 1993, pp. 1-10.

school grounds. The likelihood that skills will be learned and generalized is increased when pupils participate in activities in natural settings and using real materials.

Community-based instruction (CBI) specifically targets instruction in environments in which students learn the skills needed to live, work, and recreate in the community. Different from school field trips, CBI requires ongoing trips into the community to learn skills. For example, students may regularly travel to a public library to practice using the computer to locate a book, checking out a book, reading quietly, and interacting with the librarian. In a review of the literature, Walker, Uphold, Richter, and Test (2010) found that students with intellectual disability across all grade levels benefit from CBI and that a variety of life skills may be learned. The recommended frequency and duration of CBI for elementary learners with a disability appear in Table 10.5.

TECHNOLOGY-BASED INSTRUCTION

In recent years, technology-based instructional strategies were studied extensively when used by students with intellectual disability (Cannella-Malone et al., 2011; Cannella-Malone, Mizrachi, Sabielny, & Jimenez, 2013; Charlop-Christy, Le, & Freeman, 2000; Taber-Doughty et al., 2011; see Chapter 6 for a complete discussion of assistive technology to support students with intellectual disability). These are highly effective strategies for teaching a variety of skills, including academic and life skills, to students with intellectual disability, and practitioners need an awareness of such technologies to successfully integrate them into daily instruction (Ayres, Mechling, & Sansosti, 2013). Instructional strategies that incorporate technology include video modeling, video prompting, computer simulation (or virtual reality), and augmented reality. Video prompting and modeling provide video clips of tasks or behaviors being performed and serve as a visual model for students. With video prompting, a student watches a video clip of the first step of a task and then performs that step. Once that step is completed, the student watches each subsequent step individually before performing it. With video modeling, a pupil watches an entire activity being performed (entire task chain) and then performs the task. For example, after watching a video clip for using a blender to make a smoothie, the student adds fruit, juice, ice, and yogurt to the blender cup; attaches a lid; and turns on the blender to make the smoothie without additional prompts.

Computer simulation, also known as **virtual reality**, is another strategy used to teach life skills to students with intellectual disability. Virtual reality replicates an actual environment that reproduces an individual's physical presence in real or imagined worlds. For example, Ayres, Langone, Boon, and Norman (2006) used computer-based software (Project Shop) to teach secondary students with intellectual disability to use money to make a purchase. Here, students physically interacted with a virtual cashier and money to pay for small purchases. Similarly, elementary students with moderate intellectual disability were taught to use the dollar-plus strategy when making a purchase after using a computer-based instruction package (Ayres & Langone, 2002). Simulation programs are available online and provide students an opportunity to practice a variety of skills such as exploring learning environments (e.g., Model Me Going Places 2 [Model Me Kids, 2012; www.modelmekids .com]; Toca Boca apps [Toca Boca, 2016; https://tocaboca.com]); counting and learning about money (e.g., Jungle Coins [Short, 2016; http://jungleeducation.com/app/jungle-coins]); concepts such as big/small, empty/full, and same/different (e.g., A Day With a Difference app [Unit11, 2015; www .unit11apps.com]; What Goes Together app [Different Roads to Learning, 2012; www.difflearn.com/Apps]); and telling time (e.g., Bamba Clock app [Mezmedia, 2016; www.bambatown.com]) prior to using them in the actual setting and situation.

Related to computer simulation is instruction using **augmented reality**. Augmented reality is a live view of a task, activity, or setting that is augmented by computer-generated sensory input (for example, sound, video, graphics, GPS data) (Cassella, 2009). Figure 10.5 illustrates where augmented reality fits in the continuum of mixed reality (the blending of real and virtual instruction). While it is relatively new to special education, it is used across a number of fields including architecture, art, construction, gaming, medicine, and sports. In education, student learning during inquiry-based science units was examined as elementary students used an augmented reality game (Squire & Jan, 2007) and adults with physical and intellectual disabilities learned to participate in independent leisure activities (Weiss, Bialik, & Kizony, 2003). In special education, Chang, Kang, and Huang (2013) used augmented reality to teach three students with intellectual disability to complete vocational skills while Brown et al. (2013) taught eight individuals with intellectual disability to use augmented reality to physically navigate their way between two points on a map. Current resources for augmented reality include apps such as Aurasma (Aurasma, 2016; www.aurasma.com) and Layar—Augmented Reality (Layar B.V., 2016; www.layar.com) that allow users to create augmented reality in the classroom. Additionally, web resources such as Two Guys and Some iPads (twoguysandsomeipads.com) and the MIT Education Arcade (education.mit .edu) provide teachers direct access to augmented reality programs that may be used immediately in their classrooms with all students. Minock and Nesloney (2013) identified numerous ways in which teachers might use augmented reality in the classroom. One example, embedding video on homework pages, especially lends itself to providing additional visual prompts for a student with an intellectual disability. For instance, a student uses a digital device (tablet or smartphone) to scan her assignment page for entering activities on her daily calendar. Scanning the page opens an instructional video on the device that prompts the student through the task. When learning to engage in choice making, students might also scan the lunch menu to reveal digital pictures of their lunch choices for the day.

FIGURE 10.5 Milgram's Reality-Virtuality Continuum

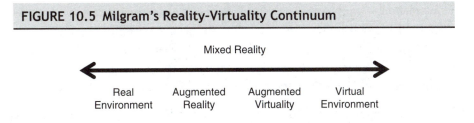

NOTE: Adapted from D. Drascic and P. Milgram, "Perceptual issues in augmented reality. "*Electronic Imaging: Science & Technology,* 2653, 1996, pp. 123-134.

COMPONENTS OF A LIFE SKILLS CURRICULUM FOR ELEMENTARY-AGE STUDENTS

Life skills may be taught within the context of the general education curriculum or as part of a modified curriculum. Specific skills may be taught in general education classroom settings or in community settings. For students with intellectual disability, life skills are critical to facilitating greater independence. Within the general education curriculum, life skills may be taught within all content areas including mathematics, science, social studies, language arts, and health education. For example, when teaching about idioms during third-grade language arts, a teacher might have students demonstrate, describe, or draw a picture about the meaning of "It's raining cats and dogs," "Pig out," or "A little birdie told me." Highlighting the difference between literal meanings and figures of speech will aid students as they interact with others across daily activities as well as provide them the ability to expand on communicative meanings. When teaching a unit in social studies about geography, the teacher might have students identify states as they play "State Stumper" (available at pbskids.org). Knowing where states are located will facilitate understanding about current events and the weather.

MATHEMATICS

Individuals use mathematics skills in every environment from setting an alarm clock to purchasing snack items from a vending machine. Mathematics skills for elementary students include money skills (counting money, money math, vocabulary), time-based skills (time management, units of time, time telling), basic calculations (adding, subtracting, understanding fractions), and measurement (using a calculator and ruler, using measuring cups, using a scale). As students progress through each academic year, increased mathematics skills will be required. Including students in the general education instruction as well as introducing the life skill equivalents will facilitate greater success in subsequent years. Table 10.6 presents a list of mathematics life skills adapted from the National Council of Teachers of Mathematics standards that may be appropriate for teaching early and late elementary-age students with intellectual disability.

Various strategies are used to teach mathematics life skills to elementary students with intellectual disability. The Next Dollar Up method, matching-to-sample, and systematic instruction through the use of task analysis are a

TABLE 10.6 Mathematics Life Skills

SKILL AREA	EARLY ELEMENTARY	LATE ELEMENTARY
Money	• Counting money • Earning money • Spending plans/saving	• Allowances and spending • Money management • Comparison shopping
Time	• Telling time on a digital clock • Following a schedule • Identifying when activities begin	• Telling time on an analog clock • Beginning and ending times (e.g., movies, sports events) • Setting an alarm clock
Basic Calculations	• Number correspondence • Addition and subtraction	• Using a calculator • Reading charts
Measurement	• Calendar • Dry and liquid ingredients • Weight • Distance	• Using a ruler • Sizing a recipe • Weighing oneself • Reading temperature

few strategies that may be used for teaching money or time-telling skills. For example, when learning to make a small purchase of less than $5.00, students would be presented with single dollar bills and the cost of an item. The Next Dollar Up method requires learners to consider the cost of their purchase and pay with one more dollar than the final total. When used, if a small toy costs $3.28, the student would count out and pay with $4.00 and then keep his hand held out to receive his change. If purchasing ice cream for $1.25 in the lunchroom, the student would pay with $2.00 and wait for change. When learning to tell time using an analog clock, matching-to-sample is a logical place to start. Teachers can pair clock faces illustrating target times with a picture of the specific school events that occur daily. As well, teachers might have students count the numbers on the face of the clock, count the minutes, and count by fives, tens, and fifteen- and thirty-minute intervals while simultaneously moving the "big hand" around the clock. Analog time can then be translated to the paired time on a digital clock. Pupils would use varying examples of timepieces (digital and analog watches, the classroom analog clock, digital alarm clocks, clocks on digital devices such as phones) during instruction to facilitate the generalization of these skills to other devices.

SCIENCE

Science skills in the areas of inquiry and process, physical science, life science, and earth science are the focus of most elementary science curricula. Embedded within each of these areas are numerous life skills. For example, science inquiry and process involves exploring the environment, making observations, asking questions, and engaging in efforts of discovery or problem solving. If an individual smells something burning, she might seek out the source, ask herself if something is on fire, observe the burning item, and seek to extinguish it or call for assistance. Physical, life, and earth science include the study of physics, chemistry, astronomy, living organisms, and science related to the planet Earth. Life skills can be tied to most areas of science and are easily embedded within the general education curriculum. Table 10.7 provides a list of sample life skills adapted from the Next Generation Science Standards (Next Generation Science Standards, 2013) that would be appropriate for teaching elementary-age students.

One strategy for teaching science life skills to students with intellectual disability is through project-based learning. **Project-based learning** (also known

TABLE 10.7 Science Life Skills

SKILL AREA	EARLY ELEMENTARY	LATE ELEMENTARY
Inquiry and Process	• Observes using five senses • Records findings	• Generates questions based on observations • Makes accurate measurements
Physical Science	• Describes physical aspects of objects (color, shape, size) • Wears headphones when environment is noisy	• Uses heat (microwave) to make snacks
Life Science	• Identifies plants and animals • Feeds/waters animals and plants	• Identifies food sources (meats, plants)
Earth Science	• Describes seasons • Observes weather patterns and what to do for severe weather • Identifies tools to measure temperature	• Identifies tools to measure precipitation • Determines when to wear sunscreen

SOURCE: Adapted from Next Generation Science Standards, *Next Generation Science Standards: For States, By States* (Washington, DC: The National Academies Press, 2013).

as problem-based learning) is a hands-on approach in which students actively engage in identifying problems and discovering solutions to those problems (Wolpert-Gawron, 2015). Often taught in collaborative groups, students use critical thinking, creativity, and problem-solving skills to generate solutions related to a problem. For example, for a unit on recycling during fifth-grade science, students are looking to solve the school's recycling issues. The physical compositions of school products that are used require many forms of recycling and therefore should be sorted differently for up-cycling or down-cycling. Students work in teams to identify effective and efficient recycling systems that may be used within the school. While a student with intellectual disability would work within a team to create school recycling solutions, the teacher may ensure that individualized functional skills are embedded in this science instruction. For example, as team members begin their research on recycling methods, the target student with an intellectual disability might use the computer to type simple notes for the team. When the group begins identifying recycling tools, she might demonstrate how to use a can crusher and how to sort classroom recyclables while wearing safety gear (goggles, gloves).

SOCIAL STUDIES

Social studies consist of history, civics and government, geography, and economics. As students actively participate in their school and community, understanding basic social studies skills will influence how they interact with others and make informed decisions. For example, a student who is knowledgeable about goods and services will have future options of where to purchase those items for the best price. Knowing and following rules and laws will assist the individual in developing positive relationships, remaining safe, and developing into a law-abiding member of the community. Instruction in social studies skills also prepares pupils to participate as active community citizens in voting and as responsible friends and family members in remembering and participating in special events (holidays, birthdays, other family events). Table 10.8 provides a list of sample social studies life skills adapted from the National Standards for Social Studies Teachers (National Council for the Social Studies, 2002) that would be appropriate for teaching elementary-age students.

Several tools that may prove useful for teaching social studies life skills to students with intellectual disability include differentiated instructional strategies such as graffiti boards, tiered learning experiences, and descriptive videos

TABLE 10.8 Social Studies

SKILL AREA	EARLY ELEMENTARY	LATE ELEMENTARY
History	• Develops a timeline of important events (birthdays and holidays) • Identifies family members across generations	• Creates and develops a timeline of school and other activities • Describes relationship between self and family
Civics and Government	• Identifies school and classroom rules	• Describes basic community laws (for example, no smoking in certain places, no stealing)
Geography	• Identifies and describes locations throughout the school building • Provides simple directions to a location	• Uses map to locate various places and walking distances in the neighborhood and community
Economics	• Identifies services that known individuals provide (for example, teacher, cafeteria worker, custodian)	• Keeps a personal budget (such as saving and spending)

SOURCE: Adapted from the National Council for the Social Studies, *National Standards for Social Studies Teachers—Revised* (Silver Spring, MD: Author, 2002).

(Evmenova & Behrmann, 2011). Graffiti boards are usually large sheets of paper in which students engage in a written conversation about a given topic. Elementary students might participate by contributing one or two words or drawing a picture to illustrate their contribution to the topic of discussion. To ensure that life skills are addressed, this strategy provides an opportunity for students to practice basic writing skills and articulate their thoughts on a topic with their peers. Tiered learning experiences (Tomlinson, 2014) allow a teacher to meet students' learning needs according to their current level of learning. For example, when learning about state capitals, struggling learners might identify each capital by locating it on a map as well as identifying travel routes to reach that location while some of their peers are researching the governmental structure within a state. Finally, descriptive videos (with closed-captioning) may be used to reinforce reading skills while concurrently introducing information about community rules and laws such as using crosswalks instead of jaywalking, knowing your *Miranda* rights, and recognizing safe and unsafe behaviors.

ENGLISH/LANGUAGE ARTS

According to the National Council of Teachers of English (NCTE), language arts encompass instruction in both language and reading. Language is described as incorporating "visual communication in addition to spoken and written forms of expressing" while reading involves "listening and viewing in addition to print-oriented reading" (National Council of Teachers of English & International Reading Association, 1996, p. 2). At the elementary level, language arts includes instruction in language, reading foundations, reading informational text, literature, speaking and listening, and writing. As students progress through each grade level and participate more in other school and community environments, these skills become crucial for future academic success and community independence. Table 10.9 provides a list of sample language arts–based life skills adapted from the NCTE that would be appropriate for teaching elementary-age students.

TABLE 10.9 English Language Arts

SKILL AREA	EARLY ELEMENTARY	LATE ELEMENTARY
Language Mechanics	• Recognizes printed name	• Accurately interprets figurative language when used during social interactions
Reading Foundations	• Reads simple directions that include both pictures and printed words	• Reads unknown words based on context clues
Reading Informational Text	• Follows simple printed or picture instructions • Interprets pictures to solve problems	• Follows a multi-step printed or visual schedule • Uses digital sources to locate answers
Literature	• Describes details of an event	• Demonstrates understanding of impact of actions on others
Speaking and Listening	• Takes turns speaking and listening when interacting with others	• Asks questions and receives answers to accurately complete an activity
Writing	• Writes or types name and address	• Writes or types important events into a personal calendar

SOURCE: Adapted from the National Council of Teachers of English & International Reading Association, *Standards for the English Language Arts* (Urbana, IL: Author, 1996).

Strategies for increasing life skills in language arts include using graphic organizers, chunking information, and explicit instruction. **Graphic organizers** are visual displays that allow students to organize information into flow charts, word maps, and diagrams to understand and learn information (Lee et al., 2006). They may be used across multiple content areas to facilitate literacy, science, social studies, and mathematics learning. When acquiring reading and text comprehension life skills, children with intellectual disability are able to use pictures and/or basic vocabulary words and physically organize them to form sentences, develop a daily schedule of activities, or communicate wants and needs as they pertain to IEP planning (Cullinan, Galda, & Strickland, 1993). **Chunking** involves linking related content to improve recall efforts (Lee et al., 2006). For a student who is learning to read words she encounters daily in the school building, chunking would be used to connect similar words. For example, when learning the word *and*, a child reads that word as well as others in which it is chunked such as *land*, *sand*, *grand*, and *brand* (Ward, 2005). Explicit instruction is synonymous with systematic and specific instruction in that educational approaches are planned and organized to facilitate learning. When teaching functional reading, teachers might provide opportunities for repetition in words and instructional language, adjust the instructional pace, and introduce motivating activities and strategies (Allor, Champlin, Gifford, & Mathes, 2010). For example, one motivational strategy, a **mnemonic** (pattern of letters, words, or ideas combined to help an individual remember), might be developed to recall the rule for spelling words when the letters *i* and *e* are contained within the word. The mnemonic "*I* before *e* except after *c*" is frequently used to remind spellers of the general order of these two letters when writing words in which they are contained.

HEALTH

A health education curriculum addresses behaviors, habits, and skills that lead to a healthy and safe lifestyle and helps to build students' knowledge and attitudes about health. It focuses on physical, mental, emotional, and social health and motivates students to be healthy, prevent disease, and reduce risky behaviors. General topics addressed within a comprehensive health education curriculum include instruction on wellness (general healthy behaviors, tooth brushing, skin protection), prevention (first aid, hygiene, handling health problems), growth and development (body changes), personal and physical safety (following safety rules, reading safety labels), self-management (using appropriate

TABLE 10.10 Health Skills

SKILL AREA	EARLY ELEMENTARY	LATE ELEMENTARY
Wellness	• Washes hands and covers mouth when coughing or sneezing	• Applies sunscreen or uses other skin protection
Prevention	• Uses sidewalks and crosswalks when in the community	• Uses healthy hygiene when having a cold or illness
Growth and Development	• Names or points to body parts	• Uses deodorant
Personal and Physical Safety	• Follows safety drill instructions	• Uses cell phone to call parent
Self-Management	• Maintains appropriate personal space	• Uses appropriate vocal levels according to environment
Nutrition and Physical Activity	• Selects healthy snacks	• Engages in energetic physical activity each day
Environmental Influences	• Recognizes strangers and refuses their offers	• Locates valid health information on the Internet

SOURCE: Adapted from the Joint Committee for National Health Education Standards, *Achieving Health Literacy*, 1995. Available at http://www.longwood.edu/assets/education/NHES.pdf

vocabulary, respecting personal space), nutrition and physical activity (making healthy food choices, food safety, engaging in active rather than passive physical activity), and environmental influences (peers, media, culture). Health instruction begins in the very first years of school and continues throughout a student's formal education. Table 10.10 presents a set of sample health-related life skills for early and late elementary-age students.

Effective instructional strategies for teaching life skills within the context of health education include direct instruction, simulation instruction, and opportunistic instruction. **Direct instruction** is a planned, multi-step approach to delivering instruction that includes defining the skill, identifying the prompts to use, and describing how skill reinforcement and generalization will be taught (Browder, Wood, Thompson, & Ribuffo, 2014; Smith, Polloway, Taber-Doughty, Patton, & Dowdy, 2016). During a physical education class, a teacher might teach body parts and have the student follow instructions when teaching a team sport. For example, the teacher would instruct the student to "Put your helmet on your head," "Velcro the flag belt around your waist," or "Use your right hand to bounce the ball" within the context of various team activities. **Simulation instruction** involves opportunities to practice skills that will ultimately be used in real-world settings (Collins & Wolery, 2012). For example, students pretend that there is a fire in the building to practice emergency procedures. **Opportunistic instruction** is making use of any opportunity in which a student may acquire or practice a skill (Annenberg Learner, 2015). For example, when provided a choice of food items at lunch, the student would be asked about why she chose those foods. She would be prompted to describe whether they were fruits, vegetables, proteins, or junk food and whether or not her choices were healthy options.

LIFE SKILLS ACROSS FUNCTIONAL DOMAINS

While it is important to identify how life skills align with the general education curriculum and content expectations, it is also critical to consider the domestic, community, recreation/leisure, and vocational instructional domains when planning for meeting the individual needs of elementary students with intellectual disability. These are the areas and activities in which life skills will be used, and thus instruction in the specific activities within each domain is crucial for facilitating skill acquisition and generalization. Many students with intellectual disability will require additional instruction in the skills within each domain and may be taught in general education settings or in alternate environments such as their home, school, or local community. Instruction within these functional domains are individually determined and based on each pupil's current and future environments. As needed skills are identified, long- and short-term goals and objectives are written and included in the student's IEP.

DOMESTIC DOMAIN

Elementary-level skills included in the domestic domain pertain to those that are completed in home environments and include self-care, grooming, and hygiene; preparing and storing food; caring for clothing; managing personal finances; maintaining a household; and yard maintenance (Fuchs, 2007). At an elementary level, students are expected to assume increased responsibilities in their own home as well as demonstrate increasing levels of independence. Young children are able to prepare their own cereal breakfast, dress themselves, and put away their toys. As they get older, elementary-age children are able to help with household chores, feed a pet, and use some appliances including a vacuum cleaner, microwave oven, or blender. For these activities, embedded skills such as motor, personal/social, communication, or academic skills may be addressed within the context of the activity. An example would be if a 10-year-old is responsible for taking trash cans and recycling bins to the curb (motor skill), he might need to ask (communication skill) if it is the correct day for trash pickup. As well, when preparing a simple snack in the microwave oven, he might need to follow simple printed instructions (academic skill) on the package of popcorn to avoid burning. At school, teachers may teach and reinforce domestic skills across classroom and school settings. Students may be responsible for putting on their own coats at recess, cleaning their desks and personal spaces, using a napkin when eating lunch, or attending to personal needs in the restroom. They may also learn to communicate their wants and needs when engaged in each of these activities. Specific domestic skills, activities, and embedded skills appropriate for elementary-age students appear in Table 10.11.

COMMUNITY DOMAIN

Skills within the community domain for elementary students provide an opportunity to develop the foundational skills needed for successfully functioning across novel and familiar settings. Instruction in these settings also contributes to increased skill generalization (Branham, Collins, Schuster, & Kleinert, 1999) and prepares students for future community success. Community-based settings in which instruction can occur include any location outside of a pupil's home. Parks (playground, picnic area), public services (post office, library), community businesses (toy store, restaurants, shopping malls), transportation modes (riding a bike or public bus with an adult), and general community skills (crossing a parking lot or street, walking down a sidewalk) are all skill areas that would be addressed with elementary-age students within this domain. When in a school setting, community skills may be taught using simulation activities and combined with community-based instruction and field trips. For example, a teacher might preview the expected activities and tasks that a student might complete or encounter while on a field trip to the museum using digital video to illustrate the skills, settings, and people in that setting. Students would rehearse the safety skills for riding the bus, remaining with their teacher, and using a cell phone to call for assistance if they become separated from their group. They might also practice paying

TABLE 10.11 Sample Domestic Domain Life Skills

SKILL	ACTIVITY	EMBEDDED SKILLS
Self-Care	• Requests more toilet paper	• Communication
	• Washes hands	• Motor
	• Takes a bath	• Motor
	• Selects outfit in correct size	• Motor/academic
	• Combs/brushes hair	• Motor
	• Brushes teeth	• Motor
Food/Nutrition	• Heats snack in the microwave oven	• Academic/motor
	• Puts milk into refrigerator	• Academic/motor
	• Sets a table	• Academic/motor
	• Remains with grown-up when shopping	• Motor
	• Orders snack from a snack bar	• Communication/academic
	• Feeds pets	• Motor
Clothing	• Puts away clean clothes	• Motor/personal/social
	• Stores dirty clothes in hamper	• Motor/personal/social
	• Dresses for the weather	• Academic/motor
Personal Finances	• Saves money	• Academic
	• Completes assigned chores for an allowance	• Personal/social
Household Maintenance	• Dusts	• Motor
	• Makes own bed	• Motor
	• Vacuums	• Motor
	• Washes dishes	• Motor
	• Clears dirty dishes from table	• Motor
	• Sweeps	• Motor
Yard Maintenance	• Rakes leaves	• Motor
	• Takes out trash	• Motor

for a ticket and using the museum directory. Upon returning from the field trip, pictures or video might be used again to reinforce the skills and concepts encountered during the experience. Learners might demonstrate how they located a specific exhibit using a museum map or describe the rules they followed to be safe. Table 10.12 provides a sample list of community-based life skills and activities for elementary students.

TABLE 10.12 Sample Community Life Skills

SKILL	ACTIVITY	EMBEDDED SKILLS
Travel Training	• Knows pedestrian and bike safety	• Motor/academic
	• Gives directions	• Academic/communication
Safety	• Recognizes stranger danger	• Personal/social
	• Asks for assistance	• Communication
	• Reads community signs	• Academic
Purchasing	• Makes small purchases	• Academic/personal/social
	• Carries items in a store	• Motor
Using Resources	• Locates and checks out book at public library	• Academic/motor
	• Purchases a stamp at post office	• Academic/communication

RECREATION/LEISURE DOMAIN

To enhance their quality of life, it is necessary for individuals to engage in constructive and personally satisfying recreation and leisure activities. However, individuals with disabilities demonstrate limited repertoires in this area (Schleien, Germ, & McAvoy, 1996). The ability to participate in leisure activities in a socially valued and acceptable manner may have a significant impact on where a person is able to live, job functioning, and relationships that develop with family, neighbors, and others in the community. Elementary students with intellectual disability should be expected to spend their free time in a variety of settings with their peers without a disability. For example, elementary students play in the park and on playgrounds; participate as team members on soccer, T-ball, and baseball teams; play video games individually or with their peers; and engage in activities alone (reading, completing a puzzle, watching a favorite cartoon). The major goal areas the recreation/leisure domain should include are physical fitness; activities to do at home, alone, and in the neighborhood; activities to do with family and friends in the community or neighborhood; and school and extracurricular activities. Table 10.13 provides a sample list of recreation/leisure life skills appropriate for elementary-age students.

Incorporating recreation/leisure skills instruction within the academic day requires teachers to identify those times in which similar or parallel activities are occurring. For example, while all children are playing at recess, target students may be paired with a group to play a team game. A reading or computer

TABLE 10.13 Sample Recreation/Leisure Life Skills

SKILL	ACTIVITY	EMBEDDED SKILLS
Physical Fitness	• Rides bicycle • Plays catch • Participates in team sports	• Motor • Motor/social • Motor/social/communication
Home Activities	• Plays computer games • Works puzzles • Goes fishing	• Academic/motor • Academic/motor • Motor
Community/Neighborhood Activities	• Goes to park • Goes skating • Plays at friend's house	• Motor/academic • Motor • Social/communication
School/Extracurricular Activities	• Reads, looks at books • Shoots baskets • Plays board games	• Academic • Motor • Academic/motor/social

center may be established in a classroom, allowing students to work independently on self-selected activities during earned free time. Learning to ride a bicycle or bounce a basketball may be taught during physical education class. Teachers might also pair academic instruction with recreation and leisure skills by teaching additional skills where all students participate in board or card games and alternate keeping score. In all, recreation and leisure skills are easily embedded within classroom and school routines to encourage the development of cooperative play, independence, and even academic learning.

VOCATIONAL DOMAIN

Gainful employment is the ultimate end goal for all students, and prekindergarten through twelfth-grade education involves preparation for that eventuality. For elementary students, the vocational domain is focused on building the early work-related skills that will one day lead to successful employment. Students should be aware of different kinds of workers, the jobs they do, and the environments in which they work. As well, they should acquire and experience the various prevocational skills required for future employment. In general, pupils should attain skills that will be applicable across a variety of job descriptions (line leader, teacher helper, peer helper) and develop general work adjustment behaviors related to vocational tasks (sorting, following

TABLE 10.14 Sample Vocational Life Skills

SKILL	BEHAVIOR	TEACHING TIPS
General Work Adjustment	• Increase student stamina and endurance	• Allow students to earn reinforcement for increasing their time on task without a break
	• Follow instructions to conclusion	• Use single or multiple picture or word instructions when presenting a new activity
	• Accept feedback and correction	• Provide direct feedback on a task such as "That's wrong. Do it again"
	• Accept changes in a task or schedule	• Interrupt a student's ability to fully complete a task during a designated time
		• Expose students to multiple distractors (visitors, other activities in the setting) when they attempt to complete tasks and remain focused
	• Maintain on-task behavior	• Establish a token system in which students may earn privileges or free time
	• Work for delayed gratification	
	• Follow a sequence when working with materials	• Provide instructions—start to finish, left to right, top to bottom, first to last, empty to full—that facilitate learning sequence
	• Follow a schedule	• Use picture, written, and/or clock-based schedules to illustrate daily activities
	• Compare a completed product to a model	• Provide concrete or picture models of completed products during arts and crafts
	• Understand quantities	• Require students to differentiate concepts—more/less, a lot/a little, numbers and concrete equivalents, one more/one less, basic addition/subtraction
On-the-Job Training and Retraining	• Match to sample	• Label classroom materials to facilitate matching labels, words, numbers, or letters
	• Sort	• Provide opportunities for students to sort by size, use, color, or function (clean/dirty, used/unused, wet/dry)
	• Imitate a model	• Demonstrate both physically and verbally how to open a milk carton
	• Assemble/disassemble items	
	• Perform specific motor actions	• Place items in containers, letters in envelopes
	• Gather and lay out materials according to a list	• Require students to complete motor activities—in/out, open/close, on/off, placements (here/there, up/down)
		• Provide material checklists and require students to check off items from a list as retrieved
	• Clean or clear a workstation	• Require students to clean their work area, put away unused items, and throw away trash

SOURCE: Adapted from P. Alberto, N. Elliott, T. Taber, N. Houser, and P. Andrews, "Vocational content for students with moderate and severe disabilities in elementary and middle grades," *Focus on Exceptional Children*, 25(9), 1993, pp. 1-10.

instructions, accepting feedback). Each of these skills should be addressed within the context of naturally occurring activities, encourage natural supports, and focus on general rather than job-specific skills (Alberto, Elliott, Taber, Houser, & Andrews, 1993). Three primary areas are the focus of the vocational domain: personal behaviors, general work-adjustment behaviors, and on-the-job training and retraining skills. Personal behaviors include using manners when eating, self-management (self-recording, observation, instruction, monitoring), independent use of public restrooms, and self-control of vocal and motor behaviors. Examples of vocational life skills and teaching tips for elementary students appear in Table 10.14. Each teaching tip should result in providing each student positive reinforcement for engaging in target behaviors.

CONCLUSION

Elementary-age students with intellectual disability are very similar to their typically developing peers in terms of the content they need to learn as part of the general education curriculum, especially in the early elementary years. Yet, as they age, academic gaps are often observed, and life skill needs are identified for greater independent functioning. While students continue to require instruction across the general education curriculum (instruction in the traditional academic content areas), instruction in life skills ensures each acquires the necessary skills for living, working, and recreating across integrated school and community environments with their peers.

Chapter Summary

- Most students with intellectual disability spend less than 40 percent of their school day in the general education classroom where they access instruction in the general education curriculum.

- Life skills enable students to access and participate in everyday activities in their current and future environments.

- The instructional domains for life skills are domestic, vocational, recreation/leisure, and community domains. Embedded within each of these domains are functional academic, communication, personal/social, and motor skills.

- When prioritizing instruction for elementary students with intellectual disability, consideration must be given to the age of the individual; his or her current and future learning needs; the student's present learning strengths and challenges; the preferences of the pupil, family, and teacher; whether a skill is socially significant and will lead to increased access in future environments; and safety issues.

- General instructional approaches typically used to teach life skills include task analysis; group instruction; least/most prompting; simulation and in vivo, community-based instruction; and technology-based instruction.

- Life skills instruction may be addressed across the general education curriculum and taught within the contexts of mathematics, science, English/language arts, social studies and health education, and others.

Review Questions

1. Define life skills and discuss why they are taught to students with intellectual disability.

2. Describe how adaptations and modifications are used to accommodate instruction for teaching life skills to elementary

students with intellectual disability.

3. Explain how embedded communication, social/behavioral, academic, and motor skills are taught within the life skill domains.

Key Terms

life skills (page 268)
instructional domains (page 268)
embedded skills (page 268)
accommodations (page 275)
modifications (page 275)
in vivo (page 278)
community-based instruction (CBI) (page 281)
virtual reality (page 282)

augmented reality (page 282)
project-based learning (page 286)
graphic organizers (page 290)
chunking (page 290)
mnemonic (page 290)
direct instruction (page 291)
simulation instruction (page 292)
opportunistic instruction (page 292)

Organizations Concerned With Intellectual Disability

American Association for Intellectual and Developmental Disability

http://aaidd.org

Association of University Centers on Disabilities

www.aucd.org

Developmental Disabilities Resource Center

www.ddrcco.com

Division on Autism and Developmental Disabilities, Council for Exceptional Children

http://daddcec.org

Center for Parent Information and Resources

www.parentcenterhub.org/repository/intellectual/

TASH

http://member. tash.org

PART V

Adolescents and Young Adults With Intellectual Disability

CHAPTER 11

Teaching Academic Skills to Secondary Students With Intellectual Disability

Jordan Shurr and Teresa Taber Doughty

Learning Objectives

After reading Chapter 11, you should be able to:

- Discuss curricular accommodations and differentiated instruction.

- Describe strategies for effectively including students with intellectual disability in academic content classes at the secondary level.

- Discuss how general and special education supports and resources work together to effectively deliver instruction at the secondary level.

- Identify general instructional approaches to teaching academic skills to secondary students with intellectual disability.

College and career readiness is the focal outcome for all students as they enter and complete secondary education (Callan, Finney, Kirst, Usdan, & Venezia, 2006). This preparation is mostly the same for secondary students with intellectual disability and includes active participation in academic subjects, extracurricular activities, and vocational preparation. Special educators seek to ensure that these students are prepared not only for the vocational demands that follow high school but also for the cognitive demands as they pursue work, postsecondary education, community living, and social participation. In this chapter, we will examine the foundations of secondary education, existing secondary education models and curriculum, and how these result in positive post-school outcomes for students with intellectual disability, general instructional strategies for accessing secondary academics, and specific academic content.

TEACHING ACADEMIC SKILLS TO STUDENTS WITH INTELLECTUAL DISABILITY

The Education for All Handicapped Children Act of 1975 (PL 94–142) opened the doors of all public schools to students with disabilities. Subsequent legislation (the No Child Left Behind Act of 2001 and the Individuals with Disabilities Education Improvement Act of 2004 [IDEA 2004]) further defined how students with disabilities were to be included in statewide assessments related to core academic state standards and provided access to the general education curriculum. As a result, a shift in instructional thinking toward a more explicit academic focus and integrated post-school outcomes began for students with intellectual disability. Today it is expected that these students will be educated in integrated core academic content areas, participate in standardized assessments, and pursue post-school outcomes similar to their peers without a disability (see Figure 11.1 for a non-exhaustive listing of secondary content areas).

The U.S. Department of Education (2015) recently noted that students with intellectual disability represent 7.1 percent of all pupils with disabilities who attend school programs in the United States. The vast majority of these students exhibit mild intellectual disability (Gargiulo & Bouck, 2018), and a considerable number (over 43%) of these individuals are served in general education classrooms for a large part of the school day. This report also indicated that while 17.9 percent of secondary students with intellectual disability dropped out of school in 2012–2013 almost 43 percent graduated with a regular high school diploma at the same time (see Figure 11.2 for a description of high school completion options). For these students and others who receive instruction in general education settings, aptitude in academic content such as mathematics, reading, and writing is positively linked with higher rates of employment (Bouck & Joshi, 2012).

FIGURE 11.1 Secondary Content Areas

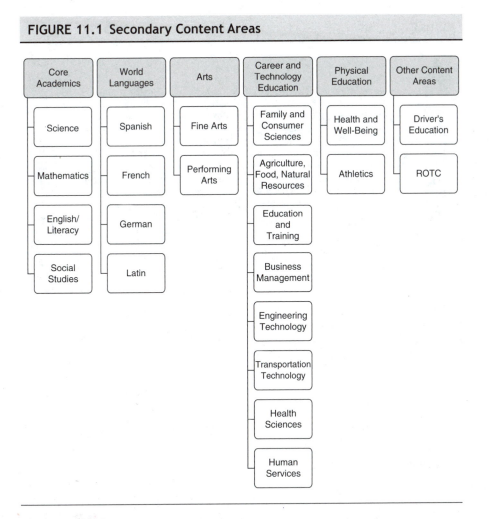

Access to the general education curriculum is a right of every student. Because each student's cognitive potential is unknown, exposure to and participation in the general curriculum is available to all (Courtade, Spooner, Browder, & Jimenez, 2012). By the nature and responsibility of schooling, it also can be considered personally relevant and enriching to life as students learn to apply knowledge to their everyday experiences (Courtade et al., 2012). An example of an activity that reflects enriched learning and experiences is using science inquiry on a walk down the street to better understand the impact of water on plant life when considering why some plants in the shade look healthier than those scorching in the hot sun. Another is studying a map and wondering how long it would take to travel from one point to another using different forms of

FIGURE 11.2 High School Completion Options

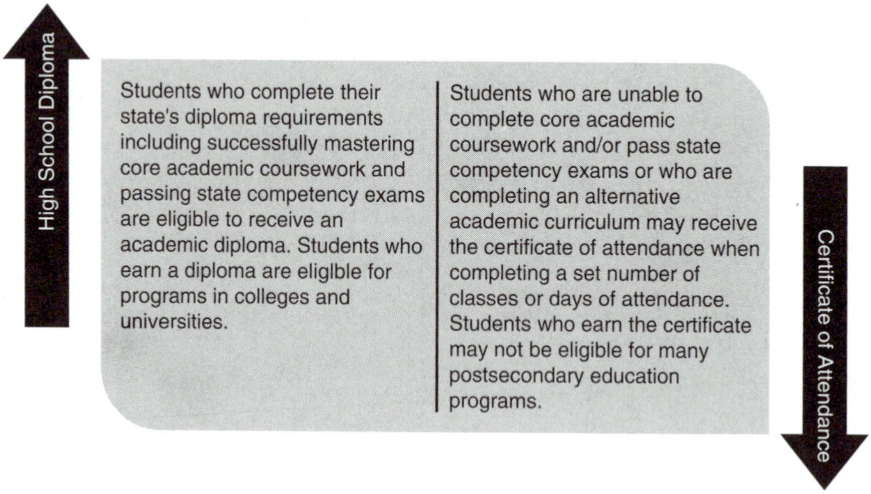

High School Diploma

Students who complete their state's diploma requirements including successfully mastering core academic coursework and passing state competency exams are eligible to receive an academic diploma. Students who earn a diploma are eliglble for programs in colleges and universities.

Students who are unable to complete core academic coursework and/or pass state competency exams or who are completing an alternative academic curriculum may receive the certificate of attendance when completing a set number of classes or days of attendance. Students who earn the certificate may not be eligible for many postsecondary education programs.

Certificate of Attendance

SOURCE: D. Johnson, M. Thurlow, and M. Schuelka, *Diploma Options, Graduation Requirements, and Exit Exams for Youth With Disabilities: 2011 National Study* (Minneapolis, MN: National Center on Educational Outcomes, 2012).

transportation. Such meaningful academic thoughts are common occurrences in everyday life. While they may not be tangibly valuable by way of economic benefit, they are nonetheless important and promote active participation in all aspects of adult life. Thus, exposure to the general academic curriculum may enhance not only academic achievement but life-enriching content as well.

As students with intellectual disability are included in the general education curriculum, they are also included in district- and statewide standardized assessments to determine their annual achievement on grade-level learning goals and instructional effectiveness. During the 2012–2013 academic year, 38.3 percent and 38.4 percent of high school students with a disability participated in regular math assessments with and without accommodations respectively. Likewise, 39.3 percent of secondary students were assessed in reading with accommodations while 37.7 percent were evaluated without accommodations (U.S. Department of Education, 2015). Under the 2015 Every Student Succeeds Act (PL 114–95), the reauthorization of the Elementary and Secondary Education Act/No Child Left Behind, annual measures of academic achievement and student growth are required for all students with not more than 1 percent completing an alternative assessment. While the purpose of

FIGURE 11.3 Emphasis Within the Secondary Curriculum Leading to Post-School Outcomes

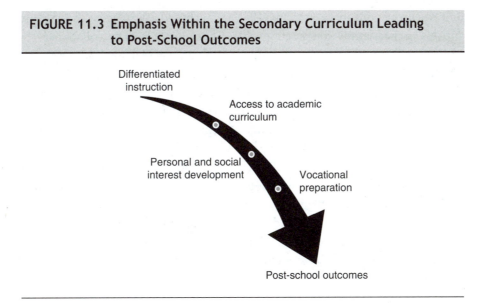

Differentiated instruction

Access to academic curriculum

Personal and social interest development

Vocational preparation

Post-school outcomes

these standardized assessments is to determine the effectiveness of instruction and student learning (Duckworth, Quinn, & Tsukayama, 2012), they also highlight the link between intelligence and performance and serve as predictors of important life outcomes (Kuncel, Ones, & Sackett, 2010). As such, participation in general education content classes with access to and instruction in the academic curriculum is even more important for students with intellectual disability as they prepare for postsecondary education, employment, and active community participation.

SECONDARY INSTRUCTIONAL EMPHASIS

Preparation for life after high school for students with a disability is specifically described in the IDEA-mandated areas of transition including employment, education and training, and community living, when applicable. Access to academic instruction, the use of differentiated instruction, vocational preparation, and opportunities for personal and social development throughout secondary schooling allow students to progress toward meeting their individualized needs and desires in each of these transition areas (see Figure 11.3). Where does the student want to work? What further training or education is needed or desired? How will the student travel in the community? Where will the student live? And, how and where will the student have opportunities to develop and maintain relationships? These are questions that a secondary individualized education program (IEP) team should ask to assist the student and his or her family for meeting post-school goals as they collaboratively work to build an appropriate educational program (see Chapter 13 for an in-depth discussion on transition planning). While access and targeted instruction within a rigorous academic curriculum are critical for developing content knowledge (Courtade et al., 2012), the need remains for a curricular balance with individually relevant functional skills (Ayres, Douglas, Lowrey, & Sievers, 2011). Hunt, McDonnell, and Crockett (2012) suggested "an ecological approach focusing on quality of life outcomes must be reconciled with the development and implementation of standards-based academic curricula" (p. 141). Simply put, academic content access, the central life goal of students with intellectual disability, should be considered. This includes those required areas of transition planning but also, as Hunt and her colleagues argued, content that is deemed by the student and his or her transition team to be "life enriching" (p. 141).

To meet the desired post-school outcomes for teenagers with intellectual disability, it is important to determine the educational pathway that each student should follow to increase success in those next settings. Figure 11.4 highlights the decision-making process for students when determining the secondary curriculum to follow in preparation for transition. Students seeking to transition to traditional postsecondary education programs in community colleges or universities will focus on an academic curriculum with completion of grade-level content with a secondary focus on life skills and real-world content (Bouck, 2012). Students who choose to pursue competitive employment following high school would focus on academic and real-world content with an emphasis on vocational preparation. In addition to the academic coursework, those students might complete internships or community-based training in local businesses to gain specific employment-related skills during their high school career. Finally, students who may enter supported employment would primarily focus on a life skills curriculum while also participating in the general education curriculum. Chapter 12 provides a more in-depth discussion of the life skills curricular approach for secondary students with intellectual disability.

Whether planning for higher education or employment following completion of their secondary education, students with intellectual disability also must be prepared to effectively interact with others in a diverse community. This is done through active participation in academic, social, and extracurricular activities where individuals with intellectual disability can demonstrate their social

FIGURE 11.4 Secondary Curriculum Decision-Making Process

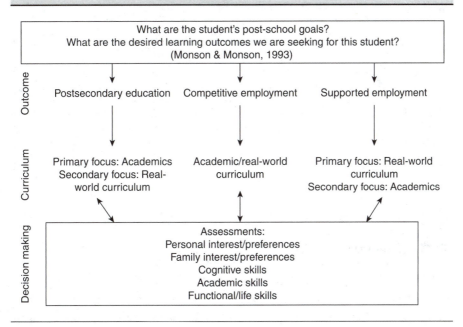

SOURCE: Adapted from E. Bouck, "Secondary Curriculum and Transition." In P. Wehman (Ed.), *Life Beyond the Classroom*, 5th ed. (Baltimore, MD: Paul H. Brookes, 2012), pp. 215-233.

skills, academic strengths, and personal competencies. Recent studies examined peer attitudes toward students with intellectual disability and found that while many middle school peers perceived students with intellectual disability as less capable of mastering academic content or complex tasks, positive perceptions increased as individuals with intellectual disability demonstrated competencies (Patel & Rose, 2014). Thus, the more competencies demonstrated by an individual with an intellectual disability, the more that she or he will be perceived positively by peers. This idea extends to post-school settings in which academic and vocational competency are valued along with social competencies and lead to greater positive perceptions and interactions by and with peers and colleagues (Griffin, Summer, McMillan, Day, & Hodapp, 2012). Thus, at the secondary level, instruction in social skills should be intentionally and systematically embedded throughout the academic and vocational curriculum to facilitate competency development, positive attitudes, and relationship development between peers. Figure 11.5 provides a list of competency areas that should be addressed within a student's educational curriculum to increase the opportunity to increase skills in these areas.

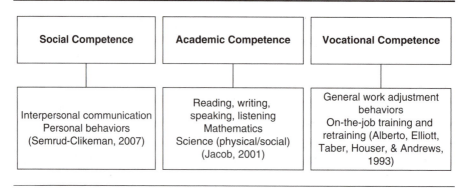

FIGURE 11.5 Social, Academic, and Vocational Competencies

Social Competence	Academic Competence	Vocational Competence
Interpersonal communication Personal behaviors (Semrud-Clikeman, 2007)	Reading, writing, speaking, listening Mathematics Science (physical/social) (Jacob, 2001)	General work adjustment behaviors On-the-job training and retraining (Alberto, Elliott, Taber, Houser, & Andrews, 1993)

Social competencies are value judgments of others based on how well an individual performs social tasks (McFall, 1982). Acceptable social competencies facilitate interactions with peers, lead to the development of friendships (Semrud-Clikeman, 2007), and directly influence an individual's ability to effectively interact with peers throughout the school day (Hughes et al., 2012). They include interpersonal communication skills (use of language and ability to have a conversation; ability to work with others, learn, and take another's perspective) (Semrud-Clikeman, 2007) and personal behaviors (physical self-control, keeping track of time, independent use of public facilities, acceptable grooming and hygiene, self-management skills, eating with appropriate manners) (Alberto et al., 1993), which result in socially important outcomes (Gresham, Sugai, & Horner, 2001).
Academic competencies are those required for successful movement through the grade-level curriculum and include success in learning language arts (reading, writing, speaking, listening), mathematics, and physical and social science (Jacob, 2001). Finally, **vocational competencies** include those skills related to successful employment such as general work adjustment behaviors (following a schedule, working for delayed gratification, accepting feedback and correction, understanding quantities) and on-the-job training and retraining (sorting, matching-to-sample, imitating a model, assembling and disassembling, performing specific motor actions, gathering materials, cleaning workstation) (Alberto et al., 1993). The ability to demonstrate proficiency in each of these areas contributes to others perceiving an individual as competent. For people with an intellectual disability, this also may increase their likelihood for success in relationship development.

For individuals with intellectual disability who matriculate to a postsecondary institution, secondary curricular emphasis must extend beyond academics.

Access and success in postsecondary settings require that secondary instruction focus on self-advocacy during IEP meetings, participation in preferred extracurricular activities to build socialization and problem-solving skills, the ability to use technology, and the receipt of guidance from high school counselors who can assist students in identifying their career and other post-school goals (Kleinert, Jones, Sheppard-Jones, Harp, & Harrison, 2012). With the reauthorization of the Higher Education Opportunity Act of 2008, the transition of students with a disability to postsecondary education received greater emphasis with financial support available when students are enrolled in a comprehensive transition and postsecondary program (Kleinert et al., 2012; Plotner & Marshall, 2015). From 1990 to 2005, the percentage of individuals with intellectual disability enrolling in advanced education programs increased from 8 to 28 percent (Newman, Wagner, Cameto, Knokey, & Shaver, 2010) in over 220 postsecondary programs (Plotner & Marshall, 2015). Their participation in postsecondary education resulted in reported positive increases in emotional well-being, interpersonal relationships, social inclusion (Hughson, Moodie, & Uditsky, 2006), improved academic learning, career development, and self-determination skills (Lynch & Gretzel, 2013), and when combined with vocational preparation, it resulted in positive employment outcomes (Migliore, Butterworth, & Hart, 2009).

GENERAL INSTRUCTIONAL STRATEGIES

Instructional strategies that result in achievement of academic content as well as increased visibility of overall student competence are desired goals for secondary programming. Numerous strategies are identified as effective in teaching academic competencies when used with students with an intellectual disability, including co-teaching (Villa, Thousand, & Nevin, 2013), varying instructional groupings (Hollo & Hirn, 2015; Wehmeyer et al., 2014), use of technology in instruction (Ayres, Mechling, & Sansosti, 2013), differentiated instruction (Zigmond, 2015), and using simulations and games (McMahon, Smith, Cihak, Wright, & Gibbons, 2015). As well, strategies for increasing social competencies include participation in extracurricular activities (Brooks, Floyd, Robins, & Chan, 2015), social problem solving, and conversational skills training, along with peer modeling (Hughes et al., 2012) and direct instruction (Morrison, Kamps, Gargia, & Parker, 2001).

Co-teaching. One prevalent model for serving children with a disability in inclusive classroom settings, particularly at the secondary level, is the use of co-teaching. Also known as collaborative or team teaching, **co-teaching** is the teaming of general and special education educators to jointly provide instruction and supports to all who receive instruction in the general education classroom (Dieker & Murawski, 2003). Both teachers plan and teach together, develop and provide accommodations together, and assess their students' progress in the academic content area being taught (Villa et al., 2013). A combination of various co-teaching formats is used in inclusive classroom settings that include the following: supportive co-teaching, parallel co-teaching, complementary co-teaching, and team teaching (Villa, 2016). Table 11.1 provides a description of each co-teaching format. Co-teaching results in a positive effect on student achievement; students with a disability learn more and demonstrate increased performance in academic assessments when in co-teaching classes (Walsh, 2012).

TABLE 11.1 Formats for Co-Teaching

CO-TEACHING FORMAT	DESCRIPTION
Supportive Co-teaching	Previously known as "one-teach, one-observe" and "one-teach, one-assist" models, supportive co-teaching allows one teacher to lead the overall class in instruction while the other either observes student learning or moves through the classroom setting and provides individual assistance to students as needed.
Parallel Co-teaching	This may include station teaching where students rotate through small-group learning stations and complete different tasks focused on the same instructional content. Co-teachers coordinate the tasks across the different stations and may lead activities at different stations. Overall, parallel co-teaching involves each teacher working with a different heterogeneous group of students to teach content simultaneously.
Complementary Co-teaching	Here, one team teacher provides supplementary or complementary instruction to students. This may be in the form of enrichment activities for higher-achieving students or remedial instruction for students who require additional instructional assistance.
Team Teaching	When team teaching occurs, both teachers instruct together while being jointly responsible for all aspects of preparation and delivering instruction as well as assessing student acquisition of content.

SOURCE: Adapted from R. Villa, *Effective Co-teaching Strategies*. Available at http://www.teachhub.com/effective-co-teaching-strategies

Instructional arrangements. The use of various instructional arrangements is also demonstrated to be effective for increasing learning and perceptions of student competencies (Carter & Hughes, 2005). **Instructional arrangements** are the groupings in which students might be taught and include one-on-one and small groups, whole-class instruction, cooperative learning groups, and peer modeling/tutoring (Logan, Bakeman, & Keefe, 1997). For example, a student with an intellectual disability might participate in a lesson with just the teacher (individual instruction), with a group of two to three other students and the teacher (small group), with the entire class (whole-class instruction), within a cooperative learning group of peers, or with a single peer (peer tutoring/modeling/instruction). Table 11.2 provides a description of each grouping model. Individual and small-group instruction are frequently more effective than large-group arrangements, allow for greater individualization of instruction, and are better predictors of access to the general curriculum (Stenhoff & Lignugaris/Kraft, 2007). Peer modeling/tutoring and cooperative learning groups were also found to be evidence-based practices for successfully teaching students with intellectual disability (Stenhoff & Lignugaris/Kraft, 2007).

TABLE 11.2 Instructional Groupings

INSTRUCTIONAL ARRANGEMENT	DESCRIPTION
Individual, One-on-One Instruction	Instruction is provided to an individual student by the teacher. Allows for specialized accommodations and instructional adjustments based on student needs (Osewalt, 2016).
Small-Group Instruction	Teachers work with two to four students to provide instruction on specific learning objectives (Meador, 2015).
Whole-Class, Large-Group Instruction	The same instruction is provided to the entire class simultaneously with little to no differentiation of instruction for individuals (Meador, 2016).
Cooperative Learning Groups, Small-Group Learning	A small number of students work together to complete a common task. Allows for positive interdependence, individualized interaction, and individual and group accountability (Johnson & Johnson, 1999).
Peer Instruction, Modeling, Tutoring	Peers serve as tutors and tutees to acquire and/or review instructional content. Includes class-wide, cross-age, reciprocal, and same-age peer tutoring (Hott & Walker, 2012).

Because of the complexity of secondary academic content classes and the differing needs of participating students, alternating a variety of instructional arrangements may increase the overall engaged behavior and learning of those with intellectual disability (Logan et al., 1997).

Technology. As technology advances, so too do the instructional strategies available to all students. In recent years, numerous technologies were effectively used by individuals with intellectual disability to learn various academic content and functional skills (Wehmeyer, Smith, Palmer, & Davies, 2004). Computer-assisted instruction (Coleman, Hurley, & Cihak, 2012), virtual manipulatives (Bouck, Satsangi, Doughty, & Courtney, 2014), digital navigation aids (McMahon, Smith, Cihak, Wright, & Gibbons, 2015), and video modeling (Burton, Anderson, Prater, & Dyches, 2013) are examples of some of the technologies that were successfully integrated into instruction. Using these technologies, students with intellectual disability acquired sight words, mathematics skills, the ability to navigate complex locations, and increased academic responding. When integrated into a secondary curriculum, technology has the potential to considerably influence the classroom, how teachers teach, and how students learn (Mouza & Lavigne, 2013). The basic types of **technologies for the classroom** include technology for student support and technology for instructional support (Halverson & Smith, 2010). These technologies integrate visualization tools, serious games, and networked technologies (Mouza & Lavigne, 2013), and when they are used by and with students with an intellectual disability, students are able to immediately access information related to the content topic, interact with that content, and communicate their learning. For example, students may blog about a specific topic to practice their writing skills in a language arts/English class, learn about U.S. geography through a serious/smart game on the American Revolution during a social studies class. Table 11.3 provides a description of these technology types and how they might be used in a secondary academic setting for students with an intellectual disability. See Chapter 6 for a more in-depth discussion of technology to support students with intellectual disability.

Differentiated instruction. Differentiated instruction is the theoretical approach that instruction should vary and adaptations should occur in response to individual student needs (Hall, Vue, Strangman, & Meyer, 2004). Introduced as a full model in the mid-1990s (Tomlinson, 1995), it serves as a teaching method for groups of students with teachers designing lessons around needs of each group (Osewalt, 2016). Differentiated instruction requires teachers to

TABLE 11.3 Technology Examples for Academic Settings

TECHNOLOGY	DESCRIPTION	HOW USED IN SECONDARY ACADEMICS
Visualization Tools—Virtual/ Augmented Reality	Digital tools that illustrate simple and complex representations of information and can be used by students to "view, analyze, manipulate, and/or communicate complex information" (Carnegie Mellon, 2016)	Students in a biology class use virtual frog dissection application software when studying the internal organs of amphibians.
Serious Games	Digital and video games that integrate challenge, fantasy, curiosity, and control and are focused on specific and intentional learning of content that results in specific and measurable outcomes (Derryberry, 2007)	DragonBox Algebra 12+ (WeWantToKnow, 2016; http://dragonbox.com/home) helps students solve algebraic equations and improve their skills in algebra
Networked Technologies	Tools that allow for the ability to maintain connections with people and information and enable supported learning	Interactive whiteboards can be used to teach individual, small, or large groups of students to actively engage with content and electronically communicate their learning with others (SMART Technologies, 2006). Social media can include writing to or responding to blogs using Word-Press or Weebly, YouTube can be used to post student presentations for feedback, and Twitter accounts may be used to post updates about school projects. Each can be incorporated in and across the academic curriculum.

be flexible in their teaching and accommodate for each individual student's learning needs (Zigmond, 2015). The idea is that all students learn differently and, thus, methods and materials should vary (Mastropieri & Scruggs, 2007). For students with intellectual disability participating in secondary academic classes, differentiated instruction provides "avenues for students to acquire content, to process information and ideas, and to develop products" (Allan & Goddard, 2010, p. 1). Differentiation may include within-classroom differentiation (flexible groupings, individualized supports) and structural differentiation (specialized services for specific students) within the context of the academic classroom setting (Allan & Goddard, 2010). For example, an adolescent with an intellectual disability might use an app on a handheld electronic device to view a video model before engaging in a lab experiment in a biology class (within-classroom differentiation). In another example, a special education teacher might work directly with a small group of students with an intellectual disability to review and reinforce content from a world history class (structural differentiation). In both instances, students receive the instructional supports needed to successfully achieve in the general education curriculum.

Differentiated instruction is similar, in some respects, but different from universal design for learning (UDL) (CAST, 2013). UDL, which is discussed in greater detail in Chapter 3, is more proactive in the sense that the accessibility and opportunities for *all* students are developed and implemented at the beginning—or, in other words, as a preventative measure. Differentiated instruction is more about individual student access (CAST, 2013).

Social skills. Since acceptable social competencies are crucial to an increased quality of life for individuals with intellectual disability (Gresham et al., 2001), specific instruction in social skills must be embedded within and across the general curriculum. In a review of the literature on social skills instruction among adolescents with intellectual disability, Carter and Hughes (2005) identified numerous intervention studies that reported positive reports. These studies indicated two primary intervention types: skill-based interventions (self-management and social interaction instruction, collateral skill instruction, communication book and social interaction instruction), and support-based interventions (general education class participation, peer support arrangements, instructional groupings, peer training). **Skill-based interventions** are those in which students are taught to use specific skills that facilitate social skills learning. For example, a student would be taught to use a picture prompt to initiate a conversation with a peer or how to play a serious video game with a peer while making socially acceptable comments. These interventions can take place throughout each school day and should be incorporated into the fabric of daily classroom activities. **Support-based interventions** are those that are teacher initiated and facilitate increased social interactions between peers with and without a disability. Table 11.4 provides an example of each intervention type.

Extracurricular activities. In addition to specific social skill interventions that may originate with the teacher, providing opportunities to participate in

TABLE 11.4 Social Skill Interventions

SKILL-BASED INTERVENTIONS	DESCRIPTIONS
Self-Management and Social Interaction	Self-prompting or self-initiating conversations and social interactions
Collateral Skill Instruction	Interacting with peers and others in various formats such as when playing computer games
Communication Book Instruction	Often used by individuals who are nonverbal, students are taught to initiate and maintain conversations using topic-appropriate pictures in conversational turn taking
Social Interaction Instruction	May include the use of appropriate greetings and social comments

SUPPORT-BASED INTERVENTIONS	DESCRIPTIONS
General Education Class Participation	Enrollment in academic and extracurricular classes with same-age peers without disabilities
Peer Support Arrangements	Pairing students with and without a disability during academic and nonacademic activities
Instructional Groupings	Organizing the classroom into cooperative learning groups
Peer Training	Pairing a peer with and without a disability for academic and/or social skills training; both peers alternate serving as the trainer

nonacademic areas may lead to an increase in social skills and perceived social competencies. Studies report that active participation in extracurricular activities alongside peers without disabilities led to the development of increased social skills while passive participation in inclusive or mainstreamed classrooms resulted in limited increases in social skills (Brooks et al., 2015). The multitude of extracurricular activities available at the secondary level offer social opportunities for peers with and without a disability to be engaged with one another (Abells, Burbridge, & Minnes, 2008). While studies report that individuals with intellectual disability were less active in extracurricular activities than their same-age peers (Bedell et al., 2013), their participation in structured school-related functions (student organizations, athletic events, performing arts events) and unstructured social activities outside of school (hanging out with friends, listening to music, going to the mall or gym) increased their likelihood of developing valued social skills (Ghosh & Datta, 2012; Siperstein, Glick, & Parker, 2009).

ACADEMIC INSTRUCTION

Academic Content. Although mathematics, language arts, social studies, and science are all typical components of secondary school programming, deciding what to teach students with intellectual disability rests on the IEP team and is guided by grade-level academic standards as well as the students' transition goals. While students should receive instruction in each of the academic content areas, the specific foci or application of standards will likely differ for each student based on his or her transition goals and needs. Every grade-level academic standard may not be appropriate for each student with intellectual disability, depending on individuals' transition goals and necessary prerequisite skills. However, students with intellectual disability can and should have both broad and focused access to academic content due to the inherent benefits in each of the core transition areas as well as the general enrichment to quality of life such access can afford. Due to the need for dual focus on academic access and successful transition to life after school, each of the academic content areas will be described in terms of both academic content and contexts as well as practical and functional applications for daily life. In other words, this section of the chapter will focus on academics as well as the relationship between academics and daily living for secondary students with intellectual disability. Instructional approaches for teaching academic content will be highlighted, including systematic instruction, natural supports and embedded instruction, and technology (see Table 11.5 for examples of these approaches across the core content areas). It should be noted that teachers often integrate these approaches for increased student support.

LANGUAGE ARTS

The primary goal of language arts instruction is to teach students to employ language skills to learn content, communicate clearly, solve problems, self-reflect, self-advocate, and gain multiple perspectives (Shea, 1989). For secondary students, these goals are especially important as they directly relate to an individual's quality of life. Lifelong learning; communicating with peers, employers, and family; and gaining a better understanding of the perspectives of others is not only life enriching, but also critical for the development

TABLE 11.5 Sample Supports for Core Academic Content

TOPIC	ACTIVITY	SUPPORT STRATEGY	EXAMPLE
Language Arts	Write a book report	Natural supports—peers	Have a classmate review the student's report draft and provide content and technical edit suggestions.
Math	Understand probability	Systematic instruction—task analysis	Use a task analysis sequence of steps to daily track the weather report likelihood of rain and actual daily rain occurrence. These data can be used to understand how probability can be used to predict occurrences.
Social Studies	Locate Civil War battle sites on map	Systematic instruction—least to most prompts	Use least to most prompting (gesture, verbal, visual, etc.) to help the student successfully match a note card with a picture and the name of a battlefield on it with the corresponding location on a map.
Science	Identify constellations	Technology	Use a tablet or smartphone and web-based app (for example, SkyView [Terminal Eleven, 2010; www.terminaleleven.com]) pointed to the night sky to identify constellations. Have the student practice identifying constellations without the device and then use it to check his or her work.

of academic and functionally oriented skills. For example, students who are taught to identify their unique strengths and desires in future employment and to communicate clearly with their teachers and family are likely to receive the directed support and training to pursue and achieve their career goals.

The content area of **language arts** comprises five essential components including reading, writing, listening, speaking, and language (Common Core State Standards Initiative, 2016a). These can be further grouped into receptive-oriented language arts skills—those skills that involve internal student process and comprehension (that is, reading and listening)—and expressive-oriented skills—those skills that focus on student output to create, comment, or question (that is, writing and speaking). The fifth component, language, focuses on grammar, rules, and conventions, and permeates each of the other four content areas. While taught in dedicated courses, language arts content, arguably more

TABLE 11.6 Activity-Based Examples of Supported Language Arts Components

LANGUAGE ARTS COMPONENT	ACTIVITY	SYSTEMATIC INSTRUCTION	NATURAL AND EMBEDDED SUPPORTS	TECHNOLOGY
Reading/ Listening— Academic	Read *To Kill a Mockingbird* for a language arts course	Teacher uses representative photos for each chapter and uses constant time delay to teach students to correctly order the photos by occurrence in the text.	Peer reads the chapter while introducing the relevant photos.	Student uses a dictionary pen to highlight and audibly define unfamiliar words.
Reading/ Listening— Community	Read a public transportation map to get to work	Teacher uses the system of least prompts to teach student to identify correct bus route and stop on map.	Peer models reading the map and identifying routes and stops in a video for the student.	Student uses public transportation web-based app to identify correct route and stop.
Writing— Academic	Write a persuasive essay	Teacher uses a graphic organizer to help student visually plan the essay structure.	Peer works with student to complete graphic organizer.	Student writes essay with speech-to-text software.
Writing— Community	Write a work-related e-mail requesting time off	Teacher provides template e-mail and uses most to least prompting to teach student how to fill in each blank.	Student writes draft e-mail and shares with peer for help with edits.	Student writes e-mail and uses software (for example, *Grammarly* (2016; www .grammarly.com) to suggest spelling and grammatical edits.
Speaking— Academic	Present a book report	Teacher uses representative photos and constant time delay to teach identification of key concepts from the book.	Student prepares and pre-sents report with a peer.	Student creates a video-based book report to present.
Speaking— Community	Order food at a restaurant	Teacher uses a task analysis to teach how to place an order.	Student points to the desired item on the menu.	Student uses a speech-generating augmentative and alternative communication (AAC) device to place order.

than any other, is part of most, if not all, areas of school and life (for example, participation in one's community). Practical examples of these school and life applications of language arts include, for example, solving problems, communicating clearly, accessing and learning content, and self-advocacy. Table 11.6 provides some examples of how language arts may be supported during instruction for secondary students with intellectual disability, when considering both academic and community foci.

As noted, instruction in language arts is important for secondary students with intellectual disability for school and/or academic reasons. However, instruction and access to language arts instruction for secondary pupils with intellectual disability is equally important given the connection between strong skills in reading, writing, speaking, and listening and positive post-school outcomes or adult life skills. Hence, instruction in language arts should also support students' transition and postschool goals. Table 11.7 provides examples of transition-relevant activities for each of the language arts components.

Receptive language arts skills. The National Reading Panel (2000) identified five key areas of focus for empirically based reading instruction: phonemic awareness, phonics, fluency, vocabulary, and comprehension (see Table 11.8). Prior research indicates that students with intellectual disability are able to

TABLE 11.7 Examples of Language Arts Components in Transition-Relevant Context

LANGUAGE ARTS COMPONENT	EDUCATION AND TRAINING	EMPLOYMENT	COMMUNITY LIVING	ENRICHMENT
Reading	Reading course texts	Reading an employee handbook	Reading a recipe	Reading a magazine article for leisure
Writing	Taking a fill-in-the-blank test	Writing a work-related e-mail	Making a grocery list	Writing a postcard
Listening	Following group activities in class	Understanding a supervisor's verbal instructions	Listening to a weather report	Listening to sports radio
Speaking	Contributing to a class discussion	Asking a question	Ordering food at a restaurant	Talking to a friend about your day

TABLE 11.8 National Reading Panel Reading Components, Descriptions, and Examples

READING COMPONENT	DEFINITION	SECONDARY EXAMPLE
Phonemic Awareness	The ability to identify sound units in words	Rhyme words to complete a poem
Phonics	The ability to sound out words	Sound out unfamiliar words to read countries on a map
Fluency	Pace and precision of reading	Read game instructions aloud to a peer group
Vocabulary	Number of words known	Differentiate between different key action words in cooking (for example, *mix, stir, sift*)
Comprehension	The ability to understand what is read	Complete a new job when given verbal or written instructions by a supervisor

gain meaningful skills in all areas of reading (Browder et al., 2009; Browder, Wakeman, Spooner, Ahlgrim-Delzell, & Algozzine, 2006; Hudson, Browder, & Wood, 2013).

The most salient evidence-based strategy to increase the receptive language arts abilities of students with intellectual disability is systematic instruction (Hudson, Browder, & Wood, 2013; Hudson & Test, 2011). **Systematic instruction** is a form of direct instruction that uses specifically arranged instructional trials to allow for structured, supported, and repeated practice of a skill (the reader can also refer to Chapter 9 regarding systematic instruction). This includes strategies such as the system of most to least or least to most prompts, time delay, and task analysis instruction (Collins, 2012). Prompting refers to any help provided during a student's performance of a skill or activity. This could include showing the student representative photos to help him or her remember the steps for an activity. Also, this could include a gesture toward the required materials or even physical assistance in obtaining materials. Prompting is generally thought of as an array of help from least (gestural) to most (full physical) intrusive. Figure 11.6 illustrates the array of prompts and directions of the progression from least to most (gesture, verbal, visual, etc.) and most to least (full physical, partial physical, model, etc.). Task analysis instruction is the act of breaking down a skill into small steps for focused step-by-step instruction. For instance, writing a book review could include such steps as

FIGURE 11.6 Prompting Systems

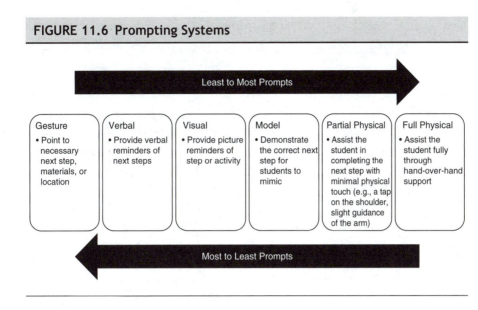

(1) creating an outline, (2) writing an introductory paragraph, (3–5) writing three paragraphs, (6) writing a conclusive paragraph, (7) editing for content, and (8) editing for grammar, spelling, and punctuation.

In many cases, reading and listening activities can occur simultaneously. Rather than independently reading or reading a printed text with support, some students with intellectual disability benefit from accessing reading materials via listening. Listening access can be achieved through technology or teacher or peer read-aloud to enable access to materials that will be read in the traditional sense by a student with intellectual disability's peers (Browder et al., 2009). For example, for assigned chapter readings that most students would read independently at home, students with intellectual disability and reading difficulty may benefit from listening to the recorded readings or listening to the readings while watching the read words highlighted via a screen-reading computer program (for example, NaturalReader [NaturalSoft Limited, 2016; www.naturalreaders.com/index.html]). Also, students may access texts as read to them by peers or read aloud to the class by a general education teacher. Accessing printed text via technology (that is, listening) can occur by using books on tape (or CD), digital books or e-books, or text-to-speech or screen readers (see Chapter 6 for additional information regarding the use of technology to support reading for students with intellectual disability). Reading via a teacher or peer is often referred to as read-alouds or shared stories (Hudson & Test, 2011). Intuitively, as it sounds, read-alouds or shared stories involve hearing stories read out loud, often stories that include text that exceeds an individual's reading ability.

To help support students with intellectual disability more independently access printed text or more meaningfully participate in shared stories, reading materials can be adapted or modified. Common research-supported practices to develop **adapted text** for students with intellectual disability include incorporating visual symbols or objects before, during, and after reading the story; implementing a task analysis for teacher story-based interactions with the student (Browder, Trela, & Jimenez, 2007); using a combination of pictures and discussion (Shurr & Taber-Doughty, 2016); teaching text vocabulary; implementing a structure for student questions during the reading (Wood, Browder, & Flynn, 2015); and shortening or rewriting the text to a lower reading level (Hudson, Browder, & Wakeman, 2013). For instance, a course reading of Alice Walker's novel *The Color Purple* could be adapted to meet the access needs of a student with intellectual disability through the use of representative photos or objects related to the characters, topics, and events from the chapters. Additionally, the text could be read aloud to the student either in its current form with the support of representative pictures and discussion or in an adapted form—rewritten to reflect a lower reading level.

Expressive language arts skills. Writing involves both the technical components of handwriting, spelling, and grammar and the more process-orientated components of writing including the writing purposes, learning to write various types of text, and writing with clarity and purpose (Common Core State Standards Initiative, 2016a). Writing is an important and integral component of both academic and functional life as students use writing to show what they know and to communicate with others. Writing can be supported through systematic instruction, such as direct teacher instruction in the writing process of POWER: planning, organizing, writing, editing, and reviewing. Additionally, **natural supports** such as peer sharing or editing drafts of a written product can increase student success in writing (Sturm, 2012). Finally, technology, such as speech-to-text or electronic dictionaries, can support the writing of students with disabilities. See Chapter 6 for additional information regarding assistive technology to support writing. For example, a personal daily journal-writing activity could be supported through systematic instruction such as task analysis instruction for the steps of brainstorming, organizing, writing, and editing a journal entry. Also, recent photos of a student completing a favorite or routine activity could be used to elicit and support a journal entry topic. Peers could be used to model the writing process or co-write an entry, transcribe a student's entry, proofread, or discuss relevant journal topics. Technology such as speech-to-text could allow the students to write an entry without relying on handwriting or typing. Additional technology to support creating a journal entry could include general editing technology (for example, Grammarly, 2016), organizational technology such as a graphic organizer to assist in brainstorming and organization, and web-based technology such as online photo libraries to insert pictures into a journal entry to relay a message without text.

The sub–language arts area of speaking in the academic context can be described as contributing to both small- and large-group discussion with clarity and thoughtfulness (Common Core State Standards Initiative, 2016a). Speaking skills are commonly grouped into the area of communication or social skills and span both functional and academic settings. For students with more severe intellectual disability and/or comorbid communication difficulties, expression is often supported through augmentative and alternative communication (AAC). (See Chapter 6 for a more in-depth discussion regarding AAC.)

MATHEMATICS

For most states, the standards for mathematics at the Common Core State Standards (CCSS) (see Chapters 3 and 9 for more in-depth information relative to the CCSS in general or the application to students with intellectual disability more specifically). The CCSS in mathematics at the high school level focus on the mathematical concepts of number and quantity, algebra, functions, modeling, geometry, and statistics and probability (Common Core State Standards Initiative, 2016b). Mathematics education is important for students with intellectual disability for the academic as well as the functional benefits (see Chapter 12 for an in-depth discussion of teaching life skills to secondary students with intellectual disability). Many aspects of adult living require mathematics (for example, grocery shopping, paying bills). Learning academic aspect of mathematics can support the independence and adult life outcomes of students with intellectual disability (see Table 11.9 for examples of the connection between mathematics concepts and skills and functional applications). Despite the importance of mathematics education, the existing research base on teaching mathematics to students with intellectual disability focuses almost exclusively on the mathematical domain of numbers and operations.

TABLE 11.9 Connection Between Mathematics Concepts and Functional Applications

CONCEPT AND SKILL EXAMPLES	FUNCTIONAL APPLICATION EXAMPLES
• Use fractions to solve problems • Use ratios to solve problems	• Determine the sale price of items in a store • Double the ingredients in a recipe
• Generalize patterns from tables • Use an algebraic equation to represent a situation	• Determine the appropriate amount of medicine to take by weight and age • Determine the original price of a sale item
• Apply geometric concepts in art • Use geometric concepts to solve problems	• Create a ceramic bowl • Find an appropriate-sized shipping box for an item
• Understand metric measurement • Estimate measurement	• Accurately dispense medication in metric measurement • Select clothing based on estimation of appropriate size
• Collect data about a population • Understand and apply probability	• Collect lunch orders for office colleagues • Use the weather report to select appropriate attire

Numbers and operations. As previously noted, most of the research teaching mathematics to students with intellectual disability focuses on numbers and operations. This content area includes basic mathematical concepts and skills such as addition, subtraction, multiplication, and division using single- and multi-digit whole numbers, fractions, and decimals. This area of instruction can be supported through natural supports such as peer learning groups, community-based instruction, and peer tutoring in general education and community settings. For example, students with intellectual disability may work in the school bookstore using skills in this area to complete sales. Systematic instruction, such as using task analysis and the system of most prompts, can enable a student with intellectual disability to complete an equation. Use of technology, such as a calculator, can help students compute mathematical problems such as finding the total sum of a series of items for purchase.

Algebra, geometry, measurement, data analysis, and probability. Research in algebra, geometry, and measurement, as well as data analysis and probability instruction, is still in the emerging stages for students with intellectual disability. Instructional techniques such as systematic instruction, natural and embedded supports, and technology integration continue to serve as effective support strategies for academic learning. However, what the field has learned about the capabilities of individuals with intellectual disability to learn academic content is most often bounded by our ability to adequately support and nurture such learning. Examples of systematic instruction include using a task analysis and prompt fading to teach algebraic equations (Jimenez, Browder, & Courtade, 2008) and most to least prompting to teach geometry and measurement skills (Hord & Xin, 2015). This includes using a task analysis approach to break down the activity into several individual and sequential steps. These steps, such as identifying the radius line of a circle or x in an algebraic equation, can then be individually taught and supported through prompting (hand-over-hand guidance to find the x or radius). In terms of technology, using visual models (or concrete manipulatives), virtual manipulatives, games, computer-assisted instruction, and video modeling can be beneficial to supporting skill practice and acquisition. Video self-modeling, for example, can be used to teach secondary students to complete a task analysis for completing algebraic story problems (Burton et al., 2013). In this case, the teacher would video record a student completing the steps for solving a story problem while providing the necessary prompts for accurate performance. The teacher could then edit out the prompts and create a final video for the student that depicts a model of him- or herself completing each of the necessary steps. Using self-modeling in instruction, such as this, can be highly effective in increasing a student's task accuracy and overall task confidence.

SCIENCE

The field of science instruction is organized on three different dimensions including practices, crosscutting concepts, and core ideas. The first dimension, **science practices**, refers to both scientific and engineering practices involved in the processes of science including asking questions, creating models, investigating, analyzing data, using mathematics, hypothesizing, defending a hypothesis, and assessing and reporting results. **Science concepts** that are considered to be crosscutting with other disciplines include "patterns, cause and effect, scale, proportion, and quantity, systems and system models, energy and matter, structure and function, and stability and change" (National Research Council, 2012, p. 3). And the four disciplinary **science ideas** identified include physical science (physics, chemistry), life science (biology, ecology), earth and space science (geology, planetary science), and the area of engineering, technology, and applications of science, which is integrated into all areas (National Research Council, 2012).

The research on science instruction for individuals with intellectual disability focuses on scientific concepts applied in functional contexts (for example, community navigation, weather concepts) as well as science content and processes in the traditional academic sense. A discussion on the science-related application of functional life skills in science can be found in Chapter 12. Table 11.10 provides examples of secondary science content along with the functional application of each concept in each of the core areas.

Similar to other areas of academic instruction, acquisition of science skills and concepts should be supported by use of systematic instruction, technology, and natural and embedded supports. Similar to math instruction, systematic instruction can be a natural fit to the methodical procedures of the scientific method. Students with intellectual disability benefit from such explicit and direct stepwise guidance to complete daily and academic tasks. Breaking scientific procedures into specific components can have a beneficial effect for pupils with intellectual disability as they learn the content. For example, a chemistry experiment would likely involve a series of precise and sequential steps in order to achieve the desired end result. This series of steps can be used to guide the individual throughout the process. Depending on the student's needs, adding

TABLE 11.10 Science Concept Examples and Functional Applications

CONTENT	CONCEPT AND SKILL EXAMPLES	FUNCTIONAL APPLICATION EXAMPLES
Physical Science	• Create and analyze chemical reactions • Understand and apply principles of thermal energy transfer	• Safely mix cleaning solutions • Select appropriate materials to remove a hot item from the oven
Life Sciences	• Understand and apply principles of photosynthesis • Understand and identify the impact of ecosystem changes on populations	• Select best placement for house plants • Properly care for animals
Earth and Space Science	• Understand the apparent movement of the sun, moon, and stars • Understand concepts of the earth's orbit and tilt	• Use sun position to estimate the time • Apply knowledge of seasons to home gardening

representative photos to the steps could also be helpful in understanding and accurately performing the procedures. Natural and embedded supports through the use of peer partners and general education and community settings can also be used to enhance access to and skills in science content. In a study of ecology and local water sources, students with intellectual disability could work in groups to take water samples from a community river for water-quality analysis in the school lab. In terms of technology-oriented supports, access to scientific content can be supported through various technology-related integration such as science-based web quests, video models, or the use of three-dimensional manipulatives. In a lesson on anatomy, prior to a lab animal dissection, students with intellectual disability may practice the procedures and identification skills using online resources (for example, www2.sd35.bc.ca/uconnect/salmon/DissectionGame.html; http://frog.edschool.virginia.edu/Frog2/Dissection/Setup/setup1.html). Also, pupils may use photos found on the Internet to answer earth-science-related questions on a worksheet.

SOCIAL STUDIES

Social studies education was most recently defined in four distinct dimensions, or processes, including (a) developing questions and planning inquires, (b) applying disciplinary tools and concepts, (c) evaluating sources and using evidence, and (d) communicating conclusions and taking informed action (National Council for the Social Studies, 2013). The first dimension refers specifically to the activity of initiating an inquiry. This could include a specific question about a certain aspect of the Civil War or making a strategy to find the necessary information to answer the question. The second dimension refers to the four basic content areas within social studies education including civics, economics, geography, and history. Table 11.11 provides examples of secondary social studies content in each of the core areas and how each would be functionally applied. The third dimension refers to the process of obtaining and assessing information for credibility and synthesizing it to better understand a particular issue or event. Finally, the fourth dimension relates to the activity of sharing information and making informed choices (National Council for the Social Studies, 2013).

Like all other academic areas previously described, systematic instruction can be used to provide structure for student understanding and application of social-studies-related strategies such as locating and comprehending primary sources or locating a border on a map. Because of the link between social studies and language arts, much of the same supports can be applied in this context

TABLE 11.11 Social Studies Concept Examples and Functional Applications

CONTENT	CONCEPT AND SKILL EXAMPLES	FUNCTIONAL APPLICATION EXAMPLES
Civics	• Understand civic roles of citizens • Analyze public-governing rules and laws	• Pay taxes • Create house rules for living with roommates
Economics	• Understand principles of innovation and entrepreneurship • Understand competition in markets	• Create a small business to meet a community need • Put in a competitive bid for a particular job
Geography	• Understand the role of technology in dissemination of cultural ideas • Use maps to communicate information about location	• Connect via technology to an international pen pal • Use a map to give directions to your house
History	• Understand the role of history on perspective • Compile historical evidence to create a statement about the past	• Have an informed conversation with someone from another generation • Make informed work-based decisions

including task analysis, prompting systems, technology application, and peer supports. Likewise, similar to reading and listening supports, pupils may gain access to texts through the aid of technological supports such as books on tape, video depictions of historical scenes, or text-to-speech software, among others.

NON-CORE ACADEMIC AREAS

In addition to the core academic areas of language arts, mathematics, science, and social studies, secondary students with intellectual disability may meet their IEP goals and increase general academic skills through participation in content and coursework such as foreign language, art, career and technical education, physical education, and other non-core (or academically related) curricular areas. Support described in the core academic areas can be extended to these non-core areas. For example, systematic instruction could be used to help students learn how to develop photos in a darkroom, how to greet a friend in his or her native language, or how to take care of their own body. Table 11.12 provides examples of transition and adult life-relevant non-core academic content.

TABLE 11.12 Non-Core Academic Area Benefits to Skill Acquisition or Learning Relative to Transition or Adult Life Skills

ACADEMIC CONTENT AREA	SKILL ACQUISITION OR LEARNING THAT BENEFITS STUDENTS FOR TRANSITION AND/OR ADULT LIFE
World Languages	Greetings in another language provide access to people and experiences of other cultures, which could positively impact work opportunities (e.g., speaking with non-native English co-workers or customers) and community experiences (e.g., engaging in cultural community events, meeting new people).
Arts	Skills in the arts can provide practice in gross and fine motor precision and creativity through activities such as choreographed dance or pottery. Artistic skills in this activity can be beneficial for both community engagement (e.g., develop friendships through shared interests; community performance), and employment (e.g., selling made goods; use of gross and fine motor precision in relevant work activities).
Career and Technology Education	Acquisition of computer and technology-related skills such as coding or technology problem solving can be beneficial for both employment outcomes (e.g., employment in technology or computer dependent position) and community engagement (social connection through web-based platforms—e.g., Facebook, Twitter, YouTube, Match.com).
Physical Education (PE)	Physical education skills such as sport and exercise can be beneficial to a student's overall life health including physical and emotional health. Pupils may increase social connections due to participation in sports or shared interest in exercise. Physical education skills may also benefit a student's stamina in employment through routines of exercise and conditioning (e.g., lifting boxes, standing for long periods of time, moving quickly).
Health	Education in concepts and skills related to health are vital to successful and healthy transition and adult life. Skills in sexuality, healthy eating, and bodily care can be vital to successful and healthy community engagement as young adults navigate friendships, romantic relationships, and independent living. Such health-related concepts can also be helpful in employment as students learn to navigate the social elements of the workplace.

Conclusion

Secondary students with intellectual disability are often taught in grade-level academic classes and are included in the general education curriculum. The goal for these students is to prepare them for their desired post-school options that include postsecondary education, employment, and community participation. Thus, active participation within the secondary curriculum along with the expectation that these students will make progress in these academic areas will increase the likelihood for successfully meeting their transition outcomes.

Chapter Summary

- Secondary education includes instruction in the middle school, junior high school, and senior high school levels and includes students in Grades 6 through 12.

- Secondary students with intellectual disability represent 7.3 percent of all children who attend middle and high school programs in the United States with the majority of those with a mild disability served in regular education classes.

- The instructional emphasis for students with intellectual disability at the secondary level is on preparation for life after high school and includes a focus on academic access, differentiated instruction, vocational preparation, and personal and social interest development.

- Core academic content areas at the secondary level include language arts, mathematics, science, and social studies. Non-core academic areas should also be considered when planning how to meet a student's postschool goals.

Review Questions

1. Why is academic access important for secondary students with intellectual disability?

2. What is life-enriching content? Give an example in regard to academic instruction.

3. What is the process for determining what academic content should be taught to secondary students with intellectual disability?

4. How do instructional arrangements contribute to increased academic and social skill development for secondary students with intellectual disability?

5. What are effective accommodations for students with intellectual disability as they are taught in academic content areas?

6. What are the major components of language arts instruction, and how can they be relevant to transition or life after school?

7. Identify an example of systematic instruction used in each of the core academic content areas.

8. Why is it important for students with intellectual disability to access non-core academic content? What are some examples?

Key Terms

social competencies (page 310)

academic competencies (page 310)

vocational competencies (page 310)

co-teaching (page 311)

instructional arrangements
(page 313)

technologies for the classroom
(page 314)

differentiated instruction (page 314)

skill-based interventions (page 316)

support-based interventions
(page 316)

language arts (page 319)

systematic instruction (page 322)

adapted text (page 324)

natural supports (page 324)

science practices (page 327)

science concepts (page 327)

science ideas (page 327)

Organizations and Associations Concerned With Academic Standards

American Council on the Teaching of Foreign Languages

www.actfl.org

Association for Career and Technical Education

www.acteonline.org

Common Core State Standards

www.corestandards.org

National Art Education Association

www.arteducators.org

National Council for the Social Studies

www.socialstudies.org

National Council of Teachers of English

www.ncte.org

National Council of Teachers of Mathematics

www.nctm.org

National Science Teachers Association

www.nsta.org

Society of Health and Physical Educators (SHAPE America)

www.shapeamerica.org

CHAPTER 12

Life Skills for Secondary Students With Intellectual Disability

Teresa Taber Doughty and Jordan Shurr

Learning Objectives

After reading Chapter 12, you should be able to:

- Describe the functional learning needs of secondary-age students with intellectual disability.

- Discuss the curricular focus for secondary students with intellectual disability.

- Define transition planning and services and their linkage to life skills instruction.

- Identify some general instructional approaches to teaching life skills to secondary students with intellectual disability.

- Describe the primary components of a secondary-level life skills curriculum.

The transition to adulthood is the primary instructional focus for secondary students with mild/moderate and moderate/severe intellectual disability. The time they spend in secondary education should be centered on their preparation for living autonomously in the community, obtaining and maintaining employment in a desired vocation, and actively participating as an adult within their community. In this chapter, we will examine the learning needs of secondary students with intellectual disability when preparing for their transition to post-school settings; describe the life skills typically targeted for these individuals; discuss the various settings in which instruction takes place and the general instructional approaches that are effective when preparing young adults for living, working, and recreating in integrated post-school environments; and the specific components of a life skills curriculum and how these may be embedded within the special education curriculum or solely within a life skills curriculum to meet individualized student needs.

OVERVIEW OF LIFE SKILLS FOR SECONDARY STUDENTS WITH INTELLECTUAL DISABILITY

Individuals with intellectual disability represent approximately 7 percent of students who attend public schools in the United States (National Center for Education Statistics, 2016). Of these, approximately 91 percent participate in varying degrees in general education placements (National Center for Education Statistics, 2015). Most of these students at the secondary level are served in a combination of special education classrooms—resource, self-contained, and community-based environments. While in these settings, they participate in the general education curriculum and learn the functional academics and life skills to meet post-school needs. Because individuals with intellectual disability are at risk for unemployment or underemployment, a particular focus at the secondary level is preparation for postsecondary education and employment (Petner-Arrey, Howell-Moneta, & Lysaght, 2015).

Chapter 10 described life skills as those skills that result in an individual's active participation in everyday activities in the areas of daily living, recreation and leisure, community functioning, and employment. In an instructional program in which students with intellectual disability are exposed to life skills as part of their preschool and elementary curriculum, they are better prepared to engage in increasingly complex activities that integrate academics with functional skills at the secondary level (Agran & Hughes, 2014). While making

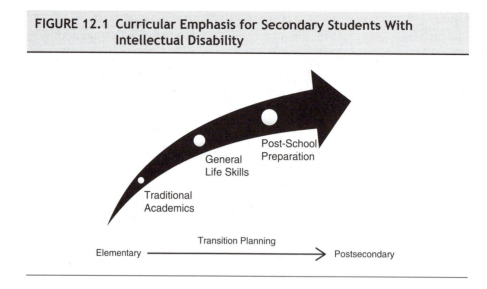

FIGURE 12.1 Curricular Emphasis for Secondary Students With Intellectual Disability

Post-School Preparation

General Life Skills

Traditional Academics

Transition Planning

Elementary ⟶ Postsecondary

progress in the general education curriculum remains important for older students with intellectual disability, the instructional emphasis moves to life skills as they progress toward the post-school environment (Wandry, Wehmeyer, & Glor-Scheib, 2013). More specifically, instruction shifts from acquiring the foundational academic skills for classroom success to the specific life skills that will lead to post-school goal attainment in home, community, and work settings. Figure 12.1 illustrates this movement from elementary to post-school settings.

The National Longitudinal Transition Study-2 (NLTS2) was conducted between 2000 and 2009 and documented the in-school and post-school experiences of individuals with disabilities who started and then exited secondary school during the time frame. NLTS2 data revealed that students with intellectual disability were less likely to pursue postsecondary education or obtain competitive employment after leaving high school (Grigal, Hart, & Migliore, 2011). Investigators who analyzed these data also found low rates of independent living and confirmed low employment among individuals with intellectual disability (Newman, Wagner, Cameto, & Knokey, 2009). Over the same period, studies verified the positive impact of life skills programming for students with intellectual disability, reporting increased employment, life satisfaction, graduation rates, and postsecondary education participation (Benz, Lindstrom, & Yovanoff, 2000; Miller & Chan, 2008). While instructional programming in the NLTS2 was not described in detail, reports indicated that students with intellectual disability were taught in both general education classrooms and self-contained settings with curricular emphasis varying between the general education curriculum and functional life skills (Bouck, 2012; Bouck & Joshi, 2012). Yet, Bouck (2010) found that increasingly fewer pupils with intellectual disability have access to life skills training at the secondary level. As such, emphasis must center on preparing individuals to meet their post-school goals and include instruction in life skills.

The philosophical foundation for focusing instruction on life skills for students with intellectual disability is grounded in the ideals of social role valorization (Wolfensberger, 1983). Three central concepts are embedded within this model and include the criterion of ultimate functioning (Brown, Nietupski, & Hamre-Nietupski, 1976), the dignity of risk (Perske, 1972), and the competency–deviancy hypothesis (Gold, 1980). These concepts concentrate on the core values and philosophies that drive today's service delivery for individuals with intellectual disability. Each concept also reinforces the necessity for providing life skills to those who might not naturally acquire these skills and who are at risk for community isolation and devaluation.

Social role valorization (SRV) is the practice of creating or supporting socially valued roles for all individuals at risk of social devaluation so that they are afforded the benefits provided to valued citizens (Wolfensberger, 1983). These benefits include enhancement of their social image in physical settings (where they live and participate with other valued individuals), relationships (social integration), activities (age-appropriate and integrated activities), language (labels), and image (personal appearance). Ultimately, it is about attributing value and positively communicating about each person who otherwise might be considered undesirable or without value. The practice of using person-first language when referring to an individual with a disability is one outcome of social role valorization.

Couched within the social role valorization framework is the **criterion of ultimate functioning** in which an individual possesses the skills to "function as productively and independently as possible in socially, vocationally, and domestically integrated community environments" (Brown et al., 1976, p. 11). Educational assumptions and practices that deviate from an individual's active and autonomous participation in these environments should be avoided. For example, denying a student access to interactions in integrated settings with typically developing peers because his or her behavior is not considered

TABLE 12.1 Questions for Determining the Criterion of Ultimate Functioning

1. Why should we engage in this activity?
2. Is this activity necessary to prepare students to ultimately function in complex heterogeneous community settings?
3. Could students function as adults if they did not acquire this skill?
4. Is there a different activity that will allow students to approximate realization of the criterion of ultimate functioning more quickly and more efficiently?
5. Will this activity impede, restrict, or reduce the probability that students will ultimately function in community settings?
6. Are the skills, materials, tasks, and criteria of concern similar to those encountered in adult life?

SOURCE: L. Brown, J. Nietupski, and S. Hamre-Nietupski, The criterion of ultimate functioning and public school services for severely handicapped students. In M. Thomas (Ed.), *Hey, Don't Forget About Me: Education's Investment in the Severely, Profoundly, and Multiply Handicapped* (Reston, VA: Council for Exceptional Children, 1976), pp. 2-15.

acceptable will lead to missed opportunities to teach and use appropriate social, behavioral, and communication skills within natural contexts. Because secondary students with intellectual disability are nearing their transition to post-school settings, training in life skills should take precedence. Table 12.1 presents the questions that should be asked when determining the criterion of ultimate functioning for individuals and will help determine whether or not an activity or skill is appropriate.

The desire to protect individuals from potential harm is one reason people with intellectual disability are denied opportunities to engage in activities, environments, and interactions in integrated settings without direct oversight from someone without a disability. For example, persons with intellectual disability are often prevented from choosing where they live, what and when they eat, what they do during their free time, or with whom they socialize by caregivers or others who fear for their safety or their exposure to risk. Yet, children, teenagers, and adults without a disability are regularly provided these opportunities. The **dignity of risk** purports that there is human dignity afforded to persons who take risks and that in doing so they are not restricted from actively participating in an integrated society (Perske, 1972). As students with intellectual disability progress through elementary and secondary settings in preparation for post-school environments, they should be expected to take risks, engage in self-determined behaviors, and make decisions and choices based on their own preferences with greater constancy. While precautions can be taken to decrease

TABLE 12.2 Dignity of Risk Principles

1. Adults should make their own decisions and be afforded the opportunity to do so.

2. Reasonable supports and assistance to make independent decisions should be provided before others assume that responsibility.

3. Adults have the right to make decisions that are opposed to the decisions of others. They also have the right to experience the consequences based on those decisions including failure.

4. An individual's best interests and preferences must be considered for any decision made on behalf of that individual and must not infringe on his or her "basic rights and freedoms."

SOURCE: Adapted from the Dignity of Risk Project, *Our Perspective on the Dignity of Risk and the Care of Older Adults*. Retrieved October 2, 2016, from www.qorf.org.au/what-is-the-dignity-of-risk/

the likelihood of negative consequences from taking risks, no one should be denied the opportunity to participate in the human experience as "there can be a dehumanizing indignity in safety" (Perske, 1972, p. 26). Table 12.2 describes the basic principles to consider when working with those considered at risk.

The **competency–deviancy hypothesis** (Gold, 1980) is the third concept tied to the social role valorization paradigm that addresses the impact of how we prepare students with a disability for integrated society and for how they will be perceived by others. This hypothesis describes the tolerance of community members for behaviors that attract negative attention when demonstrated by individuals typically at risk for being devalued. For example, the ability to successfully care for oneself, interact with others, manage personal finances, complete a job, and independently move throughout the community (walk, drive, ride the bus) are all life skills that facilitate an image of competence. Thus, when a person is regularly able to display competent and valued behaviors and skills in public daily life, society will have greater tolerance when unusual or different behaviors may be exhibited. When considering this idea within the context of social role valorization, priority must be given to preparing all students to display not only socially acceptable behaviors but also those that convey a message of competence. These critical life skills are described later in this chapter.

The settings in which secondary students with intellectual disability receive instruction are similar to those described for elementary pupils in Chapter 10. Instructional settings are dependent on each student's learning needs and where best to meet those needs. While some secondary pupils may spend extensive time learning content in subject-specific classes (Spooner & Browder, 2015), others will receive instruction in alternative school and community-based settings. According to McLeskey, Landers, Williamson, and Hoppey (2012), as students with intellectual disability get older, they receive less instruction in general classroom settings. This may be attributed to meeting individual learner goals and teaching them in those settings in which target skills will be used. As such, educators must continually balance a student's right to access the general education curriculum with the impending necessity to acquire the skills that lead to successful community living and access, employment, and social relationships (Ayres, Lowrey, Douglas, & Sievers, 2011).

When individuals with intellectual disability are taught in general education classes, the instructional focus is often on actively participating in and learning the content being taught. However, to be effective, these learners may require instructional accommodations to learn the academic content due to the "emphasis on verbal skills, ability to recall information quickly, and the ability to focus on a teacher standing at the front of the room" (Downing, 2010, p. 5). While they can acquire anything (Spooner & Browder, 2015; Taber-Doughty, 2015), the majority who receive content instruction in secondary general education classes are frequently those with a mild intellectual disability whereas those with more severe levels are mostly taught in alternative school and community environments (McLeskey et al., 2012). When life skills are addressed in subject-specific classes, they may be embedded within the context of instruction. For example, a student included in a first-year foreign language class might learn the English version of the basic vocabulary that his classmates are learning in Spanish. When a spelling test over vocabulary words occurs at the end of the week, the target student demonstrates his mastery of new words by reading each word to his classmates so that they may translate it on their test. By embedding life skills, teachers are able to link developmentally appropriate curricular content with meaningful skills.

For learners taught in alternative school and community-based environments, the instructional focus typically centers on either academic remediation or life skills with a specific emphasis on preparing for post-school employment (Ayres, Mechling, & Sansosti, 2013). **Community-based instruction (CBI)** and **community-based vocational instruction (CBVI)** are the models used to teach students skills such as using public transportation, banking, shopping, and job-specific work behaviors. Different from field trips, which are single outings into the community (such as a trip to the museum or zoo), community-based instruction and community-based vocational instruction allow for ongoing training in the real environments in which skills will be used and provide natural opportunities for life skills practice. Community-based instruction also facilitates the use of age-appropriate activities and the generalization of skills across multiple environments. When preparing students for competitive employment, community-based vocational instruction will center on general work adjustment behaviors and on-the-job training (remaining focused on a task, performing specific motor functions) within the context of real job settings. Table 10.14 in Chapter 10 (page 297) provides a list of vocational skills and behaviors as well as life skills examples. (See also page 281 for more on CBI and page 350 for more on CBVI.)

Performance success while participating across environments for students who participate in a life skills curriculum may be determined by their ability to fully or partially partake in activities. Secondary learners with intellectual disability vary greatly in their capacity to complete tasks autonomously or with accuracy. For those who generally acquire life skills quickly and are able to apply them to a variety of situations, the potential for post-school achievement is good. Yet, individuals who struggle with fully participating in activities with independent success may require an alternate criterion for participation. The **principle of partial participation** describes how individuals who are unable to complete all aspects of a task or activity still may be actively engaged or contributing by completing only parts of it (Baumgart et al., 1982). In other words, all students with intellectual disability, regardless of severity, can at least partially take part in any activity. Within the context of preparing for postsecondary and/or community involvement, this principle suggests that even partial participation will promote students' self-determination that may contribute to later quality of life (Wehmeyer, 2007; Wehmeyer & Schwartz, 1998).

TRANSITION PLANNING AND SERVICES

The Individuals with Disabilities Education Act (1990) (PL 101–476) provided the impetus for post-school planning by requiring that **transition services** be identified for all students with a disability. According to this legislation, transition services are

> a coordinated set of activities for a child with a disability that is designed to be within a results-oriented process, that is focused on

improving the academic and functional achievement of the child with a disability to facilitate the child's movement from school to post-school activities, including postsecondary education, vocational education, integrated employment (including supported employment), continuing and adult education, adult services, independent living, or community participation; is based on the individual child's needs . . . ; and includes instruction, related services, community experiences, the development of employment and other post-school adult living objectives, and, if appropriate, acquisition of daily living skills and provision of a functional vocational evaluation. (34 C.F.R. Part 300/A/§ 300.43)

These services must begin no later than when a student reaches age 16 but may be included in his or her individualized education program (IEP) prior to that age. Because these services foster preparing students to enter and participate in integrated post-school settings, ensuring that life skills are addressed at this time holds even greater importance.

Teachers of secondary students with intellectual disability should always begin their instructional planning around a young adult's **individualized transition plan (ITP)**. This plan is a part of a student's IEP and specifically identifies the post-school outcomes that students want to achieve. Transition recommendations are made within the ITP for postsecondary training and adult living, community experiences, daily living, instruction, employment, and related services. Once these are identified, annual IEP goals and objectives are then determined for a student. (Under IDEA 2004, short-term objectives are only required in an IEP for students who take alternate assessments aligned with alternate achievement standards.) For example, if 16-year-old Daniel indicates that he wants to live in his own apartment with a roommate after graduation, work in a job in the movie theater industry, hang out with friends on the weekend, and ride a bicycle to various community localities, instruction will center on preparing him for ultimately achieving these desired goals. Thus, the ITP/IEP will determine the focus and location of instruction. The resources and supports needed to meet transition outcomes will be identified and included in the transition services process. See Figure 12.2 for sample transition recommendations for a student with a moderate intellectual disability. (For a full discussion of supported employment, see Chapter 13.)

FIGURE 12.2 Transition Recommendations and Related IEP Goals and Objectives

Student: Tina Thomas

Initial Transition Plan Date: April 13, 2012

Date(s) Transition Plan Reviewed/Revised: 4/12/13, 4/18/14, 4/15/15, 4/15/16

Student Preferences, Needs, and Interests

Tina attended her IEP meeting and expressed her post-school preferences. She indicated that she was interested in graduating with her class at age 18 and then going to work following graduation. Therefore, Tina will need a supported employment position in which a full-time job coach is available for initial and some follow-up training. She also indicated her desire to have her own apartment one day but, at this time, wants to continue to live at home with increased responsibilities. Information needs to be provided to Tina and her family regarding residential support services that Tina may need in the future. Tina has several friends from school, and activities she would like to continue with her friends include working out at the local gym, going to the movies, eating out, and doing crafts. Tina will therefore need assistance with transportation to and from social activities.

Needed Transition Services

Instruction:

1. Enroll in community-based instruction and community-based vocational instruction program. School will be responsible for providing transportation and instruction in community settings.

2. Enroll in exercise program at the local YWCA. Parents will be responsible for transportation and costs.

Related Services

1. Receive support/training services from the speech-language pathologist in communication and speech skills. These services should be provided across school, community, and home settings. The school will be responsible for ensuring these services.

2. Special education staff will provide transportation training and mobility skills (walking routes). School staff and parents will be responsible for training and providing opportunities for practice.

Community Experiences

1. Schedule visits with local residential service providers. School will provide Tina and her family with a listing of residential service providers in the area. Tina and her family will be responsible for scheduling visiting.

2. Receive specific training in community safety skills such as avoiding risks, stranger danger, asking for assistance, and emergencies. School staff and parents will be responsible for providing specific training.

Employment and Other Post-School Adult Living Objectives

1. Enroll in vocational rehabilitation services. School will invite the vocational rehabilitation counselor to the IEP meeting. Parents and Tina will be responsible for completing the intake process with the vocational rehabilitation counselor.

(Continued)

FIGURE 12.2 (Continued)

2. Financial supports are needed. Tina will complete the application for receiving Social Security. In addition, her salary in her employment position needs to be above minimum wage. School staff will provide Tina and her family with Social Security information and phone numbers and will assist in the application process. The job coach will locate a supported employment position with an appropriate salary.

Daily Living Skills

1. Increase responsibilities at home. School and parents will provide instruction and opportunities to practice meal preparation, clothing care, general housekeeping, and yard maintenance.

2. Self-medicate. Establish a schedule and train Tina to follow in taking diabetes medication. School, parents, and family physician will work collaboratively to establish a schedule and train Tina.

Functional Vocational Evaluation

1. Complete modified vocational interest inventories to assist in the selection of a supported employment position. Special education staff and the school counselor will be responsible for conducting the vocational interest inventories with Tina.

What to Teach Secondary Students With Intellectual Disability

When determining what to teach secondary students with intellectual disability, consideration should be given to their needs identified by assessment and in each IEP and ITP. Planning for and providing recommendations for instruction, related services, community experiences, employment, adult living, and daily living in the transition plan will drive the decisions about what to teach to these secondary students. Transition assessment plays a valuable role in identifying students' needs as they prepare for post-school participation. The Division on Career Development and Transition of the Council for Exceptional Children describes **transition assessment** as a process for gathering information about an individual as it specifically relates to activities in current and future environments (Walker, Kortering, Fowler, Rowe, & Bethune, 2013). It is a formal and informal process that includes multiple measures where results are used to prioritize planning and instruction as students prepare for their transition to work, postsecondary education, community living, and recreational activities. Numerous resources exist for determining what assessments might be appropriate for transition. For example, the Transition Assessment Matrix (Northeast Indiana Cadre of Transition Leaders,

2015) provides users a list of transition assessments specific for transition domains (employment, independent living, education/training), student grade level, and disability. The key to gathering meaningful information about an individual's transition needs is to use multiple measures that include information from the student, family members, teachers, and others who are familiar with the individual. Once information is gathered and results are reviewed, IEP/ITP recommendations are generally developed. Figure 12.3 provides an example of how IEP annual goals and short-term objectives may be aligned to the transition recommendations for each life skill domain. Within each goal and objective, the foci for instruction lead to meeting the post-school outcomes needed.

To address the transition recommendations within each of the life skill domains, instruction should include a focus on self-determination skills. **Self-determination** is an individual's ability to make his or her own life decisions and is illustrated by the following for components of behavior: autonomy, self-regulation, psychological empowerment, and self-realization (Flexer, Baer, Luft, & Simmons, 2013; Wehmeyer & Schwartz, 1997). **Autonomy** refers to behaviors that are directed by personal choice and decision making (Niemiec & Ryan, 2009). Students who are autonomous are able to express their choices and make decisions about their wants, needs, likes, and dislikes. **Self-regulation** is the ability to plan for the future, manage one's own behavior, and solve problems. When individuals self-regulate, they are able to save their money for desired purchases, demonstrate socially acceptable public and private behaviors, and determine a solution for getting to work on time when the bus is late. Individuals who are self-determined also learn that what they do and say is important and that others will respond accordingly. This state of mind is known as **psychological empowerment** in which individuals believe that their thoughts and actions matter and have an impact on their daily life (Wehmeyer & Schwartz, 1997). Finally, **self-realization** is the ability to recognize one's own strengths and limitations (Wehmeyer & Schalock, 2001). Individuals who understand self-realization are able to highlight their strengths to others and ask for accommodations where they may have challenges.

Overall, self-determination is a critical component of life skills instruction for secondary students with intellectual disability due to its beneficial effect on post-school outcomes including employment, independent living, and financial independence (Wehmeyer & Palmer, 2003; Wehmeyer & Schwartz, 1997). Specific

COMMUNITY DOMAIN

Transition Outcome Recommendation

Use self-advocacy skills at home, on the job, and in various community settings

IEP Annual Goal

- Tamara will identify her own vocational strengths, weaknesses, and necessary accommodations.

Short-Term Objectives

- Tamara will verbally indicate three of her vocational strengths and weaknesses when asked by an interviewer, coworker, or teacher in both real and role-playing situations in school and vocational settings, independently in eight of ten opportunities.
- During role-playing activities with teachers and novel individuals in school and community settings, Tamara will state her need for additional lighting at her workstation independently in eight of ten opportunities.

Instructional Strategies

- Tamara's teacher verbally confirms Tamara's vocational strengths and weaknesses during classroom and vocational activities. He asks Tamara to identify her strengths during multiple occasions. As well, Tamara completes a daily checklist that identifies task success and challenges. During role-playing and actual vocational activities, Tamara is asked to refer to her checklist and then verbally describe her strengths and weaknesses. Coaching is provided to simplify descriptions and offer solutions to accommodate any weaknesses.
- When there is a need for additional lighting, the teacher will prompt Tamara to verbally state, "I need more light to see my work." Tamara also will be prompted to approach her direct supervisor (paraprofessional, teacher, or co-worker) to make her verbal request.

VOCATIONAL DOMAIN

Transition Outcome Recommendation

Obtain a supported employment position in the food services industry

IEP Annual Goal

- Charles will participate in three community-based vocational training sites for the 2016-2017 school year.

Short-Term Objectives

- With indirect supervision, Charles will train in the food services cluster working on dishwashing skills for a range of 6 to 8 hours per week, for six out of eight training sessions, for no more than 215 hours.
- Given a picture prompt, Charles will identify and correct errors 80 percent of the time for five days in a variety of community sites (restaurants, library, post office).

Instructional Strategies

- Charles will practice loading trays in the school cafeteria and in the classroom kitchen. He will also use the industrial sink sprayer to rinse dishes before loading them onto trays for washing.

- Charles will practice using picture prompts for completing familiar and unfamiliar tasks in the classroom and community.

RECREATION/LEISURE DOMAIN

Transition Outcome Recommendation

- Participate in a variety of recreation/leisure activities at home and in the community

IEP Annual Goal

- Ellen will participate in at least three school- and community-based recreation/leisure activities during the school year.

Short-Term Objectives

- During gym, Ellen will increase the amount of weight she lifts by 5 percent over baseline performance over a six-week period.

- While in the community, Ellen will maneuver her wheelchair up and down ramps without assistance during 100 percent of opportunities for the entire school year.

Instructional Strategies

- Across the school day, the teacher will prompt Ellen to lift and retrieve her own materials around instructional settings to complete tasks. Furthermore, during physical activities in the community such as bowling, she will be prompted to lift and roll bowling balls of increasing weights over time.

- Ellen will be provided practice in maneuvering herself when transitioning from the school bus to the building, moving between classes, and crossing streets.

DOMESTIC DOMAIN

Transition Outcome Recommendations

- Live semi-independently in an apartment with a roommate with supervision provided by Acme Residential Supports

IEP Annual Goal

- Sally will learn to prepare simple meals in a variety of settings.

Short-Term Objectives

- Sally will operate independently a microwave oven to prepare a meal at home, at school, and on the vocational training site for two days each week for twelve weeks.

- Given a list of five items needed to prepare a simple meal, Sally will locate and purchase these items with indirect supervision one time per week for twelve weeks.

(Continued)

FIGURE 12.3 (Continued)

Instructional Strategies

- Digital pictures and video prompts will be used to teach Sally to operate a microwave oven. Different microwave ovens will be operated according to the environment (school, work-site break room). Picture prompts will be shared with parents to be used at home to facilitate learning.
- Self-recorded audio prompts will be used in school and grocery settings to facilitate accurate grocery shopping skills.

self-determination skills include choice and decision making, problem solving, goal setting, independence, self-management, self-instruction, self-advocacy, and self-awareness (Wehmeyer & Schalock, 2001). Instruction in these and other related self-determination skills should be interwoven with functional life skill practice and acquisition. Embedding these skills will not only help to make them practical and relevant for the student, but will also help to bridge the gap between initial learning and later generalization of the skill for use among multiple contexts. Table 12.3 provides the definitions of each self-determination skill and examples of how these may look in a life skills curriculum.

GENERAL INSTRUCTIONAL APPROACHES

The general instructional approaches described in Chapter 10 continue to be relevant and effective strategies for secondary students with intellectual disability. Using a task analysis approach, group, simulation, in vivo, and community- and technology-based instruction are all grounded in research to support their continued use with these students as they prepare for the transition to post-school settings and activities. However, of particular importance are those strategies related to expanded community-based experiences and those within vocational settings. Test et al. (2009) noted that experiences within community settings were one of sixteen predictors for achieving post-school outcomes for students with a disability. Cimera (2010) indicated that, when employed, young adults with intellectual disability who participated in community-based vocational instruction while in a secondary program required fewer supports. Thus, specific instructional methods should be emphasized including simulation approaches, technology-based strategies, and natural supports to increase the likelihood of meeting post-school outcomes.

TABLE 12.3 Self-Determination Skills: Definitions and Examples

SELF-DETERMINATION SKILL	DEFINITION	EXAMPLES OF PROVIDING INSTRUCTION
Choice making	Identify the most appropriate and/or desired option between two or more viable options	• Student is prompted to choose a lab partner in science class.
Decision making	Make a decision based on the best information available	• During a writing activity for sending an e-mail response, student completes a checklist to identify critical information before composing her e-mail.
Problem solving	Identify a problem and a workable solution	• Student decides what to do when she incorrectly solves a math problem. • Student adapts to a change in the schedule.
Goal setting	Articulate dreams and desires into manageable goals	• During consumer science class, student engages in interview role-playing to describe current and future employment goals.
Independence	Manage environments with minimal assistance	• Student uses a picture prompting system to retrieve specific athletic materials (balls, hoops, cones) during physical education class.
Self-management	Control one's own behavior	• Student carries and refers to a behavior card in his pocket as a reminder of acceptable classroom behaviors.
Self-instruction	Learn new information and skills without the direct help of others	• Student uses a self-operated video modeling system to locate desired books in the school library.
Self-advocacy	Make one's own needs and desires known	• When encountering difficulty completing a math assignment, student asks for peer assistance and describes his difficulty.
Self-awareness	Understand one's own unique strengths and limitations	• During a career exploration class, student searches Internet websites for employment opportunities that match his strengths and interests.

Community-based instruction (CBI) and **community-based vocational instruction (CBVI)**. An effective CBI program requires multiple trips into the community for instruction and preparing students to generalize the skills they are learning. Yet, financial challenges may exist that prohibit multiple excursions per week. As such, **simulation** might be used when access to community-based settings is limited (Mechling & O'Brien, 2010). While not a replacement for CBI or CBVI, simulation is an approach that is used to replicate and reinforce the instruction and community environment where skills will be learned and activities will take place (Bouck, Taber-Doughty, & Savage, 2015). Its benefit is that it allows for repeated practice and reinforcement of community skills. Simulations may be in the form of artificial or modified materials and settings such as a digital video of a task being performed in the actual environment, interactive simulations used in virtual and augmented reality programs, static picture systems, and a modified environment that provides opportunities to practice skills with real materials such as purchasing a newspaper from a newspaper stand temporarily located in the classroom (Alberto, Cihak, & Gama, 2005; Cuvo & Davis, 1983; Mechling & Ortega-Hurndon, 2007).

When developing a CBI/CBVI program, planning should center on addressing students' IEPs and ITPs within community contexts. Planning should include obtaining parental consent and making specific arrangements regarding daily procedures, prioritizing skills, and data collection (Bouck et al., 2015). Obtaining parent consent for their son or daughter to receive instruction in settings outside of the school building should be the first step in facilitating CBI or CBVI. Within the form for consent, information should be given about the rationale for CBI, the types of skills students will learn, and the environments in which instruction will take place when requested from parents. Establishing a weekly or monthly calendar of instructional events and locations to be shared with parents and other stakeholders (school staff or administrators) is helpful for communicating the activities that will take place, where instruction will occur, and the specific skills that will be taught.

In addition to receiving consent and informing parents and others of CBI/CBVI activities, daily procedures must be established to ensure student safety in community settings. These include emergency procedures (emergency contact information, medical information, how to respond to and report emergency situations to parents and school office) and student preparation (carrying official identification, how to seek assistance if lost or in trouble, how to dress appropriately for the community setting) (Bouck et al., 2015). Table 12.4 summarizes additional areas of consideration when preparing for and prioritizing skills for CBI and CBVI. As foundational procedures are set in place and tailored to each individual school situation, preparation for targeted instructional skills and data to be gathered is then determined. In addition, recommendations for the amount of time students should spend participating in CBI are provided in Table 12.5.

Skills identified as priorities for training are derived from previous measurements (ecological inventories and transition assessments) and are included in

TABLE 12.4 Community-Based Instruction/Community-Based Vocational Instruction Priorities

1. Skills that are frequently required or performed by the individual in community settings

2. Skills critical to health and safety when in the community

3. Costs for purchases in the community, transportation, etc.

4. Opportunities to learn and practice skills over time in the community

5. Location of community-based instruction in the students' communities to increase the opportunities for practice and skill generalization

SOURCE: Adapted from E. Bouck, T. Taber-Doughty, and M. Savage, *Footsteps Toward the Future: Implementing a Real-World Curriculum for Students With Developmental Disabilities* (Arlington, VA: Council for Exceptional Children, 2015).

TABLE 12.5 Recommended Community-Based Instruction Frequency and Duration for Secondary Students

GRADE/AGE	FREQUENCY	DURATION
Grades 6-8	2 days per week	90 minutes per day
Ages 14-16/17/18	2-3 days per week	90 minutes to 2 hours per day
Ages 18-22	4-5 times per week	2 or more hours per day

SOURCE: Adapted from P. Alberto, N. Elliott, T. Taber, E. Houser, and P. Andrews, "Vocational content for students with moderate and severe disabilities in elementary and middle grades," *Focus on Exceptional Children*, 25(9), 1993, pp. 1-10.

each student's IEP. As specific instructional skills are targeted for community settings, data must be gathered on student performance to first determine student learning and second evaluate the effectiveness of instruction. A challenge for recording data in community settings is portability. Thus, instructors should consider using data recording cards (index card size) that can fit in a shirt pocket or bag or data collection software available on an electronic device. A general practice for any time a student participates in CBI/CBVI is that when IEP-related goals/objectives are addressed, data will be gathered on student performance. Examples of two data collection formats, task analysis and self-graphing trial-by-trial recording forms, are presented in Figure 12.4.

Technology-based strategies include those that incorporate low or high technology and require limited or lengthy training and setup (Lane & Mistrett, 1996). In recent years, digital video, virtual reality, and augmented reality were used more frequently with students with intellectual disability to

FIGURE 12.4 Sample Data Collection Formats

Student __June__ Task/Behavior __Order in a fast-food restaurant__

SESSIONS	1	2	3	4	5	6	7	8	9	10
Locate end of line and wait for turn	V	I	I	I	I					
Select items from menu	M	M	M	M	V					
Order desired food items	V	V	V	I	I					
Pay for purchase	P	P	P	M	M					
Retrieve tray with meal	V	V	I	I	I					
Locate an available seat	V	V	V	V	V					

Task analysis data card key: I = Independent, V = Verbal Prompts, G = Gesture, M = Model, P = Physical Prompt.

Student	Jarvis			Task/Behavior		Selecting correct clothing size			
10	10	10	10	10	10	10	10	10	10
9	9	9	9	9	9	9	9	9	9
8	8	8	8	8	8	8	8	8	8
7	7	7	7	7	7	7	7	7	7
6	6	6	6	6	(6)	(6)	6	6	6
5	5	5	5	5	5	5	5	5	5
4	4	(4)	4	(4)	4	4	(4)	4	4
(3)	(3)	3	3	3	3	3	3	3	3
2	2	2	(2)	2	2	2	2	2	2
1	1	1	1	1	1	1	1	1	1
0	0	0	0	0	0	0	0	0	0

Self-graphing trial-by-trial across sessions data card (number of steps correct per trial).

SOURCE: Adapted from E. Bouck, T. Taber-Doughty, and M. Savage, *Footsteps Toward the Future: Implementing a Real-World Curriculum for Students With Developmental Disabilities* (Arlington, VA: Council for Exceptional Children, 2015, p. 79).

not only facilitate skill acquisition while in the community but also practice those skills before and after community-based instruction experiences. For example, Cihak, Alberto, Taber-Doughty, and Gama (2006) compared static pictures and video prompting simulation in a classroom setting with middle school students with intellectual disability to preview purchasing and banking skills before they were used in the real setting. In addition, virtual reality was successfully used to teach vocational tasks to secondary learners with intellectual disability (Chang, Kang, & Huang, 2013). As technology continues to evolve and innovative technology-based strategies and tools are introduced, educators should continue to determine their effectiveness in promoting learning.

Three frequently used technology-based strategies are self-operated picture, auditory, and video prompting systems. Teachers develop these self-instructional delivery systems to enable students to learn and/or engage in tasks or behaviors with greater autonomy (Bouck et al., 2015). Applying the most recent technology, these prompts are generally developed using electronic apps or software and are delivered via smartphones and tablets. However, static pictures and audio/video recordings may also be used if newer technology is unavailable.

When developing a self-operated prompting system, consideration should be given to a student's preferred instructional format. Does she prefer to listen to verbal directions or view a video model of a task being completed? Is her preference to follow a series of pictures in a step-by-step process? Once this is determined, the preferred type of prompting should be created. When developed, a detailed task analysis should guide the prompts provided (Bouck et al., 2015). For example, for purchasing a soda from a vending machine using an auditory prompting system, clear verbal steps should be articulated for each step the student will complete ("locate price of soda," "count your change or dollars," "insert your money," "press your selection," "retrieve your soda," "check for change"). Table 6.7 in Chapter 6 (page 161) illustrates the steps for developing self-operated picture, auditory, and video systems.

Finally, using **natural supports** is critical to learner success in integrated settings. Natural supports generally refer to the peers and co-workers who are learning and working within the same integrated environment and who might provide prompting and other learning support to others. Individuals with intellectual disability often benefit from instruction that is more natural and less systematic as may be provided by colleagues. For example, when teachers provide positive reinforcement as students learn and respond to instruction, they often use systematic and planned responses such as prompts, verbal reinforcement, modeling, and gesturing. Yet, when peers or coworkers provide supports, it is less planned and occurs more naturally. Peer-delivered reinforcement might not be provided for each instance of correct behavior and instruction. Rather, instructions might be more abrupt such as "Go get that for me" or "Put that here" without any reinforcement. A "high-five" might be offered when a task is completed, or nothing might happen and the individual with intellectual disability needs to continue on with his or her schedule of activities. These types of supports are what individuals will typically encounter in integrated settings and often result in positive experiences.

When natural supports are provided in school, community, and/or work settings, student success is noted. For example, evidence illustrates that when adolescents with and without intellectual disability were paired in a community-based fitness program, students with intellectual disability experienced health benefits, independence, and friendships with their exercise buddies (Stanish & Temple, 2012). In vocational settings, co-workers also serve an important support role. They may provide natural supports and on-the-job training as workers with intellectual disability learn and generalize vocational skills (Storey & Certo, 1996). Evidence also suggests that coworker involvement positively impacts employment retention for adults with intellectual disability (Cimera, 2001) and can result in cost reductions for supported employment services (Cimera, 2007). Overall, when teachers are able to integrate both peers and coworkers into the learning and support landscape, adolescents with intellectual disability benefit.

While simulation, technology-based strategies, and natural supports provide a methodological foundation for life skills instruction, considerable planning and organization is necessary to ensure that successful learning will occur in community-based and vocational settings. Specifically, procedures must be in place for selecting instructional settings, identifying needed supports, ensuring communication with families and school administration, organizing transportation, arranging for instruction and data collection, and preparing staff for delivering instruction in community settings. However, this all begins with conducting a transition assessment to determine where to emphasize instruction.

COMPONENTS OF A LIFE SKILLS CURRICULUM FOR SECONDARY STUDENTS WITH INTELLECTUAL DISABILITY

When secondary students with intellectual disability participate in a life skills curriculum, instruction will center on domestic, recreation/leisure, community, and vocational domains. Additionally, instruction in self-determination will be integrated across the domains and educational curriculum. Thus, students will learn skills specific to their transition needs across the environments in which those skills will be used, while practicing the act of asserting their personal will and making their choices known. Within the domestic domain, secondary students will focus on adult skills related to personal management (making appointments, seeing a doctor, grooming), personal finance (banking, budgeting, purchasing goods and services), food preparation and storage (cooking, food safety, cooking safety), and household management (yard maintenance, home cleaning, laundry) among other home-related activities (Bouck et al., 2015). Within the recreation and leisure domain, students will learn skills related to personal fitness, team sports, individual activities, and other leisure pursuits such as gaming, gardening, or photography. Basically, activities in this domain represent those in which an individual would engage during his or her free time. Activities that might be learned in the community domain include mobility training (traveling training throughout the neighborhood, city, or long distance such as walking, driving, bicycle riding, or using public transportation) and consumer-related skills (shopping, requesting services, eating in restaurants). Finally, vocational domain skills are directly related to preparing for, locating, participating in, and maintaining future employment. This could include skills such as following a schedule in a work setting, learning how to interact with customers and co-workers, setting an alarm clock at home to arrive on time to work, and job-specific skills. Throughout secondary programming, students with intellectual disability should not only be afforded multiple opportunities to acquire the many skills associated with each domain but also be provided numerous occasions for practicing these skills over time. For example, for a student who is learning how to do laundry, opportunities should be provided at school, such as using the gym machines to wash uniforms or the classroom washer to launder towels, and in the community, such as visiting a coin Laundromat to wash classroom or personal items. Skills such as measuring soap, machine operation, and counting money would all be taught as part of the instructional routine. Table 12.6 provides a list of sample life skills for each instructional domain and how and where these skills may be taught.

Because secondary students with intellectual disability also participate in integrated educational settings and access the general education curriculum, life skills may be addressed within the context of content-area subject matter (see Table 12.7). While these individuals will continue to participate in community-based instruction and community-based vocational instruction to acquire and practice the skills needed for postsecondary success, opportunities to reinforce meaningful skills may be afforded in general education subject matter. For example, the secondary general education curriculum is focused on increasingly complex academics that serve as the basis for postsecondary education and vocational achievement. Mastery of advanced mathematics (statistics, algebra, geometry), science (biology, chemistry, physics), language arts (writing, reading, vocabulary development, speaking, listening media literacy), and social studies (history, civics, geography, economics) is the foundation for numerous future vocations. While individuals with intellectual disability may never use some of this academic content in future employment, skills related to each subject will be critical for future success. In today's world, adults need to be proficient in using electronic communication (English), understanding finances (social studies), measurement (mathematics), and life science (science).

TABLE 12.6 Secondary Life Skills per Instructional Domain

DOMAIN	SKILLS	HOW AND WHERE TO TEACH
Domestic	• Grooming/dressing/hygiene—self-care, shaving, brushing hair and teeth, using deodorant, tying shoes, washing laundry, bathing • Food preparation—making small meals and snacks, using kitchen appliances, purchasing food, storing food, preparing a sack lunch • Home maintenance—cleaning home, tending outdoor spaces, changing air filters, replacing broken items	• In physical education class, practice to dress/undress is provided. • During lunch in a vocational setting, student learns to use the break room microwave to heat her lunch. • Student cares for outdoor class garden and indoor plants.
Recreation/leisure	• Things to do alone—work out at the gym/exercise, read, play computer games, do arts and crafts • Things to do with others—attend parties and social events, play on a team, hang out with friends	• Student engages in and charts his workout routine in the school or local gym. • Between classes, student interacts with friends in the hallway.
Community	• Traveling through the community—ride a public bus, walk routes, ride a bicycle to community locations • Shopping—use money, know clothing sizes, use a shopping list • Eating out—wear appropriate clothing for the restaurant, order from a menu, leave a tip, use manners • Interacting with others—at social events, at work, with store clerks, with emergency personnel	• During CBI, student uses the public bus to travel to community site. • Student follows a picture list at the grocery store. • Student wears rubber-sole shoes when attending a CBVI restaurant site. • Student uses an augmentative and alternative communication device to converse with cashier at department store.
Vocational	• Working autonomously or with co-workers • Using break room facilities • Working until task completion • Transitioning between work tasks • Setting an alarm clock to get up for work or school • Dressing appropriately for workplace	• Student remains on task when stocking shelves at a CBVI site. • Student receives support provided in operating snack machines and returning to work within the break time limit. • Student works for delayed reinforcement in school and CBVI settings. • Student uses a self-operated prompting system to transition between tasks at school and in CBVI settings. • Student learns to set different types of alarm clocks in the classroom. • Student selects and dresses in appropriate attire for different work sites (restaurant, hospital, recycling center, office).

TABLE 12.7 Alignment of Secondary Life Skills With Content Areas

CONTENT AREA	LIFE SKILLS	HOW TO EMBED
English	• Writing—uses e-mail, writes and sends text messages, writes a shopping list, writes a chore list • Reading—reads simple instructions for cooking, reads and understands warning labels, reads e-mails and text messages • Vocabulary—uses age-appropriate terminology when at the doctor's office, at work, and across home and community settings; interprets and recognizes sarcasm, euphemisms, and oxymorons • Speaking and listening—actively listens and adjusts use of spoken language to effectively communicate with different audiences; communicates information with supporting evidence in emergencies • Media literacy—differentiates between accurate and inaccurate information presented in the media including visual and verbal messages	• During an essay writing activity in class, student uses her iPad to write and send an e-mail to the teacher. • On library research day, student locates cookbooks and identifies recipe ingredients. • During group activity, students identify and translate common euphemisms. • When acting out scenes from a play literature text, student rehearses and uses correct dialogue along with classmates. • When conducting Internet research for a writing project, student questions the accuracy of information provided via various websites.
Social Studies	• History—celebrates national holidays and understands their meanings such as the Fourth of July, Memorial Day, Labor Day, and Martin Luther King Day • Civics and government—knows *Miranda* rights, participates in voting for class officers • Geography—identifies locations on a map or globe, follows travel directions in the community • Economics—saves money, pays taxes when making a purchase, understands the concept of interest when purchasing using a credit card	• Student maintains a personal calendar with holidays and participates in class discussion about their meanings. • During a mock trial, student is able to recite his rights as a citizen. • When examining current events in the newspaper, student identifies the event location on the map for classmates. • Student prepares a simple savings budget during class exercise about saving for the future.

Mathematics	• Number sense—examines receipt to evaluate if charges are correct • Computation—calculates taxes, tips, or interest • Algebra and functions—calculates the amount of time to travel between two distances • Geometry and measurement—cuts enough wrapping paper to wrap a gift, measures ingredients to bake brownies • Data analysis—prepares for the weather according to the local weather chart • Statistics and probability—calculates calories for daily consumption	• When solving number sense problems, target student examines sample prices to determine if the cost is too high ($100 or $0.50 for a banana). • While class is solving algebraic problems, target student uses a calculator to determine percentages. • In a lesson examining lines and line segments, student works with a group to determine the fastest travel routes on a map. • Student records completion of task steps using an electronic device during class activities. • During a lesson on interpreting data, student reviews weather predictions and identifies clothing needed each day.
Science	• Earth and space—recycles materials in the home, at work, and at school • Life science—plants vegetables, flowers, and herbs • Science, technology, and engineering—packs boxes, suitcases, and other containers so that all necessary items are included within	• Student uses a calculator to determine amount of recycling materials produced per science class period. • Student grows different plants in biology class lab under different environmental conditions. • Student stores class materials in original containers.

CONCLUSION

The educational focus for secondary students with intellectual disability is to meet their post-school wants and needs. These may include postsecondary education, employment, community living, or recreational and leisure pursuits. The instructional curriculum in place in secondary school must be flexible enough to ensure that these individuals continue to gain access to the general education curriculum and their typically developing peers while concurrently learning and practicing the life skills they will need as adults who participate in an integrated community. When this occurs, young adults with intellectual disability are better prepared to be active and participating citizens in their neighborhoods and communities.

Chapter Summary

- A primary instructional focus for students with intellectual disability at the secondary level is meeting transition outcomes and preparing for postsecondary education and employment.

- Secondary students with intellectual disability are served across a variety of instructional settings including grade-level content classes, general community environments, and vocational sites.

- As individuals with intellectual disability progress through secondary programs, they spend increasing amounts of time in community-based settings.

- Transition planning is critical for ensuring that each student with an intellectual disability has an educational experience that is developed that focuses on making him or her ready to meet his or her post-school wants and needs.

- Self-determination components include autonomy, self-regulation, psychological empowerment, and self-realization. Instruction that facilitates each individual's mastery of these elements will contribute to his or her ability to live a self-determined life.

Review Questions

1. Why is a life skills focus important for students with intellectual disability at the secondary level?

2. Why are the elements of social role valorization important to consider when planning instruction for secondary students with intellectual disability?

3. How are transition services aligned with each student's IEP goals? Provide an example.

4. How should a life skills curriculum be determined for each secondary student with an intellectual disability?

5. What is self-determination, and how is instruction for these skills embedded within a life skills curriculum?

Key Terms

social role valorization (SRV), (page 337)
criterion of ultimate functioning (page 337)
dignity of risk (page 338)
competency–deviancy hypothesis (page 339)
community-based instruction (CBI) (page 340)
community-based vocational instruction (CBVI) (page 340)
principle of partial participation (page 341)
transition services (page 341)

individualized transition plan (ITP) (page 342)
transition assessment (page 344)
self-determination (page 345)
autonomy (page 345)
self-regulation (page 345)
psychological empowerment (page 345)
self-realization (page 345)
simulation (page 350)
technology-based strategies (page 352)
natural supports (page 354)

Organizations Concerned With Secondary Students With Intellectual Disability and Life Skills

National Association of Councils on Developmental Disabilities

www.nacdd.org

National Center on Secondary Education and Transition

www.ncset.org

PACER Center

www.pacer.org

The Arc

www.thearc.org

CHAPTER 13

Transition Planning for Secondary Students With Intellectual Disability

Michael L. Wehmeyer and Karrie A. Shogren

Learning Objectives

After reading Chapter 13, you should be able to:

- Explain how transition is defined, critical transition periods, and federal requirements pertaining to transition services.
- Discuss critical components of transition assessment and planning.
- Define and describe best practice to promote self-determination and student involvement.
- Describe opportunities for postsecondary education for students with intellectual disability.

The transitions from adolescence to young adulthood, from high school to work or postsecondary education, and, often, from one's parents' home to a dorm or apartment are significant events in the lives of all young people. Transition is also the most frequent outcome of the process of **individuation**, the term developmental psychologists use to describe the movement from being dependent on others (typically one's parents) to being dependent primarily on oneself in day-to-day life activities (Wehmeyer & Lee, 2007). Such transitions are no less important for youth with intellectual disability as they become adults in society, and yet, for a variety of reasons we will discuss in this chapter, they occur less frequently or less successfully than for most young people. This chapter will discuss transition and transition planning, the importance of transition and transition planning for youth and young adults with intellectual disability, and research- and evidence-based practices in transition and transition planning that enable adolescents with intellectual disability to become self-determined young people and pursue valued life outcomes in their communities.

TRANSITION AND TRANSITION STAGES

Transition, broadly, refers simply to movement and change, and in the lives of students with intellectual disability, it refers more specifically to times during which significant changes occur, typically associated with school- and education-related movements. There are several important transition periods during a child's education: from early childhood to elementary school, from elementary school to middle school, and then from middle school to high school. However, the focus of this chapter is the transition from high school to adult life, including postsecondary education, employment, community living, and so forth. It is worth, however, briefly discussing transitions between other school and life phases before narrowing the focus on adolescent transitions from school to adult life.

TRANSITION FROM EARLY CHILDHOOD TO ELEMENTARY EDUCATION

Best practices in promoting a successful transition from early childhood to elementary education, according to the National Early Childhood Transition Center (www.hdi.uky.edu/nectc/NECTC/Home.aspx), include the identification of a primary contact person for the transition within each program or school, the development of a transition plan as part of the child's individualized education program (IEP) that has active involvement by parents, coordination of curricular objectives between the early childhood agency and kindergarten curriculum, and the opportunity for children to visit the kindergarten class and for kindergarten teachers to visit the child in the preschool setting (Rous, Hallam, McCormick, & Cox, 2010). Rous and colleagues (2010) examined practices used by kindergarten teachers that promote an effective transition and identified several as effective, including visiting a child's home or calling the home before school starts and after the school year has begun, participation in kindergarten registration activities, visits to the incoming student's preschool program, and coordinating curricular objectives with the preschool teacher.

TRANSITION FROM ELEMENTARY SCHOOL TO MIDDLE SCHOOL

The transition from elementary school to middle school has long been seen as one of the more difficult transitions for all students, and coincides with acceleration of adolescent development, puberty, and maturity that mark the middle school years. Some of the issues that impact students are obvious; middle schools are larger than elementary schools, more departmentalized, and more academically demanding. Researchers identified a myriad of factors influencing transition success. Gender plays a role, with both males and females having increased anxiety and concerns associated with physical attractiveness and athletic prowess in addition to making friends and fitting in (Niesen & Wise, 2004). Not surprisingly, peer acceptance and friendship are strong predictors of adjustment to the transition to middle school (Kingery, Erdley, & Marshall, 2011). The quality of classrooms and the structure of schools (that is, size, composition) also predict youth adjustment outcomes, with larger schools associated with lower engagement levels. Positive teacher connectedness, likewise, results in higher satisfaction, and puberty-related health issues can detrimentally impact adjustment and satisfaction (Forrest, Bevans, Riley, Crespo, & Louis, 2013). Echoing a theme that we will emphasize in the transition of adolescents with intellectual disability, Shoshani and Slone (2013) determined adolescent character strengths and positive affect predicted more positive school adjustments in the transition from elementary school to middle school.

There are, unfortunately, only a limited number of studies addressing this transition phase for students with disabilities, and almost none focusing on students with intellectual disability. Some research exists that examines this transition for students with disabilities, most of which focuses on the role of problem behavior in making the transition and the importance of positive behavioral approaches to ensuring success (Lane, Oakes, Carter, & Messenger, 2015). In a review of the literature on transitioning, Hughes, Banks, and Terras (2013) found children with disabilities transitioning from elementary school to middle school have more concerns about bullying and experience victimization more than their typical classmates. Hughes and colleagues also found pupils with disabilities feel greater loneliness and anxiety.

There should be no reason to assume the factors that influence this transition for students without disabilities will not be equally important for students with disabilities. Given the limited research on this transition for students with disabilities, and considering issues pertaining to the transition to middle school of students with intellectual disability, it seems clear that one must keep factors such as social isolation, teacher/school supports, friendship and peer networks, and strengths-based interventions in mind as facilitating such transitions. Thus, as is far too often the case, when students with intellectual disability move from a more inclusive elementary school into a more segregated middle school, one has to consider the impact on student perceptions of strengths, quality of classroom instruction, and so forth.

Best practice for middle school administrators and teachers with regard to ensuring a smooth transition includes scheduling a student's classes to be close together, identifying teachers who work well with students with disabilities as a priority for assignment, teaching students to use a daily planner to assist in self-monitoring and tracking their schedule, teaching students the routines at the middle school, and including a transition plan in the IEP. Implementing practices such as positive behavior interventions and supports (PBIS) and, increasingly, multi-tiered systems of support (MTSS) that emphasize high-quality social and academic instruction for all students may be particularly important to students with intellectual disability in the transition to middle school, particularly given the importance of dealing with social issues to ensure a successful transition (Shogren, Wehmeyer, Lane, & Quirk, in press). Teachers can also play a role in helping to ensure a smooth transition—at least initially—by having the middle school special education teacher attend the transition IEP as well as visit the student while in elementary school. A visit to the middle school should be arranged for a student with an intellectual disability as well prior to starting middle school, so the student gets an opportunity to try out using a locker, navigate the school, and understand the bells and changing of classes.

TRANSITION FROM MIDDLE SCHOOL TO HIGH SCHOOL

Given the paucity of research pertaining to the transition from primary education to secondary education, it should not be a surprise that there is relatively little research that has examined the transition from middle school to high school. The National High School Center issued a report on easing the transition to high school (Kennelly & Monrad, 2007) and noted that there is a disproportionate number of ninth-grade students in high schools, in part because a greater number of students fail to be promoted out of ninth grade than out of any other grade and because of the relatively high number of students who drop out after ninth grade. The report suggested establishing data and monitoring systems to identify students who are struggling, personalizing the learning environment to reduce the sense of anonymity associated with the transition from the smaller middle school to the larger high school, and creating networks and connections to help students find homes within the larger high school.

What little research exists examining this transition period for students with disabilities follows themes discussed with the transition to middle school: the role of problem behavior and adequate supports for success (McIntosh, Flannery, Sugai, Braun, & Cochrane, 2008) through practices such as PBIS and MTSS (Shogren, Wehmeyer, Lane, et al., in press). The supports introduced in the literature at this point, which, again, will be central to this chapter, involve promoting the self-determination of youth with intellectual and developmental disabilities so as to better enable them to be successful in high school (Eisenman, 2007).

ADOLESCENT TRANSITION AND TRANSITION PLANNING

The term *transition* refers, most frequently, to adolescent transition and, thus, to the "life changes, adjustments, and cumulative experiences that occur in the lives of young adults as they move from school environments to independent living and work environments" (Wehman, 2006, p. 4). Transition from secondary education to adulthood "represents a period during which adolescents with disabilities face multiple responsibilities and changing roles that include establishing independence, attending postsecondary education or training, developing social networks, choosing a career, participating in their communities, and managing healthcare and financial affairs" (Wehmeyer & Webb, 2012, p. 3).

The issues and topics covered under the umbrella of adolescent transition are beyond the scope of the current chapter, but include (simply by way of example)

- issues pertaining to policy;
- transition planning and IEP development;
- student involvement in transition planning and processes;
- transition assessment;
- family involvement;
- life skills and community-based instruction;
- workforce, employment, and career development;
- self-determination and self-advocacy;
- social skills and social networks;
- technology use;
- transition-related academics;
- transition education for diverse populations;
- postsecondary education; and
- interagency collaborations.

By necessity, we chose to focus in this chapter on issues and topics that are most pertinent to teachers and students with intellectual disability, while acknowledging that none of the topics listed above are irrelevant to these learners. This chapter will focus on research- and evidence-based practices in transition in areas pertaining to self-determination, student involvement in transition planning, innovative transition to employment, and transition to postsecondary education.

FEDERAL TRANSITION REQUIREMENTS AND TRANSITION PLANNING

One important aspect for considering secondary education and transition for adolescents with intellectual disability involves the requirements in the Individuals with Disabilities Education Act (IDEA) pertaining to transition planning and transition services. The transition services requirements in

IDEA first appeared in the 1997 reauthorization (PL 105–17) (see Johnson, 2012, for extensive discussion of the history of transition services within special education and other federal laws impacting transition). The 2004 reauthorization of IDEA (PL 108–446) introduced some modifications to these original mandates. IDEA does not define transition, but instead stipulates a number of requirements pertaining to **transition services**, which are defined as

> a coordinated set of activities for a child with a disability that (1) is designed to be within a results-oriented process, that is focused on improving the academic and functional achievement of the child with a disability to facilitate the child's movement from school to post-school activities, including postsecondary education, vocational education, integrated employment (including supported employment), continuing and adult education, adult services, independent living, or community participation; (2) is based on the individual child's needs, taking into account the child's strengths, preferences and interests; and includes instruction, related services, community experiences, the development of employment and other post-school adult living objectives, and, if appropriate, acquisition of daily-living skills and functional vocational evaluation. (34 C.F.R. Part 300/A/§ 300.43)

IDEA requires, beginning no later than the first IEP meeting after the student turns 16 (or younger, if deemed by the IEP team as appropriate) and updated annually, that the IEP include measurable postsecondary goals based on transition assessments related to training, education, employment, and independent living skills and that transition services be provided as needed to assist the child in reaching those goals. See Table 13.1 for an example of a transition goal. Table 13.2 provides guidance to educators to evaluate the quality of postsecondary transition goals on the IEP. If transition services are to be discussed in an IEP, the student must be invited to the meeting. In other words, adolescent transition education should focus on academic and functional achievement that facilitates the movement from school to post-school activities, including ongoing education options (postsecondary education, vocational education, adult or continuing education), community-based employment, independent living, and community participation. Transition goals must be based on the student's individual needs, taking into account his or her strengths, preferences, and interests. See Table 13.3 for a component of an IEP devoted to transition planning.

TABLE 13.1 Example of an IEP Goal Statement

POSTSECONDARY GOAL	IEP GOALS	TRANSITION ACTIVITIES/ SERVICES
Upon completion of high school, Liz will learn to use public transportation, including the public bus and subway systems.	• When using public transportation with her class or during independent travel instruction, Liz will sit quietly and refrain from talking to strangers at least two times across three opportunities. • When using public transportation with her class or during independent travel instruction, Liz will plan which bus route or subway line she will be taking and what stop she will be getting off at prior to getting on the bus or subway at least two times across three opportunities.	• Travel instruction, including reading a map and planning a route • Math instruction related to money usage to pay for transportation • Math instruction related to telling time on a variety of watches and clocks • Literacy instruction related to sight word identification • Literacy instruction related to reading signs • Instruction related to community safety and self-defense

SOURCE: Adapted from *Transition Goals in the IEP*. Available at http://www.parentcenterhub.org/repository/transition-goals/

Transition planning, thus, refers, at a minimum, to the involvement of students in IEP team meetings that discuss and set transition service goals. Of course, there is much more to planning than just showing up to a meeting. Setting goals requires knowledge about student transition skills and knowledge, as well as student preferences and interests, strengths, and limitations. With regard to the former (assessment information), we will return to this topic next. With regard to the latter, the requirements that transition services be based on student strengths, preferences, and interests and that students be invited to the meeting have come to be referred to as the **student involvement** mandates in IDEA, and have led to a series of practices that promote active student involvement in transition planning. We will discuss these practices in a subsequent section focused on promoting self-determination and student involvement.

Transition assessment. As is the case with all planning activities, effective transition planning requires information and data from multiple sources. Again, some of these sources are simply out of the scope of this chapter, particularly assessments focused on vocational and employment skills typically conducted through agencies such as vocational rehabilitation, including performance

TABLE 13.2 National Secondary Transition Technical Assistance Center Indicator 13 Checklist: Form B

QUESTIONS	POSTSECONDARY SKILLS		
	EDUCATION TRAINING	EMPLOYMENT	INDEPENDENT LIVING
1. Is there a measurable postsecondary goal or goals in this area?	Y | N	Y | N	Y | N

Can the goal(s) be counted?
Will the goal(s) occur after the student graduates from school?
Based on the information available about this student, does (do) the postsecondary goal(s) seem appropriate for this student?

• If yes to all three, circle Y, *or* if a postsecondary goal(s) is (are) not stated, circle N.

2. Is (are) the postsecondary goal(s) updated annually?	Y | N	Y | N	Y | N | NA

Was (were) the postsecondary goal(s) addressed/updated in conjunction with the development of the current IEP?

• If yes, circle Y, *or* if the postsecondary goal(s) was (were) not updated with the current IEP, circle N.

3. Is there evidence that the measurable postsecondary goal(s) were based on age-appropriate transition assessment?	Y | N	Y | N	Y | N | NA

Is the use of transition assessment(s) for the postsecondary goal(s) mentioned in the IEP or evident in the student's file?

• If yes, circle Y, *or* if no, circle N.

4. Are there transition services in the IEP that will reasonably enable the student to meet his or her postsecondary goal(s)?	Y | N	Y | N	Y | N

Is a type of instruction, related service, community experience, or development of employment and other post-school adult living objectives, and if appropriate acquisition of daily living skills, and provision of a functional vocational evaluation listed in association with meeting the postsecondary goal(s)?

• If yes, circle Y, *or* if no, circle N.

5. Do the transition services include courses of study that will reasonably enable the student to meet his or her postsecondary goal(s)?	Y | N	Y | N	Y | N

Do the transition services include courses of study that align with the student's postsecondary goal(s)?

• If yes, circle Y, *or* if no, circle N.

6. Is (are) there annual IEP goal(s) related to the student's transition services needs?	Y | N	Y | N	Y | N

(Continued)

TABLE 13.2 (Continued)

QUESTIONS	POSTSECONDARY SKILLS		
	EDUCATION TRAINING	EMPLOYMENT	INDEPENDENT LIVING

Is (are) an annual goal(s) included in the IEP that is (are) related to the student's transition services needs?

- If yes, circle Y, *or* if no, circle N.

QUESTIONS	EDUCATION TRAINING	EMPLOYMENT	INDEPENDENT LIVING
7. Is there evidence that the student was invited to the IEP team meeting where transition services were discussed?	Y | N	Y | N	Y | N

For the current year, is there documented evidence in the IEP or cumulative folder that the student was invited to attend the IEP team meeting?

- If yes, circle Y, *or* if no, circle N.

QUESTIONS	EDUCATION TRAINING	EMPLOYMENT	INDEPENDENT LIVING
8. If appropriate, is there evidence that a representative of any participating agency was invited to the IEP team meeting with the prior consent of the parent or student who has reached the age of majority?	Y | N | NA	Y | N | NA	Y | N | NA

For the current year, is there evidence in the IEP that representatives of any of the following agencies/services were invited to participate in the IEP development including but not limited to *postsecondary education, vocational education, integrated employment (including supported employment), continuing and adult education, adult services, independent living, or community participation* for this postsecondary goal?

Was consent obtained from the parent (or student, for a student the age of majority)?

- If yes to both, circle Y.
- If no invitation is evident and a participating agency is likely to be responsible for providing or paying for transition services and there was consent to invite them to the IEP meeting, circle N.
- If it is too early to determine if the student will need outside agency involvement, or no agency is likely to provide or pay for transition services, circle NA.
- If parent or individual student consent (when appropriate) was not provided, circle NA.

Does the IEP meet the requirements of Indicator 13? (Circle one)

Yes (all *Y*s or *NA*s for each item [1-8] on the checklist included in the IEP are circled) or **No** (one or more *N*s circled)

SOURCE: U.S. Department of Education, Office of Special Education Programs Grant No. H326J050004. This product is public domain. Authorization to reproduce it in whole or in part is granted.

TABLE 13.3 Example of an IEP Transition Plan

STUDENT: JAMES C. STEVENS   GRADE: 11   STUDENT ID NUMBER: 194710
DATE OF BIRTH: MAY 3, 1999   TEACHER: MELANIE SANTORO

Background Information:

James is a student with Down syndrome who has moderate intellectual disability. He participates in special education classes with the support of a paraprofessional. His areas of strength include receptive language abilities, long-term memory skills, and a love of animals. Verbal outbursts with accompanying profanity and occasional inappropriate comments to female classmates and teachers are areas of concern. A behavior intervention plan has been developed to address these issues. His parents are actively involved in his education.

Date of IEP Meeting: June 14, 2016

Participants:

Samuel Slade	General Education Teacher
Melanie Santoro	Special Education Teacher
Jerome Worthington	Rehabilitation Specialist
Candice Monroe	Assistant Principal
Larry Decker	County Special Education Coordinator
Victoria Emerson	School Psychologist
Christina Peabody	Coordinator, Independent Living Center
Martha Stevens	Parent
Richard Stevens	Parent
James Stevens	Student

TRANSITION PLAN

Course of Study: Special education certificate

Career Goals: Working with small animals in a veterinary clinic, pet sitter

Postsecondary Employment Goal: Employment in the community with the assistance of a job coach

Needed Transition Services:

1. Ability to utilize public and para-transportation systems

2. Develop appropriate interpersonal skills for working with employer, customers, and clients

3. Postsecondary instruction for continued development of adaptive behavior skills, vocational skills, and functional academics

Postsecondary Community Living Goal: Upon graduation, residence in a group home in his neighborhood

Needed Transition Services:

1. Personal hygiene skills appropriate for independent living

2. Access to and ability to use community recreational facilities

3. Cooking skills appropriate for making himself breakfast and lunch

Identify Interagency Responsibilities: A case manager from Vocational Rehabilitation Services will be assigned in addition to a case manager from the Independent Living Center.

Community Linkages: State Vocational Rehabilitation Office, Independent Living Center, Specialized Employment Services Inc.

work sampling. However, teachers of students with intellectual disability may work in tandem with job development professionals and other transition educators to examine aspects of work, living, postsecondary, and community environments using task analysis procedures, observations, and interviews to determine what employment, living, schooling, or participation options exist; what modifications might be necessary for a student to participate in them; and what skills the student might need to be successful (Neubert, 2012).

Transition assessment, broadly, employs multiple methods to get information and data, from direct observations to interviews to self-report measures to records reviews. Clark (1996) identified informal assessment processes from which transition-related decisions can be made, including

- situational or observational learning styles assessments;
- curriculum-based assessment;
- observational reports from teachers, employers, and family members;
- situational assessments in home, community, and work settings;
- environmental assessments;
- personal-future planning activities;
- structured interviews with students;
- structured interviews with parents, guardians, advocates, or peers;
- adaptive, behavioral, or functional skill inventories;
- social histories;
- employability, independent living, and personal/social skills rating scales; and
- technology or vocational education skills assessments.

Though there are a limited number of standardized transition assessments, two more recent and comprehensive systems are the Transition Assessment and Goal Generator (TAGG) (Martin, Hennessey, McConnell, Terry, & Willis, 2015) and the Transition Planning Inventory (TPI) (Patton & Clark, 2014). Both tools are intended for use by teachers. The TAGG is an online transition assessment (although there is a paper version) developed for secondary-age youth with disabilities. The TAGG measures eight nonacademic skills and behaviors associated with attainment of transition outcomes: strengths and limitations, disability awareness, persistence, interacting with others, goal setting and attainment, employment, student involvement in the IEP, and support community. There are three versions of the TAGG: Professional, Family, and Student. The TPI provides an assessment of a student's knowledge, skills, and behaviors in nine critical functioning areas identified in federal law and/or determined to be important for successful adult outcomes in the transition process (Rehfeldt, Clark, & Lee, 2012). The nine domains include employment, further education, daily living, leisure activities, community participation, health, self-determination, communication, and interpersonal relations. The computer version of the TPI generates a strengths-based profile to use in planning.

Assessing self-determination. Measurement in the field of transition services, which has a life skills and life span focus and, as noted earlier, involves multiple methods and sources, is by its nature future oriented. Such efforts should focus on ability, not deficits; emphasize strengths, not limitations; and be outcomes oriented. A supports focus, to be discussed in a subsequent section, emphasizes the identification of supports that youth need to successfully function in typical environments, and should be a critical component of transition planning that is futures oriented and ability focused. Another critical assessment area pertains to **self-determination**. There are two standardized measures that are widely used, designed for teachers to administer, and applicable for students with intellectual disability, The Arc's Self-Determination Scale (SDS) (Wehmeyer & Kelchner, 1995) and the American Institutes for Research (AIR) Self-Determination Assessments (Wolman, Campeau, Dubois, Mithaug, & Stolarski, 1994). The Arc's SDS is a seventy-two-item self-report measure of global self-determination. An overall self-determination score, as well as subscale scores for each of four essential characteristics of self-determined behavior—autonomy, self-regulation, psychological empowerment, and self-realization—can be calculated.

The AIR Self-Determination Assessments (Wolman et al., 1994), designed for students, educators, and parents, assess student capacity and opportunity for self-determination. The student version consists of twenty-four questions and yields capacity and opportunity subscale scores. The capacity subscale consists of questions related to things students do related to self-determination ("Things I Do" subscale) and how students feel about performing these self-determined behaviors ("How I Feel" subscale). The opportunity subscale consists of questions regarding students' perceptions of their opportunities to perform self-determined behaviors at home and at school. The parent and educator versions parallel the structure of the student version. Shogren et al. (2008) showed that while the SDS and the AIR student assessment are related, they measure distinct aspects of the self-determination construct. The SDS measures current self-determination status, independent of why a student has high or low levels of self-determination, while the AIR assessment measures student capacity and opportunity for self-determination.

Shogren, Wehmeyer, Little, and colleagues (in press) are in the initial stages of validating a new measure of self-determination—the Self-Determination Inventory: Self-Report version—that includes items from The Arc's Self-Determination Scale, but expands assessment to include associated domains identified by Shogren, Wehmeyer, Palmer, Forber-Pratt, Little, and Lopez (2015) pertaining to causal agency theory (to be discussed subsequently). When field testing is completed, the measure will be available at www.self-determination.org.

Person-centered, self-directed transition planning. There is general consensus in the field that transition planning should, at some level, involve **person-centered planning**. According to Seabrooks-Blackmore and Williams (2012), a person-centered planning approach "involves a systematic process that focuses on an understanding of the needs of the person with disabilities and not the system that serves them" (p. 91). Person-centered planning processes "share common beliefs and attempt to put those shared beliefs into a planning framework" (Wehmeyer, 2002, p. 56). Schwartz, Jacobson, and Holburn (2000) used a consensus process to define person-centeredness, identifying eight hallmarks of a person-centered planning process:

1. The person's activities, services, and supports are based on his or her dreams, interests, preferences, strengths, and capacities.

2. The person and people important to him or her are included in lifestyle planning, and have the opportunity to exercise control and make informed decisions.

3. The person has meaningful choices, with decisions based on his or her experiences.

4. The person uses, when possible, natural and community supports.

5. Activities, supports, and services foster skills to achieve personal relationships, community inclusion, dignity, and respect.

6. The person's opportunities and experiences are maximized, and flexibility is enhanced within existing regulatory and funding constraints.

7. Planning is collaborative and recurring and involves an ongoing commitment to the person.

8. The person is satisfied with his or her relationships, home, and daily routine. (p. 238)

Seabrooks-Blackmore and Williams (2012) identified a number of frequently used person-centered planning processes that provide a structure for planning meetings that embody the above hallmark characteristics, including Personal Futures Planning (Mount & Zwernik, 1990); the McGill Action Planning System, or Making Action Plans (MAPS) (Vandercook, York, & Forest, 1989); Planning Alternative Tomorrows with Hope (PATH) (Pearpoint, O'Brien, & Forest, 1998); Group Action Planning (Turnbull et al., 1996); and Essential Lifestyle Planning (O'Brien & O'Brien, 2000).

Wehmeyer (2002) argued that person-centered planning processes and student-directed or self-directed planning processes differ, not in the values undergirding the process, which share considerable overlap, but in the priority assigned to those values. Wehmeyer noted:

> To some degree, the ingredients to these two processes are the same, but they are mixed differently, with varying proportions of each value reflected in each respective process. For example, in person-centered planning, both currently and historically, there has been a greater emphasis on the role of significant others in plan making than exists in student-directed planning, while student-directed planning processes have placed greater emphasis on building student capacity to set or track goals or make decisions than has person-centered planning. (p. 57)

This is not to be critical of either planning approach, but to suggest that the best approach would be a person-centered, student-directed approach in which the values, processes, and intent of both person-centered and student-directed planning are merged. Wehmeyer (2002) identified the Group Action Planning model as an example of a person-centered planning process that has built in student-directed components. The Group Action Planning process includes multiple components that emphasize connections among families, the student, and professionals; setting high expectations; problem solving; and celebrating success.

Supports planning. In recent years, assessments of support needs, defined as the "pattern and intensity of supports necessary for a person to participate in activities linked with normative human functioning," were developed that have applicability to age-appropriate transition assessment (Thompson et al., 2009, p. 135). Supports assessment and planning differ from traditional assessment in that the focus is the support needed for someone to be successful in a particular life domain, not the skills, knowledge, abilities, or actions of the person (in other words, a measure of personal competency). There are now two versions of the widely used Supports Intensity Scale that can provide information for a supports plan to be included within the transition planning process: the Supports Intensity Scale—Adult Version (SIS-A) (Thompson, Bryant et al., 2016) and the Supports Intensity Scale—Children's Version (SIS-C) (Thompson, Wehmeyer et al., 2016). Both norm-referenced measures provide data pertaining to the intensity of support needed for a person to be successful across multiple domains (SIS-A: Home Living, Community Living, Lifelong Learning, Employment, Health and Safety, Social, and Protection and Advocacy; SIS-C: Home Living, Community and Neighborhood, School Participation, School Learning, Health and Safety, Social Activities, and Advocacy).

During the transition years, the SIS-C can be used by educators and other IEP team members to develop a supports plan that can be used in a person-centered planning process to determine needed supports for students to be successful in contexts pertinent to their school years, while the SIS-A can be used by the IEP team to determine supports needed for future environments and domains. Seo and colleagues (in press) examined the comparability of the two versions, and found alignment of the specific set of items across parallel activity domains and score comparability across the two assessments.

Figure 13.1 provides an example of how the inclusion of supports planning in the transition IEP planning process might occur. The process "starts with assessing personal interests and needs for support, proceeds to team planning and implementation, is followed by careful monitoring of implementation, and ends with an evaluation of outcomes" (Thompson et al., 2009, p. 143). The process is iterative as it calls for planning teams to return to earlier components based on monitoring and evaluation activities.

Family involvement in transition planning. It should go without saying that family involvement in transition planning is crucial. Wandry and Pleet (2012) provided solid evidence of the importance of active family and parental

FIGURE 13.1 Supports Planning Process

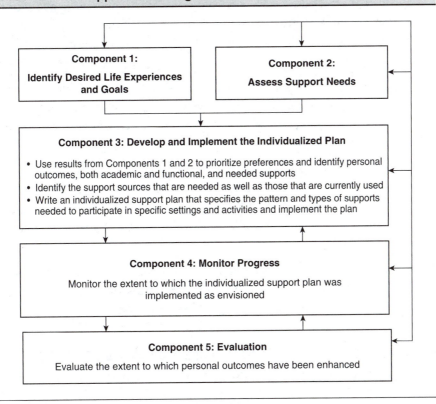

SOURCE: Adapted from J. Thompson, M. Wehmeyer, and C. Hughes, "Mind the Gap! Implications of Person-Environment Fit Models of Intellectual Disability for Students, Educators, and Schools," *Exceptionality, 18*(4), 2010, pp. 168-181.

involvement in a child's school life, and this is especially important during the transition years. Family participation in transition planning has been linked with increased graduation rates, employment, and achievement of post-school outcomes (Wandry & Pleet, 2012). Such involvement, though, must be meaningful, with open communication and engagement in shared decision making among the family and the student, and responsive to family needs and cultural/linguistic/ethnic differences and preferences.

Wehmeyer, Morningstar, and Husted (1999) provided several recommendations to teachers for increasing family involvement:

- *Learning to listen.* The transition planning process and the transition implementation process are more effective if teachers know what family members prefer. Of course, this is done along with efforts to involve students themselves. Teachers should determine family goals and visions for current and future vocational, living, and other transition-related options, and should ask families how they want to be involved.

- *Inviting involvement.* Teachers should not expect parents and family members to shoulder all responsibility for their involvement. Instead, professionals should actively seek parental and family advice and involvement, and reach out to parents to ensure their meaningful participation.

- *Provide examples.* Most family members have only limited information and knowledge about transition and what options exist for students after public school. Teachers should provide information that shows families a variety of examples leading to positive transition outcomes for youth.

- *Help connect.* Teachers can be critical in linking families and students to adult support providers and other resources that are important for successful transition.

CURRENT TRANSITION OUTCOMES FOR ADOLESCENTS AND YOUNG ADULTS WITH INTELLECTUAL DISABILITY

Before discussing research- and evidence-based practices to promote successful transition for adolescents and young adults with intellectual disability, it is worth briefly documenting what we know about current transition outcomes for this population. The take-home message is that although things have improved, such outcomes are still less positive for youth with intellectual disability than for their nondisabled peers and, by and large, for their peers with other types of disabilities. This is documented by results from the National Longitudinal Transition Study-2, or NLTS2, a ten-year longitudinal study of transition outcomes for youth with disabilities funded by the federal government.

Shogren and Plotner (2012) examined the transition planning experiences of students with intellectual disability, autism, or other disabilities (all other disability groups in NLTS2 combined, including learning disabilities, emotional and behavior disorders, speech and language disorders, etc.) as reported in the NLTS2. With regard to the primary goal of students' education program for post-school preparation, only 10 percent of students with intellectual disability had any goals pertaining to postsecondary education, and 20 percent still had goals pertaining to segregated employment. Only half or just under half of students had goals pertaining to independent living and functional independence. Students with intellectual disability had the lowest rates of enrollment in any postsecondary program, including vocational or technical school, compared to every other disability category. Not surprisingly, only 38 percent of students with intellectual disability were actually employed at the time of the NLTS2 interview, and only 36 percent of students with intellectual disability were living independently or semi-independently after graduation. In other words, there is much work yet to be done to achieve the outcome that youth with intellectual and developmental disabilities transition to rich, full lives in their community.

EVIDENCE-BASED PRACTICES TO PROMOTE SUCCESSFUL TRANSITION FOR ADOLESCENTS AND YOUNG ADULTS WITH INTELLECTUAL DISABILITY

As we have emphasized throughout this chapter, what is to be known about transition far exceeds the space allotted in this chapter. To determine what was covered, and particularly with regard to what practices we included, we drew from a couple of sources. First, Wehmeyer and Patton (2012) identified a number of guiding principles essential to the transition process for all youth:

- Transition efforts should start early.
- Planning must be comprehensive.
- Planning processes must consider a student's preferences and interests.
- The transition planning process should be considered a capacity-building activity (that is, consider a student's strengths).
- Student participation throughout the process is essential.
- Family involvement is desired, needed, and crucial.
- The transition planning process must be sensitive to diversity.
- Supports and services are useful, and we all use them.
- Community-based activities provide extremely beneficial experiences.
- Interagency commitment and coordination is essential.

Second, the federally funded National Secondary Transition Technical Assistance Center (2010) identified evidence-based practices in secondary transition for students with disabilities (see Table 13.4) as well as sixteen evidence-based predictors of post-school employment, education, and independent living success (see Table 13.5 on p. 384). By knowing what transition supports and services predict or support particular post-school outcomes, educators and transition IEP teams make informed decisions about the educational programming of secondary students with intellectual disability. For example, social skills were a predictor for both post-school employment and postsecondary education; instruction social skills were also considered an evidence-based practice (National Secondary Transition Technical Assistance Center, 2010). This suggests social skills instruction should be an element of secondary programming for students with intellectual disability, particularly for students who need any support or additional skills in this area. (See Chapter 11 for additional discussion of teaching social skills.)

Again, many of the skills listed in these tables are covered in other chapters, but drawing from the priorities listed by Wehmeyer and Patton (2012) and the National Secondary Transition Technical Assistance Center (2010) evidence-based predictors and practices, we examine practices in adolescent transition for students with intellectual disability in the areas of self-determination and student involvement, postsecondary education, and career and employment practices.

SELF-DETERMINATION AND STUDENT INVOLVEMENT

Promoting the self-determination of adolescents with intellectual disability emerged as a best practice for a variety of reasons, from studies linking enhanced self-determination to more positive school and adult outcomes and more positive quality of life to the prominence of self-determination in the disability rights movement (Wehmeyer & Abery, 2013). As noted in Tables 13.4 and 13.5, elements of promoting self-determination and student involvement have strong evidence for their importance and have established promoting self-determination and student involvement as evidence-based practices in the field of special education.

What is self-determination? Self-determination has been defined as a

dispositional characteristic manifested as acting as the causal agent in one's life. Self-determined people (i.e., causal agents) act in service

TABLE 13.4 Evidence-Based Practices in Secondary Transition

TRANSITION DOMAIN	EVIDENCE-BASED PRACTICES
Student-Focused Planning	• Involving students in the IEP process • Using the *Whose Future Is It Anyway?* process • Using the *Self-Directed IEP*

Student Development	• Instruction in the following skills:
	  ○ Functional life skills
	  ○ Banking skills
	  ○ Restaurant meal-purchasing skills
	  ○ Employment skills using computer-assisted instruction
	  ○ Grocery shopping skills
	  ○ Home maintenance skills
	  ○ Leisure skills
	  ○ Personal health skills
	  ○ Job-specific employment skills
	  ○ Purchasing using the "one more than" strategy
	  ○ Life skills using computer-assisted instruction
	  ○ Life skills using community-based instruction
	  ○ Self-care skills
	  ○ Safety skills
	  ○ Self-determination skills
	  ○ Goal-setting and goal attainment skills using the *Self-Determined Learning Model of Instruction*
	  ○ Self-management for life skills
	  ○ Self-management for employment skills
	  ○ Self-advocacy skills
	  ○ Purchasing skills
	  ○ Functional reading skills
	  ○ Functional math skills
	  ○ Social skills
	  ○ Purchasing skills
	  ○ Skills for completing a job application
	  ○ Job-related social communication skills
	  ○ Cooking and food preparation skills
	  ○ Employment skills using community-based instruction

Family Involvement	• Training parents about transition services
Program Structure	• Extending services beyond secondary school (e.g., publicly funded school services for students ages 18 to 21 in community college or another postsecondary setting, vocational training, etc.) • Using *Check and Connect* (a dropout prevention program) • Providing community-based instruction

SOURCE: *Evidence-Based Practices and Predictors in Secondary Transition: What We Know and What We Still Need to Know* (Charlotte, NC: National Secondary Transition Technical Assistance Center, 2010).

TABLE 13.5 Evidence-Based Predictors of Post-School Employment, Education, and Independent Living Success

PREDICTORS/OUTCOMES	EDUCATION	EMPLOYMENT	INDEPENDENT LIVING
Career Awareness	X	X	
Community Experiences		X	
Exit Exam Requirements/High School Diploma Status		X	
Inclusion in General Education	X	X	X
Interagency Collaboration	X	X	
Occupational Courses	X	X	
Paid Employment/Work Experience	X	X	X
Parental Involvement		X	
Program of Study		X	
Self-Advocacy/Self-Determination	X	X	
Self-Care/Independent Living	X	X	X
Social Skills	X	X	
Student Support	X	X	X
Transition Program	X	X	
Vocational Education	X	X	
Work Study		X	

SOURCE: *Evidence-Based Practices and Predictors in Secondary Transition: What We Know and What We Still Need To Know* (Charlotte, NC: National Secondary Transition Technical Assistance Center, 2010).

to freely chosen goals. Self-determined actions function to enable a person to be the causal agent in his or her life. (Shogren, Wehmeyer, Palmer, Forber-Pratt et al., 2015, p. 258)

A dispositional characteristic is an enduring tendency used to characterize and describe differences between people; it refers to a tendency to act or think in a particular way, but presumes contextual variance (that is, socio-contextual supports and opportunities and threats and impediments). Broadly defined, causal agency implies that it is the individual who makes or causes things to happen

TABLE 13.6 Component Elements of Self-Determined Behavior and Instructional Focal Points

COMPONENT ELEMENT	TEACHING FOCUS
Choice-making skills	Infuse opportunities to make choices throughout the school day
Decision-making skills	Teach students to identify decision options, identify consequences of each option, assess probability of consequence occurring, consider preferences and values associated with the decision, and choose an option
Problem-solving skills	Teach students to identify and define the problem, list possible solutions, and identify the best solution
Goal-setting and goal attainment skills	Teach students to identify and define a goal clearly, develop objectives to achieve goal, create action plan to achieve goal, and track progress toward goal
Self-regulation and self-management skills	Teach strategies such as self-monitoring, self-instruction, self-evaluation, self-scheduling, and picture prompting
Self-advocacy and leadership skills	Teach students skills to advocate for themselves, including how to be assertive, how to communicate effectively, and how to negotiate and compromise
Self-awareness and self-knowledge	Teach students about their skills and abilities and how to get the supports they need to be successful

SOURCE: M. Wehmeyer, S. Palmer, N. Garner, M. Lawrence, J. Soukup, K. Shogren, . . . J. Kelly, *The Self-Determined Learning Model of Instruction: A Teacher's Guide,* 2nd ed. (Lawrence, KS: Beach Center on Disability, 2009).

in his or her life. Self-determined actions enable a person to act as a causal agent in his or her life.

Self-determination emerges across the life span as individuals learn skills and develop attitudes and beliefs that enable them to be causal agents in their lives. These are the component elements of self-determined behavior, and include choice making, problem solving, decision making, goal setting and attainment, self-advocacy, and self-management, among other skills. It is at this level that intervention operates. Evidence-based practices to promote self-determination are discussed in a subsequent section, but the first level of instructional focus for educators wanting to promote the self-determination of students with intellectual disability is to provide explicit instruction on each of these component elements. Table 13.6 provides a list of critical component elements and focal points for instruction in self-determination.

Importance of promoting self-determination. There is, by now, considerable evidence supporting the importance of promoting self-determination. Meta-analyses of the literature support that when students with disabilities are taught component skills leading to self-determination, such as those identified in Table 13.6, they do successfully acquire those skills (Algozzine, Browder, Karvonen, Test, & Wood, 2001), and that when provided instruction to promote self-determination, students become more self-determined (Wehmeyer, Palmer, Shogren, Williams-Diehm, & Soukup, 2012; Wehmeyer, Shogren et al., 2012). Further, when students are more self-determined, they attain more positive school and community outcomes, including greater access to the general education curriculum and more positive employment and community living outcomes (Powers et al., 2012; Shogren, Palmer, Wehmeyer, Williams-Diehm, & Little, 2012; Shogren, Wehmeyer, Palmer, Rifenbark, & Little, 2015).

Importance of promoting student involvement. The 1992 transition mandates in IDEA required that when transition services are discussed in a student's IEP meeting, students must be invited. This so-called student involvement mandate resulted in the development and evaluation of numerous programs, and processes to promote student involvement in transition planning and research subsequent to these requirements have established the importance of such involvement and shown the effectiveness of several transition planning programs. The **Self-Directed IEP**, for example, enables students to learn the leadership skills necessary to manage their IEP meeting and publicly disclose their interests, skills, limits, and goals identified through Choosing Goals lessons. Rather than be passive participants at their IEP meetings, students learn to lead these meetings to the greatest extent of their ability. Martin et al. (2006) determined that students with disabilities who received instruction using the Self-Directed IEP

- attended more IEP meetings;
- increased their active participation in the meetings;
- showed more leadership behaviors in the meetings;
- expressed their interests, skills, and support needs across educational domains; and
- remembered their IEP goals after the meeting at greater rates than did students who received no such instruction.

Wehmeyer, Palmer, Lee, Williams-Diehm, and Shogren (2011) studied the impact of another student involvement intervention, **Whose Future Is It Anyway?**, on self-determination and transition knowledge and skills of students with intellectual disability. The training consisted of thirty-six sessions introducing students to the concept of transition and transition planning and enabling students to self-direct instruction related to

- self- and disability awareness;

- making decisions about transition-related outcomes;

- identifying and securing community resources to support transition services;

- writing and evaluating transition goals and objectives;

- communicating effectively in small groups; and

- developing skills to become an effective team member, leader, or self-advocate.

Wehmeyer et al. (2011) found instruction using the Whose Future Is It Anyway? process resulted in significant, positive differences in self-determination and that students who received instruction gained transition knowledge and skills.

Evidence-based practices to promote self-determination and student involvement. There are now a number of methods, materials, and strategies to promote self-determination that meet standards for evidence-based practice. The **Self-Determined Learning Model of Instruction** is a multicomponent intervention to enable teachers to teach students to self-regulate problem solving to set a goal, create an action plan to achieve that goal, self-monitor and self-evaluate progress toward the goal, and revise the action plan or goal as needed so as to attain the goal. Implementation of this model consists of a three-phase instructional process. Each instructional phase presents a problem to be solved by the student. The student solves each problem by answering a series of four student questions per phase that students learn, modify to make their own, and apply to reach self-set goals. Each question is linked to a set of teacher objectives, and each instructional phase includes a list of educational supports teachers can use to teach or support students to self-direct learning. Figures 13.2, 13.3, and 13.4 provide flow charts for the instructional sequence described next.

FIGURE 13.2 Phase 1 of the Self-Determined Learning Model of Instruction

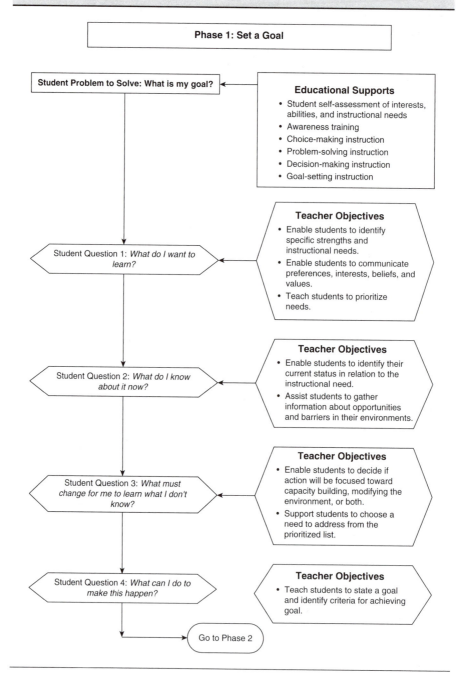

Phase 1: Set a Goal

Student Problem to Solve: What is my goal?

Educational Supports
- Student self-assessment of interests, abilities, and instructional needs
- Awareness training
- Choice-making instruction
- Problem-solving instruction
- Decision-making instruction
- Goal-setting instruction

Student Question 1: *What do I want to learn?*

Teacher Objectives
- Enable students to identify specific strengths and instructional needs.
- Enable students to communicate preferences, interests, beliefs, and values.
- Teach students to prioritize needs.

Student Question 2: *What do I know about it now?*

Teacher Objectives
- Enable students to identify their current status in relation to the instructional need.
- Assist students to gather information about opportunities and barriers in their environments.

Student Question 3: *What must change for me to learn what I don't know?*

Teacher Objectives
- Enable students to decide if action will be focused toward capacity building, modifying the environment, or both.
- Support students to choose a need to address from the prioritized list.

Student Question 4: *What can I do to make this happen?*

Teacher Objectives
- Teach students to state a goal and identify criteria for achieving goal.

Go to Phase 2

FIGURE 13.3 Phase 2 of the Self-Determined Learning Model of Instruction

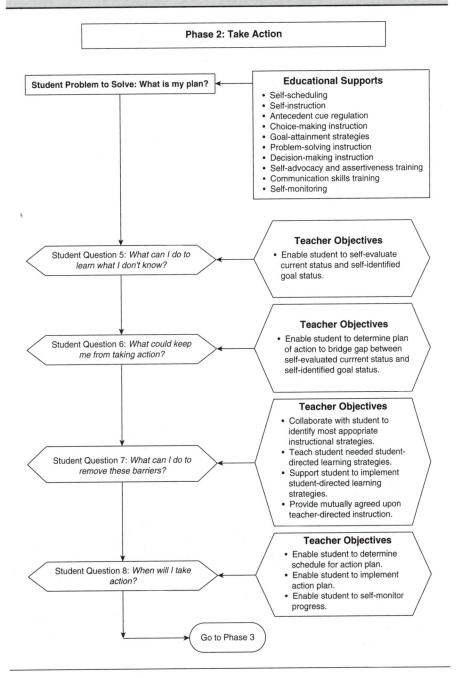

Phase 2: Take Action

Student Problem to Solve: What is my plan?

Educational Supports
- Self-scheduling
- Self-instruction
- Antecedent cue regulation
- Choice-making instruction
- Goal-attainment strategies
- Problem-solving instruction
- Decision-making instruction
- Self-advocacy and assertiveness training
- Communication skills training
- Self-monitoring

Student Question 5: *What can I do to learn what I don't know?*

Teacher Objectives
- Enable student to self-evaluate current status and self-identified goal status.

Student Question 6: *What could keep me from taking action?*

Teacher Objectives
- Enable student to determine plan of action to bridge gap between self-evaluated currrent status and self-identified goal status.

Student Question 7: *What can I do to remove these barriers?*

Teacher Objectives
- Collaborate with student to identify most appopriate instructional strategies.
- Teach student needed student-directed learning strategies.
- Support student to implement student-directed learning strategies.
- Provide mutually agreed upon teacher-directed instruction.

Student Question 8: *When will I take action?*

Teacher Objectives
- Enable student to determine schedule for action plan.
- Enable student to implement action plan.
- Enable student to self-monitor progress.

Go to Phase 3

FIGURE 13.4 Phase 3 of the Self-Determined Learning Model of Instruction

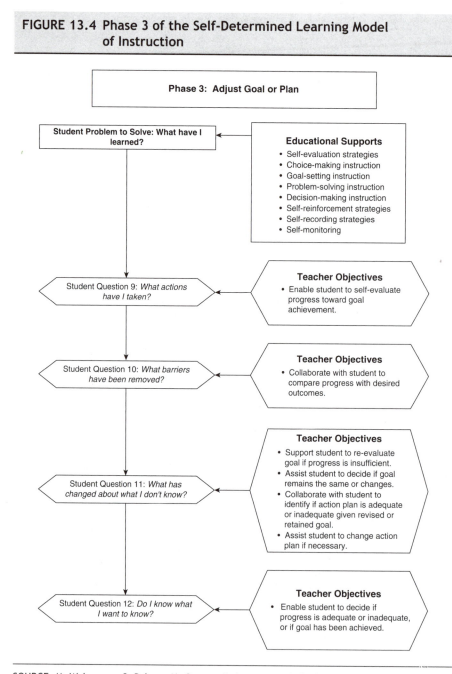

SOURCE: M. Wehmeyer, S. Palmer, N. Garner, M. Lawrence, J. Soukup, K. Shogren, . . . J. Kelly, *The Self-Determined Learning Model of Instruction: A Teacher's Guide,* 2nd ed. (Lawrence, KS: Beach Center on Disability, 2009).

The student questions are constructed to direct the student through a problem-solving sequence in each instructional phase. The four questions differ in each phase, but represent identical steps in the problem-solving sequence: (a) identify the problem, (b) identify potential solutions to the problem, (c) identify barriers to solving the problem, and (d) identify consequences of each solution. These steps are the fundamental steps in any problem-solving process, and they form the means–end problem-solving sequence represented by the student questions in each phase and enable the student to solve the problem posed in each instructional phase (What is my goal? What is my plan? What have I learned?). The evidence pertaining to the impact of this process on student self-determination and school-/transition-related outcomes has been described already. In addition, Shogren, Plotner, Palmer, Wehmeyer, and Paek (2014) found teachers who implemented this strategy raised their expectations of students with intellectual disability as a function of the outcomes.

POSTSECONDARY EDUCATION

As mentioned earlier, the federal transition mandates require that transition services be intended to improve the academic and functional skills that support the transition from school to post-school activities, one of which is postsecondary education. As documented when looking at current transition outcomes for youth with intellectual disability, postsecondary education has not been an outcome traditionally available for these young people, despite the fact that it is well recognized that later employment and earning capacity is directly linked to postsecondary education for all young people. This is, however, changing, and although the evidence of the impact of postsecondary education for youth with intellectual disability is preliminary at best, there are a growing number of community college and university programs for youth with intellectual disability that have emerged in the past several years. Think College (2016) provides a searchable database of postsecondary education opportunities specifically designed for students with disabilities at two-year, four-year, and vocational/technical schools. See Table 13.7 for examples of postsecondary education programs specifically designed to support the needs of students with intellectual disability.

Postsecondary educational opportunities for students with intellectual disability include multiple models. Some postsecondary programs are ones that substantially separate; these programs are not inclusive or integrated. Other

TABLE 13.7 Example Postsecondary Education Programs for Students With Intellectual Disability

POSTSECONDARY EDUCATION TYPES	POSTSECONDARY EDUCATION OPTIONS
After high school, residential, four-year university	• Launch at the University of Arkansas (www.lifestylesinc.org/services/college-for-living/launch/) • UI REACH at the University of Iowa (www.education.uiowa.edu/services/reach/)
After high school, nonresidential, four-year university	• FUTURE at the University of Tennessee (http://futureut.utk.edu/)
After high school, two-year college	• Dual Enrollment With Individualized Supports (DEIS) at the University of Hawaii (www.cds.hawaii.edu/deis/)

models are inclusive individual support programs in which the students with disabilities are fully integrated or included into all facets of the postsecondary educational setting. Finally, there are hybrid models in which inclusion and integration within the traditional postsecondary educational setting (for example, classes) are occurring but the students with disabilities may also take classes just among themselves (Cook, Hayden, Wilczenski, & Poynton, 2015; Hart & Grigal, 2010; Neubert & Moon, 2006). Within these different models, postsecondary education programs can also be day programs or residential, where students live at the postsecondary institution similar to peers without disabilities. Programs can also be separated based on students attending them after high school or while they are still in high school (Think College, 2016).

CAREER AND EMPLOYMENT PRACTICES

Employment outcomes for students with intellectual disability lag behind even those for other students with disabilities, despite the fact that there are numerous strategies that have been shown to improve employment results. Table 13.5 (page 384) showed an evidence base for a number of activities that promote employment and career skills, including skills for completing a job application, job-related social communication skills, and employment skills using community-based instruction, as well as paid work experiences during high school. Life skills such as social and communication skills, academic skills, and personal care skills are all, of course, critical for achieving positive employment and career outcomes (Hanley-Maxwell & Izzo, 2012). Table 13.8 provides the

TABLE 13.8 Content and Skills Needed for the Twenty-First-Century Workforce

Life Skills

- Personal care
- Transportation
- Physical/mental health
- Safety
- Communication

Core Academic Skills

- English
- Mathematics
- Sciences
- History

Career Skills

- Abilities
- Interests
- Limitations
- Values
- Accommodation needs

Information, Media, and Technology Skills

- Can find and analyze information
- Computer and Internet skills
- Uses media
- Work technologies
- Communication technologies

Social Skills

- Hygiene
- Dresses appropriately
- Daily living skills
- Follows social rules

Self-Determination Skills

- Self-knowledge
- Self-direction
- Plans and sets goals
- Self-regulates
- Problem solving
- Self-advocacy

Personal Values Skills

- Responsible
- Respectful
- Collaborates
- Cooperates
- Ethical
- Continuously learns

Career Planning Skills

- Interest assessment
- Self-assessment
- Vocational training
- Mentoring
- Career exploration
- Postgraduation/IEP planning
- Career portfolios

Job Search Skills

- Community-based instruction
- Work experience
- Service learning
- Job clubs
- Apprenticeships and internships

SOURCE: Adapted from C. Hanley-Maxwell and M. Izzo, "Preparing Students for the 21st Century Workforce," in M. Wehmeyer and K. Webb (Eds.), *Handbook of Adolescent Transition and Disability* (New York, NY: Taylor & Francis, 2012), pp. 139-155.

skills Hanley-Maxwell and Izzo (2012) identified as critical for students to learn during the school years.

There is a limited evidence base pertaining to career and employment practices for students with intellectual disability, although research points to the critical nature of career planning and job search skills. Grigal and Deschamps (2012) identified indicators of quality work-based learning experiences for students with intellectual disability as including (a) clear expectations of student activity at the workplace, (b) clearly defined roles of teachers and work-site supervisors, and (c) well-structured feedback on student performance.

There are a number of employment support models shown to effectively promote the transition to employment for youth with intellectual disability. Teachers may not be directly responsible for implementing these models, but should have a working knowledge of them so as to promote collaboration between school- and community-based agencies. The best known models involve **supported employment**, defined as "competitive employment in a community business with individualized assistance by a skilled job coach who helps a person find a job, learn how to do the job, and provides follow-along support to assist with keeping their job" (Parent-Johnson, 2012, p. 330). Among the components of supported employment are job development and creation strategies, job carving, and providing workplace accommodations. **Customized employment** is an extension of supported employment, emphasizing the person's involvement in planning for work activities. Parent-Johnson (2012) noted these two models share the common elements of (a) customer choice, (b) the belief that individuals should be viewed from an abilities versus disabilities perspective, (c) workplace integration, (d) jobs/careers of choice, (e) competitive/prevailing wages, and (f) consumer-directed services with individualized workplace supports.

A final model used is **self-employment**, often combined with resource ownership. Self-employment focuses on setting a person with intellectual disability up as a small business owner (for example, owning a series of vending machines, operating a lawn care service), while resource ownership involves "purchasing of equipment, machinery, or other items that an individual owns and brings to the workplace as part of their employment, offering an additional advantage to the employer" (Parent-Johnson, 2012, p. 332). The role of the teacher is, typically, to work with vocational rehabilitation and job placement experts in the implementation of these models and to ensure that students are prepared for the twenty-first-century workforce, as emphasized by Hanley-Maxwell and Izzo (2012).

CONCLUSION

As we have noted throughout this chapter, there is far more to cover pertaining to the transition from school to adulthood for students with intellectual disability. In many ways, transition-related skills have been a focus of the education of students with intellectual disability since the earliest years of special education. And yet, the adult outcomes experienced by youth with intellectual disability remain poor. There are, however, research- and evidence-based practices that can improve postsecondary outcomes. In many cases, it is a matter of prioritizing such instruction and having high expectations for students.

Chapter Summary

- The transition to adulthood and the process of individuation are important life phases for all students, including students with intellectual disability.

- There are multiple transition phases during a child's education, from early childhood to elementary school, from elementary school to middle school, and then from middle school to high school.

- Multiple factors, including the level of support from and involvement by school personnel and parents and families and the quality of early childhood experiences, impact the successful transition from early childhood special education to elementary education.

- Peer acceptance, gender issues, friendships, and the quality and structure of schools predict more positive outcomes for the transition from elementary school to middle school.

- There is limited research on the transition to high school from middle school, and what little research exists emphasizes the role of problem behavior and supports for success as critical factors.

- Federal mandates for transition include the requirements for transition services planning and student involvement in transition planning.

- Transition assessment involves multiple methods, from direct observations to interviews to standardized assessments, but emphasizes data pertaining to current and future functioning, preferences, and interests.

- Transition planning should be person centered and student directed and incorporate information to create a support plan to identify needed supports for success across transition domains.

- Despite three decades of a focus on transition, the transition-related outcomes of youth with intellectual disability remain less positive than desired.

- There are evidence-based practices that can reverse the negative outcomes for youth with intellectual disability pertaining to promoting self-determination,

career and employment strategies, and postsecondary education.

- Promoting self-determination has shown to have a causal impact on more positive school and employment outcomes for youth with intellectual disability.

- There are emerging programs supporting youth with intellectual disability in postsecondary education settings.

- Career and employment strategies focus on generic skills needed to be successful in the workforce as well as innovative employment support models, including supported and customized employment and self-employment.

Review Questions

1. Discuss the transition services mandates in IDEA and how these impact students with intellectual disability.

2. What are current transition outcomes for youth with disabilities, and why might they not be as positive as desired?

3. Identify research- and evidence-based practices that can promote more positive transition outcomes, and discuss how they might be infused into the educational programs of students with intellectual disability.

Key Terms

individuation (page 363)
transition (page 364)
transition services (page 369)
student involvement (page 370)
self-determination (page 375)
person-centered planning
    (page 376)
Self-Directed IEP (page 386)

Whose Future Is It Anyway?
    (page 387)
Self-Determined Learning Model
    of Instruction (page 387)
supported employment (page 394)
customized employment (page 394)
self-employment (page 394)

Organizations Concerned With Transition

**National Gateway to
Self-Determination**

http://ngsd.org

**National Technical Assistance
Center on Transition**

http://transitionta.org

Think College

www.thinkcollege.net

Transition Coalition

http://transitioncoalition.org

**U.S. Department of Education—
Transition of Students With
Disabilities to Postsecondary
Education: A Guide for High
School Educators**

www2.ed.gov/about/offices/list/ocr/
transitionguide.html

Appendix

COUNCIL FOR EXCEPTIONAL CHILDREN

PROFESSIONAL STANDARDS

Initial Special Education Developmental Disabilities Specialty Set

Standard 1. Learner Development and Individual Learning Differences

KNOWLEDGE STANDARD		CHAPTER												
		1	2	3	4	5	6	7	8	9	10	11	12	13
ISCI 1 K1	Typical and atypical human growth and development	•	•											
ISCI 1 K2	Similarities and differences among individuals with exceptionalities		•											
ISCI 1 K3	Educational implications of characteristics of various exceptionalities		•											
ISCI 1 K4	Family systems and the role of families in supporting development													
ISCI 1 K5	Cultural perspectives influencing the relationships among families, schools, and communities as related to instruction													
ISCI 1 K6	Variations in beliefs, traditions, and values across and within cultures and their effects on relationships among individuals with exceptionalities, family, and schooling													
ISCI 1 K7	Characteristics and effects of the cultural and environmental milieu of the individual with exceptionalities and the family													
ISCI 1 K8	Similarities and differences of individuals with and without exceptionalities		•											

KNOWLEDGE STANDARD		CHAPTER												
		1	2	3	4	5	6	7	8	9	10	11	12	13
ISCI 1 K9	Effects of various medications on individuals with exceptionalities													
ISCI 1 K10	Effects an exceptional condition(s) can have on an individual's life	•												
ISCI 1 K11	Impact of learners' academic and social abilities, attitudes, interests, and values on instruction and career development		•	•	•	•	•	•	•	•	•	•		•
ISCI 1 K12	Differing ways of learning of individuals with exceptionalities, including those from culturally diverse backgrounds and strategies for addressing these differences		•	•	•	•	•	•	•	•		•		•
ISCI 1 K13	Effects of cultural and linguistic differences on growth and development													
ISCI 1 K14	Characteristics of one's own culture and use of language and the ways in which these can differ from other cultures and uses of languages													
ISCI 1 K15	Ways of behaving and communicating among cultures that can lead to misinterpretation and misunderstanding													
DDA1 K1	Medical aspects and implications for learning for individuals with developmental disabilities/autism spectrum disorders		•											
DDA1 K2	Core and associated characteristics of individuals with developmental disabilities/autism spectrum disorders		•											
DDA1 K3	Coexisting conditions and ranges that exist at a higher rate than in the general population	•	•											
DDA1 K4	Sensory challenges of individuals with developmental disabilities/autism spectrum disorders													

(Continued)

KNOWLEDGE STANDARD		CHAPTER												
		1	2	3	4	5	6	7	8	9	10	11	12	13
DDA1 K5	Speech, language, and communication of individuals with developmental disabilities/autism spectrum disorders													
DDA1 K6	Adaptive behavior needs of individuals with developmental disabilities/autism spectrum disorders					•								
DDA1 K7	Impact of theory of mind, central coherence, and executive function on learning and behavior													
DDA1 K8	Impact of neurological differences on learning and behavior													
DDA1 K9	Impact of self-regulation on learning and behavior											•		•

Standard 2. Learning Environments

KNOWLEDGE STANDARD		CHAPTER												
		1	2	3	4	5	6	7	8	9	10	11	12	13
ISCI 2 K1	Demands of learning environments				•	•	•	•	•	•	•	•	•	•
ISCI 2 K2	Basic classroom management theories and strategies for individuals with exceptionalities					•								
ISCI 2 K3	Effective management of teaching and learning	•		•	•	•	•	•	•	•	•	•		
ISCI 2 K4	Teacher attitudes and behaviors that influence behavior of individuals with exceptionalities													
ISCI 2 K5	Social skills needed for educational and other environments						•		•		•		•	
ISCI 2 K6	Strategies for crisis prevention and intervention					•								

KNOWLEDGE STANDARD		1	2	3	4	5	6	7	8	9	10	11	12	13
ISCI 2 K7	Strategies for preparing individuals to live harmoniously and productively in a culturally diverse world													
ISCI 2 K8	Ways to create learning environments that allow individuals to retain and appreciate their own and each other's respective language and cultural heritage													
ISCI 2 K9	Ways cultures are negatively stereotyped													
ISCI 2 K10	Strategies used by diverse populations to cope with a legacy of former and continuing racism													

SKILL STANDARD		1	2	3	4	5	6	7	8	9	10	11	12	13
ISCI 2 S1	Create a safe, equitable, positive, and supportive learning environment in which diversities are valued													
ISCI 2 S2	Identify realistic expectations for personal and social behavior in various settings						•		•		•		•	
ISCI 2 S3	Identify supports needed for integration into various program placements			•										
ISCI 2 S4	Design learning environments that encourage active participation in individual and group activities						•	•	•	•	•	•	•	
ISCI 2 S5	Modify the learning environment to manage behaviors					•								
ISCI 2 S6	Use performance data and information from all stakeholders to make or suggest modifications in learning environments				•									

(Continued)

(Continued)

SKILL STANDARD		CHAPTER												
		1	2	3	4	5	6	7	8	9	10	11	12	13
ISCI 2 S7	Establish and maintain rapport with individuals with and without exceptionalities													
ISCI 2 S8	Teach self-advocacy													•
ISCI 2 S9	Create an environment that encourages self-advocacy and increased independence												•	•
ISCI 2 S10	Use effective and varied behavior management strategies					•								
ISCI 2 S11	Use the least intensive behavior management strategy consistent with the needs of the individual with exceptionalities					•								
ISCI 2 S12	Design and manage daily routines							•	•	•	•	•		•
ISCI 2 S13	Organize, develop, and sustain learning environments that support positive intracultural and intercultural experiences													
ISCI 2 S14	Mediate controversial intercultural issues among individuals with exceptionalities within the learning environment in ways that enhance any culture, group, or person													
ISCI 2 S15	Structure, direct, and support the activities of paraeducators, volunteers, and tutors													
ISCI 2 S16	Use universal precautions													
DDA2 S1	Plan instruction for independent functional life skills and adaptive behavior								•		•		•	

Standard 3. Curricular Content Knowledge

SKILL STANDARD		CHAPTER												
		1	2	3	4	5	6	7	8	9	10	11	12	13
ISCI 3 S1	Identify and prioritize areas of the general curriculum and accommodations for individuals with exceptionalities													
ISCI 3 S2	Integrate affective, social, and life skills with academic curricula							•	•	•	•		•	•
DDA3S1	Provide pragmatic language instruction that facilitates social skills													
DDA3S2	Provide individuals with developmental disabilities/ autism spectrum disorders strategies to avoid and repair miscommunications													
DDA3S3	Plan instruction for independent functional life skills and adaptive behavior								•		•		•	
DDA3S4	Plan and implement instruction and related services for individuals with developmental disabilities/ autism spectrum disorders that are both age appropriate and ability appropriate						•	•	•	•	•		•	•
DDA3S5	Use specialized instruction to enhance social participation across environments					•			•		•		•	
DDA3S6	Plan systematic instruction based on learner characteristics, interests, and ongoing assessment				•	•		•	•	•	•		•	•

Standard 4. Assessment

KNOWLEDGE STANDARD		CHAPTER												
		1	2	3	4	5	6	7	8	9	10	11	12	13
ISCI 4 K1	Basic terminology used in assessment				•									
ISCI 4 K2	Legal provisions and ethical principles regarding assessment of individuals			•	•									

KNOWLEDGE STANDARD		CHAPTER												
		1	2	3	4	5	6	7	8	9	10	11	12	13
ISCI 4 K3	Screening, prereferral, referral, and classification procedures			•	•									
ISCI 4 K4	Use and limitations of assessment instruments				•									
ISCI 4 K5	National, state or provincial, and local accommodations and modifications			•	•						•			

SKILL STANDARD		CHAPTER												
		1	2	3	4	5	6	7	8	9	10	11	12	13
ISCI 4 S1	Gather relevant background information				•									
ISCI 4 S2	Administer nonbiased formal and informal assessments				•									
ISCI 4 S3	Use technology to conduct assessments				•									
ISCI 4 S4	Develop or modify individualized assessment strategies				•									
ISCI 4 S5	Interpret information from formal and informal assessments				•									
ISCI 4 S6	Use assessment information in making eligibility, program, and placement decisions for individuals with exceptionalities, including those from culturally and/or linguistically diverse backgrounds			•	•									
ISCI 4 S7	Report assessment results to all stakeholders using effective communication skills			•	•									
ISCI 4 S8	Evaluate instruction and monitor progress of individuals with exceptionalities				•			•	•	•		•	•	
ISCI 4 S9	Create and maintain records					•								

Standard 5. Instructional Planning and Strategies

KNOWLEDGE STANDARD		CHAPTER												
		1	2	3	4	5	6	7	8	9	10	11	12	13
ISCI 5 K1	Roles and responsibilities of the paraeducator related to instruction, intervention, and direct service													
ISCI 5 K2	Evidence-based practices validated for specific characteristics of learners and settings	•						•	•	•	•	•	•	•
ISCI 5 K3	Augmentative and assistive communication strategies						•							

SKILL STANDARD		CHAPTER												
		1	2	3	4	5	6	7	8	9	10	11	12	13
ISCI 5 S1	Develop and implement comprehensive, longitudinal, individualized programs in collaboration with team members			•										•
ISCI 5 S2	Involve the individual and family in setting instructional goals and monitoring progress	•	•				•	•	•	•	•	•	•	•
ISCI 5 S3	Use functional assessments to develop intervention plans				•	•								
ISCI 5 S4	Use task analysis				•	•				•	•	•	•	
ISCI 5 S5	Sequence, implement, and evaluate individualized learning objectives							•	•	•	•	•		•
ISCI 5 S6	Develop and select instructional content, resources, and strategies that respond to cultural, linguistic, and gender differences							•	•	•	•	•	•	
ISCI 5 S7	Incorporate and implement instructional and assistive technology into the educational program						•	•	•	•	•	•		•
ISCI 5 S8	Prepare lesson plans													
ISCI 5 S9	Prepare and organize materials to implement daily lesson plans													

SKILL STANDARD		CHAPTER												
		1	2	3	4	5	6	7	8	9	10	11	12	13
ISCI 5 S10	Use instructional time effectively													
ISCI 5 S11	Make responsive adjustments to instruction based on continual observations													
ISCI 5 S12	Prepare individuals to exhibit self-enhancing behavior in response to societal attitudes and actions												•	
ISCI 5 S13	Use strategies to facilitate integration into various settings													
ISCI 5 S14	Teach individuals to use self-assessment, problem-solving, and other cognitive strategies to meet their needs													
ISCI 5 S15	Select, adapt, and use instructional strategies and materials according to characteristics of the individual with exceptionalities							•	•	•	•	•	•	
ISCI 5 S16	Use strategies to facilitate maintenance and generalization of skills across learning environments					•		•	•	•	•	•	•	
ISCI 5 S17	Use procedures to increase the individual's self-awareness, self-management, self-control, self-reliance, and self-esteem					•								
ISCI 5 S18	Use strategies that promote successful transitions for individuals with exceptionalities												•	
ISCI 5 S19	Use strategies to support and enhance communication skills of individuals with exceptionalities													

(Continued)

(Continued)

SKILL STANDARD		CHAPTER												
		1	2	3	4	5	6	7	8	9	10	11	12	13
ISCI 5 S20	Use communication strategies and resources to facilitate understanding of subject matter for individuals with exceptionalities whose primary language is not the dominant language													
ISCI 5 S21	Modify instructional practices in response to ongoing assessment data				•			•	•	•	•		•	

Standard 6. Professional Learning and Ethical Practice

KNOWLEDGE STANDARD		CHAPTER												
		1	2	3	4	5	6	7	8	9	10	11	12	13
ISCI 6 K1	Models, theories, philosophies, and research methods that form the basis for special education practice			•		•		•	•	•	•		•	•
ISCI 6 K2	Laws, policies, and ethical principles regarding behavior management planning and implementation					•								
ISCI 6 K3	Relationship of special education to the organization and function of educational agencies			•									•	
ISCI 6 K4	Rights and responsibilities of individuals with exceptionalities; parents, teachers, and other professionals; and schools related to exceptionalities			•										
ISCI 6 K5	Issues in definition and identification of individuals with exceptionalities, including those from culturally and linguistically diverse backgrounds	•		•										

KNOWLEDGE STANDARD		CHAPTER												
		1	2	3	4	5	6	7	8	9	10	11	12	13
ISCI 6 K6	Issues, assurances, and due process rights related to assessment, eligibility, and placement within a continuum of services			•	•									
ISCI 6 K7	Family systems and the role of families in the educational process													
ISCI 6 K8	Historical points of view and contribution of culturally diverse groups													
ISCI 6 K9	Impact of the dominant culture on shaping schools and the individuals who study and work in them													
ISCI 6 K10	Potential impact of differences in values, languages, and customs that can exist between the home and school													
ISCI 6 K11	Personal cultural biases and differences that affect one's teaching													
ISCI 6 K12	Importance of the teacher serving as a model for individuals with exceptionalities													
ISCI 6 K13	Continuum of lifelong professional development													
ISCI 6 K14	Methods to remain current regarding research-validated practice													

SKILL STANDARD		CHAPTER												
		1	2	3	4	5	6	7	8	9	10	11	12	13
ISCI 6 S1	Practice within the CEC Code of Ethics and other standards of the profession													
ISCI 6 S2	Uphold high standards of competence and integrity and exercise sound judgment in the practice of the professional													

SKILL STANDARD		CHAPTER												
		1	2	3	4	5	6	7	8	9	10	11	12	13
ISCI 6 S3	Act ethically in advocating for appropriate services													
ISCI 6 S4	Conduct professional activities in compliance with applicable laws and policies													
ISCI 6 S5	Demonstrate commitment to developing the highest education and quality-of-life potential of individuals with exceptionalities													
ISCI 6 S6	Demonstrate sensitivity for the culture, language, religion, gender, disability, socioeconomic status, and sexual orientation of individuals													
ISCI 6 S7	Practice within one's skill limits and obtain assistance as needed													
ISCI 6 S8	Use verbal, nonverbal, and written language effectively													
ISCI 6 S9	Conduct self-evaluation of instruction													
ISCI 6 S10	Access information on exceptionalities													
ISCI 6 S11	Reflect on one's practice to improve instruction and guide professional growth													
ISCI 6 S12	Engage in professional activities that benefit individuals with exceptionalities, their families, and one's colleagues													
ISCI 6 S13	Demonstrate commitment to engage in evidence-based practices			•			•	•	•	•	•	•		•
ISCI 6 S14	Articulate personal philosophy of special education													

Standard 7. Collaboration

SKILL STANDARD		CHAPTER												
		1	2	3	4	5	6	7	8	9	10	11	12	13
ISCI 7 K1	Models and strategies of consultation and collaboration													
ISCI 7 K2	Roles of individuals with exceptionalities, families, and school and community personnel in planning of an individualized program			•										
ISCI 7 K3	Concerns of families of individuals with exceptionalities and strategies to help address these concerns			•										•
ISCI 7 K4	Culturally responsive factors that promote effective communication and collaboration with individuals with exceptionalities, families, school personnel, and community members													

SKILL STANDARD		CHAPTER												
		1	2	3	4	5	6	7	8	9	10	11	12	13
ISCI 7 S1	Maintain confidential communication about individuals with exceptionalities													
ISCI 7 S2	Collaborate with families and others in assessment of individuals with exceptionalities				•									
ISCI 7 S3	Foster respectful and beneficial relationships between families and professionals													
ISCI 7 S4	Assist individuals with exceptionalities and their families in becoming active participants in the educational team			•										•

(Continued)

(Continued)

SKILL STANDARD		CHAPTER												
		1	2	3	4	5	6	7	8	9	10	11	12	13
ISCI 7 S5	Plan and conduct collaborative conferences with individuals with exceptionalities and their families													
ISCI 7 S6	Collaborate with school personnel and community members in integrating individuals with exceptionalities into various settings													•
ISCI 7 S7	Use group problem-solving skills to develop, implement, and evaluate collaborative activities													
ISCI 7 S8	Model techniques and coach others in the use of instructional methods and accommodations													
ISCI 7 S9	Communicate with school personnel about the characteristics and needs of individuals with exceptionalities													
ISCI 7 S10	Communicate effectively with families of individuals with exceptionalities from diverse backgrounds													
ISCI 7 S11	Observe, evaluate, and provide feedback to paraeducators													

NOTE: K = Knowledge standard, S = Skill standard. The number designates the sequential placement of the standard.

ISCI = Initial specialty common item standard.

SOURCE: Adapted from https://www.cec.sped.org/Standards/Special-Educator-Professional-Preparation-Standards/CEC-Initial-and-Advanced-Specialty-Sets

References

CHAPTER 1

American Association on Intellectual and Developmental Disabilities. (2015). *Diagnostic Adaptive Behavior Scale*. Retrieved January 4, 2015, from www.aaidd.org/intellectual-disability/diagnostic-adaptive-behavior-scale#.V17L6CvF-So

Beirne-Smith, M., Patton, J., & Kim, S. (2006). *Mental retardation* (7th ed.). Upper Saddle River, NJ: Pearson Education.

Blatt, B., & Kaplan, F. (1966). *Christmas in purgatory*. Boston, MA: Allyn and Bacon.

Drew, C., & Hardman, M. (2007). *Intellectual disabilities across the lifespan* (9th ed.). Upper Saddle River, NJ: Pearson Education.

Dugdale, R. (1877). *"The Jukes": A study in crime, pauperism, disease and heredity*. New York, NY: Putnam.

Gargiulo, R. (1985). *Working with parents of exceptional children*. Boston, MA: Houghton Mifflin.

Gargiulo, R. (2012). *Special education in contemporary society* (4th ed.). Thousand Oaks, CA: Sage.

Goddard, H. (1912). *The Kallikak family: A study in the heredity of feeblemindedness*. New York, NY: Macmillan.

Grossman, H. (1973). *Manual on terminology and classification in mental retardation*. Washington, DC: American Association on Mental Deficiency.

Grossman, H. (1983). *Classification in mental retardation*. Washington, DC: American Association on Mental Deficiency.

Hardman, M., Drew, C., & Egan, M. (2014). *Human exceptionality* (11th ed.). Belmont, CA: Wadsworth/Cengage Learning.

Heber, R. (1961). A manual on terminology and classification in mental retardation (Rev. ed.). *Monograph Supplement to the American Journal of Mental Deficiency, 64.*

Hickson, L., Blackman, L., & Reis, E. (1995). *Mental retardation: Foundations of educational programming*. Boston, MA: Allyn and Bacon.

Kaufman, A., & Kaufman, N. (2004). *Kaufman Assessment Battery for Children* (2nd ed.). Circle Pines, MN: American Guidance Service.

Lindman, F., & McIntyre, K. (1961). *The mentally disabled and the law*. Chicago, IL: University of Chicago Press.

Luckasson, R., Borthwick-Duffy, S., Buntinx, W., Coulter, D., Craig, E., Reeve, A., . . . Tassé, M. (2002). *Mental retardation: Definition, support, and systems of supports* (10th ed.). Washington, DC: American Association on Mental Retardation.

Luckasson, R., Coulter, D., Polloway, E., Reiss, S., Schalock, R., Snell, M., . . . Stark, J. (1992). *Mental retardation: Definition, classification, and systems of supports* (9th ed.). Washington, DC: American Association on Mental Retardation.

Morrison, G., & Polloway, E. (1995). Mental retardation. In E. Meyen & T. Skirtic (Eds.), *Special education and student disability* (4th ed., pp. 213–269). Denver, CO: Love.

Nirje, B. (1969). The normalization principle and its human management implications. In R. Kugel & W. Wolfensberger (Eds.), *Changing patterns in residential services for the mentally retarded* (pp. 179–195). Washington, DC: President's Committee on Mental Retardation.

Richards, S., Brady, M., & Taylor, R. (2015). *Cognitive and intellectual disabilities* (2nd ed.). New York, NY: Routledge.

Roid, G. (2003). *Stanford-Binet Intelligence Scales* (5th ed.). Itasca, IL: Riverside.

Schalock, R. (2015). *Bob Schalock interview.* Retrieved January 2, 2015, from http://www.aaidd .org/intellectual-disability/videos/bob-schalock#.VJQRPI4AKA

Schalock, R., Borthwick-Duffy, S., Bradley, V., Buntinx, W., Coulter, D., Craig, E., . . . Yeager, M. (2010). *Intellectual disability: Definition, classification, and systems of supports* (11th ed.). Washington, DC: American Association on Intellectual and Developmental Disabilities.

Scheerenberger, R. (1983). *A history of mental retardation.* Baltimore, MD: Paul H. Brookes.

Scheerenberger, R. (1987). *A history of mental retardation: A quarter century of concern.* Baltimore, MD: Paul H. Brookes.

Smith, T., Polloway, E., Patton, J., & Dowdy, C. (2008). *Teaching students with special needs in inclusive settings* (5th ed.). Needham Heights, MA: Allyn and Bacon.

U.S. Department of Education. (2015). *Thirty-seventh annual report to Congress on the implementation of the Individuals with Disabilities Education Act, 2015.* Washington, DC: U.S. Government Printing Office.

Wechsler, D. (2014). *Wechsler Intelligence Scale for Children* (5th ed.). San Antonio, TX: Psychological Corp.

Wehmeyer, M. (2003). Defining mental retardation and ensuring access to the general curriculum. *Education and Training in Developmental Disabilities, 38*(3), 271–282.

Winzer, M. (1993). *The history of special education.* Washington, DC: Gallaudet University Press.

Wolfensberger, W. (1972). *Normalization: The principle of normalization in human services.* Toronto, ON: National Institute on Mental Retardation.

CHAPTER 2

Alevriadou, A., & Grouios, G. (2007). Distractor interference effects and identification of safe and dangerous road-crossing sites by children with and without mental retardation. In E.

Heinz (Ed.), *Mental retardation research advances* (pp. 75–87). New York, NY: Nova Science Publishers.

Batshaw, M., Gropman, A., & Lanpher, B. (2013). Genetics and developmental disabilities. In M. Batshaw, N. Roizen, & G. Lotrecchiano (Eds.), *Children with disabilities* (7th ed., pp. 3–24). Baltimore, MD: Paul H. Brookes.

Batshaw, M., & Lanpher, B. (2013). Inborn errors of metabolism. In M. Batshaw, N. Roizen, & G. Lotrecchiano (Eds.), *Children with disabilities* (7th ed., pp. 319–332). Baltimore, MD: Paul H. Brookes.

Bybee, J., & Zigler, E. (1998). Outer-directedness in individuals with and without mental retardation: A review. In J. Burack, R. Hodapp, & E. Zigler (Eds.), *Handbook of mental retardation and development* (pp. 434–460). Cambridge, England: Cambridge University Press.

Drew, C., & Hardman, M. (2007). *Intellectual disabilities across the lifespan* (9th ed.). Upper Saddle River, NJ: Pearson Education.

Fergus, K. (2016, June 30). *Maternal age-related risks for Down syndrome and other trisomies*. Retrieved August 28, 2016, from www.downsyndrome.about.com/od/diagnosingdownsyndrome/a/Matagechart.htm

Friend, M., & Bursuck, W. (2015). *Including students with special needs* (7th ed.). Upper Saddle River, NJ: Pearson Education.

Gargiulo, R. (2015). *Special education in contemporary society* (5th ed.). Thousand Oaks, CA: Sage.

Gleason, J., & Ratner, N. (2013). *The development of language* (8th ed.). Boston, MA: Allyn & Bacon.

Hardman, M., Drew, C., & Egan, M. (2014). *Human exceptionality* (11th ed.). Belmont, CA: Wadsworth/Cengage Learning.

Hendricks, D., & Wehman, P. (2009). Transition from school to adulthood for youth with autism spectrum disorders. *Focus on Autism and Other Developmental Disabilities, 24*(2), 77–88.

Jarrold, C., & Brock, J. (2012). Short-term and working memory in mental retardation. In J. Burack, R. Hodapp, G. Iarocci, & E. Zigler (Eds.), *The Oxford handbook of intellectual disability and development* (pp. 109–124). New York, NY: Oxford University Press.

Jones, K., Smith, D., Ulleland, C., & Streissguth, A. (1973). Pattern of malformation in offspring of chronic alcoholic mothers. *Lancet, 1*(7815), 1267–1271.

Kids Health. (2015). *Fetal alcohol syndrome*. Retrieved March 10, 2015, from http://www.kidshealth.org/parent/medical/brain/fas.html

Lejune, J., Gautier, M., & Turpin, R. (1959). Études des chromosomes somatiques de neuf enfants mongoliers. *Academie de Science, 248*, 1721–1722.

Luckasson, R., Borthwick-Duffy, S., Buntinx, W., Coulter, D., Craig, E., Reeve, A., . . . Tassé, M. (2002). *Mental retardation: Definition, support, and systems of supports* (10th ed.). Washington, DC: American Association on Mental Retardation.

March of Dimes. (2015a). *Down syndrome*. Retrieved March 2, 2015, from http://www.marchofdimes.org/baby/down-syndrome.aspx

March of Dimes. (2015b). *Fragile X*. Retrieved March 2, 2015, from http://www.marchofdimes.org/baby/fragile-x-syndrome.aspx

March of Dimes. (2015c). *Maternal PKU*. Retrieved March 9, 2015, from http://www.marchofdimes.org/pregnancy/maternal-pku.aspx

National Down Syndrome Society. (2015a). *An introduction to Alzheimer's disease*. Retrieved March 2, 2015, from http://www.ndss.org/Resources/Aging-Matters/Alzheimers-Disease/An-Introduction-to-Alzheimers-Disease/

National Down Syndrome Society. (2015b). *Down syndrome facts*. Retrieved March 2, 2015, from http://www.ndss.org/Down-Syndrome/Down-Syndrome-Facts/

National Fragile X Foundation. (2015). *Fragile X syndrome*. Retrieved March 8, 2015, from https://fragilex.org/fragile-x-associated-disorders/fragile-x-syndrome/

National Heart, Lung, and Blood Institute. (2015). *What is Rh incompatibility?* Retrieved March 9, 2015, from www.nhlbi.nih.gov/health/health-topics/topics/rh

National Institutes of Health. (2015). *Phenylketonuria*. Retrieved March 9, 2015, from http://www.nlm.nih.gov/medlineplus/phenylketonuria.html

National Organization on Fetal Alcohol Syndrome. (2015). *FASD: What everyone should know*. Retrieved March 10, 2015, from http://www.nofas.org/wp-content/uploads/2014/08/Factsheet-what-everyone-should-know_old_chart-new-chart1.pdf

Owens, R. (2009). Mental retardation/intellectual disabilities In D. Bernstein & E. Tiegerman-Farber (Eds.), *Language and communication disorders in children* (6th ed., pp. 246–313). Boston, MA: Pearson Education.

Owens, R. (2014). *Language disorders* (6th ed.). Boston, MA: Pearson Education.

Paulson, J. (2013). Environmental toxicants and neurocognitive development. In M. Batshaw, N. Roizen, & G. Lotrecchiano (Eds.), *Children with disabilities* (7th ed., pp. 37–46). Baltimore, MD: Paul H. Brookes.

Pellegrino, J. (2013). Newborn screening: Opportunities for prevention of developmental disabilities. In M. Batshaw, N. Roizen, & G. Lotrecchiano, (Eds.), *Children with disabilities* (7th ed., pp. 61–72). Baltimore, MD: Paul H. Brookes.

Prader-Willi Syndrome Association. (2016a). *About Prader-Willi syndrome*. Retrieved September 1, 2016, from http://www.pwsausa.org/about-pws/#1443576754481-86156423-bded

Prader-Willi Syndrome Association. (2016b). *PWS basic facts*. Retrieved September 1, 2016, from http://www.pwsausa.org/about-facts/

Richards, S., Brady, M., & Taylor, R. (2015). *Cognitive and intellectual disabilities* (2nd ed.). New York, NY: Routledge.

Roizen, N. (2013). Down syndrome. In M. Batshaw, N. Roizen, & G. Lotrecchiano (Eds.), *Children with disabilities* (7th ed., pp. 307–318). Baltimore, MD: Paul H. Brookes.

Schonberg, R. (2013). Birth defects and prenatal diagnosis. In M. Batshaw, N. Roizen, & G. Lotrecchiano (Eds.), *Children with disabilities* (7th ed., pp. 47–60). Baltimore, MD: Paul H. Brookes.

Shapiro, B., & Batshaw, M. (2013). Developmental delay and intellectual disability. In M. Batshaw, N. Roizen, & G. Lotrecchiano (Eds.), *Children with disabilities* (7th ed., pp. 291–306). Baltimore, MD: Paul H. Brookes.

Shogren, K., Bovaird, J., Palmer, S., & Wehmeyer, M. (2010). Examining the development of locus of control orientation in students with intellectual disability, learning disabilities, and no disabilities: A latent growth curve analysis. *Research and Practice for Persons With SevereDisabilities, 35*(3–4), 80–92.

Simpson, K. (2013). Syndromes and inborn errors of metabolism. In M. Batshaw, N. Roizen, & G. Lotrecchiano (Eds.), *Children with disabilities* (7th ed., pp. 757–801). Baltimore, MD: Paul H. Brookes.

Smith, T., Polloway, E., Taber-Doughty, T., Patton, J., & Dowdy, C. (2016). *Teaching students with special needs in inclusive settings* (7th ed.). Upper Saddle River, NJ: Pearson Education.

Taylor, R., Smiley, L., & Richards, S. (2015). *Exceptional students* (2nd ed.). New York, NY: McGraw-Hill Education.

Turnbull, A., Turnbull, R., Wehmeyer, M., & Shogren, K. (2016). *Exceptional lives* (8th ed.). Upper Saddle River, NJ: Pearson Education.

Vaughn, S., Bos, C., & Schumm, J. (2014). *Teaching students who are exceptional, diverse, and at risk* (6th ed.). Upper Saddle River, NJ: Pearson Education.

CHAPTER 3

Armstrong v. Kline, 476 F. Supp. 583 (E.D. Pa. 1979), aff'd in part and remanded *sub nom*.

Aron, L., & Loprest, P. (2012). Disability and the education system. *The Future of Children, 22*(1), 97–122.

Ayres, K., Lowrey, K., Douglas, K., & Sievers, C. (2011). I can identify Saturn but I can't brush my teeth: What happens when the curricular focus for students with severe disabilities shifts. *Education and Training in Autism and Developmental Disabilities, 46(4)*, 11–21.

Billingsley, F., & Albertson, L. (1999). Finding a future for functional skills. *The Journal of the Association for Persons With Severe Handicaps, 24*, 298–302.

Bouck, E. (2009). *No Child Left Behind*, the *Individuals with Disabilities Education Act* and functional curricula: A conflict of interest? *Education and Training in Developmental Disabilities, 44(1)*, 3–13.

Bouck, E. (2012). Secondary curriculum and transition. In P. Wehman (Ed.), *Life beyond the classroom: Transition strategies for young people with disabilities* (5th ed., pp. 215–233). Baltimore, MD: Paul H. Brookes.

Bouck, E., Taber-Doughty, T., & Savage, M. (2015). *Footsteps towards the future: Implementing a real-world curriculum for students with disabilities*. Arlington, VA: Council for Exceptional Children.

Bradshaw, C., Koth, C., Bevans, K., Ialongo, N., & Leaf, P. (2008). The impact of school-wide positive behavioral interventions and supports (BPIS) on the organizational health of elementary schools. *School Psychology Quarterly, 23(4)*, 463–473.

Branstad, T., Acosta, A., Bartlett, S., Berdine, W., Butterfield, P., Chambers, J., . . . Wright, K. (2002). *A new era: Revitalizing special education for children and their families*. Washington, DC: U.S. Department of Education.

Browder, D., Ahlgrim-Delzwell, L., Spooner, F., Mims, P., & Baker, J. (2009). Using time delay to teach literacy to students with severe developmental disabilities. *Exceptional Children, 75*(3), 343–364.

Browder, D., & Cooper-Duffy, K. (2003). Evidence-based practices for students with severe disabilities and the requirement for accountability in "No Child Left Behind." *Journal of Special Education, 37(3)*, 157–163.

Browder, D., Flowers, C., Ahlgrim-Delzell, L., Karvonen, M., Spooner, F., & Algozzine, R. (2004). The alignment of alternate assessment content with academic and functional curricula. *The Journal of Special Education, 37(4)*, 211–223.

Brown, L., Bronston, M., Hamre-Nietupski, S., Pumpiam, I., Certo, N., & Gruenewald, L. (1979). A strategy for developing chronological-age-appropriate and functional curricular content for severely handicapped adolescents and young children. *The Journal of Special Education, 13(1)*, 81–90.

Burling, K. (2007). *Pearson Educational Measurement Bulletin, 4*. Retrieved September 18, 2008, from http://www.pearsonedmeasurement.com/bulletin/Bulletin_4_FINAL.pdf

Burns, M., & Gibbons, K. (2012). *Implementing response-to-intervention in elementary and secondary schools: Procedures to assure scientific-based practices* (2nd ed.). New York, NY: Routledge.

Center on Standards and Assessment Implementation & National Center on Educational Outcomes. (2014). *Successfully transitioning away from the 2% assessment: Frequently asked questions*. Retrieved April 25, 2015, from http://csai-online.org/sites/default/files/resource/151/AA_MAS_FAQ_2014_0.pdf

Collins, B. (2013). What happened to functional curriculum? In W. Heward (Ed.), *Exceptional children: An introduction to special education* (10th ed., pp. 436–437). Upper Saddle River, NJ: Pearson Education.

Common Core State Standards Initiative. (2015). *Application to students with disabilities*. Retrieved April 3, 2015, from http://www.corestandards.org/wp-content/uploads/Application-to-Students-with-Disabilities-again-for-merge1.pdf

Council for Exceptional Children. (2008). *New flexibility in testing students with disabilities a positive step*. Retrieved September 18, 2008, from http://www.cec.sped.org/AM/Template.cfm?Section=Home&CONTENTID=6247&TEMPLATE=/CM/ContentDisplay.cfm

Council for Exceptional Children. (2005). *Universal Design for Learning: A guide for teachers and education professionals*. Boston, MA: Pearson Education.

Council of Chief State School Officers. (2010, June 2). *National Governors Association and state education chiefs launch common state academic standards*. Retrieved April 27, 2015, from http://

www.ccsso.org/News_and_Events/Press_Releases/national_governors_association_and_state_education_chiefs_launch_common_state_academic_standards_.html

Courtade, G., & Browder, D. (2011). *Aligning IEPs to the Common Core State Standards for students with moderate and severe disabilities.* Verona, WI: Attainment Co.

Courtade, G., Spooner, F., & Browder, D. (2007). Review of studies with students with significant cognitive disabilities which link to science standards. *Research & Practice for Persons With Severe Disabilities, 3(4)*, 43–49.

Courtade, G., Spooner, F., Browder, D., & Jimenez, B. (2012). Seven reasons to promote standards-based instruction for students with severe disabilities: A reply to Ayres, Lowrey, Douglas, & Sievers (2011). *Education and Training in Autism and Developmental Disabilities, 47*(1), 3–13.

Cronin, M., & Patton, J. (1993). *Life skills instruction for all students with special needs: A practical guide for integrating real-life content into the curriculum.* Austin, TX: Pro-Ed.

Cusumano, D., Algozzine, K., & Algozzine, B. (2014). Multi-tiered system of supports for effective inclusion in elementary schools. In J. McLeskey, N. Waldron, F. Spooner, & B. Algozzine (Eds.), *Handbook of effective inclusive schools: Research and practice* (pp. 197–209). New York, NY: Routledge.

Daniel R. R. v. State Board of Education, 874 F.2d 1036 (5th Cir. 1989).

Dynamic Learning Maps. (2016). *Essential elements.* Retrieved August 29, 2016, from http://dynamiclearningmaps.org/content/essential-elements

Gargiulo, R. (2015). *Special education in contemporary society: An introduction to exceptionality* (5th ed.). Thousand Oaks, CA: Sage.

Gargiulo, R., & Bouck, E. (2018). *Special education in contemporary society* (6th ed.). Thousand Oaks, CA: Sage.

Gargiulo, R., & Metcalf, D. (2017). *Teaching in today's inclusive classrooms* (3rd ed.). Boston, MA: Cengage Learning.

Gartin, B., & Murdick, N. (2005). IDEA 2004: The IEP. *Remedial and Special Education, 26*(6), 327–331.

Giangreco, M., Cloninger, C., & Iverson, V. (1998). *Choosing outcomes for accommodations for children: A guide to educational planning for students with disabilities.* Baltimore, MD: Paul H. Brookes.

Gibb, G., & Dyches, T. (2016). *IEPs: Writing quality individualized education programs.* Boston, MA: Pearson Education.

Harlacher, J., Sakelaris, T., & Kattelman, N. (2014). Multi-tiered systems of support. In *Practitioner's guide to curriculum-based evaluation in reading.* New York, NY: Springer.

Hitchcock, C., Meyer, A., Rose, D., & Jackson, R. (2002). Providing new access to the general curriculum: Universal Design for Learning. *Teaching Exceptional Children, 35*(2), 8–17.

Hudson, M., Browder, D., & Wood, L. (2012). Review of experimental research on academic learning by students with moderate and severe intellectual disability in general education. *Research & Practice for Persons With Severe Disabilities, 38*(1), 17–29.

Jimenez, B., Courtade, G., & Browder, D. (2013). *Six successful strategies for teaching Common Core State Standards to students with moderate to severe disabilities*. Verona, WI: Attainment Co.

Kolstoe, O. (1970). *Teaching educable mentally retarded children*. New York, NY: Holt, Rinehart, & Winston.

Larry P. v. Riles, 495 F. Supp. 926 (N.D. Cal. 1979), aff'd in part, rev'd in part, 793 F.2d 969 (9th Cir. 1986).

Lazarus, S., Thurlow, M., Christensen, L., & Cormier, D. (2007). *States' alternate assessments based on modified achievement standards (AA-MAS) in 2007* (Synthesis Report 67). Minneapolis: University of Minnesota, National Center on Educational Outcomes.

Lipkin, P., & Schertz, M. (2008). Early intervention and its efficacy. In P. Accardo (Ed.), *Capute & Accardo's neurodevelopmental disabilities in infancy and childhood* (3rd ed., Vol. 1, pp. 519–551). Baltimore, MD: Paul H. Brookes.

National Center on Educational Outcomes. (2014). Considerations for consortia as states transition away from the AA-MAS. *NCEO Brief, 7*. Retrieved April 15, 2015, from http://www.cehd.umn.edu/NCEO/onlinepubs/briefs/brief07/NCEOBrief7.pdf

National Education Association. (2015). *Are you a "highly qualified" paraprofessional?* Retrieved March 26, 2015, from http://www.nea.org/home/19145.htm

No Child Left Behind Act of 2001, Pub. L. No. 107–110, 115 Stat. 1425 (2002).

Patton, J., Cronin, M., & Jairrels, V. (1997). Curricular implications of transition: Life skills as an integral part of transition education. *Remedial and Special Education, 18(5)*, 294–306.

Pennsylvania Association for Retarded Children v. Commonwealth of Pennsylvania, 343 F. Supp. 279 (E.D. Pa. 1972).

Perner, D. (2007). No Child Left Behind: Issues of assessing students with the most significant cognitive disabilities. *Education and Training in Developmental Disabilities, 42(4)*, 243–251.

Public Schools of North Carolina. (2016). *Extended Common Core State Standards: English/language arts 6–8*. Retrieved August 29, 2016, from http://www.ncpublicschools.org/docs/acre/standards/extended/ela/6-8.pdf

Pugach, M., & Warger, C. (2001). Curriculum matters: Raising expectations for students with disabilities. *Remedial and Special Education, 22(4)*, 194–196.

Rehabilitation Act of 1973, Section 504 Regulations, 34 C.F.R. § 104.1 *et seq.*

Rose, D., Hasselbring, T., Stahl, S., & Zabala, J. (2005). Assistive technology and Universal Design for Learning: Two sides of the same coin. In D. Edyburn, K. Higgins, & R. Boone (Eds.), *Handbook of special education technology research and practice* (pp. 507–518). Whitefish Bay, WI: Knowledge by Design.

Rose, D., & Meyer, A. (2002). *Teaching every student in the Digital Age: Universal design for learning*. Alexandria, VA: Association for Supervision and Curriculum Development.

Rosenfeld, S. J. (1996). *Section 504 and IDEA: Basic similarities and differences*. Retrieved March 31, 2015, from http://eric.ed.gov/?id=ED427487

Sailor, W. (2015). Advances in schoolwide inclusive school reform. *Remedial and Special Education, 36(2)*, 94–99. DOI: 10.1177/0741932514555021

Sailor, W., Wolf, N., Choi, H., & Roger, B. (2009). Sustaining positive behavior support in a context of comprehensive school reform. In W. Sailor, G. Dunlap, G. Sugai, & R. Horner (Eds.), *Handbook of positive behavior support* (pp. 633–670). New York, NY: Springer.

Saunders, A., Spooner, F., Browder, D., Wakeman, S., & Lee, A. (2013). Teaching the Common Core in English language arts to students with severe disabilities. *Teaching Exceptional Children, 46*(2), 22–33.

Simpson, R., LaCava, P., & Graner, P. (2004). The No Child Left Behind Act: Challenges and implications for educators. *Intervention in School and Clinic, 40*(2), 67–75.

Smith, T. (2005). IDEA 2004: Another round in the reauthorization process. *Remedial and Special Education, 26*(6), 314–319.

Spooner, F., Knight, V., Browder, D., & Smith, B. (2012). Evidence-based practice for teaching academics to students with severe developmental disabilities. *Remedial and Special Education, 33*(6), 374–387.

Storey, K., & Miner, C. (2011). *Systematic instruction of functional skills for students and adults with disabilities.* Springfield, IL: Charles C Thomas.

Sugai, G., & Horner, R. (2009). Responsiveness-to-intervention and school-wide positive behavior supports: Integration of multi-tiered system approaches. *Exceptionality, 17*(4), 223–237.

Turnbull, H., III. (2005). Individuals with Disabilities Education Act reauthorization: Accountability and personal responsibility. *Remedial and Special Education, 26*(6), 320–326.

U.S. Department of Education. (2002, October). *Evidence-based education.* Presented at the Student Achievement and School Accountability Conference. Retrieved April 2, 2015, from http://www.ed.gov/nclb/methods/whatworks/eb/edlite-slide003.html

U.S. Department of Education. (2003, December 9). *Title I—Improving the Academic Achievement of the Disadvantaged;* Final Rule, 68 Federal Registry 268 (codified at 34 C.R.F. pt. 200).

U.S. Department of Education. (2007, May 20). *Final regulations on modified academic achievement standards.* Retrieved April 15, 2015, from http://www.ed.gov/policy/speced/guid/modachieve-summary.html

U.S. Department of Education. (2015). *Thirty-seventh annual report to Congress on the implementation of the Individuals with Disabilities Education Act, 2015.* Washington, DC: Office of Special Education and Rehabilitative Services. Retrieved September 5, 2016, from http://www2.ed.gov/about/reports/annual/osep/2015/parts-b-c/37th-arc-for-idea.pdf

Wakeman, S., Browder, D., Meier, I., & McColl, A. (2007). The implications of No Child Left Behind for students with developmental disabilities. *Mental Retardation and Developmental Disabilities Research Reviews, 13(2),* 143–150.

Wehmeyer, M., Lattin, D., & Agran, M. (2001). Achieving access to the general education curriculum for students with mental retardation: A curriculum decision-making model. *Education and Training in Mental Retardation and Developmental Disabilities, 36(4),* 327–342.

West, E., McCollow, M., Kidwell, J., Umbarger G., & Cote, D. (2013). Current status of evidence-based practice for students with intellectual disability and autism spectrum disorder. *Education and Training in Autism and Developmental Disabilities, 48*(4), 443–455.

Yell, M. (2016). *The law and special education* (4th ed.). Boston, MA: Pearson Education.

Yell, M., & Drasgow, E. (2005). *No Child Left Behind: A guide for professionals*. Upper Saddle River, NJ: Prentice Hall.

Chapter 4

American Association on Intellectual and Developmental Disabilities. (2013). *Definition of intellectual disability*. Retrieved December 10, 2015, from http://aaidd.org/intellectual-disability/definition#.VmnPiHvKKX0

Brigance, A. (2004). *BRIGANCE® Inventory of Early Development* (2nd ed.). North Billerica, MA: Curriculum Associates.

Brigance, A. (2010a). *BRIGANCE® Comprehensive Inventory of Basic Skills* (2nd ed.). North Billerica, MA: Curriculum Associates.

Brigance, A. (2010b). *BRIGANCE® Transition Skills Inventory*. North Billerica, MA: Curriculum Associates.

Browder, D., Liberty, K., Heller, M., & D'Huyvetters, K. (1986). Self-management by teachers: Improving instructional decision-making. *Professional School Psychology, 1*(3) 165–175.

Browder, D., Spooner, F., & Jimenez, B. (2011). Standards-based individualized education plans and progress monitoring. In D. Browder & F. Spooner (Eds.), *Teaching students with moderate to severe disabilities* (pp. 42–91). New York, NY: Guilford Press.

Brown, F., & Snell, M. (2011). Measuring student performance. In M. Snell & F. Brown (Eds.), *Instruction of students with severe disabilities* (7th ed., pp. 186–223). Upper Saddle River, NJ: Pearson Education.

Brown, L., Branston, M., Hamre-Nietupski, S., Pumpian, I., Certo, N., & Gruenwald, L. (1979). A strategy for developing chronologically-age-appropriate and functional curricular content for severely handicapped adolescents and young adults. *Journal of Special Education, 13*(1), 81–90.

Brown, L., Sherbenou, R., & Johnsen, S. (2010). *Test of Nonverbal Intelligence* (4th ed.). Austin, TX: Pro-Ed.

Cannella-Malone, H., Sabielny, L., Jimenez, E., & Miller, M. (2013). Pick one! Conducting preference assessments with students with significant disabilities. *Teaching Exceptional Children, 45*(6), 16–23.

Capizzi, A. (2008). From assessment to annual goal: Engaging a decision-making process in writing measurable IEPs. *Teaching Exceptional Children, 41*(1), 18–25.

Cohen, L., & Spenciner, L. (2015). *Assessment of children and youth with special needs* (5th ed.). Upper Saddle River, NJ: Pearson Education.

Collins, B. (2007). *Moderate and severe disabilities: A foundational approach*. Upper Saddle River, NJ: Pearson Education.

Cooper, J., Heron, T., & Heward, W. (2007). *Applied behavior analysis* (2nd ed.). Upper Saddle River, NJ: Pearson Education.

Council of Chief State School Officers. (2008). *Attributes of effective formative assessment.* Retrieved December 3, 2015, from http://ccsso.org/Documents/2008/Attributes_of_Effective_2008.pdf

Council of Chief State School Officers. (2013). *High quality summative assessment principles for ELA/Literacy and mathematics assessments aligned to College and Career Readiness Standards.* Retrieved December 3, 2015, from http://www.ccsso.org/Documents/2013/CCSSO%20Assessment%20Quality%20Principles%2010-1-13%20FINAL.pdf

DeLeon, I., & Iwata, B. (1996). Evaluation of a multiple-stimulus presentation format for assessing reinforcer preferences. *Journal of Applied Behavior Analysis, 29*(4), 519–533.

Etscheidt, S. (2006). Progress monitoring: Legal issues and recommendations for IEP teams. *Teaching Exceptional Children, 38*(3), 56–60.

Evans, S., & Evans, W. (1986). A perspective on assessment for instruction. *Pointer, 30*(2), 9–12.

Fisher, W., Piazza, C., Bowman, L., Hagopian, L., Owens, J., & Sleving, I. (1992). A comparison of two approaches for identifying reinforcers for persons with severe and profound disabilities. *Journal of Applied Behavior Analysis, 25*(2), 491–498.

Fuchs, L., & Fuchs, D. (2000). Analogue assessment of academic skills: Curriculum-based measurement and performance assessment. In E. Shapiro & T. Kratchowill (Eds.), *Behavioral assessment in schools* (2nd ed., pp.168–201). New York, NY: Guilford Press.

Giangreco, M., Cloninger, C., & Iverson, V. (2011). *Choosing outcomes and accommodations for children* (3rd ed.). Baltimore, MD: Paul H. Brookes.

Harrison, P., & Oakland, T. (2015). *Adaptive Behavior Assessment System* (3rd ed.). San Antonio, TX: Psychological Corporation.

Heward, W. (2013). *Exceptional children: An introduction to special education* (10th ed.). Upper Saddle River, NJ: Pearson Education.

Higbee, T., Carr, J., & Harrison, C. (1999). The effects of pictorial versus tangible stimuli in stimulus-preference assessments. *Research in Developmental Disabilities, 20* (1), 63–72.

Hosp, M., Hosp, J., & Howell, K. (2007). *The ABC's of CBM: A practical guide to curriculum-based measurement.* New York, NY: Guilford Press.

Individuals with Disabilities Education Act Amendments of 1997, PL 105–17, 20 U.S.C §§ 1400 *et seq.*

Individuals with Disabilities Education Improvement Act, 20 U.S.C. § 1400 (2004).

Janney, R., & Snell, M. (2011). Designing and implementing instruction for inclusive classes. In M. Snell & F. Brown (Eds.), *Instruction of students with severe disabilities* (7th ed., pp. 224–256). Upper Saddle River, NJ: Pearson Education.

Kaufman, A., & Kaufman, N. (2014). *Kaufman Test of Educational Achievement* (3rd ed.). San Antonio, TX: Pearson Clinical.

Kazdin, A. (2011). *Single-case research designs: Methods for clinical and applied settings* (2nd ed.). New York, NY: Oxford University Press.

Kentucky Department of Education. (2014, February)., *Inclusion of special populations in the state-required assessment and accountability programs: 703 KAR 5:070.* Retrieved December 3, 2015, from http://education.ky.gov/districts/legal/Documents/5070%20doc.pdf

Kleinert, H., Quenemoen, R., & Thurlow, M. (2010). An introduction to alternate assessments: Historical foundations, parameters, and guiding principles. In H. Kleinert & J. Farmer Kearns (Eds.), *Alternate assessment of students with significant cognitive disabilities: An educator's guide* (pp. 3–18). Baltimore, MD: Paul H. Brookes.

Lane, J., & Ledford, J. (2014). Using interval-based systems to measure behavior in early childhood special education and early intervention. *Topics in Early Childhood Special Education, 34*(2), 83–93.

National Center on Education Outcomes. (2013). *Alternate assessment for students with disabilities: Frequently asked questions.* Retrieved December 3, 2015, from http://www.cehd.umn.edu/NCEO/TopicAreas/AlternateAssessments/altAssessFAQ.htm

National Center on Education Outcomes. (2014). *Alternate assessments based on alternate achievement standards (AA-AAS) overview.* Retrieved December 3, 2015, from http://nceo.info/Assessments/aa-aas

No Child Left Behind Act of 2001, PL 107–110, 115 Stat. 1425, 20 U.S.C. §§ 6301 *et seq.*

Northup, J. (2000). Further evaluation of the accuracy of reinforcer surveys: A systematic replication. *Journal of Applied Behavior Analysis, 33*(3), 335–338.

Northup, J., George, T., Jones, K., Broussard, C., & Vollmer, T. (1996). A comparison of reinforcer assessment methods: The utility of verbal and pictorial choice procedures. *Journal of Applied Behavior Analysis, 29*(2), 201–212.

Overton, T. (2016). *Assessing learners with special needs* (8th ed.). Upper Saddle River, NJ: Pearson Education.

Pace, G., Ivancic, M., Edwards, G., Iwata, B., & Page, T. (1985). Assessment of stimulus preference and reinforcer value with profoundly retarded individuals. *Journal of Applied Behavior Analysis, 18*(3), 249–255.

Powell, J., Martindale, A., & Kulp, S. (1975). An evaluation of time-sample measures of behavior. *Journal of Applied Behavior Analysis, 8*(4), 463–469.

Public Schools of North Carolina. (2016). *North Carolina Extended Common Core State Standards: English/language arts 6–8.* Retrieved August 29, 2016, from http://www.ncpublicschools.org/docs/acre/standards/extended/ela/6-8.pdf

Quenemoen, R., Lehr, C., Thurlow, M., & Massanari, C. (2001). *Students with disabilities in standards-based assessment and accountability systems: Emerging issues, strategies, and recommendations* (Synthesis Report 37). Minneapolis: University of Minnesota, National Center on Educational Outcomes. Retrieved December 3, 2015, from http://education.umn.edu/NCEO/OnlinePubs/Synthesis37.html

Roid, G. (2003). *Stanford-Binet Intelligence Scales* (5th ed.). Itasca, IL: Riverside.

Roid, G., Miller, L., Pomplun, M., & Koch, C. (2013). *Leiter International Performance Scale* (3rd ed.). Wood Dale, IL: Stoelting.

Salvia, J., Ysseldyke, J., & Bolt, S. (2007). *Assessment in special and inclusive education* (10th ed.). Boston, MA: Houghton Mifflin.

Sautter, R., LeBlanc, L., & Gillet, J. (2008). Using free operant preference assessments to select toys for free play between children with autism and siblings. *Research in Autism Spectrum Disorders, 2*(1), 17–27.

Shapiro, E. (1989). *Academic skills problems: Direct assessment and intervention.* New York, NY: Guilford Press.

Sparrow, S., Balla, D., & Cicchetti, D. (2007). *Vineland Adaptive Behavior Scales* (2nd ed.). Circle Pines, MN: American Guidance Services.

Spinelli, C. (2006). *Classroom assessment for students in special and general education* (2nd ed.). Upper Saddle River, NJ: Pearson Education.

Spooner, F., Browder, D., & Richter, S. (2011). Community and job skills. In D. Browder & F. Spooner (Eds.), *Teaching students with moderate and severe disabilities* (pp. 342–363). New York, NY: Guilford Press.

Sundberg, M. (2008). *Verbal behavior milestones assessment and placement program: The VB-MAPP.* Concord, CA: AVB Press.

Taylor, R. (2009). *Assessment of exceptional students: Educational and psychological procedures* (8th ed.). Upper Saddle River, NJ: Pearson Education.

U.S. Department of Education. (2005). *Alternate achievement standards for students with the most significant cognitive disabilities: Non-regulatory guidance.* Washington, DC: Author.

Vargas, J. (2013). *Behavior analysis for effective teaching* (2nd ed.). New York, NY: Routledge.

Wechsler, D. (2014). *Wechsler Intelligence Scale for Children* (5th ed.). San Antonio, TX: Psychological Corp.

Woodcock, R., Schrank, F., McGrew, K., & Mather, N. (2014). *Woodcock-Johnson Tests of Achievement* (4th ed.). Rolling Meadow, IL: Houghton Mifflin Harcourt-Riverside.

Wright, J. (2007). *The RTI toolkit: A practical guide for schools.* Port Chester, NY: National Professional Resources.

Wright, J. (2013). *How to: Assess reading speed with CBM: Oral reading fluency passages.* Retrieved December 3, 2015, from http://www.jimwrightonline.com/mixed_files/lansing_IL/_Lansing_IL_Aug_2013/2_CBA_ORF_Directions.pdf

CHAPTER 5

Alberto, P., & Troutman, A. (2013). *Applied behavior analysis for teachers* (9th ed.). Upper Saddle River, NJ: Pearson Education.

Bailey, J., & Burch, M. (2011). *Ethics for behavior analysts* (2nd ed.). New York, NY: Routledge.

Bambara, L., & Knoster, T. (2009). *Designing positive behavior support plans* (2nd ed.). Washington, DC: American Association on Intellectual and Developmental Disabilities.

Behavior Analyst Certification Board. (2010). *Guidelines for responsible conduct for behavior analysts.* Littleton, CO: Author.

Benedict, E., Horner, R., & Squires, J. (2007). Assessment and implementation of positive behavior support in preschools. *Topics in Early Childhood Special Education, 27*(3), 174–192.

Bledsoe, R., Myles, B., & Simpson, R. (2003). Using a social story intervention to improve mealtime skills of an adolescent with Asperger syndrome. *Autism, 7*(3), 289–295.

Boden, L., Ennis, R., & Jolivette, K. (2012). Implementing check in/check out for students with intellectual disability in self-contained classrooms. *Teaching Exceptional Children, 45*(1), 32–39.

Boutot, E. (2009). Using "I will" cards and social coaches to improve social behaviors of students with Asperger syndrome. *Intervention in School and Clinic, 44*(5), 276–281.

Boutot, E., & Hume, K. (2012). Beyond time out and table time: Today's applied behavior analysis for students with autism. *Education and Training in Autism and Developmental Disabilities, 47*(1), 23–38.

Byiers, B., Dimian, A., & Symons, F. (2014). Functional communication training in Rett syndrome: A preliminary study. *American Journal on Intellectual and Developmental Disabilities, 19*(4), 340–350.

Carr, E., & Durand, V. (1985). Reducing behavior problems through functional communication training. *Journal of Applied Behavior Analysis, 18*(2), 111–126.

Carter, D., Carter, G., Johnson, E., & Pool, J. (2013). Systematic implementation of a Tier 2 behavior intervention. *Intervention in School and Clinic, 48*(4), 223–231.

Cooper, J., Heron, T., & Heward, W. (2007). *Applied behavior analysis* (2nd ed.). Upper Saddle River, NJ: Prentice Hall.

Crone, D., Hawken, L., & Horner, R. (2015). *Building positive behavior support systems in schools: Functional behavior assessment* (2nd ed.). New York, NY: Guilford.

Davis, T., III, Kurtz, P., Gardner, A.,& Carman, N. (2006). Cognitive-behavioral treatment for specific phobias with a child demonstrating severe problem behavior and developmental delays. *Research in Developmental Disabilities, 28*(6), 546–558.

Dunlap, G., & Liso, D. (2004). *Using choice and preference to promote improved behavior.* Center on the Social and Emotional Foundations for Early Learning. Retrieved December 2, 2015, from http://csefel.vanderbilt.edu/briefs/wwb15.pdf

Durand, V. (1990). *Severe behavior problems: A functional communication training approach.* New York, NY: Guilford.

Durand, V. (1999). Functional communication training using assistive devices: Recruiting natural communities of reinforcement. *Journal of Applied Behavior Analysis, 32*(3), 247–267.

Emerson, E., Kiernan, C., Alborz, A., Reeves, D., Mason, H., Swarbrick, R., . . . Hatton, C. (2001). The prevalence of challenging behaviors: A total population study. *Research in Developmental Disabilities, 22*(1), 77–93.

Filcheck, H., McNeill, C., Greco, L., & Bernard, R. (2004). Using a whole-class token economy and coaching of teacher skills in a preschool classroom to manage disruptive behavior. *Psychology in the Schools, 41*(3), 351–361.

Filter, K., McKenna, M., Benedict, E., Horner, R., Todd, A., & Watson, J. (2007). Check in/check out: A post-hoc evaluation of an efficient, secondary-level targeted intervention for reducing problem behaviors in schools. *Education and Treatment of Children, 30*(1), 69–84.

Green, V., Drysdale, H., Boelema, T., Smart, E., van der Meer, L., Achmadi, D., . . . Lancioni, G. (2013). Use of video modeling to enhance positive peer interactions of four preschool children with social skills difficulties. *Education and Treatment of Children, 36*(2), 59–85.

Hanley, G., Piazza, C., Keeney, K., Blakeley-Smith, A., & Worsdell, A. (1998). Effects of wrist weights on self-injurious and adaptive behaviors. *Journal of Applied Behavior Analysis, 31*(2), 307–310.

Individuals with Disabilities Education Improvement Act, 20 U.S.C. § 1400 (2004).

Iwata, B., DeLeon, I., & Roscoe, E. (2013). Reliability and validity of the Functional Analysis Screening Tool. *Journal of Applied Behavior Analysis, 46*(1), 271–284.

Jolivette, K., Stichter, J., & McCormick, K. (2002). Making choices-improving behavior-engaging in learning. *Teaching Exceptional Children, 34*(3), 24–29.

Keen, K., Sigafoos, J., & Woodyatt, G. (2001). Replacing prelinguistic behaviors with functional communication. *Journal of Autism and Developmental Disorders, 31*(4), 385–398.

Kelm, J., McIntosh, K., & Cooley, S. (2014). Effects of implementing school-wide positive behavioural interventions and supports on problem behaviour and academic achievement in a Canadian elementary school. *Canadian Journal of School Psychology, 29*(3), 195–212.

Knight, V., Sartini, E., & Spriggs, A. (2015). Evaluating visual activity schedules as evidence-based practice for individuals with autism spectrum disorder. *Journal of Autism and Developmental Disorders, 45*(1), 157–178.

Kokina, A., & Kern, L. (2010). Social Story™ interventions for students with autism spectrum disorders: A meta-analysis. *Journal of Developmental Disorders, 40*(7), 812–826.

Lalli, J., Livezey, K., & Kates, K. (1996). Functional analysis and treatment of eye poking with response blocking. *Journal of* Applied *Behavior Analysis, 29*(1), 129–132.

Lancioni, G., Singh, N., O'Reilly, M., & Sigafoos, J. (2009). An overview of behavioral strategies for reducing hand-related stereotypies of persons with severe to profound intellectual and multiple disabilities: 1995–2007. *Research in Developmental Disabilities, 30*(1), 20–43.

Lancioni, G., Singh, N., O'Reilly, M., Sigafoos, J., Oliva, D., Severini, L., . . . Tamma, M. (2007).Microswitch technology to promote adaptive responses and reduce mouthing in two children with multiple disabilities. *Journal of Visual Impairment and Blindness, 101*(10), 628–636.

Lee, L., Harrington, R., Chang, J., & Connors, S. (2008). Increased risk of injury in children with developmental disabilities. *Research in Developmental Disabilities, 29*(3), 247–255.

Lequia, J., Machalicek, W., & Rispoli, M. (2012). Effects of activity schedules on challenging behavior exhibited in children with autism spectrum disorders: A systematic review. *Research in Autism Spectrum Disorders, 6*(1), 480–492.

Luiselli, J. (2006). *Antecedent assessment and intervention: Supporting children and adults with developmental disabilities in community settings*. Baltimore, MD: Paul H. Brookes.

Mancil, G., Conroy, M., Nakao, T., & Alter, P. (2006). Functional communication training in the natural environment: A pilot investigation with a young child with autism spectrum disorder. *Education and Treatment of Children, 29*(4), 615–633.

Martinez, C., & Betz, A. (2013). Response interruption and redirection: Current research trends and clinical application. *Journal of Applied Behavior Analysis, 46*(2), 549–554.

Matson, J., Dixon, D., & Matson, M. (2005). Assessing and treating aggression in children and adolescents with developmental disabilities: A 20-year overview. *Educational Psychology, 25*(2–3), 151–181.

McClelland, M., Acock, A., & Morrison, F. (2006). The impact of kindergarten learning-related skills on academic trajectories at the end of elementary school. *Early Childhood Research Quarterly, 21*(4), 471–490.

McCormick, K., Jolivette, K., & Ridgley, R. (2003). Choice making as an intervention strategy for young children. *Young Exceptional Children, 6*(2), 3–10.

McDonald, J., Wilder, D., & Dempsey, C. (2002). Brief functional analysis and treatment of eye poking. *Behavioral Interventions, 17*(4), 261–270.

McIntyre, L., Blacher, J., & Baker, B. (2006). The transition to school adaptation in children with and without developmental delays. *Journal of Intellectual Disability Research, 50*(5), 349–361.

Mechling, L., Ayres, K., Bryant, K., & Foster, A. (2014). Continuous video modeling to assist with completion of multi-step home living tasks by young adults with moderate intellectual disability. *Education and Training in Autism and Developmental Disabilities, 49*(3), 368–380.

Mechling, L., & Swindle, C. (2012). Fine and gross motor task performance when using computer-based video models by students with autism and moderate intellectual disability. *Journal of Special Education, 47*(3), 135–147.

Myles, B., Trautman, M., & Schelvan, R. (2004). *The hidden curriculum.* Shawnee Mission, KS: Autism Asperger Publishing Company.

O'Neill, R., Horner, R., Albin, R., Sprague, J., Storey, K., & Newton, J. (1997). *Functional assessment of problem behavior: A practical assessment guide.* Pacific Grove, CA: Brooks/Cole.

Paulus, M., & Moore, C. (2014). The development of recipient-dependent sharing behavior and sharing expectations in preschool children. *Developmental Psychology, 50*(3), 914–921.

Reynhout, G., & Carter, M. (2007). Social Story™ efficacy with a child with autism spectrum disorder and moderate intellectual disability. *Focus on Autism and Other Developmental Disabilities, 22*(3), 173–182.

Rooker, G., Jessel, J., Kurtz, P., & Hagopian, L. (2013). Functional communication training with and without alternative reinforcement and punishment: An analysis of 58 applications. *Journal of Applied Behavior Analysis, 46*(4), 708–722.

Schieltz, K., Wacker, D., Harding, J., Berg, W., Lee, J., Dalmau, Y., . . .Ibrahimović, M. (2011). Indirect effects of functional communication training on non-targeted disruptive behavior. *Journal of Behavioral Education, 20*(1), 15–32.

Smith, T., Polloway, E., Taber-Doughty, T., Patton, J., & Dowdy, C. (2016). *Teaching students with special needs in inclusive settings* (7th ed.). Upper Saddle River, NJ: Pearson Education.

Taber-Doughty, T., Patton, S., & Brennan, S. (2008). Simultaneous and delayed video modeling: An examination of system effectiveness and student preferences. *Journal of Special Education Technology, 23*(1), 2–18.

Travers, J., Whitby, P., Tincani, M., & Boutot, E. (2014). Alignment of sexuality education with self-determination for people with significant disabilities: A review of research and future directions. *Education and Training in Autism and Developmental Disabilities, 49*(2), 232–247.

Tymchuk, A. (1971). Token economy and motivating environment for mildly retarded adolescent boys. *Mental Retardation, 9*(6), 8.

U.S. Department of Education. (2012). *Restraint and seclusion: Resource document*. Washington, DC: Author.

Wacker, D., Steege, M., Northup, J., Sasso, G., Berg, W., Reimers, T., . . . & Donn, L. (1990). A component analysis of functional communication training across three topographies of severe behavior problems. *Journal of Applied Behavior Analysis, 23*(4), 417–429.

Wilder, D., Myers, K., Fischetti, A., Leon, Y., Nicholson, K., & Allison, J. (2012). An analysis of modifications to the three-step guided compliance procedure necessary to achieve compliance among preschool children. *Journal of Applied Behavior Analysis, 45*(1), 121–130.

Winborn, L., Wacker, D., Richman, D., Asmus, J., & Geier, D. (2002). Assessment of mand selection for functional communication training packages. *Journal of Applied Behavior Analysis, 35*(3), 295–298.

Winborn-Kemmerer, L., Ringdahl, J., Wacker, D., & Kitsukawa, K. (2009). A demonstration of individual preference for novel mands during functional communication training. *Journal of Applied Behavior Analysis, 42*(1), 185–189.

Wong, C., Odom, S., Hume, K., Cox, C., Fettig, A., Kurcharczyk, S., . . . Schultz, T. (2015). Evidence-based practices for children, youth, and young adults with autism spectrum disorder: A comprehensive review. *Journal of Autism and Developmental Disorders, 45*(7), 1951–1966.

Woods, M. (1971). Development of a pay for recreation procedure in a token economy. *Mental Retardation, 9*(1), 54–57.

Zuluaga, C., & Normand, M. (2008). An evaluation of the high-probability instruction sequence with and without programmed reinforcement for compliance with high probability instructions. *Journal of Applied Behavior Analysis, 41*(3), 453–457.

Chapter 6

ABCya.com. (2014). *Virtual manipulatives!* (Version 1.4). Retrieved September 13, 2016, from https://itunes.apple.com/us/app/virtual-manipulatives!/id471341079?mt=8 www.abcya.com/fraction_percent_decimal_tiles.htm

Ackerman, A., & Shapiro, E. (1984). Self-monitoring and work productivity with mentally retarded adults. *Journal of Applied Behavior Analysis, 17(3)*, 403–407.

Adylitica. (2014). *Do it (tomorrow)* (Version 2.0.6). Retrieved September 13, 2016, from https://itunes.apple.com/us/app/do-it-tomorrow/id381651376?mt=8

Agran, M. (1997). *Student-directed learning: Teaching self-determination skills*. Pacific Grove, CA: Brooks/Cole.

American Speech-Language-Hearing Association. (2015). *Augmentative and alternative communication (AAC)*. Retrieved April 14, 2015, from http://www.asha.org/public/speech/disorders/AAC/

Appest Limited. (2016). *Tick Tick* (Version 3.0.70). Retrieved September 13, 2016, from https://itunes.apple.com/us/app/ticktick-your-to-do-list-task/id626144601?mt=8

Apple. (2016). *Dictation*. Retrieved September 13, 2016, from https://support.apple.com/en-us/ HT202584

Applied Human Factors. (2016). *SoothSayer word prediction*. Retrieved September 13, 2016, from http://newsite.ahf-net.com/soothsayer/

Assistive Ware. (2016). *Proloquo2Go* (Version 4.3). Retrieved September 13, 2016, from https:// itunes.apple.com/us/app/proloquo2go/id308368164?mt=8

Attainment Company. (2016). *GoTalk button*. Retrieved September 13, 2016, from http://www .attainmentcompany.com/gotalk-button

Ayres, K., Mechling, L., & Sansosti, F. (2013). The use of mobile technologies to assist with life skills/independence of students with moderate/severe intellectual disability and/or autism spectrum disorders: Considerations for the future of school psychology. *Psychology in the Schools, 50*(3), 259–271.

Barton, E., Reichow, B., Schnitz, A., Smith, I., & Sherlock, D. (2015). A systematic review of sensory-based treatments for children with disabilities. *Research in Developmental Disabilities, 37(1)*, 64–80. DOI: 10.1016/j.ridd.2014.11.006

Bedesem, P., & Dieker, L. (2014). Self-monitoring with a twist: Using cell phones to cell monitor on-task behavior. *Journal of Positive Behavior Interventions, 16*(4), 246–254. DOI: 10.1177/1098300713492857

Bee Visual. (2016). *Choiceworks*. Retrieved September 13, 2016, from https://itunes.apple.com/ us/app/choiceworks/id486210964?mt=8

Behrmann, M., & Jerome, M. (2002). Assistive technology for students with mild disabilities: Update 2002. *ERIC Digest*. Retrieved April 14, 2015, from http://www.gpo.gov/fdsys/pkg/ ERIC-ED463595/pdf/ERIC-ED463595.pdf

Behrmann, M., & Schaff, J. (2001). Assisting educators with assistive technology: Enabling children to achieve independence in living and learning. *Children and Families, 42*(3), 24–28.

Blackhurst, A. (1997). Perspectives on technology in special education. *Teaching Exceptional Children, 29*(5), 41–48.

Blackhurst, A. (2005a). Historical perspectives about technology applications for people with disabilities. In D. Edyburn, K. Higgins, & R. Boone (Eds.), *Handbook of special education technology research and practice* (pp. 3–30). Whitefish Bay, WI: Knowledge by Design.

Blackhurst, A. (2005b). Perspectives on applications of technology in the field of learning disabilities. *Learning Disability Quarterly, 28*(2), 175–178.

Bolkan, J. (2012, December 19). Research: IT predictions for 2013. *THE Journal*. Retrieved from http://thejournal.com/articles/2012/12/19/research-it-predictions-for-2013.aspx?admgarea= News1

Bondy, A., & Frost, L. (1994). The Picture-Exchange Communication System. *Focus on Autistic Behavior, 9*(3), 1–19.

Bondy, A., & Frost, L. (2001). The Picture Exchange Communication System. *Behavior Modification, 2(5)*, 725–744.

Bornman, J. (2011). Low technology. In O. Wendt, R. W. Quist, & L. L. Lloyd (Eds.), *Assistive technology: Principles and applications for communication disorders and special education* (pp. 175–220). Bingley, United Kingdom: Emerald.

Bouck, E., Bassette, L., Taber-Doughty, T., Flanagan, S., & Szwed, K. (2009). Pentop computers as tools for teaching multiplication to students with mild intellectual disabilities. *Education and Training in Developmental Disabilities, 4(3),* 367–380.

Bouck, E., & Flanagan, S. (2010). Virtual manipulatives: What are they and how can teachers use them? *Intervention in School and Clinic, 45(3),* 186–191.

Bouck, E., Flanagan, S., Miller, B., & Bassette, L. (2012). Technology in action: Rethinking everyday technology as assistive technology to meet students' IEP goals. *Journal of Special Education Technology,* 27(4), 47–57.

Bouck, E., Jasper, A., Bassette, L., Shurr, J., & Miller, B. (2013). Applying TAPE: Rethinking assistive technology for students with physical disabilities, multiple disabilities, and other health impairment. *Physical Disabilities: Education and Related Services, 32*(1), 31–54.

Bouck, E., Satsangi, R., Bartlett, W., & Weng, P. (2012). Promoting independence through assistive technology: Evaluating audio recorders to support grocery shopping. *Education and Training in Autism and Developmental Disabilities, 47(4),* 462–473.

Bouck, E., Taber-Doughty, T., & Savage, M. (2015). *Footsteps towards the future: Implementing a real-world curriculum for students with disabilities.* Arlington, VA: Council for Exceptional Children.

Brownlee, A. (2015). Augmentative communication. *ALS Association.* Retrieved April 14, 2015, from http://www.alsa.org/als-care/augmentative-communication/

Bryant, D., & Bryant, B. (2012). *Assistive technology for people with disabilities* (2nd ed.). Boston, MA: Allyn & Bacon.

Bryant, B., Seok, S., Ok, M., & Bryant, D. (2012). Individuals with intellectual and/or developmental disability use of assistive technology devices in support provisions. *Journal of Special Education Technology, 27*(2), 41–57.

BryTech. (2016). *Note teller 2.* Retrieved September 13, 2016, from http://www.brytech.com/noteteller/

Burgstahler, S. (2012). *Working together: People with disabilities and computer technology.* Retrieved February 9, 2015, from http://www.washington.edu/doit/working-together-people-disabilities-and-computer-technology

Cannon, L., Dorward, J., Duffin, J., & Heal, B. (2004). National Library of Virtual Manipulatives. *The Mathematics Teacher, 97*(2), 158–159.

Cook, A., & Polgar, J. (2015). *Assistive technologies: Principles and practice* (4th ed.). St. Louis, MO: Elsevier.

Council for Exceptional Children. (2005). *Universal design for learning: A guide for teachers and education professionals.* Boston, MA: Pearson Company.

Dell, A., Newton, D., & Petroff, J. (2012). *Assistive technology in the classroom: Enhancing the school experience for students with disabilities.* Boston, MA: Pearson Education.

Drescher, P. (2009). Access to computers for students with physical disabilities. In J. Gierach (Ed.), *Assessing students' needs for assistive technology (ASNAT): A resource manual for school district teams* (5th ed.). Milton: Wisconsin Assistive Technology Initiative. Retrieved from http://www.wati.org/content/supports/free/pdf/Ch4-ComputerAccess.pdf

Don Johnston. (2016). *Co:Writer 7*. Retrieved September 13, 2016, from http://donjohnston.com/cowriter-7

Douglas, K., Ayres, K., Langone, J., Bell, V., & Meade, C. (2009). Expanding literacy for learners with intellectual disabilities: The role of supported eText. *Journal of Special Education Technology*, *24*(3), 35–45.

Edyburn, D. (2001). Models, theories, and frameworks: Contributions to understanding special education technology. *Special Education Technology Practice*, *4*(2), 16–24.

Edyburn, D. (2004). Rethinking assistive technology. *Special Education Technology Practice*, *5*(4), 16–23.

Edyburn, D. (2005). Assistive technology and students with mild disabilities: From consideration to outcomes measurement. In D. Edyburn, K. Higgins, & R. Boone (Eds.), *Handbook of special education technology research and practice* (pp. 239–270). Whitefish Bay, WI: Knowledge by Design.

Englert, C., Zhao, Y., Dunsmore, K., Collings, N., & Wolbers, K. (2007). Scaffolding the writing of students with disabilities through procedural facilitation: Using an Internet-based technology to improve performance. *Learning Disability Quarterly*, *30*(1), 9–29.

eType. (2016). *eType*. Retrieved September 13, 2016, from http://www.etype.com/

Flower, L., & Hayes, J. (1981). A cognitive process theory of writing. *College Composition and Communication, 32*(4), 365–387.

Gargiulo, R. (2015). *Special education in contemporary society* (5th ed.). Thousand Oaks, CA: Sage.

Gierach, J. (Ed.). (2009). *Assessing students' needs for assistive technology (ASNAT): A resource manual for school district teams* (5th ed.). Retrieved April 14, 2015, from http://www.wati.org/content/supports/free/pdf/ASNAT5thEditionJun09.pdf

Ginger Labs. (2016). *Notability* (Version 6.3.0). Retrieved September 13, 2016, from https://itunes.apple.com/us/app/notability/id360593530?mt=8

Ginger Software. (2016). *Ginger*. Retrieved September 13, 2016, from http://www.gingersoftware.com/

goQ. (2016). *wordQ+speakQ*. Retrieved September 13, 2016, from http://www.goqsoftware.com/wordQspeakQ.php

Gray, C., & Garand, J. (1993). Social stories: Improving responses of students with autism with accurate social information. *Focus on Autistic Behavior, 8(1)*, 1–10.

Green, J. (2014). *Assistive technology in special education: Resources for education, intervention, and rehabilitation* (2nd ed.). Waco, TX: Prufrock Press.

Handhold Adaptive. (2016). *StoryMaker™ for social stories* (Version 4.3.01). Retrieved September 13, 2016, from https://itunes.apple.com/us/app/storymaker-for-social-stories/id570007786?mt=8

Hanline, M., Nunes, D., & Worthy, M. (2007). Augmentative and alternative communication in the early childhood years. *Beyond the Journal: Young Children on the Web*, 1–6. Retrieved April 14, 2015, from https://www.naeyc.org/files/yc/file/200707/BTJHanline.pdf

Higgins, E., & Raskind, M. (2005). The compensatory effectiveness of the Quicktionary Reading Pen II on the reading comprehension of students with learning disabilities. *Journal of Special Education Technology*, *20*(1), 31–40.

Idea4e. (2015). *Timer forkids* (Version 1.3.1). Retrieved September 13, 2016, from https://itunes.apple.com/us/app/kids-countdown-visual-timer/id786114488?mt=8

I Get It. (2016). *i Create . . . social skills stories* (Version 3.8.5). Retrieved September 13, 2016, from https://itunes.apple.com/us/app/i-create...-social-skills/id513666306?mt=8

inClass. (2016). *inClass*. Retrieved September 13, 2016, from http://www.inclassapp.com/

Individuals with Disabilities Education Improvement Act, 20 U.S.C. § 1400 (2004).

Inspiration Software. (2016a). *Inspiration 9*. Retrieved September 13, 2016, from http://www.inspiration.com/

Inspiration Software. (2016b). *Kidspiration 3*. Retrieved April 14, 2015, from http://www.inspiration.com/Kidspiration

Institute for Human & Machine Cognition. (2014). *Cmap Tools* (Version 6.02). Retrieved September 13, 2016, from http://cmap.ihmc.us/

Johnson, L., Beard, L., & Carpenter, L. (2007). *Assistive technology: Access for all students*. Upper Saddle River, NJ: Pearson Education.

Jones, V., & Hinesman-Matthews, L. (2014). Effective assistive technology considerations and implications for diverse students. *Computers in the Schools*, *31*(3), 220–232.

Kassardjian, A., Leaf, J., Ravid, D., Leaf, J., Alcalay, A., Dale, S., . . . Oppenheim-Leaf, M. (2014). Comparing the teaching interaction procedure to social studies: A replication study. *Journal of Autism and Developmental Disorders*, *44*(9), 2329–2340.

Kelly, J., Kratcoski, A., & McClain, K. (2006). The effects of word processing software on the writing of students with special needs. *Journal of the Research Center for Educational Technology*, *2*(2), 32–43.

Koehler, L. (2011). Assistive technology for daily living. In O. Wendt, R. Quist, & L. Lloyd (Eds.), *Assistive technology: Principles and applications for communication disorders and special education* (pp. 447–478). Bingley, United Kingdom: Emerald.

Kurzweil Education. (2016). *Kurzweil 3000 + firefly*. Retrieved September 13, 2016, from www.kurzweiledu.com/k3000-firefly/overview.html

Lee, H., & Templeton, R. (2008). Ensuring equal access to technology: Providing assistive technology for students with disabilities. *Theory Into Practice*, *47*(3), 212–219.

Leong, H., Carter, M., & Stephenson, J. (2015). Meta-analysis of research on sensory integration therapy for individuals with developmental and learning disabilities. *Journal of Developmental and Physical Disabilities*, *27*(2), 183–206.

Limited Cue. (2016). *Stories about me* (Version 1.5). Retrieved September 13, 2016, from https://itunes.apple.com/us/app/stories-about-me/id531603747?mt=8

Loeding, B. (2011). Assistive technology for visual and dual-sensory impairments. In O. Wendt, R. Quist, & L. Lloyd (Eds.), *Assistive technology: Principles and applications for communication disorders and special education* (pp. 367–412). Bingley, United Kingdom: Emerald.

LookTel. (2016). *Money reader.* Retrieved September 13, 2016, from www.looktel.com/moneyreader

Love Learning. (2015). *What's today* (Version 1.2.2). Retrieved September 13, 2016, from https://itunes.apple.com/us/app/whats-today/id647286448?mt=8&ign-mpt=uo%3D4

MacArthur, C. (2009). Reflections on research on writing and technology for struggling writers. *Learning Disabilities Research and Practice, 24*(2), 93–103.

Maccini, P., & Gagnon, J. (2000). Best practices for teaching mathematics to secondary students with special needs. *Focus on Exceptional Children, 32*(5), 1–22.

Maccini, P., & Gagnon, J. (2006). Mathematics instructional practice and assessment accommodations by secondary special and general educators. *Exceptional Children, 72*(2), 217–234.

Madraso, J. (1993). Proofreading: The skill we've neglected to teach. *English Journal, 82*(2), 32–41.

Mariage, T., & Bouck, E. (2004). Scaffolding literacy learning for students with mild needs. In A. Rodgers & E. Rodgers (Eds.), *Scaffolding literacy instruction: Strategies for K–4 classrooms* (pp. 36–74). Portsmouth, NH: Heinemann.

Mariage, T., Englert, C., & Garmon, M. (2000). The teacher as "more knowledgeable other" in assisting literacy learning with special needs students. *Reading and Writing Quarterly, 16*(4), 299–336.

Marino, M., Marino, E., & Shaw, S. (2006). Making informed assistive technology decisions for students with high incidence disabilities. *Teaching Exceptional Children, 38*(6), 18–25.

McDougall, D., Morrison, C., & Awana, B. (2011). Students with disabilities use tactile cued self-monitoring to improve academic productivity during independent tasks. *Journal of Instructional Psychology, 39*(2), 119–130.

Microsoft. (2016). *Windows Speech Recognition.* Retrieved September 13, 2016, from https://support.microsoft.com/en-us/help/17208

National Commission on Writing for America's Families, Schools, and Colleges. (2005). *Writing: A powerful message from state government.* Retrieved April 13, 2015, from http://www.collegeboard.com/prod_downloads/writingcom/powerful-message-from-state.pdf

National Council of Teachers of Mathematics. (2016). *Illuminations.* Retrieved September 13, 2016, from http://illuminations.nctm.org

NaturalSoft Limited. (2016). *NaturalReader* (Version 14.0). Retrieved September 13, 2016, from http://www.naturalreaders.com/

Netherton, D., & Deal, W. (2006). Assistive technology in the classroom. *The Technology Teacher, 66*(1), 10–15.

Notion. (2014). *Popplet* (Version 2.1). Retrieved September 13, 2016, from https://itunes.apple
.com/us/app/popplet/id374151636?mt=8

n2y. (2016). *News-2-You.* Retrieved April 14, 2015, from https://www.n2y.com/products/
news2you

Nuance. (2016). *Dragon NaturallySpeaking.* Retrieved September 13, 2016, from http://www
.nuance.com/dragon/index.htm

Parette, H., Blum, C., & Quesenberry, A. (2013). The role of technology for young children in
the 21st century. In H. P. Parette & C. Blum (Eds.), *Instructional technology in early childhood*
(pp. 1–28). Baltimore, MD: Paul H. Brookes.

Parette, P., Peterson-Karlan, G., & Wojcik, B. (2005). The state of assistive technology services
nationally and implications for future development. *Assistive Technology Outcomes and Benefits, 2*(1), 13–24.

Pilone, P. (2016). *iHomework 2* (Version 1.6.3). Retrieved September 13, 2016, from https://
itunes.apple.com/us/app/ihomework-2/id1052937170?mt=8

PockeySoft. (2016). *UPAD 3* (Version 3.29). Retrieved September 13, 2016, from https://itunes
.apple.com/us/app/upad/id401643317?mt=8

Ptomey, L., Sullivan, D., Lee, J., Goetz, J., Gibson, C., & Donnelly, J. (2015). The use of technology for delivering a weight loss program for adolescents with intellectual and developmental
disabilities. *Journal of the Academy of Nutrition and Dietetics, 115*(1), 112–118.

Rafferty, L., & Raimondi, S. (2009). Self-monitoring of attention versus self-monitoring of
performance: Examining the differential effects among students with emotional disturbance
engaged in independent math practice. *Journal of Behavioral Education, 18(4),* 279–299.

Reed, F.., Hyman, S., & Hirst, J. (2011). Applications of technology to teach social skills to children with autism. *Research in Autism Spectrum Disorders, 5(3),* 1003–1010.

Reid, R. (1996). Research in self-monitoring with students with learning disabilities: The present, the prospects, the pitfalls. *Journal of Learning Disabilities, 29(3),* 317–331.

Reid, R., Trout, A., & Schartz, M. (2005). Self-regulation interventions for children with attention deficit/hyperactivity disorder. *Exceptional Children, 71(4),* 361–377.

Remember the Milk. (2016). *Remember the milk.* Retrieved September 13, 2016, from https://
www.rememberthemilk.com/

Rewordify. (2016). *Rewordify.* Retrieved September 13, 2016, from https://rewordify.com/

Savage, M. (2014). Self-operated auditory prompting systems: Creating and using them to support students with disabilities. *Teaching Exceptional Children, 47*(1), 266–275.

Scott, R., Collins, B., Knight, V., & Kleinert, H. (2013). Teaching adults with moderate intellectual disability ATM use via the iPod. *Education and Training in Autism and Developmental
Disabilities, 48*(2), 190–199.

Shodor. (2016). Inter*activate.* Retrieved September 13, 2016, from www.shodor.org/interactivate

Shurr, J., & Taber-Doughty, T. (2012). Increasing comprehension for middle school students with moderate intellectual disability on age-appropriate texts. *Education and Training in Autism and Developmental Disabilities, 47*(3), 359–372.

6 Wunderkinder. (2016). *Wunderlist* (Version 3.4.4). Retrieved September 13, 2016, from https://itunes.apple.com/app/wunderlist-to-do-list-tasks/id410628904

Skywise. (2016). *Kids timer* (Version 3.0). Retrieved September 13, 2016, from https://play.google.com/store/apps/details?id=nl.skywise.kidstimer&hl=en

Soft Grup Construct SRL. (2016). *Turbo Type* (Version 1.39.004). Retrieved September 13, 2016, from http://www.easytousetools.com/turbo_type/

Studious. (2016). *Studious*. Retrieved September 13, 2016, from https://www.studiousapp.com/

Taber-Doughty, T. (2005). Considering student choice when selecting instructional strategies: A comparison of three prompting systems. *Research in Developmental Disabilities, 26(5),* 411–432.

Taber-Doughty, T., Bouck, E., Tom, K., Jasper, A., Flanagan, S., & Bassette, L. (2011). Video modeling and prompting: A comparison of two strategies for teaching cooking skills to students with mild intellectual disabilities. *Education and Training in Autism and Developmental Disabilities, 46(4),* 499–513.

Tapfun. (2014). *Base ten blocks math* (Version 1). Retrieved September 13, 2016, from https://itunes.apple.com/us/app/base-ten-blocks-math/id878351349?mt=8

Texthelp. (2016). *Read&Write Gold* (Version 1.2.1). Retrieved September 13, 2016, from https://itunes.apple.com/us/app/read-write-for-ipad/id934749270?mt=8

Tufts University. (2015). *Visual Understanding Environment* (Version 3.3.0). Retrieved September 13, 2016, from http://vue.tufts.edu/

Tuthill, J. (2014, June). Get real with visual scene displays. *The ASHA Leader, 19*, 34–35. DOI: 10.1044/leader.APP.19062014.34

Vanderheiden, G. (1984). High and light technology approaches in the development of communication systems for the severely physically handicapped person. *Exceptional Education Quarterly, 4*(4), 40–56.

Walsall Academy. (2016). *Too Noisy Pro* (Version 5.03). Retrieved September 13, 2016, from https://itunes.apple.com/us/app/too-noisy-pro/id521646496?mt=8

Wehmeyer, M. (1988). National survey of the use of assistive technology by adults with mental retardation. *Mental Retardation, 36*(1), 44–51.

Wehmeyer, M. (1999). Assistive technology and students with mental retardation: Utilization and barriers. *Journal of Special Education Technology, 14*(1), 48–58.

Wehmeyer, M., Tassé, M., Davies, D. , & Stock, S. (2012). Support needs of adults with intellectual disability across domains: The role of technology. *Journal of Special Education Technology, 27*(2), 11–21.

Weng, P., & Bouck, E. (2014). Using video prompting to teach price comparison to adolescents with autism. *Research in Autism Spectrum Disorders, 8*(10), 1405–1415.

Weng, P., Savage, M., & Bouck, E. (2014). iDIY: Video-based instruction using iPads. *Teaching Exceptional Children, 47*(1), 231–239. DOI: 10.1177/0040059914542764

WizcomTech. (2014). *Quicktionary2*. Retrieved September 13, 2016, from www.wizcomtech.com/product-catalog/products-english

Yakubova, G., & Bouck, E. (2014). Not all created equally: Exploring calculator use by students with mild intellectual disability. *Education and Training in Autism and Developmental Disabilities, 4(1)*, 111–126.

York, C., & Fabrikant, K. (2011). High technology. In O. Wendt, R. W. Quist, & L. L. Lloyd (Eds.), *Assistive technology: Principles and applications for communication disorders and special education* (pp. 221–264). Bingley, United Kingdom: Emerald.

Chapter 7

Bruns, D., & Pierce, C. (2007). Let's read together: Tools for early literacy development for all children. *Young Exceptional Children, 10*(2), 2–10.

Carle, E. (1969). *The very hungry caterpillar*. New York, NY: Penguin Putnam.

Cook, R., Klein, M., & Chen, D. (2016). *Adapting early childhood curricula for children with special needs* (9th ed.). Upper Saddle River, NJ: Pearson Education.

Division for Early Childhood. (2014, April 14). *DEC recommended practices in early intervention/early childhood special education 2014*. Retrieved January 3, 2016, from http://www.dec-sped.org/recommendedpractices

Dunst, C., Gorman, E., & Hamby, D. (2010). Effectiveness of adult contingent responsiveness on increases in infant vocalizations. *CELLreviews, 3*(1), 1–11.

Dunst, C., Hamby, D., Trivette, C., Raab, M., & Bruder, M. (2000). Everyday family and community life and children's naturally occurring learning opportunities. *Journal of Early Intervention, 23*(3), 151–164.

Dunst, C., Jones, T., Johnson, M., Raab, M., & Hamby, D. (2011). Role of children's interests in early literacy and language development. *CELLreviews, 4*(5), 1–18.

Dunst, C., Trivette, C., Masiello, T., Roper, N., & Robyak, A. (2006). Framework for developing evidence-based early literacy learning practices. *CELLpapers, 1*(1), 1–12.

Dunst, C., Trivette, C., & Raab, M. (2013). An implementation science framework for conceptualizing and operationalizing fidelity in early childhood intervention studies. *Journal of Early Intervention, 35*(2), 85–101.

Gargiulo, R. (2015). *Special education in contemporary society* (5th ed.). Thousand Oaks, CA: Sage.

Gargiulo, R., & Kilgo, J. (2014). *An introduction to young children with special needs* (4th ed.). Belmont, CA: Wadsworth/Cengage Learning.

Goldstein, H. (2011). Knowing what to teach provides a roadmap for early intervention. *Journal of Early Intervention, 33*(4), 268–280.

Guo, Y., Sawyer, B., Justice, L., & Kadervek, J. (2013). Quality of the literacy environment in inclusive special education classrooms. *Journal of Early Intervention, 35*(1), 40–60.

Koppenhaver, D., & Yoder, D. (1993). Classroom literacy instruction for children with severe speech and physical impairments (SSPI): What is and what might be. *Topics in Language Disorders, 13*(2), 1–15.

Linder, T. (2008). *Transdisciplinary play-based intervention* (2nd ed.). Baltimore, MD: Paul H. Brookes.

Massaro, D. (2004). On the road to reading fluently: Where is the science in helping us find the best balance between meaning-oriented and skills-oriented approaches? *American Journal of Psychology, 117*(2), 300–316.

McGee, L., & Richgels, D. (2014). *Designing early literacy programs* (2nd ed.). New York, NY: Guilford Press.

National Early Literacy Panel. (2008). *Developing early literacy: Report of the National Early Literacy Panel.* Washington, DC: National Institute for Literacy.

Noonan, M., & McCormick, L. (2006). *Young children with disabilities in natural environments.* Baltimore, MD: Paul H. Brookes.

Odom, S., Buysse, V., & Soukakou, E. (2011). Inclusion for young children with disabilities: A quarter century of research perspectives. *Journal of Early Intervention, 33*(4), 344–356.

Pretti-Frontczak, K., & Bricker, D. (2004). *An activity based approach to early intervention* (3rd ed.). Baltimore, MD: Paul H. Brookes.

Raab, M., & Dunst, C. (2006). Influence of child interests on variations in child behavior and functioning. *Winterberry Press, 1*(24), 1–22.

Robyak, A., Masiello, T., Trivette, C., Roper, N., & Dunst, C. (2007). Mapping the contemporary landscape of early literacy learning. *CELLreviews, 1*(1), 1–10.

Schertz, H., Reichow, B., Tan, P., Vaiouli, P., & Yildirim, E. (2012). Intervention for children with autism spectrum disorders: An evaluation of research evidence. *Journal of Early Intervention, 34*(3), 166–189.

Wolery, M. (2005). DEC recommended practices: Child-focused practices. In S. Sandall, M. Hemmeter, B. Smith, & M. McLean (Eds.), *DEC recommended practices: A comprehensive guide for practical application for early intervention/early childhood special education.* Missoula, MT: Division for Early Childhood.

Wolery, M., & Hemmeter, M. (2011). Classroom instruction: Background, assumptions, and challenges. *Journal of Early Intervention, 33*(4), 371–380.

Zero to Three. (2016). *Help your child develop early math skills.* Retrieved September 9, 2016, from https://www.zerotothree.org/resources/299-help-your-child-develop-early-math-skills

CHAPTER 8

Ackerman, D., & Barnett, W. (2005, March). *Prepared for kindergarten: What does "readiness" mean?* Retrieved August 4, 2015, from http://nieer.org/resources/policyreports/report5.pdf

Alberto, P., & Troutman, A. (2013). *Applied behavior analysis for teachers* (9th ed.). Upper Saddle River, NJ: Pearson Education.

American Montessori Society. (2015). *Introduction to Montessori Method.* Retrieved September 19, 2015, from https://amshq.org/Montessori-Education/Introduction-to-Montessori

Barnett, W., Friedman-Krauss, A., Gomez, R., Horowitz, M., Weisenfeld, G., & Squires, J. (2016). *The state of preschool 2015*. New Brunswick, NJ: National Institute for Early Education Research.

Bouck, E., Taber-Doughty, T., & Savage, M. (2015). *Footsteps toward the future: Implementing a real-world curriculum for students with developmental disabilities*. Arlington, VA: Council for Exceptional Children.

Connors-Tadros, L., Dunn, L., Martella, J., & McCauley, C. (2015). *Incorporating early learning strategies in the school improvement grants (SID) program: How three schools integrated early childhood strategies into school turnaround efforts to improve instruction for all students*. New Brunswick, NJ: National Institute for Early Education Research.

Daily, S., Burkhauser, M., & Halle, T. (2010). A review of school readiness practices in the states: Early learning guidelines and assessments. *Early Childhood Highlights, 1*(2), 1–12.

Danaher, J. (2011, January). Eligibility polices and practices for young children under Part B of IDEA. *NECTAC Notes, 27*, 1–6. Retrieved September 19, 2015, from http://www.nectac .org/~pdfs/pubs/nnotes27.pdf

Deiner, P. (2013). *Inclusive early childhood education: Development, resources, and practice* (6th ed.). Belmont, CA: Wadsworth/Cengage Learning.

Division for Early Childhood. (2014, April 14). *DEC recommended practices in early intervention/ early childhood special education 2014*. Retrieved August 28, 2015, from http://www.dec-sped .org/recommendedpractices

Division for Early Childhood. (2015, April 18). *DEC recommended practices in early intervention and early childhood special education glossary 2015*. Retrieved August 28, 2015, from http:// www.dec-sped.org/recommendedpractices

Dunst, C., Bruder, M., Trivette, C., Raab, M., & McLean, M. (2001). Natural learning opportunities for infants, toddlers and preschoolers. *Young Exceptional Children, 4*(2), 18–25.

Georgeson, J., & Payler, J. (2013). *International perspectives on early childhood education and care*. New York, NY: McGraw-Hill.

Glenn-Applegate, K. (2011). *Caregivers' preschool selection factors and their degree of agency in selecting high quality preschools* (Unpublished doctoral dissertation). The Ohio State University, Columbus.

Gutek, G. (2004). *The Montessori Method*. New York, NY: Rowman & Littlefield.

Hohmann, M., Banet, B., & Weikart, D. (1979). *Young children in action: A manual for preschool educators*. Ypsilanti, MI: High/Scope Press.

Hohmann, M., & Weikart, D. (1995). *Educating young children: Active learning practices for preschool and child care programs*. Ypsilanti, MI: HighScope Press.

Individuals with Disabilities Education Act, 20 U.S.C. § 1400 (2004).

Klein, A. (2008). Creating peaceful environmental designs for the classroom. *EarlychildhoodNews*. Retrieved September 5, 2015, from http://www.earlychildhoodnews.com/earlychildhood/ article_view.aspx?ArticleID=390

Linder, T. (2008). *Transdisciplinary play-based assessment* (2nd ed.). Baltimore, MD: Paul H. Brookes.

McCormick, K., Stricklin, S., Nowak, T., & Rous, B. (2008). Using eco-mapping to understand family strengths and resources. *Young Exceptional Children, 11*(2), 17–28.

McWilliam, R. (2009a). *Goal Functionality Scale III*. Chattanooga, TN: Siskin Children's Institute.

McWilliam, R. (2009b). *Protocol for the Routines-Based Interview*. Chattanooga, TN: Siskin Children's Institute.

McWilliam, R. (2012). Implementing and preparing for home visits. *Topics in Early Childhood Special Education, 31*(4), 224–231.

McWilliam, R., Casey, A., & Sims, J. (2009). The routines-based interview: A methods for gathering information and assessing needs. *Infants & Young Children, 22*(3), 224–233.

Milbourne, S., & Campbell, P. (2007). *CARA's Kit: Creating adaptations for routines and activities.* Philadelphia, PA: Child and Family Studies Research Programs, Thomas Jefferson University.

Murphy, J., Pagano, M., Ramirez, A., Anaya, A., Nowlin, C., & Jellinek, M. (1999). Validation of the Preschool and Early Childhood Functional Assessment Scale. *Journal of Children and Family Studies, 8*(3), 343–356.

National Association for the Education of Young Children. (2009). *Developmentally appropriate practice in early childhood programs serving children from birth through age 8: Position statement.* Washington, DC: Author.

National Association for the Education of Young Children. (2015). *10 effective DAP teaching strategies*. Retrieved September 4, 2015, from http://www.naeyc.org/dap/10 -effective-dap-teaching-strategies

Nesloney, T., & Minock, D. (2013, November 4). Augmented reality brings new dimensions to learning. *Edutopia*. Retrieved September 18, 2015, from http://www.edutopia.org/blog/ augmented-reality-new-dimensions-learning-drew-minock

North American Montessori Teachers' Association. (2015). *How much does Montessori cost?* Retrieved August 14, 2015, from http://www.montessori-namta.org/FAQ/ Montessori-Education/How-much-does-Montessori-cost

Odom, S., Peck, C., Hanson, M., Beckman, P., Kaiser, A., Lieber, J., . . . Schwartz, I. (2015). *Inclusion at the preschool level: An ecological systems analysis*. Retrieved April 11, 2015, from http:// education.jhu.edu/PD/newhorizons/Exceptional%20Learners/Inclusion/General%20 Information/inclusion_preschool.htm

Pacer Center. (2011). What is the difference between an IFSP and an IEP? *Pacer Center Action Information Sheet*. Retrieved August 29, 2015, from http://www.pacer.org/parent/php/ PHP-c59.pdf

Robbins, T., Stagman, S., & Smith, S. (2012). *Young children at risk: National and state prevalence of risk factors.* New York, NY: National Center for Children in Poverty, Columbia University.

U.S. Department of Education. (1999, March). *Use of "developmental delay" by states and LEAs: Topic brief.* Retrieved August 10, 2015, from http://www2.ed.gov/policy/speced/leg/idea/ brief7.html

U.S. Department of Education. (2012). *Serving preschool children through Title I Part A of the Elementary and Secondary Education Act of 1965.* Washington, DC: Author.

U.S. Department of Health and Human Services. (2015). *Getting started with the Head Start early learning outcomes framework: Ages birth to five.* Retrieved August 10, 2015, from http:// eclkc.ohs.acf.hhs.gov/hslc/hs/sr/approach/pdf/getting-started.pdf

Weikart, D., Rogers, L., Adcock, L., & McClelland, D. (1971). *The cognitively oriented curriculum: A framework for preschool teachers.* Washington, DC: National Association for the Education of Young Children.

Woods, J., & Lindeman, D. (2008). Gathering and giving information with families. *Infants & Young Children, 21*(4), 272–284.

CHAPTER 9

Armbruster, B., Lehr, F., & Osborn, J. (2003). *Putting reading first: The research building block for teaching children to read.* Washington, DC: Center for Improvement of Early Reading Achievement and National Institute for Literacy.

Aykut, C. (2012). Effectiveness and efficiency of constant-time delay and most-to-least prompt procedures in teaching daily living skills to children with intellectual disabilities. *Educational Sciences: Theory and Practice, 12*(1), 366–373.

Bloom, B. (Ed.). (1956). *Taxonomy of educational objectives book 1: Cognitive domain.* White Plains, NY: Longman.

Browder, D., Ahlgrim-Delzell, L., Flowers, C., & Baker, J. (2012). An evaluation of a multicomponent early literacy program for students with severe developmental disabilities. *Remedial and Special Education, 33*(4), 237–246.

Browder, D., Ahlgrim-Delzell, L., Spooner, F., Mims, P., & Baker, J. (2009). Using time delay to teach literacy to students with severe developmental disabilities. *Exceptional Children, 75*(3), 343–364.

Browder, D., Gibbs, S., Ahlgrim-Delzell, L., Courtade, G., & Lee, A. (2007). *Early literacy skills builder.* Verona, WI: Attainment Company.

Browder, D., Hudson, M., & Wood, L. (2013). Teaching students with moderate intellectual disability who are emergent readers to comprehend text. *Exceptionality, 38*(4), 17–29.

Browder, D., Jimenez, B., & Trela, K. (2012). Grade-aligned math instruction for secondary students with moderate intellectual disabilities. *Education and Training in Autism and Developmental Disabilities, 47*(3), 373–388.

Browder, D., Mims, P., Spooner, F., Ahlgrim-Delzell, L., & Lee, A. (2008). Teaching elementary students with multiple disabilities to participate in shared stories. *Research and Practice for Persons With Severe Disabilities, 33*(1), 3–12.

Browder, D., & Minarovic, T. (2000). Utilizing sight words in self-instruction training for employees with moderate mental retardation in competitive jobs. *Education and Training in Mental Retardation and Developmental Disabilities, 35*(1), 78–89.

Browder, D., & Spooner, F. (2011). *Teaching students with moderate and severe disabilities.* New York, NY: Guilford.

Browder, D., Spooner, F., Ahlgrim-Delzell, L., Harris, A., & Wakeman, S. (2008). A meta-analysis on teaching mathematics to students with significant cognitive disabilities. *Exceptional Children, 74*(4), 407–432.

Browder, D., Trela, K., Courtade, G., Jimenez, B., Knight, V., & Flowers, C. (2012). Teaching mathematics and science standards to students with moderate and severe developmental disabilities. *Journal of Special Education, 46*(1), 26–35.

Browder, D., Trela, K., & Jimenez, B. (2007). Training teachers to follow a task analysis to engage middle school students with moderate and severe developmental disabilities in grade-appropriate literature. *Focus on Autism and Other Developmental Disabilities, 22*(4), 206–219.

Browder, D., Wakeman, S., Spooner, F., Ahlgrim-Delzell, L., & Algozzine, B. (2006). Research on reading instruction for individuals with significant cognitive disabilities. *Exceptional Children, 72*(4), 392–408.

Bryan, L., & Gast, D. (2000). Teaching on-task and on-schedule behaviors to high functioning children with autism via picture activity schedules. *Journal of Autism and Developmental Disorders, 30*(6), 553–567.

Bryant, D., & Bryant, B. (2012). *Assistive technology for people with disabilities.* Upper Saddle River, NJ: Pearson Education.

Carnine, D., Silbert, J., Kaméenui, E., Traver, S., & Juongjohann, K. (2006). *Teaching struggling and at-risk readers.* Upper Saddle River, NJ: Pearson Education.

Carter, E., Sisco, L., Brown, L., Brickham, D., & Al-Khabbaz, Z. (2009). Peer interactions and academic engagement of youth with developmental disabilities in inclusive middle and high school classrooms. *American Journal on Mental Retardation, 113*(6), 479–494.

CAST. (2015). *Universal design for learning.* Retrieved December 1, 2015, from http://www.cast.org/

Chall, J. (1996). *Stages of reading development.* New York, NY: Harcourt Brace.

Collins, B. (2012). *Systematic instruction for students with moderate and severe disabilities.* Baltimore, MD: Paul H. Brookes.

Collins, B., & Stinson, D. (1994). Teaching generalized reading of product warning labels to adolescents with mental disabilities. *Exceptionality, 5*(1), 163–181.

Council of Chief State School Officers & National Governors Association. (2015). *Common Core State Standards Initiative.* Retrieved October 1, 2015, from http://www.corestandards.org/

Courtade, G., Browder, D., Spooner, F., & DiBiase, W. (2010). Training teachers to use an inquiry-based task analysis to teach science to students with moderate and severe disabilities. *Education and Training in Developmental Disabilities, 45*(3), 378–399.

Courtade, G., Test, D., & Cook, B. (2015). Evidence-based practices for learners with severe intellectual disability. *Research and Practice for Persons With Severe Disabilities, 39*(4), 305–318.

Doabler, C., & Fien, H. (2013). Explicit mathematics instruction: What teachers can do for teaching students with mathematics difficulties. *Intervention in School and Clinic, 48*, 276–285.

Doyle, P., Wolery, M., Ault, M., & Gast, D. (1990). System of least prompts: A literature review of procedural parameters. *Journal of the Association for Persons With Severe Handicaps, 13*(1), 28–40.

Fisher, M., & Meyer, L. (2002). Development and social competence after two years for students enrolled in inclusive and self-contained educational programs. *Research and Practice in Severe Disabilities, 27*(3), 165–174.

Frank, A., Wacker, D., Berg, W., & McMahon, C. (1985). Teaching selected microcomputer skills to retarded students via picture prompts. *Journal of Applied Behavior Analysis, 18*(2), 179–185.

Gargiulo, R., & Metcalf, D. (2017). *Teaching in today's inclusive classrooms: A universal design for learning approach* (3rd ed.). Boston, MA: Cengage Learning.

Hudson, M., Browder, D., & Jimenez, B. (2014). Effects of a peer-delivered system of least prompts intervention with adapted science read-alouds on listening comprehension for students with moderate intellectual disability. *Education and Training in Autism and Developmental Disabilities, 49*(1), 60–77.

Hudson, M., Browder, D., & Wood, L. (2013). Review of experimental research on academic learning by students with moderate and severe intellectual disability in general education. *Research and Practice for Persons With Severe Disabilities, 38*(1), 17–29.

Hume, K., Plavnick, J., & Odom, S. (2012). Promoting task accuracy and independence in students with autism across educational setting through the use of individual work systems. *Journal of Autism and Developmental Disorders, 42*(10), 2084–2099.

Hunt, P., McDonnell, J., & Crockett, M. (2012). Reconciling an ecological curricular framework focusing on quality of life outcomes with the development and instruction of standards-based academic goals. *Research and Practice in Severe Disabilities, 37*(3), 139–152.

Individuals with Disabilities Education Act Amendments, 20 U.S.C. § 1400 (1997).

Individuals with Disabilities Education Improvement Act, 20 U.S.C. § 1400 (2004).

Jackson, L., Ryndak, D., & Wehmeyer, M. (2009). The dynamic relationship between context, curriculum, and student learning: A case for inclusive education as a research-based practice. *Research and Practice for Persons With Severe Disabilities, 34*(1), 175–195.

Jimenez, B., Browder, D., & Courtade, G. (2008). Teaching algebra to students with moderate cognitive disabilities. *Education and Training in Developmental Disabilities, 43*(2), 266–274.

Jimenez, B., Browder, M., Spooner, F., & DiBiase, W. (2012). Inclusive inquiry science using peer mediated embedded instruction for students with moderate intellectual disability. *Exceptional Children, 78*(3), 301–317.

Knight, V., Browder, D., Agnello, B., & Lee, A. (2010). Academic instruction in ELA, math, and science for students with severe disabilities. *Focus on Exceptional Children, 42*(7), 1–14.

Knight, V., Sartini, E., & Spriggs, A. (2015). Evaluating visual activity schedules as evidence-based practice for individuals with autism. *Journal of Autism and Developmental Disorders, 45*(1), 157–178.

Knight, V., Spooner, F., Browder, D., Smith, B., & Wood, C. (2013). Using systematic instruction and graphic organizers to teach science to students with autism spectrum disorders and intellectual disability. *Focus on Autism and Other Developmental Disabilities, 28*(2), 115–126.

Koegel, R., & Koegel, L. (1995). *Teaching children with autism: Strategies for initiating positive interactions and improving learning.* Baltimore, MD: Paul H. Brookes.

McDonnell, J. (2011). Instructional contexts. In J. Kauffman & D. Hallahan (Eds.), *Handbook of special education* (pp. 532–543). New York, NY: Routledge.

Mims, P., Hudson, M., & Browder, D. (2012). Using read-alouds of grade-level biographies and systematic prompting to promote comprehension for students with moderate and severe developmental disabilities. *Focus on Autism and Other Developmental Disabilities, 27*(2), 67–80.

National Council for the Social Studies. (2002). *National standards for social studies teachers.* Washington, DC: Author.

National Council of Teachers of Mathematics. (2000). *Principles and standards for school mathematics.* Reston, VA: Author.

National Research Council. (2001). *Educating children with autism.* Washington, DC: National Academies Press.

National Research Council. (2012). *A framework for K–12 science education.* Washington, DC: National Academies Press.

National Science Teachers Association. (2003). *Standards for science teacher preparation.* Washington, DC: Author.

Neitzel, J., & Wolery, M. (2009). *Steps for implementation: Least-to-most prompts.* Chapel Hill: National Professional Development Center on Autism Spectrum Disorders, Frank Porter Graham Child Development Institute, University of North Carolina.

Next Generation Science Standards. (2013). *Appendix D—"All standards, all students": Making the Next Generation Science Standards accessible to all students.* Retrieved May 17, 2016, from http://www.nextgenscience.org/sites/default/files/Appendix%20D%20Diversity%20 and%20Equity%206-14-13.pdf

No Child Left Behind Act of 2001, 20 U.S.C. § 6319 (2008).

Pugalee, D. (2004). A comparison of verbal and written descriptions of students' problem solving processes. *Educational Studies in Mathematics, 55*(1), 27–47.

Riesen, T., McDonnell, J., Johnson, J., Polychronis, S., & Jameson, M. (2003). A comparison of constant time delay and simultaneous prompting within embedded instruction in general education classes with students with moderate to severe disabilities. *Journal of Behavioral Education, 12*(4), 241–259.

Ryndak, D., Jackson, L., & White, J. (2013). Involvement and progress in the general curriculum for students with extensive support needs: K–12 inclusive-education research and implications for the future. *Inclusion, 1*(1), 28–49.

Slavin, R. (1994). *Educational psychology* (4th ed.). Needham Heights, MA: Allyn & Bacon.

Spooner, F., Knight, V., Browder, D., Jimenez, B., & DiBiase, W. (2011). Evaluating evidence-based practice in teaching science content to students with severe developmental disabilities. *Research and Practice for Persons With Severe Disabilities, 36*(1), 62–75.

Spooner, F., Knight, V., Browder, D., & Smith, B. (2012). Evidence-based practices for teaching academics to students with severe developmental disabilities. *Remedial and Special Education, 33*(6), 374–387.

TouchMath. (2015). *What is TouchMath.* Retrieved December 1, 2015, from https://www.touchmath.com/

Walker, G. (2008). Constant and progressive time delay procedures for teaching children with autism: A literature review. *Journal of Autism and Developmental Disorders, 38*(2), 261–275.

Wolery, M. (1994). Instructional strategies for teaching young children with special needs. In M. Wolery & J. Wilbers (Eds.), *Including children with special needs in early childhood programs* (pp. 151–166). Washington, DC: National Association for the Education of Young Children.

Wolery, M., Anthony, L., Caldwell, N., Snyder, E., & Morgante, J. (2002). Embedding and distributing constant time delay in circle time and transitions. *Topics in Early Childhood Special Education, 22*(1), 14–25.

Wolery, M., Holcombe, A., Cybriwsky, C., Doyle, P., Schuster, J., Ault, M., & Gast, D. (1992). Constant time delay with discrete responses: A review of effectiveness and demographic, procedural, and methodological parameters. *Research in Developmental Disabilities, 13*(3), 239–266.

Yell, M. (2016). *The law and special education* (4th ed.). Upper Saddle River, NJ: Pearson Education.

Chapter 10

Alberto, P., Elliott, N., Taber, T., Houser, N., & Andrews, P. (1993). Vocational content for students with moderate and severe disabilities in elementary and middle grades. *Focus on Exceptional Children, 25*(9), 1–10.

Allor, J., Champlin, T., Gifford, D., & Mathes, P. (2010). Methods for increasing intensity of reading instruction for students with intellectual disabilities. *Education and Training in Autism and Developmental Disabilities, 45*(4), 500–511.

Annenberg Learner. (2015). *Key terms: Teaching Reading K–2 Workshop.* Retrieved October 25, 2015, from http://www.learner.org/workshops/readingk2/front/keyterms2.html

Aurasma. (2016). *Aurasma* [Version 5.1.1]. Retrieved September 29, 2016, from https://itunes.apple.com/us/app/aurasma/id432526396?mt=8

Ayres, K., & Langone, J. (2002). Acquisition and generalization of purchasing skills using video enhanced computer-based instructional program. *Journal of Special Education Technology, 17* (4), 15.

Ayres, K., Langone, J., Boon, R., & Norman, A. (2006). Computer-based instruction for purchasing skills. *Education and Training in Developmental Disabilities, 41*(3), 253–263.

Ayres, K., Mechling, L., & Sansosti, F. (2013). The use of mobile technologies to assist with life skills/independence of students with moderate/severe intellectual disability and/or autism spectrum disorders: Considerations for the future of school psychology. *Psychology in the Schools, 50*(3), 259–271.

Bambara, L., Ager, C., & Koper, F. (1994). The effects of choice and task preference on the work performance of adults with severe disabilities. *Journal of Applied Behavior Analysis, 27*(3), 555–556.

Bambara, L., Koger, F., Katzer, T., & Davenport, T. (1995). Embedding choice in the context of daily routines: An experimental case study. *Research and Practice for Persons With Severe Handicaps, 20*(3), 185–195.

Bouck, E., Taber-Doughty, T., & Savage, M. (2015). *Footsteps toward the future: Implementing a real-world curriculum for students with developmental disabilities.* Arlington, VA: Council for Exceptional Children.

Branham, R., Collins, B., Schuster, J., & Kleinert, H. (1999). Teaching community skills to students with moderate disabilities: Comparing combined techniques of classroom simulation, videotape modeling, and community-based instruction. *Education and Training in Mental Retardation and Developmental Disabilities, 34*(2), 170–181.

Browder, D., Jimenez, B., & Trela, K. (2012). Grade-aligned math instruction for students with moderate intellectual disability. *Education and Training in Autism and Developmental Disabilities, 47*(3), 373–388.

Browder, D., Wood, L., Thompson, J., & Ribuffo, C. (2014). *Evidence-based practices for students with severe disabilities.* Retrieved October 25, 2015, from http://ceedar.education.ufl.edu/tools/innovation-configurations/

Brown, L., Branston, M., Hamre-Nietupski, S., Pumpian, I., Certo, N., & Gruenewald, L. (1979). A strategy for developing chronological-age-appropriate and functional curricular content for severely handicapped adolescents and young adults. *The Journal of Special Education, 13*(1), 81–90.

Brown, L., Nietupski, J., & Hamre-Nietupski, S. (1976). The criterion of ultimate functioning. In M. Thomas (Ed.), *Hey, don't forget about me! Education's investment in the severely, profoundly, and multiply handicapped* (pp. 2–15). Reston, VA: Council for Exceptional Children.

Brown, D., Standen, P., Saridaki, M., Shopland, N., Roinioti, E., Evett, L., . . . Smith, P. (2013). Engaging students with intellectual disabilities through games based learning and related technologies. In C. Stephanidis & M. Antona (Eds.), *Universal access in human-computer interaction* (Part III, pp. 573–582). Berlin, Germany: Springer-Verlag.

Cannella-Malone, H., Fleming, C., Chung, Y., Wheeler, G., Basbagill, A., & Singh, H. (2011). Teaching daily living skills to seven individuals with severe intellectual disabilities: A comparison of video prompting to video modeling. *Journal of Positive Behavior Interventions, 13*(3), 144–153.

Cannella-Malone, H., Mizrachi, S., Sabielny, L., & Jimenez, E. (2013). Teaching physical activities to students with significant disabilities using video modeling. *Developmental Neurorehabilitation, 16*(3), 145–154.

Cassella, D. (2009, November 3). What is augmented reality (AR): Augmented reality defined, iPhone augmented reality apps and games and more. *Digital Trends.* Retrieved July 3, 2015, from http://www.digitaltrends.com/mobile/what-is-augmented-reality-iphone-apps-games-flash-yelp-android-ar-software-and-more/

Chang, Y., Kang, Y., & Huang, P. (2013). An augmented reality (AR)-based vocational task prompting system for people with cognitive impairments. *Research in Developmental Disabilities, 34*(10), 3049–3056.

Charlop-Christy, M., Le, L., & Freeman, K. (2000). A comparison of video modeling with in vivo modeling for teaching children with autism. *Journal of Autism and Developmental Disorders, 30*(6), 537–552.

Collins, B., & Wolery, M. (2012). *Systematic instruction for students with moderate and severe disabilities.* Baltimore, MD: Paul H. Brookes.

Collins, B., Wolery, M., & Gast, D. (1991). A survey of safety concerns for students with special needs. *Education and Training in Mental Retardation, 26,* 305–318.

Cronin, M., Patton, J., & Wood, S. (2007). *Life skills instruction: A practical guide for integrating real-life content into the curriculum at the elementary and secondary levels for students with special needs or who are placed at risk* (2nd ed.). Austin, TX: Pro-Ed.

Cullinan, B., Galda, L., & Strickland, D. (1993). *Language, literacy, and the child.* New York, NY: Harcourt Brace College.

Davies, D., Stock, S., & Wehmeyer, M. (2003). Application of computer simulation to teach ATM access to individuals with intellectual disabilities. *Education and Training in Developmental Disabilities, 38*(4), 451–456.

Different Roads to Learning. (2012). *What goes together?* [Version 2.0]. Retrieved September 22, 2016, from https://itunes.apple.com/us/app/what-goes-together/id420970889?mt=8

Drascic, D., & Milgram, P. (1996, April). Perceptual issues in augmented reality. In *Electronic Imaging: Science & Technology* (pp. 123–134). Bellingham, WA: International Society for Optics and Photonics.

Evmenova, A., & Behrmann, M. (2011). Research-based strategies for teaching content to students with intellectual disabilities: Adapted videos. *Education and Training in Autism and Developmental Disabilities, 46*(3), 315–325.

Fuchs, L. (2007). Curriculum for students with severe disabilities. In C. Reynolds & E. Fletcher-Janzen (Eds.), *Encyclopedia of special education: A reference for the education of children, adolescents, and adults with disabilities and other exceptional individuals* (p. 613). Hoboken, NJ: Wiley.

Hintz, J., Volpe, R., & Shapiro, E. (2002). Best practices in the systematic direct observation of student behavior. In A. Thomas & J. Grimes (Eds.), *Best practices in school psychology IV* (pp. 993–1006). Bethesda, MD: National Association of School Psychologists.

Hudson, M., Browder, D., & Wood, L. (2013). Review of experimental research on academic learning by students with moderate and severe intellectual disability in general education. *Research & Practice for Persons With Severe Disabilities, 38*(1), 17–29.

Joint Committee on National Health Education Standards. (1995). *National health education-standards*. Reston, VA: American School Health Association.

Killu, K., Clare, C., & Im, A. (1999). Choice vs. preference: The effects of choice and no choice of preferred and non-preferred spelling tasks on the academic behavior of students with disabilities. *Journal of Behavioral Education, 9*(3–4), 239–253.

Layar B. (2016). *Layar—Augmented Reality* [Version 8.5]. Retrieved September 29, 2016, from https://itunes.apple.com/us/app/layar-augmented-reality/id334404207?mt=8

Lee, S., Amos, B., Stelios, G., Lee, Y., Shogren, K., Theoharis, R., . . . Wehmeyer, M. (2006). Curriculum augmentation and adaptation strategies to promote access to the general curriculum for students with intellectual and developmental disabilities. *Education and Training in Developmental Disabilities, 41*(3), 199–212.

McLaughlin, M., & Allen, M. (2009). *Guided comprehension in grades 3–8*. Newark, DE: International Reading Association.

Mechling, L. (2008). Thirty year review of safety skill instruction for persons with intellectual disabilities. *Education and Training in Developmental Disabilities, 43*(3), 311–323.

Mezmedia. (2016, March 1). *Bamba clock: Learn to tell time* [Version 1.0.2]. Retrieved September 22, 2016, from https://itunes.apple.com/us/app/bamba-clock-learn-to-tell-time/id1017620167?mt=8

Miller, B., & Taber-Doughty, T. (2014). Self-monitoring checklists for inquiry problem-solving: Functional problem-solving for students with intellectual disability. *Education and Training in Autism and Developmental Disabilities, 49*(4), 555–567.

Minock, D., & Nesloney, T. (2013, November 4). *Augmentative reality brings new dimensions to learning* [Web log post]. Retrieved September 27, 2016, from http://www.edutopia.org/blog/augmented-reality-new-dimensions-learning-drew-minock

Model Me Kids. (2012). *Model Me Going Places 2* (Version 3.3). Retrieved September 22, 2016, from https://itunes.apple.com/us/app/model-me-going-places-2/id375669988?mt=8

National Center for Education Statistics. (2012). *Digest of education statistics*. Washington, DC: U.S. Department of Education.

National Center for Education Statistics. (2014a). *Condition of education*. Washington, DC: U.S. Department of Education.

National Center for Education Statistics. (2014b). *Digest of education statistics*. Washington, DC: U.S. Department of Education.

National Council for the Social Studies. (2002). *National standards for social studies teachers—revised*. Silver Spring, MD: Author.

National Council of Teachers of English & International Reading Association. (1996). *Standards for the English language arts*. Urbana, IL: Author. Retrieved September 27, 2016, from http://www.ncte.org/standards/ncte-ira

Next Generation Science Standards. (2013). *Next generation science standards: For states, by states*. Washington, DC: The National Academies Press.

Olinghouse, N. (2008). *Designing lessons for diverse learners*. Retrieved May 22, 2015, from http://education.msu.edu/te/secondary/pdf/Designing-Lessons-for-Diverse-Learners.pdf

Riggs, L., Collins, B., Kleinert, H., & Knight, V. (2013). Teaching principles of heredity to high school students with moderate and severe disabilities. *Research and Practice for Persons With Severe Disabilities, 38*(1), 30–43.

Schleien, S., Germ, P., & McAvoy, L. (1996). Inclusive community leisure services: Recommended professional practices and barriers encountered. *Therapeutic Recreation Journal, 30*(4), 260–273.

Short, A. (2016). *Jungle coins—learn coin math* [Version 7.58]. Retrieved September 22, 2016, from https://itunes.apple.com/us/app/jungle-coins-learn-coin-math/id380864501?mt=8

Smith, T., Polloway, E., Taber-Doughty, T., Patton, J., & Dowdy, C. (2016). *Teaching students with special needs in inclusive settings* (7th ed.). Upper Saddle River, NJ: Pearson Education.

Spooner, F., Knight, V., Browder, D., Jimenez, B., & DiBiase, W. (2011). Evaluating evidence-based practice in teaching science content to students with severe developmental disabilities. *Research and Practice for Persons With Severe Disabilities, 36*(1–2), 62–75.

Squire, K., & Jan, M. (2007). Mad City mystery: Developing scientific argumentation skills with a place-based augmented reality game on handheld computers. *Journal of Science Education and Technology, 16*(1), 5–29.

Stafford, A., Alberto, P., Fredrick, L., Heflin, J., & Heller, K. (2002). Preference variability and the instruction of choice making with students with severe intellectual disabilities. *Education and Training in Mental Retardation and Developmental Disabilities, 37*(1), 70–88.

Storey, K., & Miner, C. (2011). *Systematic instruction of functional skills for students and adults with disabilities*. Springfield, IL: Charles C Thomas.

Taber-Doughty, T. (2005). Considering student choice when selecting instructional strategies: A comparison of three prompting systems. *Research in Developmental Disabilities, 26*(5), 411–432.

Taber-Doughty, T., Bouck, E., Tom, K., Jasper A., Flanagan, S., & Bassette, L. (2011). Video modeling and prompting: A comparison of two strategies for teaching cooking skills to students with mild intellectual disabilities. *Education and Training in Autism and Developmental Disabilities, 46*(4), 499–513.

Taylor, R., Richards, S., & Brady, M. (2005). *Mental retardation: Historical perspectives, current practices, and future directions*. Boston, MA: Allyn & Bacon.

Toca Boca. (2016). *All of our apps*. Retrieved September 22, 2016, from http://tocaboca.com/apps/

Tomlinson, C. (2014). *The differentiated classroom: Responding to the needs of all learners* (2nd ed.) Alexandria, VA: ASCD.

Unit11. (2015). *A day with a difference* [Version 3.1]. Retrieved September 22, 2016, from https://itunes.apple.com/us/app/a-day-with-a-difference/id498266298?mt=8

Wakeman, S., Karvonen, M., & Ahumada, A. (2013). Changing instruction to increase achievement for students with moderate to severe intellectual disabilities. *Teaching Exceptional Children, 46*(2), 6–13.

Walker, A., Uphold, N., Richter, S., & Test, D. (2010). Review of the literature on community-based instruction across grade levels. *Education and Training in Autism and Developmental Disabilities, 45*(2), 242–267.

Ward, H. (2005). The use of language experiences in teaching reading to students with severe-learning disabilities. *The Reading Matrix, 5*(1), 16–20.

Wehman, P., Targett, P., & Richardson, M. (2012). Functional curriculum design. In P. Wehman & J. Kregel (Eds.), *Functional curriculum for elementary and secondary students with special needs* (pp. 1–51). Austin, TX: Pro-Ed.

Weiss, P., Bialik, P., & Kizony, R. (2003). Virtual reality provides leisure time opportunities for young adults with physical and intellectual disabilities. *CyberPsychology & Behavior, 6*(3), 335–342.

Wolpert-Gawran, H. (2015, August 13). What the heck is project-based learning? *Edutopia.* Retrieved October 15, 2015, from http://www.edutopia.org/blog/what-heck-project-based-learning-heather-wolpert-gawron

Wright, D. (2003). Common definitions: Adaptations, accommodations, modifications. *Teaching & Learning.* Retrieved July 3, 2015, from http://www.pent.ca.gov/acc/commondefinitions_accom-mod.pdf

CHAPTER 11

Abells, D., Burbridge, J., & Minnes, P. (2008). Involvement of adolescents with intellectual disabilities in social and recreational activities. *Journal on Developmental Disabilities, 14*(2), 88–94.

Alberto, P., Elliott, N., Taber, T., Houser, E., & Andrews, P. (1993). Vocational content for students with moderate and severe disabilities in elementary and middle grades. *Focus on Exceptional Children, 25*(9), 1–10.

Allan, S., & Goddard, Y. (2010). Differentiated instruction and RTI: A natural fit. *Educational Leadership, 68*(2). Retrieved October 4, 2016, from www.ascd.org/publications/educational-leadership/oct10/vol68/num02/Differentiated-Instruction-and-RTI@-A-Natural-Fit.aspx

Ayres, K., Douglas, K., Lowrey, K., & Sievers, C. (2011). I can identify Saturn but I can't brush my teeth: What happens when the curricular focus for students with severe disabilities shifts. *Education and Training in Autism and Developmental Disabilities, 46*(1), 11–21.

Ayres, K., Mechling, L., & Sansosti, F. (2013). The use of mobile technologies to assist with life skills/independence of students with moderate/severe intellectual disability and/or autism spectrum disorders: Considerations for the future of school psychology. *Psychology in the Schools, 50*(3), 259–270.

Bedell, G., Coster W., Law, M., Liljenquist, K., Kao, Y., Teplicky R., . . . Khetani, M. (2013). Community participation, supports, and barriers of school-age children with and without disabilities. *Archives of Physical Medicine and Rehabilitation, 94*(2), 315–323.

Bouck, E. (2012). Secondary curriculum and transition. In P. Wehman (Ed.), *Life beyond the classroom: Transition strategies for young people with disabilities* (5th ed., pp. 215–233). Baltimore, MD: Paul H. Brookes.

Bouck, E., & Joshi, G. (2012). Functional curriculum and students with mild intellectual disability: Exploring postschool outcomes through the NLTS2. *Education and Training in Autism and Developmental Disabilities, 47*(2), 139–153.

Bouck, E., Satsangi, R., Doughty, T., & Courtney, W. (2014). Virtual and concrete manipulatives: A comparison of approaches for solving mathematics problems for students with autism spectrum disorder. *Journal of Autism and Developmental Disorders, 44*(1), 180–193.

Brooks, B., Floyd, F., Robins, D., & Chan, W. (2015). Extracurricular activities and the development of social skills in children with intellectual and specific learning disabilities. *Journal of Intellectual Disability Research, 59*(7), 678–687.

Browder, D., Gibbs, S., Ahlgrim-Delzell, L., Courtade, G., Mraz, M., & Flowers, C. (2009). Literacy for students with severe developmental disabilities what should we teach and what should we hope to achieve? *Remedial and Special Education, 30*(5), 269–282.

Browder, D., Trela, K., & Jimenez, B. (2007). Training teachers to follow a task analysis to engage middle school students with moderate and severe developmental disabilities in grade-appropriate literature. *Focus on Autism and Other Developmental Disabilities, 22*(4), 206–219.

Browder, D., Wakeman, S., Spooner, F., Ahlgrim-Delzell, L., & Algozzine, R. (2006). A comprehensive review of reading for students with significant cognitive disabilities. *Exceptional Children, 72*(4), 392–408.

Burton, C., Anderson, D., Prater, M., & Dyches, T. (2013). Video self-modeling on an iPad to teach functional math skills to adolescents with autism and intellectual disability. *Focus on Autism and Other Developmental Disabilities, 28*(2), 67–77.

Callan, P., Finney, J., Kirst, M., Usdan, M., & Venezia, A. (2006). *Claiming common ground: State policymaking for improving college readiness and success* (National Center Report # 06-1). San Jose, CA: National Center for Public Policy and Higher Education.

Carnegie Mellon. (2016). *Information visualization tools.* Retrieved January 3, 2016, from http://www.cmu.edu/teaching/technology/tools/informationvisualization/

Carter, E., & Hughes, C. (2005). Increasing social interaction among adolescents with intellectual disabilities and their general education peers: Effective interventions. *Research and Practice for Persons with Severe Disabilities, 30*(4), 179–193.

CAST. (2013). *UDL intersections: Universal design for learning and universal design.* Retrieved September 29, 2016, from http://www.udlcenter.org/sites/udlcenter.org/files/UDL-DI%20BRIEFfinal.pdf

Coleman, M., Hurley, K., & Cihak, D. (2012). Comparing teacher-directed and computer-assisted constant time delay for teaching functional sight words to students with moderate intellectual disability. *Education and Training in Autism and Developmental Disabilities, 47*(3), 280–292.

Collins, B. (2012). *Systematic instruction for students with moderate and severe disabilities.* Baltimore, MD: Paul H. Brooks.

Common Core State Standards Initiative. (2016a). *English language arts standards.* Retrieved January 2, 2016, from http://www.corestandards.org/ELA-Literacy/

Common Core State Standards Initiative. (2016b). *Mathematics standards.* Retrieved from http://www.corestandards.org/Math/

Courtade, G., Spooner, F., Browder, D., & Jimenez, B. (2012). Seven reasons to promote standards-based instruction for students with severe disabilities: A reply to Ayres, Lowrey, Douglas, & Sievers (2011). *Education and Training in Autism and Developmental Disabilities, 47*(1), 3–13.

Derryberry, A. (2007). *Serious games: Online games for learning.* Retrieved January 3, 2016, from http://www.adobe.com/resources/elearning/pdfs/serious_games_wp.pdf

Dieker, L., & Murawski, W. (2003). Co-teaching at the secondary level: Unique issues, current trends, and suggestions for success. *The High School Journal, 86*(4), 1–13.

Duckworth, A., Quinn, P., & Tsukayama, E. (2012). What *No Child Left Behind* leaves behind: The roles of IQ and self-control in predicting standardized achievement test scores and report card grades. *Journal of Educational Psychology, 104*(2), 439–451.

Every Student Succeeds Act, Pub. L. 114-95, § 1111, 129 Stat. 1802 (2015).

Gargiulo, R., & Bouck, E. (2018). *Special education in contemporary society* (6th ed.). Thousand Oaks, CA: Sage.

Ghosh, D., & Datta, T. (2012). Functional improvement and social participation through sports activity for children with mental retardation: A field study from a developing nation. *Prosthetics & Orthotics International, 36*(3), 339–347.

Grammarly. (2016). *Grammarly.* Retrieved October 1, 2016, from https://www.grammarly.com/

Gresham, F., Sugai, G., & Horner, R. (2001). Interpreting outcomes of social skills training for students with high-incidence disabilities. *Exceptional Children, 67*(3), 331–344.

Griffin, M., Summer, A., McMillan, E., Day, T., & Hodapp, R. (2012). Attitudes toward including students with intellectual disabilities at college. *Journal of Policy and Practice in Intellectual Disabilities, 9*(4), 234–239.

Hall, T., Vue, G., Strangman, N., & Meyer, A. (2004). *Differentiated instruction and implications for UDL implementation.* Retrieved January 2, 2016, from http://aem.cast.org/about/publications/2003/ncac-differentiated-instruction-udl.html

Halverson, R., & Smith, A. (2010). How new technologies have (and have not) changed teaching and learning in schools. *Journal of Computing in Teacher Education, 26*(2), 49–54.

Hart, J., & Whalon, K. (2012). Using video self-modeling via iPads to increase academic responding of an adolescent with autism spectrum disorder and intellectual disability. *Education and Training in Autism and Developmental Disabilities, 47*(4), 438–446.

Higher Education Opportunities Act, Pub. L. 110-315, 20 U.S.C. §§ 1001 *et seq.* (2008).

Hollo, A., & Hirn, R. (2015). Teacher and student behaviors in the contexts of grade-level and instructional grouping. *Preventing School Failure, 59*(1), 30–39.

Hord, C., & Xin, Y. (2015). Teaching area and volume to students with mild intellectual disability. *Journal of Special Education, 49*(2), 118–128.

Hott, B., & Walker, J. (2012). *Peer tutoring*. Retrieved January 2, 2016, from http://www.council-for-learning-disabilities.org/peer-tutoring-flexible-peer-mediated-strategy-that-involves-students-serving-as-academic-tutors

Hudson, M., Browder, D., & Wakeman, S. (2013). Helping students with moderate and severe intellectual disability access grade-level text. *Teaching Exceptional Children, 45*(3), 14-23.

Hudson, M., Browder, D., & Wood, L. (2013). Review of experimental research on academic learning by students with moderate and severe intellectual disability in general education. *Research and Practice for Persons With Severe Disabilities, 38*(1), 17–29.

Hudson, M., & Test, D. (2011). Evaluating the evidence base of shared story reading to promote literacy for students with extensive support needs. *Research and Practice for Persons With Severe Disabilities, 36*(1–2), 34–45.

Hughes, C., Kaplan, L., Bernstein, R., Boykin, M., Reilly, C., Brigham, N., . . . Harvey, M. (2012). Increasing social interaction skills of secondary school students with autism and/or intellectual disability: A review of interventions. *Research & Practice for Persons With Severe Disabilities, 37*(4), 288–307.

Hughson, E., Moodie, S., & Uditsky, B. (2006). *The story of inclusive postsecondary education in Alberta. Final research report 2004–2005*. Edmonton, Canada: Alberta Association for Community Living.

Hunt, P., McDonnell, J., & Crockett, M. (2012). Reconciling an ecological curricular framework focusing on quality of life outcomes with the development and instruction of standards-based academic goals. *Research and Practice for Persons With Severe Disabilities, 37*(3), 139–152.

Jacob, B. (2001). Getting tough? The impact of high school graduation exams. *Educational Evaluation and Policy Analysis, 23*(2), 99–121.

Jimenez, B., Browder, D., & Courtade, G. (2008). Teaching an algebraic equation to high school students with moderate developmental disabilities. *Education and Training in Developmental Disabilities, 43*(2), 266–274.

Johnson, D., & Johnson, R. (1999). Making cooperative learning work. *Theory Into Practice, 38*(2), 67–73.

Johnson, D., Thurlow, M., & Schuelka, M. (2012). *Diploma options, graduation requirements, and exit exams for youth with disabilities: 2011 national study*. Minneapolis, MN: National Center on Educational Outcomes.

Kleinert, H., Jones, M., Sheppard-Jones, K., Harp, B., & Harrison, E. (2012). Students with intellectual disabilities going to college? Absolutely! *Teaching Exceptional Children, 44*(5), 26–35.

Kuncel, N., Ones, D., & Sackett, P. (2010). Individual differences as predictors of work, educational, and broad live outcomes. *Personality and Individual Differences, 49*(4), 331–336.

Lancioni, G., & O'Reilly, M. (2002). Teaching food preparation skills to people with intellectual disabilities: A literature overview. *Journal of Applied Research in Intellectual Disabilities, 15*(3), 236–253.

Logan, K., Bakeman, R., & Keefe, E. (1997). Effects of instructional variables on engaged behavior of students with disabilities in general education classrooms. *Exceptional Children, 63*(4), 481–497.

Lynch, K., & Gretzel, E. (2013). Assessing impact of inclusive postsecondary education using the Think College standards. *Journal of Postsecondary Education and Disability, 26*(4), 385–393.

Mastropieri, M., & Scruggs, T. (2007). *The inclusive classroom: Strategies for effective instruction* (3rd ed.). Upper Saddle River, NJ: Pearson Education.

McFall, R. (1982). A review and reformulation of the concept of social skills. *Behavioral Assessment, 4*(1), 1–33.

McMahon, D., Smith, C., Cihak, D., Wright, R., & Gibbons, M. (2015). Effects of digital navigation aids on adults with intellectual disabilities: Comparison of paper map, Google maps, and augmented reality. *Journal of Special Education Technology, 30*(3), 157–165.

Meador, D. (2015). *An investment in small group instruction will pay off.* Retrieved January 2, 2016, from http://teaching.about.com/od/s-zteachingvocabulary/g/Small-Group-Instruction.htm

Meador, D. (2016). *Exploring the value of whole group instruction.* Retrieved September 29, 2016, from http://teaching.about.com/od/W-Z/g/Whole-Group-Instruction.htm

Migliore, A., Butterworth, J., & Hart, D. (2009). Postsecondary education and employment outcomes for youth with intellectual disabilities. *Think College! Fast Facts, 1*, 1.

Monson, M. P., & Monson, R. J. (1993). Who creates curriculum: New roles for teachers. *Educational Leadership, 51*, 19–21.

Morrison, L., Kamps, D., Gargia, J., & Parker, D. (2001). Peer mediation and monitoring strategies to improve initiations and social skills for students with autism. *Journal of Positive Behavior Interventions, 3(*4), 237–250.

Mouza, C., & Lavigne, N. (2013). Introduction to emerging technologies for the classroom: A learning sciences perspective. In C. Mouza & N. Lavigne (Eds.), *Emerging technologies for the classroom* (pp.1–12). New York, NY: Springer.

National Council for the Social Studies. (2013). *The college, career, and civic life (C3) framework for social studies state standards: Guidance for enhancing the rigor of K–12 civics, economics, geography, and history.* Silver Spring, MD: Author.

National Council of Teachers of Mathematics. (2000). *Principles and standards for school mathematics.* Reston, VA: Author.

National Reading Panel. (2000). *Teaching children to read: An evidence-based assessment of the scientific research literature on reading and its implications for reading instruction.* Washington, DC: National Institute of Child Health and Human Development.

National Research Council. (2012). *A framework for K–12 science education.* Washington, DC: National Academies Press.

NaturalSoft Limited. (2016). *NaturalReader* [Version 14.0]. Retrieved October 1, 2016, from http://www.naturalreaders.com/index.html

Newman, L., Wagner, M., Cameto, R., & Knokey, A. (2009). *The post-high school outcomes of youth with disabilities up to 4 years after high school. A report from the National Longitudinal Transition Study-2 (NLTS2).* Menlo Park, CA: SRI International.

Newman, L., Wagner, M., Cameto, R., & Knokey, A., & Shaver, D. (2010). *Comparisons across time of the outcomes of youth with disabilities up to 4 years after high school. A report of findings from the National Longitudinal Transition Study (NLTS) and the National Longitudinal Transition Study-2 (NLTS2).* Menlo Park, CA: SRI International.

No Child Left Behind Act of 2001, Pub. L. No., 107–110 115 Stat.1425 *et seq.* (2002).

Osewalt, G. (2016). *Individualized instruction vs. differentiated instruction.* Retrieved January 2, 2016, from https://www.understood.org/en/school-learning/partnering-with-childs-school/instructional-strategies/individualized-instruction-vs-differentiated-instruction

Patel, M., & Rose, J. (2014). Students' attitudes towards individuals with an intellectual disability. *Journal of Intellectual Disabilities, 18*(1), 90–103.

Plotner, A., & Marshall, K. (2015). Postsecondary education programs for students with an intellectual disability: Facilitators and barriers to implementation. *Intellectual and Developmental Disabilities, 53*(1), 58–69.

Semrud-Clikeman, M. (2007). *Social competence in children.* New York, NY: Springer.

Shea, G. (1989). *The English coalition conference: Secondary.* National Council of Teachers of English. Retrieved January 3, 2016, from http://www.ncte.org/positions/statements/englishcoalitionsec

Shurr, J., & Taber-Doughty, T. (2016). The PPD intervention: Text access for high school students with moderate intellectual disability. *Focus on Autism and Other Developmental Disabilities.*

Siperstein, G., Glick, G., & Parker, R. (2009). Social inclusion of children with intellectual disabilities in a recreational setting. *Intellectual & Developmental Disabilities, 47*(2), 97–107.

SMART Technologies. (2006). *Interactive whiteboards and learning: Improving student learning outcomes and streamlining lesson planning.* Retrieved January 3, 2016, from http://downloads01.smarttech.com/media/education/pdf/interactivewhiteboardsandlearning.pdf

Stenhoff, D., & Lignugaris/Kraft, B. (2007). A review of the effects of tutoring on students with mild disabilities in secondary settings. *Exceptional Children, 74*(1), 8–30.

Sturm, J. (2012). An enriched writers' workshop for beginning writers with developmental disabilities. *Topics in Language Disorders, 32*(4), 335–360.

Terminal Eleven. (2010). *SkyView®—explore the universe [Version 3.5.0].* Retrieved October 1, 2016, from https://itunes.apple.com/us/app/skyview-explore-the-universe/id404990064?mt=8

Tomlinson, C. (1995). *How to differentiate instruction in a mixed ability classroom.* Alexandria, VA: Association for Supervision and Curriculum Development.

U.S. Department of Education. (2015). *Thirty-seventh annual report to Congress on the implementation of the Individuals with Disabilities Education Act, 2015.* Washington, DC: Author.

Villa, R. (2016). *Effective co-teaching strategies.* Retrieved January 1, 2016, from http://www.teachhub.com/effective-co-teaching-strategies

Villa, R., Thousand, J., & Nevin, A. (2013). *A guide to co-teaching: New lessons and strategies to facilitate student learning.* Thousand Oaks, CA: Corwin.

Walsh, J. (2012). Co-teaching as a school strategy for continuous improvement. *Preventing School Failure, 56*(1), 29–36.

WeWantToKnow. (2016). *DragonBox Algebra 12+* [Version 2.2.1]. Retrieved October 4, 2016, from https://itunes.apple.com/app/apple-store/id634444186?mt=8

Wehmeyer, M., Shogren, K., Verdugo, M., Nota, L., Soresi, S., Lee, S., . . . Lachapelle, Y. (2014). Cognitive impairment and intellectual disability. In A. Rotatori, J. Bakken, S. Burkhardt, F. Obiakor, & U. Sharma (Eds.), *Special education international perspectives* (Vol. 27, pp. 55–89). Bingley, United Kingdom: Emerald.

Wehmeyer, M., Smith, S., Palmer, S., & Davies, D. (2004). Technology use by students with intellectual disabilities: An overview. *Journal of Special Education Technology, 19*(4), 7–21.

Wood, L., Browder, D., & Flynn, L. (2015). Teaching students with intellectual disability to use a self-questioning strategy to comprehend social studies text for an inclusive setting. *Research and Practice for Persons With Severe Disabilities, 40*(4), 275–293.

Zigmond, N. (2015). Where should students with disabilities receive their education? In B. Bateman, J. Lloyd, & M. Tankersley (Eds.), *Enduring issues in special education: Personal perspectives* (pp. 198–214). New York, NY: Routledge.

Chapter 12

Agran, M., & Hughes, C. (2014). Promoting self-determination and self-directed learning. In M. Agran, F. Brown, C. Hughes, C. Quirk, & D. Ryndak (Eds.), *Equity and full participation for individuals with severe disabilities: A vision for the future* (pp. 75–98). Baltimore, MD: Paul H. Brookes.

Alberto, P., Cihak, D., & Gama, R. (2005). Use of static picture prompts versus video modeling during simulation instruction. *Research in Developmental Disabilities, 26*(4), 327–339.

Alberto, P., Elliott, N., Taber, T., Houser, E., & Andrews, P. (1993). Vocational content for students with moderate and severe disabilities in elementary and middle grades. *Focus on Exceptional Children, 25*(9), 1–10.

Ayres, K., Lowrey, K., Douglas, K., & Sievers, C. (2011). I can identify Saturn but I can't brush my teeth: What happens when the curricular focus for students with severe disabilities shifts. *Education and Training in Autism and Developmental Disabilities, 46*(1), 11–21.

Ayers, K., Mechling, L., & Sansosti, F. (2013). The case of mobile technologies to assist with life skills/independence of students with moderate/severe intellectual disability and/or autism spectrum disorders: Considerations for the future of school psychology. *Psychology in the Schools, 50*(3), 259–271.

Baumgart, D., Brown, L., Pumpian, I., Nisbet, J., Ford, A., Sweet, M., . . .Schroeder, J. (1982). Principal of partial participation and individualized adaptations in educational programs for severely handicapped students. *TASH Journal, 7*(2), 17–27.

Benz, M., Lindstrom, L., & Yovanoff, P. (2000). Improving graduation and employment outcomes of students with disabilities: Predictive factors and student perspectives. *Exceptional Children, 66*(4), 509–529.

Bouck, E. (2010). Reports of life skills training for students with intellectual disabilities in and out of school. *Journal of Intellectual Disability Research, 54*(12), 1093–1103.

Bouck, E. (2012). Secondary students with moderate/severe intellectual disability: Considerations of curriculum and post-school outcomes from the National Longitudinal Transition Study-2. *Journal of Intellectual Disability Research, 56*(12), 1175–1186.

Bouck, E., & Joshi, G. (2012). Functional curriculum and students with mild intellectual disability: Exploring postschool outcomes through the NLTS2. *Education and Training in Autism and Developmental Disabilities, 47*(2), 139–153.

Bouck, E., Taber-Doughty, T., & Savage, M. (2015). *Footsteps toward the future: Implementing a real-world curriculum for students with developmental disabilities.* Arlington, VA: Council for Exceptional Children.

Brown, L., Nietupski, J., & Hamre-Nietupski, S. (1976). The criterion of ultimate functioning and public school services for severely handicapped students. In M. Thomas (Ed.), *Hey, don't forget about me: Education's investment in the severely, profoundly, and multiply handicapped* (pp. 2–15). Reston, VA: Council for Exceptional Children.

Chang, Y., Kang, Y., & Huang, P. (2013). An augmented reality (AR)-based vocational task prompting system for people with cognitive impairments. *Research in Developmental Disabilities, 34*(10), 3049–3056.

Cihak, D., Alberto, P., Taber-Doughty, T., & Gama, R. (2006). A comparison of static picture prompting and video prompting simulation strategies using group instructional procedures. *Focus on Autism and Other Developmental Disabilities, 21*(2), 89–99.

Cimera, R. (2001). Utilizing coworkers as "natural supports": Evidence on cost-efficiency, job retention, and other employment outcomes. *Journal of Disability Policy Studies, 11*(4), 194–201.

Cimera, R. (2007). Utilizing natural supports to lower the cost of supported employment. *Research & Practice for Persons With Severe Disabilities, 32*(3), 184–189.

Cimera, R. (2010). Can community-based high school transition programs improve the cost-efficiency of supported employment? *Career Development for Exceptional Individuals, 33*(1), 4–12.

Conderman, G., & Katsiyannis, A. (2002). Instructional issues and practices in secondary special education. *Remedial and Special Education, 23*(3), 169–179.

Cuvo, A., & Davis, P. (1983). Behavior therapy and community living skills. In M. Hersen, R. Eisler, & P. Miller (Eds.), *Progress in behavior modification* (Vol. 14, pp. 132–156). New York, NY: Academic Press.

Downing, J. (2010). *Academic instruction for students with moderate and severe intellectual disabilities in inclusive classrooms.* Thousand Oaks, CA: Corwin.

Flexer, R., Baer, R., Luft, P., & Simmons, T. (2013). *Transition planning for secondary students with disabilities* (4th ed.). Boston, MA: Pearson Education.

Gold, M. (1980). *Did I say that? Articles and commentary on the Try Another Way system.* Champaign, IL: Research Press.

Grigal, M., Hart, D., & Migliore, A. (2011). Comparing the transition planning, postsecondary education, and employment outcomes of students with intellectual and other disabilities. *Career Development for Exceptional Individuals, 34*(1), 4–17.

Lane, S., & Mistrett, S. (1996). Play and assistive technology issues for infants and young children with disabilities: A preliminary examination. *Focus on Autism and Other Developmental Disabilities, 11*(2), 96–104.

Lee, S. (2009, October). Overview of the federal Higher Education Opportunities Act reauthorization. *Think College Insight Brief,* 1. Boston, MA: Institute for Community Inclusion, University of Massachusetts Boston. Available at www.thinkcollege.net/images/stories/HEAC_Overview(1).pdf

McLeskey, J., Landers, E., Williamson, P., & Hoppey, D. (2012). Are we moving toward educating students with disabilities in less restrictive settings? *The Journal of Special Education, 46*(3), 131–140.

Mechling, L., & O'Brien, E. (2010). Computer-based video instruction to teach students with intellectual disabilities to use public bus transportation. *Education and Training in Autism and Developmental Disabilities, 45*(2), 230–241.

Mechling, L., & Ortega-Hurndon, F. (2007). Computer-based video instruction to teach young adults with moderate intellectual disabilities to perform multiple step, job tasks in a generalized setting. *Education and Training in Developmental Disabilities, 42*(1), 24–37.

Miller, S., & Chan, F. (2008). Predictors of life satisfaction in individuals with intellectual disabilities. *Journal of Intellectual Disability Research, 52*(12), 1039–1047.

National Center for Education Statistics. (2015). *Digest of education statistics 2013.* Washington, DC: U.S. Department of Education.

National Center for Education Statistics. (2016). *Children and youth with disabilities.* Washington, DC: U.S. Department of Education. Retrieved October 1, 2016, from https://nces.ed.gov/programs/coe/indicator_cgg.asp

Newman, L., Wagner, M., Cameto, R., & Knokey, A. (2009). *The post-high school outcomes of youth with disabilities up to 4 years after high school: A report from the National Longitudinal Transition Study-2 (NLTS2).* Menlo Park, CA: SRI International.

Niemiec, C., & Ryan, R. (2009). Autonomy, competence, and relatedness in the classroom. Applying self-determination theory to educational practice. *Theory and Research in Education, 7*(2), 133–144.

Northeast Indiana Cadre of Transition Leaders. (2015). *Transition assessment matrix*. Retrieved October 23, 2015, from https://www.iidc.indiana.edu/styles/iidc/defiles/cclc/transition_matrix/transition_matrix.html

Perske, R. (1972). The dignity of risk and the mentally retarded. *Mental Retardation, 10*(1), 24–26.

Petner-Arrey, J., Howell-Moneta, A., & Lysaght, R. (2015). Facilitating employment opportunities for adults with intellectual and developmental disability through parents and social networks. *Disability and Rehabilitation, 38*(8), 789-795. DOI10.3109/09638288.2015.1061605

Spooner, F., & Browder, D. (2015). Raising the bar: Significant advances and future needs-for promoting learning for students with severe disabilities. *Remedial and Special Education, 36*(1), 28–32.

Stanish, H., & Temple, V. (2012). Efficacy of a peer-guided exercise programme for adolescents with intellectual disability. *Journal of Applied Research in Intellectual Disabilities, 25*(4), 319–328.

Storey, K., & Certo, N. (1996). Natural supports for increasing integration in the workplace for people with disabilities: A review of the literature and guidelines for implementation. *Rehabilitation Counseling Bulletin, 40*(1), 62-76.

Taber-Doughty, T. (2015). STEM for students with severe disabilities. *School Science and Mathematics, 115*(4), 153–154.

Test, D., Mazzotti, V., Mustian, A., Fowler, C., Kortering, L., & Kohler, P. (2009). Evidence-based secondary transition predictors for improving postschool outcomes for students with disabilities. *Career Development for Exceptional Individuals, 32*(3), 160–181.

Walker, A., Kortering, L., Fowler, C., Rowe, D., & Bethune, L. (2013). *Age transition assessment toolkit* (3rd ed.). Charlotte, NC: National Secondary Transition Technical Assistance Center.

Wandry, D., Wehmeyer, M., & Glor-Scheib, S. (2013). *Life centered education: The teacher's guide*. Arlington, VA: Council for Exceptional Children.

Wehmeyer, M. (2007). *Promoting self-determination in students with developmental disabilities*. New York, NY: Guilford Press.

Wehmeyer, M., & Palmer, S. (2003). Adult outcomes for students with cognitive disabilities three-years after high school: The impact of self-determination. *Education and Training in Developmental Disabilities, 38*(2), 131–144.

Wehmeyer, M., & Schalock, R. (2001). Self-determination and quality of life: Implications for special education services and supports. *Focus on Exceptional Children, 33*(8), 1–16.

Wehmeyer, M., & Schwartz, M. (1997). Self-determination and positive adult outcomes: A follow-up study of youth with mental retardation or learning disabilities. *Exceptional Children, 63*(2), 245–255.

Wehyemer, M., & Schwartz, M. (1998). The relationship between self-determination, quality of life, and life satisfaction for adults with mental retardation. *Education and Training in Mental Retardation and Developmental Disabilities, 33*(1), 3–12.

Wolfensberger, W. (1983). Social role valorization: A proposed new term for the principle of normalization. *Mental Retardation, 21*(6), 234–239.

Chapter 13

Algozzine, B., Browder, D., Karvonen, M., Test, D., & Wood, W. (2001). Effects of intervention to promote self-determination for individuals with disabilities. *Review of Educational Research, 71*(2), 219–277.

Carlson, E., Daley, T., Bitterman, A., Heinzen, H., Keller, B., Markowitz, J., . . . Rosenquist, C. (2009). *Early school transitions and the social behavior of children with disabilities: Selected findings from the Pre-Elementary Education Longitudinal Study.* Washington, DC: National Center for Special Education Research.

Clark, G. (1996). Transition planning assessment for secondary-level students with learning disabilities. In J. Patton & G. Blalock (Eds.), *Transition and students with learning disabilities: Facilitating the movement from school to adult life* (pp. 131–156). Austin, TX: Pro-Ed.

Cook, A., Hayden, L., Wilczenski, F., & Poynton, T. (2015). Increasing access to postsecondary education for students with intellectual disabilities. *Journal of College Access, 1*(1), 41–55.

Eisenman, L. (2007). Self-determination interventions: Building a foundation for school completion. *Remedial and Special Education, 28*(1), 2–8.

Forrest, C., Bevans, K., Riley, A., Crespo, R., & Louis, T. (2013). Health and school outcomes during children's transition into adolescence. *Journal of Adolescent Health, 52*(2), 186–194.

Grigal, M., & Deschamps, A. (2012). Transition education for adolescents with intellectual disability. In M. Wehmeyer & K. Webb (Eds.), *Handbook of adolescent transition and disability* (pp. 398–416). New York, NY: Taylor & Francis.

Hanley-Maxwell, C., & Izzo, M. (2012). Preparing students for the 21st century workforce. In M. Wehmeyer & K. Webb (Eds.), *Handbook of adolescent transition and disability* (pp. 139–155). New York, NY: Taylor & Francis.

Hart, D., & Grigal, M. (2010). The spectrum of options: Current practices. In M. Grigal & D. Hart (Eds.), *Think college: Postsecondary education options for students with intellectual disabilities* (pp. 49–86). Baltimore, MD: Paul H. Brookes.

Holas, I., & Huston, A. (2012). Are middle schools harmful? The role of transition timing, classroom quality and school characteristics. *Journal of Youth and Adolescence, 41*(3), 333–345.

Hughes, L., Banks, P., & Terras, M. (2013). Secondary school transition for children with special educational needs: A literature review. *Support for Learning, 28*(1), 24–34.

Johnson, D. (2012). Policy and adolescent transition education. In M. Wehmeyer & K. Webb (Eds.), *Handbook of adolescent transition and disability* (pp. 11–32). New York, NY: Taylor & Francis.

Kennelly, L., & Monrad, M. (2007). *Easing the transition to high school: Research and best practices designed to support high school learning.* Washington, DC: National High School Center.

Kingery, J., Erdley, C., & Marshall, K. (2011). Peer acceptance and friendship as predictors of early adolescents' adjustment across the middle school transition. *Merrill-Palmer Quarterly, 57*(3), 215–243.

Lane, K., Oakes, W., Carter, E., & Messenger, M. (2015). Examining behavioral risk and academic performance for students transitioning from elementary to middle school. *Journal of Positive Behavior Interventions, 17*(1), 39–49.

Martin, J., Hennessey, M., McConnell, A., Terry, R., & Willis, D. (2015). *Transition assessment and goal generator*. Norman, OK: Board of Regents of the University of Oklahoma.

Martin, J., Van Dycke, J., Christensen, W., Greene, B., Gardner, J., & Lovett, D. (2006). Increasing student participation in IEP meetings: Establishing the Self-Directed IEP as an evidenced-based practice. *Exceptional Children, 72*(3), 299–316.

McIntosh, K., Flannery, K., Sugai, G., Braun, D., & Cochrane, K. (2008). Relationships between academics and problem behavior in the transition from middle school to high school. *Journal of Positive Behavior Interventions, 10*(4), 243–255.

Mount, B., & Zwernik, K. (1990). *Making futures happen: A manual for facilitators of Personal Futures Planning*. St. Paul, MN: Minnesota Governor's Planning Council on Developmental Disabilities.

National Secondary Transition Technical Assistance Center. (2009). *Indicator 13 training materials*. Charlotte, NC: Author.

National Secondary Transition Technical Assistance Center. (2010). *Evidence-based practices and predictors in secondary transition: What we know and what we still need to know*. Charlotte, NC: Author.

Neubert, D. (2012). Transition assessment for adolescents. In M. Wehmeyer & K. Webb (Eds.), *Handbook of adolescent transition and disability* (pp. 73–90). New York, NY: Taylor & Francis.

Neubert, D., & Moon, M. (2006). Postsecondary settings and transition services for students with intellectual disabilities: Models and research. *Focus on Exceptional Children, 39*(4), 1–8.

Niesen, V., & Wise, P. (2004). *Transition from elementary to middle school: Strategies for educators*. Washington, DC: National Association of School Psychologists.

O'Brien, C., & O'Brien, J. (2000). *The origins of person-centered planning: A community of practice perspective*. Retrieved October 3, 2015, from http://citeseerx.ist.psu.edu/viewdoc/download?doi=10.1.1.502.8388&rep=rep1&type=pdf

Parent-Johnson, W. (2012). Innovative employment support models. In M. Wehmeyer & K. Webb (Eds.), *Handbook of adolescent transition and disability* (pp. 329–338). New York, NY: Taylor & Francis.

Patton, J., & Clark, G. (2014). *Transition planning inventory: Administration and resource guide* (2nd ed.). Austin, TX: Pro-Ed.

Pearpoint, J., O'Brien, J., & Forest, M. (1998). *PATH: A workbook for planning possible futures* (2nd ed.). Toronto, Canada: Inclusion Press.

Powers, L., Geenen, S., Powers, J., Pommier-Satya, S., Turner, A., Dalton, L., . . . Swand, P. (2012). My life: Effects of a longitudinal, randomized study of self-determination enhancement on the transition outcomes of youth in foster care and special education. *Children and Youth Services Review, 34*(11), 2179–2187.

Rehfeldt, J., Clark, G., & Lee, S. (2012). The effects of using the Transition Planning Inventory and a structured IEP process as a transition planning intervention on IEP meeting outcomes. *Remedial and Special Education, 33*(1), 48–58.

Rosenkoetter, S., Schroeder, C., Rous, B., Hains, A., Shaw, J., & McCormick, K. (2009). *A review of research in early childhood transition: Child and family studies* (Technical Report #5). Lexington: University of Kentucky, Human Development Institute, National Early Childhood Transition Center.

Rous, B., Hallam, R., McCormick, K., & Cox, M. (2010). Practices that support the transition to public preschool programs: Results from a national survey. *Early Childhood Research Quarterly, 25*(1), 17–32.

Schwartz, A., Jacobson, J., & Holburn, S. (2000). Defining person-centeredness: Results of two consensus methods. *Education and Training in Mental Retardation and Developmental Disabilities, 35*(3), 235–258.

Seabrooks-Blackmore, J., & Williams, G. (2012). Transition planning strategies. In M. Wehmeyer & K. Webb (Eds.), *Handbook of adolescent transition and disability* (pp. 91–101). New York, NY: Taylor & Francis.

Seo, H., Shogren, K., Wehmeyer, M., Hughes, C., Thompson, J., Little, T., . . . Palmer, S. (in press). Exploring shared measurement properties and score comparability between two versions of the Supports Intensity Scale. *Career Development and Transition for Exceptional Individuals.*

Shogren, K., Palmer, S., Wehmeyer, M., Williams-Diehm, K., & Little, T. (2012). Effect of intervention with the Self-Determined Learning Model of Instruction on access and goal attainment. *Remedial and Special Education, 33*(5), 320–330.

Shogren, K., & Plotner, A. (2012). Transition planning for students with intellectual disability, autism, or other disabilities: Data from the National Longitudinal Transition Study-2. *Intellectual and Developmental Disabilities, 50*(1), 16–30.

Shogren, K., Plotner, A., Palmer, S., Wehmeyer, M., & Paek, Y. (2014). Impact of the Self-Determined Learning Model of Instruction on teacher perceptions of student capacity and opportunity for self-determination. *Education and Training in Autism and Developmental Disabilities, 49*(3), 440–448.

Shogren, K., Wehmeyer, M., Lane, K., & Quirk, C. (in press). Embedding interventions to promote self-determination within multi-tiered systems of supports. *Exceptionality.*

Shogren, K., Wehmeyer, M., Little, T., Forber-Pratt, A., Palmer, S., & Seo, H. (in press). Preliminary validity and reliability of scores on the Self-Determination Inventory: Student Report version. *Career Development and Transition for Exceptional Individuals.*

Shogren, K., Wehmeyer, M., Palmer, S., Forber-Pratt, A., Little, T., & Lopez, S. (2015). Causal agency theory: Reconceptualizing a functional model of self-determination. *Education and Training in Autism and Developmental Disabilities, 50*(3), 251–263.

Shogren, K., Wehmeyer, M., Palmer, S., Rifenbark, G., & Little, T. (2015). Relationships between self-determination and postschool outcomes for youth with disabilities. *Journal of Special Education, 48*(4), 256–267.

Shogren, K., Wehmeyer, M., Palmer, S., Soukup, J., Little, T., Garner, N., . . . Lawrence, M. (2008). Understanding the construct of self-determination: Examining the relationship between The Arc's Self-Determination Scale and the American Institute for Research Self-Determination Scale. *Assessment for Effective Instruction, 33*(2), 94–107.

Shoshani, A., & Slone, M. (2013). Middle school transition from the strengths perspective: Young adolescents' character strengths, subjective well-being, and school adjustment. *Journal of Happiness Studies, 14*(4), 1163–1181.

Think College. (2016). Retrieved May 20, 2016, from http://www.thinkcollege.net/

Thompson, J., Bryant, B., Schalock, R., Shogren, K., Tassé, M., Wehmeyer, M., . . . Rotholz, D. (2016). *Supports Intensity Scale—Adult Version: User's manual.* Washington, DC: American Association on Intellectual and Developmental Disabilities.

Thompson, J., Buntinx, W., Schalock, R., Shogren, K., Snell, M., Wehmeyer, M., . . . Yeager, M. (2009). Conceptualizing supports and the support needs of people with intellectual disability. *Intellectual and Developmental Disabilities, 47*(2), 135–146.

Thompson, J., Wehmeyer, M., & Hughes, C. (2010). Mind the gap! Implications of person-environment fit models of intellectual disability for students, educators, and schools. *Exceptionality, 18*(4), 168–181.

Thompson, J., Wehmeyer, M., Hughes, C., Shogren, K., Seo, H., Little, T., . . . Tassé, M. (2016). *Supports Intensity Scale—Children's Version: User's manual.* Washington, DC: American Association on Intellectual and Developmental Disabilities.

Turnbull, A., Blue-Banning, M., Anderson, E., Turnbull, H., Seaton, K., & Dinas, P. (1996). Enhancing self-determination through Group Action Planning: A holistic emphasis. In D. Sands & M. Wehmeyer (Eds.), *Self-determination across the life span: Independence and choice for people with disabilities* (pp. 237–256). Baltimore, MD: Paul H. Brookes.

Vandercook, T., York, J., & Forest, M. (1989). The McGill Action Planning System (MAPS): A strategy for building the vision. *Journal of the Association for Persons With Severe Handicaps, 14*(3), 205–215.

Wandry, D., & Pleet, A. (2012). Family involvement in transition planning. In M. Wehmeyer & K. Webb (Eds.), *Handbook of adolescent transition and disability* (pp. 102–118). New York, NY: Taylor & Francis.

Wehman, P. (2006). Transition: The bridge from youth to adulthood. In P. Wehman (Ed.), *Life beyond the classroom: Transition strategies for young people with disabilities* (4th ed., pp. 3–40). Baltimore, MD: Paul H. Brookes.

Wehmeyer, M. (1996). A self-report measure of self-determination for adolescents with cognitive disabilities. *Education and Training in Mental Retardation and Developmental Disabilities, 31*(4), 282–293.

Wehmeyer, M. (2002). The confluence of person-centered planning and self-determination. In C. Holburn & C. Vietz (Eds.), *Person-centered planning: Research, practice, and future directions* (pp. 51–69). Baltimore, MD: Paul H. Brookes.

Wehmeyer, M., & Abery, B. (2013). Self-determination and choice. *Intellectual and Developmental Disabilities, 51*(5), 399–411.

Wehmeyer, M., & Kelchner, K. (1995). *The Arc's Self-Determination Scale*. Arlington, TX: The Arc of the United States.

Wehmeyer, M., & Lee, S. (2007). Educating children with intellectual disability. In A. Carr, G. O'Reilly, P. Walsh, & J. McEvoy (Eds.), *The handbook of intellectual disability and clinical psychology practice* (pp. 559–605). London, United Kingdom: Routledge.

Wehmeyer, M., Morningstar, M., & Husted, D. (1999). *Family involvement in transition planning and implementation*. Austin, TX: Pro-Ed.

Wehmeyer, M., Palmer, S., Garner, N., Lawrence, M., Soukup, J., Shogren, K., . . . Kelly, J. (2009). *The Self-Determined Learning Model of Instruction: A teacher's guide* (2nd ed.). Lawrence, KS: Beach Center on Disability.

Wehmeyer, M., Palmer, S., Lee, Y., Williams-Diehm, K., & Shogren, K. (2011). A randomized-trial evaluation of the effect of Whose Future Is It Anyway? on self-determination. *Career Development for Exceptional Individuals, 34*(1), 45–56.

Wehmeyer, M., Palmer, S., Shogren, K., Williams-Diehm, K., & Soukup, J. (2012). Establishing a causal relationship between interventions to promote self-determination and enhanced student self-determination. *Journal of Special Education, 46*(4), 195–210.

Wehmeyer, M., & Patton, J. (2012). Transition to postsecondary education, employment, and adult living. In D. Zagar, M. Wehmeyer, & R. Simpson (Eds.), *Educating students with autism spectrum disorders: Research-based principles and practices* (pp. 247–261). New York, NY: Taylor & Francis.

Wehmeyer, M., Shogren, K., Palmer, S., Williams-Diehm, K., Little, T., & Boulton, A. (2012). The impact of the *Self-Determined Learning Model of Instruction* on student self-determination. *Exceptional Children, 78*(2), 135–153.

Wehmeyer, M., & Webb, K. (2012). An introduction to adolescent transition education. In M. Wehmeyer & K. Webb (Eds.), *Handbook of adolescent transition and disability* (pp. 3–10). New York, NY: Taylor & Francis.

Wolman, J., Campeau, P., Dubois, P., Mithaug, D., & Stolarski, V. (1994). *AIR self-determination scale and user guide*. Palo Alto, CA: American Institute for Research.

Index

Page numbers in *italics* indicate figures or tables.

sensory-based technology and, 170

social skills and, 168–69

speech-to-text and, 154–55

switch device and, 152, *153, 163,* 163–65, *165*

text-to-speech and, 152–53

UDL or universal design for learning and, 148

virtual manipulatives for mathematics and, 156, 157

Web 2.0 and, 167

word prediction tool and, 155–56

writing skills and, 153–56, *155*

Assistive technology service defined, 144. *See also* Assistive technology for students

Assistive technology specialists, 144. *See also* Assistive technology for students

Assistive Ware, 159

Attention span, 41–42

Augmentative and alternative communication (AAC), 157–59, 325

Augmented reality instruction, and elementary-age students' life skills, 282–83, *283*

Authentic literacy, and preschool students' academic skills, 193

Autonomy, and secondary students' life skills, 345

AYP (adequate yearly progress) schools, 50–51

Ayres, K., 282

Banks, P., 366

Barnett, W., 206

Behavioral and social characteristics. *See also* Behavioral interventions

behavioral momentum and, 126–27, 130

behavior support from assistive technology and, 166–70

BIP or behavior intervention plan and, 114, *115–16*

learning characteristics of students and, 44, *45,* 46

social narratives and, 119–22, *120, 122,* 130

social skills and, 168–69

Behavioral interventions. *See also* Antecedent interventions; Behavioral and social characteristics; Challenging behaviors in classrooms

about and summary, 107, 140, 141

AGA or applied behavior analysis and, 109–11

antecedent interventions and, 110

BIP or behavior intervention plan and, 114, *115–16*

consequences of behavior and, 111–12

elementary-age students and, 108–9

functional behavioral assessments and, 110–12, 211–12, *212, 213*

key terms for, 142

negative reinforcement and, 110, *111*

organizations concerned with, 142

PBIS or positive behavior interventions and supports and, 112–16, *113*

positive reinforcement and, 110, *111*

preschool students and, 108

punishments and, 110

reinforcement and, 110–11, *111,* 133–35

review questions and, 141–42

secondary students and, 109

Behavioral momentum, as antecedent intervention, 126–27, *130*

Behavior intervention plan (BIP), 114, *115–16*

Behavior support, from assistive technology for students, 166–70

Betz, A., 139

BIP (behavior intervention plan), 114, *115–16*

Birth trauma, 39

Birth weight, low, 39

Blackman, L., 7

Blatt, B., 10

Bloom, B., 251, 253

Boon, R., 282

Bouck, E., 337

Breech presentation, 39

about, 51–52, 65–66, *66*

elementary-age students' academic skills and, 246, *246*, *248–50*

elementary-age students' life skills, 278

transition planning for secondary students and, 381–82, *383*, *384*, 387, *388*, *389*, *390*, 391

Explicit instruction, and elementary-age students' academic skills, 251

Expressive language arts skills, and secondary students' academic skills, 324–25

Extended Common Core State Standards, North Carolina, 101, 102

External locus of control, 43

Extinction, for challenging behaviors in classrooms, 139–40

Extracurricular activities, and secondary students' academic skills, 316–18

Family involvement, in transition planning, 378–80

FAPE (free appropriate public education), 53, 55

FAS (fetal alcohol syndrome), 39

FASD (fetal alcohol spectrum disorder), 39

FCT (functional communication training), 131–33

Federal policies (legislation), 50–56, 304. *See also specific federal policies and legislation*

Fetal alcohol spectrum disorder (FASD), 39

Fetal alcohol syndrome (FAS), 39

Fisher, M., 233

Forced-choice (paired-stimulus) assessments, 90, 91

Formal supports, and intellectual disability, 23–24

Formative assessments, 83, *84*. *See also* Assessments and evaluations, of students; Summative assessments

Foundational concepts of intellectual disability. *See* Etiology of intellectual disability; Learning characteristics of students

Fragile X syndrome, 33–34

Free appropriate public education (FAPE), 53

Functional behavioral assessments, 110–12, 211–12, *212*, *213*. *See also* Behavioral interventions

Functional communication training (FCT), 131–33

Functional curriculum

about, 69, 70

elementary-age students' life skills and, 267, 268, 270, 271, 272, 273–74, 287

Functional skills, for preschool students, 188–89

Galactosemia, 36

Gama, R., 353

General education curriculum. *See* Academic (standards-based) curriculum

Generalizing knowledge, and learning characteristics of students, 43

Generative skills, and preschool students' academic skills, 188–89

Geometry instruction, and secondary students' academic skills, *326*, 326–27

German measles (rubella), 36

Gestational disorders, 39

Gestures, as prompting strategy, 256

Gillet, J., 89–90

Goddard, H., 9

Google Chromebook, and assistive technology for students, 155

Graphic organizers for language arts instruction, and elementary-age students' life skills, 290

Graphs, for assessments and evaluations, *95*, 95–97, *96*, *97*

Grigal, M., 394

Grossman, H., 16–18, 22

Group Action Planning model, 377, 387, *388*, *389*, *390*, 391

Group instruction approach, and elementary-age students' life skills, 279

Guided compliance, for challenging behaviors in classrooms, 133

Guided practice, and elementary-age students' academic skills, 255, 262–63